CHELSEA HOUSE PUBLISHERS
Modern Critical Views

HENRY ADAMS
EDWARD ALBEE
A. R. AMMONS
MATTHEW ARNOLD
JOHN ASHBERY
W. H. AUDEN
JANE AUSTEN
JAMES BALDWIN
CHARLES BAUDELAIRE
SAMUEL BECKETT
SAUL BELLOW
THE BIBLE
ELIZABETH BISHOP
WILLIAM BLAKE
JORGE LUIS BORGES
ELIZABETH BOWEN
BERTOLT BRECHT
THE BRONTËS
ROBERT BROWNING
ANTHONY BURGESS
GEORGE GORDON, LORD BYRON
THOMAS CARLYLE
LEWIS CARROLL
WILLA CATHER
CERVANTES
GEOFFREY CHAUCER
KATE CHOPIN
SAMUEL TAYLOR COLERIDGE
JOSEPH CONRAD
CONTEMPORARY POETS
HART CRANE
STEPHEN CRANE
DANTE
CHARLES DICKENS
EMILY DICKINSON
JOHN DONNE & THE
    17th-CENTURY POETS
ELIZABETHAN DRAMATISTS
THEODORE DREISER
JOHN DRYDEN
GEORGE ELIOT
T. S. ELIOT
RALPH ELLISON
RALPH WALDO EMERSON
WILLIAM FAULKNER
HENRY FIELDING
F. SCOTT FITZGERALD
GUSTAVE FLAUBERT
E. M. FORSTER
SIGMUND FREUD
ROBERT FROST

ROBERT GRAVES
GRAHAM GREENE
THOMAS HARDY
NATHANIEL HAWTHORNE
WILLIAM HAZLITT
SEAMUS HEANEY
ERNEST HEMINGWAY
GEOFFREY HILL
FRIEDRICH HÖLDERLIN
HOMER
GERARD MANLEY HOPKINS
WILLIAM DEAN HOWELLS
ZORA NEALE HURSTON
HENRY JAMES
SAMUEL JOHNSON
BEN JONSON
JAMES JOYCE
FRANZ KAFKA
JOHN KEATS
RUDYARD KIPLING
D. H. LAWRENCE
JOHN LE CARRÉ
URSULA K. LE GUIN
DORIS LESSING
SINCLAIR LEWIS
ROBERT LOWELL
NORMAN MAILER
BERNARD MALAMUD
THOMAS MANN
CHRISTOPHER MARLOWE
CARSON MCCULLERS
HERMAN MELVILLE
JAMES MERRILL
ARTHUR MILLER
JOHN MILTON
EUGENIO MONTALE
MARIANNE MOORE
IRIS MURDOCH
VLADIMIR NABOKOV
JOYCE CAROL OATES
SEAN O'CASEY
FLANNERY O'CONNOR
EUGENE O'NEILL
GEORGE ORWELL
CYNTHIA OZICK
WALTER PATER
WALKER PERCY
HAROLD PINTER
PLATO
EDGAR ALLAN POE

POETS OF SENSIBILITY &
    THE SUBLIME
ALEXANDER POPE
KATHERINE ANNE PORTER
EZRA POUND
PRE-RAPHAELITE POETS
MARCEL PROUST
THOMAS PYNCHON
ARTHUR RIMBAUD
THEODORE ROETHKE
PHILIP ROTH
JOHN RUSKIN
J. D. SALINGER
GERSHOM SCHOLEM
WILLIAM SHAKESPEARE (3 vols.)
    HISTORIES & POEMS
    COMEDIES
    TRAGEDIES
GEORGE BERNARD SHAW
MARY WOLLSTONECRAFT SHELLEY
PERCY BYSSHE SHELLEY
EDMUND SPENSER
GERTRUDE STEIN
JOHN STEINBECK
LAURENCE STERNE
WALLACE STEVENS
TOM STOPPARD
JONATHAN SWIFT
ALFRED LORD TENNYSON
WILLIAM MAKEPEACE THACKERAY
HENRY DAVID THOREAU
LEO TOLSTOI
ANTHONY TROLLOPE
MARK TWAIN
JOHN UPDIKE
GORE VIDAL
VIRGIL
ROBERT PENN WARREN
EVELYN WAUGH
EUDORA WELTY
NATHANAEL WEST
EDITH WHARTON
WALT WHITMAN
OSCAR WILDE
TENNESSEE WILLIAMS
WILLIAM CARLOS WILLIAMS
THOMAS WOLFE
VIRGINIA WOOLF
WILLIAM WORDSWORTH
RICHARD WRIGHT
WILLIAM BUTLER YEATS

Further titles in preparation.

Modern Critical Views

EDMUND SPENSER

Modern Critical Views

EDMUND SPENSER

Edited with an introduction by

Harold Bloom

Sterling Professor of the Humanities
Yale University

1986
CHELSEA HOUSE PUBLISHERS
New York
New Haven   Philadelphia

PROJECT EDITORS: Emily Bestler, James Uebbing
ASSOCIATE EDITOR: Maria Behan
EDITORIAL COORDINATOR: Karyn Gullen Browne
EDITORIAL STAFF: Perry King, Bert Yaeger
DESIGN: Susan Lusk

Cover illustration by Peter McCaffrey

Library of Congress Cataloging in Publication Data

Edmund Spenser.
   (Modern critical views)
   Bibliography: p.
   Includes index.
   Summary: Sixteen critical essays on the
Elizabethan poet and his works.
   1. Spenser, Edmund, 1552?–1599—Criticism and
interpretation—Addresses, essays, lectures. 2. English
literature—History and criticism—Addresses, essays,
lectures. I. Bloom, Harold. II. Series.
PR2364.E36 1986   821'.3   85–25560
ISBN 0–87754–672–X

Chelsea House Publishers
Harold Steinberg, Chairman and Publisher
Susan Lusk, Vice President
A Division of Chelsea House Educational Communications, Inc.
133 Christopher Street, New York, NY 10014

Contents

Editor's Note

This volume gathers together a representative selection of the best literary criticism devoted to the poetry of Edmund Spenser during the past quarter-century, arranged in the chronological order of its publication. The editor's "Introduction," published here for the first time, actually was written in 1960, and then was lost. Recovered recently, it is offered here with only a few minor revisions, both as a general overview of Spenser's achievement, and as a commentary upon aspects of Book II of *The Faerie Queene*, and upon *Epithalamion, Prothalamion, Muiopotmos* and the *Amoretti*. Rereading it after twenty-five years, its author acknowledges how profoundly the essay is indebted to the earlier criticism of Northrop Frye, and to *Anatomy of Criticism* (1957) in particular.

My first selection, Frye's essay of 1961 on "The Structure of Imagery in *The Faerie Queene*," is therefore an appropriate beginning, since Frye, the Ruskin of our day, has been the fountainhead of so much recent criticism of Spenser. His influence is strong in the next essay, A. C. Hamilton's analysis of allegorical structure in Books I and II. With Thomas Greene's meditation upon that aspect of *The Faerie Queene*, we find ourselves in a different critical tradition, Continental and more formalistic. Greene accurately compares the poem to Joyce's *Finnegans Wake*, with its metamorphic, dreamlike nature.

Four of *The Faerie Queene*'s mythic centers are then illuminated, with Thomas P. Roche, Jr. on the marriage of the Thames and the Medway, Donald Cheney on the Gardens of Adonis, A. Bartlett Giamatti on the Bower of Bliss, and Harry Berger, Jr. on the *Mutabilitie Cantos*. Isabel G. MacCaffrey's essay on *The Shepheardes Calender* returns to Spenser's poetic beginnings to examine the relation between pastoral and allegory, a relation that comes full circle in Book VI of the poem, and is described in Patricia A. Parker's exegesis of what she calls "the romance of romance" in Spenser. Between MacCaffrey and Parker comes Angus Fletcher, the authority for our time on allegory, with his brilliant juxtaposition of Spenser's great conceptual images of the temple and the labyrinth.

This volume's final movement consists of criticism of the nineteen-eighties, commencing with Lawrence Manley on the image of the city in *Prothalamion* and related poems, Kenneth Gross on Spenser and Milton,

John Guillory on poetic authority, and Peter Sacks on "Astrophel," Spenser's beautifully modulated lament for Sir Philip Sidney. John Hollander's brilliant excursus upon Spenser's metric is followed by Donald Cheney's advanced meditation upon the structure of *The Faerie Queene*. Cheney's essay, published here for the first time, fittingly concludes this volume. It sums up many of the insights achieved in Spenser criticism during the last quarter-century, and intimates directions in which our reading of Spenser is likely to move.

Introduction

. . . if the whole man be trained perfectly, and his mind calm, consistent, and powerful, the vision which comes to him is seen as in a perfect mirror, serenely, and in consistence with the rational power; but if the mind be imperfect and ill trained, the vision is seen as in a broken mirror, with strange distortions and discrepancies, all the passions of the heart breathing upon it in cross ripples, till hardly a trace of it remains unbroken. So that, strictly speaking, the imagination is never governed; it is always the ruling and Divine power. . . . And thus Iliad, *the* Inferno, *the* Pilgrim's Progress, *(the* Faerie Queene, *are all of them true dreams; only the sleep of the men to whom they came was the deep, living sleep which God sends, with a sacredness in it, as of death, the revealer of secrets.*)

— RUSKIN

Of all the major poets in English, Edmund Spenser is, at this time, the last read and, in proportion to his merits, the least valued. As a living presence in the poetry of the last twenty years he is scarcely to be felt, for since the death of Yeats the English-speaking world has had no poet even in part educated by Spenser, no poetry directly affected by *The Faerie Queene*. Spenser has been abandoned to the academies, and within them he has become increasingly peripheral. When the critical sensibility that prevailed in Britain and America during these last decades turned to Spenser, it found little in him to justify the eminence he had held for three hundred years. His long poem was dismissed as the product of the will usurping the work of the imagination. The Shakespearean critic, Derek Traversi, may be taken as representative of still prevalent (though waning) taste when he judged Spenser to have made "splendid pieces of rhetorical decoration" devoid of deep personal content, and to have mastered a style which "tends irresistibly to become an instrument of disintegration, furthering the dissolution of the declared moral intention into mere rhythmical flow." The distance between such a verdict and an accurate judgment of Spenser's achievement is so great that a lover of Spenser's poetry is compelled to resist a reaction into overpraise of "the Prince of Poets in his time." One is tempted to maintain that a reader who cannot apprehend Spenser's voice as being at its best the voice of poetry itself is not capable of reading adequately any poetry whatsoever. But too much rhetoric of that dismissing kind has been used by critics over the past decades; admirers of Spenser, of Milton, of Blake and Wordsworth and Shelley, have been assured, all too frequently, that the life of English poetry was elsewhere, and that the Romantic and mythopoeic tradition was an aberration. It was curiously necessary for the admirers of metaphysical verse to deprecate everything in English poetry that was most unlike Donne, but the poetry of Spenser and the tradition he inaugurated are too firmly central to require any polemic against a rival tradition.

John Hughes, who edited the works of Spenser in 1715, remarked of *The Faerie Queene* that "the chief merit of this Poem consists in that surprizing Vein of fabulous Invention, which runs thro it." We no longer commend poets specifically for their invention, but that seemed the essence of poetry from the Renaissance critics through Dr. Johnson and on into the Romantic period. The manner in which the invention was handled received only equal weight with the rarity of the fictive matter itself in Renaissance criticism, but gradually has come (in modern criticism) to crowd out the proper valuing of invention. In a period of revived mythopoeic poetry, the age of Yeats and Rilke, the poets are attended as exegetes by rhetorical critics, many of them hostile to the autonomy demanded by the inventive faculty, the mythopoeic power that Spenser possessed in greater measure than any poet in English except for Blake.

Hughes observed that "Spenser's Fable, tho often wild, is . . . always emblematical," and commended his poet for thus turning romance to the uses of allegory. The conventions of romance and the problematical nature of allegory have alike provided barriers between Spenser and many modern readers, but the poet's artistry as a romantic allegorist is informed by the exuberance of his invention. To consider Spenser under the arbitrary divisions of romance, allegory and myth-making, as I shall now proceed to do, is to endanger the integrity of his sustained vision, but one of the virtues of reading and discussing Spenser is to be taught a healthy fear of discursive reduction, of the organized translation of poetry into prose that criticism can so easily become. Yet one learns also, more from Spenser than from any poet, that all criticism of poetry tends towards allegorizing, and that the consciously allegorical poet is not content to leave the reader and critic without a guide in his interpretation.

W. L. Renwick has said of Spenser that "we must regard his work as part of a cultural movement of European extent, as fruit of general and not merely personal experience." Certainly any attempt to understand the genesis of Spenser's poetry and that poetry's intentions must look on it as

Renwick suggests, yet Spenser in his best poetry stands very much apart from his fellow-poets of Renaissance Europe. There are very crucial elements in his poetry that make it more akin in certain ways to Blake and Shelley and Keats, writing two hundred years later, than to Ariosto and Du Bellay and Sidney, all of whom influenced him. To account for the emergence of those elements is perhaps not possible, since an imagination as full and powerful as Spenser's is strictly not accountable; we can see what it was and where it went but may never surmise its origins. Scholars of the history of ideas and historical critics of poetry think otherwise, but they tend to read all poetry by allegorizing it into concepts, on the implied assumption that the minds of great poets work as theirs do. It must be granted that Spenser thought of himself as being, among other things, a philosophical poet. Philosophically he was eclectic and richly confused, in the fortunate manner of his time, which could still believe in the ultimate unity of all knowledge, pagan and Christian, natural and revealed. The intricate tangle of his conceptual borrowings is a delight to the source-hunter but irrelevant to a reader who seeks what a poet alone can give him. Again, Spenser conceived of his poetic function as being a uniquely national one; he wished to write an English poem that would match if not surpass the classical epic of Homer and Virgil and the contemporary romance of Ariosto and Tasso. The thrust towards national identity and international greatness that typified Elizabethan aspiration at its most intense is a vital component in Spenser's conscious poetic purpose. But where his poem is most national, most the work of the courtier, it is least interesting as a poem, and hopelessly mired in a now disheartening historical allegory, which Dr. Johnson's "common reader" can safely ignore.

Yeats, who knew better, but was moved by an understandable Irish grudge against Spenser, spoke of him as "the first poet struck with remorse, the first poet who gave his heart to the State." Insofar as *The Faerie Queene* so gives its heart, it ceases to be a poem, and does fasten its knights and ladies "with allegorical nails to a big barn door of common sense, of merely practical virtue," as Yeats maintained. But Spenser never gave all his heart to anything less than that imaginative vision in which the unattainable ideals of Protestant humanism were displaced into a poetic world where all good things and their dialectical counterparts were made simultaneously possible. Yeats was more accurate about Spenser and the value of his poetry when he realized how Spenser's visions, supposedly forgotten, "would rise up before me coming from I knew not where." Yeats's best criticism of Spenser is in his own poetry where he makes use of him, as when *The Ruins of Time* and the *Prothalamion* together with certain stanzas in *The Faerie Queene*, help form *Leda and the Swan* and *The Wild Swans at Coole*. More is to be learned about what is most relevant to us in Spenser's poetry by seeing how it was used by Drayton, Milton, Blake, Shelley, Keats, Tennyson and Yeats than by reading the bulk of past and present Spenserian criticism. There have been excellent Spenser critics, from Hughes and Thomas Warton to C. S. Lewis and Northrop Frye, but the extraordinary sense in which Spenser is truly the poet's poet is best brought out in a great poem like Shelley's *The Witch of Atlas*, where the world of *The Faerie Queene* is relied upon as being the universe of poetry itself.

To understand the unique nature of Spenser's poetry is to understand also something vital about how poets influence one another; indeed the study of Spenser's poetry is the best introduction available to the fascinating problem of what there is about poetry that can bring more poetry into being, for no poet has made so many other men into poets as Spenser has. What so many poets have learned from Spenser is not a style of writing but a mode of poetry, and a sense of the poet's self-recognition in regard to his own poem. The mode is that of the poem as heterocosm, the other or possible world of the poem as it exists in relation to the too-probable world of the reader. Coleridge acutely noted "the marvellous independence and true imaginative absence of all particular space or time in *The Faerie Queene*. It is in the domains neither of history or geography; it is ignorant of all artificial boundary, all material obstacles; it is truly in land of Faery, that is, of mental space." Dante comes closest to Spenser in creating such a world, but Dante's three worlds are categorical and sharply distinguished from one another. The persuasiveness of Spenser's imagined world is in the treachery of its boundaries; its heavens and hells, purgatories and earthly paradises, undergo a continual transmemberment, yet its appearances are either supremely delusive or absolutely truthful and no honest reader could tell the difference between one and the other on the basis of imagistic vividness. What Spenser had, better I think than any poet before or since, was the power to project both the object of desire and the shape of nightmare with equal imaginative freedom. That power gives its possessor the control of the literary realm of romance or idealized narrative, a domain with a potential ranging from the most primordial and almost childlike to the most sophisticated of perspectives. Romance, Northrop Frye suggestively states, is the Mythos of Summer, the narrative of quest for a lost paradise, the proper story for the man of whom Wallace Stevens could say: "He had studied the nostalgias." So have we all, and when we find ourselves most impatient of romance we are most susceptible to it, rejecting the wish but falling somehow into its fulfilling dream.

Between the invaluable chaos of nostalgia and the achieved form of romance only the capable imagination can mediate, and the fully capable
imagination must be uninhibited. Why Spenser's liberty to imagine existed
at all we cannot know, but we can see how the circumstances of his life
and time conspired to make him more free than his greater disciple,
Milton, ever came to be.

Spenser, like Milton after him, is a Protestant poet, and the Spenserian tradition in English poetry has been a Protestant one, with a progressive movement to what could be called the visionary left wing; radical in
politics, individualist in religion and insisting upon the unsupported imagination as its own warrant. The movement in religion is from the moderate Puritanism of Spenser, with its prophetic strain conflicting with a
residue of medieval sacramentalism, to the militant Puritanism and prophetic self-identification of Milton on to the displaced Protestantism of
Romantic myth-making: the naturalistic humanism of Keats, the natural
supernaturalism (as M. H. Abrams terms it) of Wordsworth, the apocalyptic vitalism of Blake, and the despairing yet heroic agnosticism of the
prophetic Shelley, most Spenserian of them all in the effect of his major
poems. In our own time the Spenserian and Romantic tradition is directly
manifested in Yeats's eclectic "system" of belief, and indirectly in the
American late Romanticism of Wallace Stevens (who returns to Wordsworth and Keats) and of Hart Crane, very much the Shelley of our age
and the legitimate claimant to the sad dignity of being the Last Romantic.
Extreme as this statement is, *Notes Towards A Supreme Fiction* and *The
Bridge* are Spenserian poems, for the conception of the poem pointing to
itself as poem in *Notes* and the terrified quest of the poet in *The Bridge* are
both in lineal descent from *The Faerie Queene*. Crane trapped in the
purgatorial maze of *The Tunnel* seems a symbolic figure far removed from
Spenser's knight lost in the labyrinth of Error's wood, but the kinship is
clear enough when we consider the binding figures in the middle of the
tradition, the young poets of Shelley's *Alastor* and Keats's *Endymion*
questing through the baffling mazes of the natural world. Stevens, medi-
tating in his subtle variations on the theme of "the origin of the major
man," and uncovering at last "how simply the fictive hero becomes the
real," seems far indeed from Spenser laboring "to fashion a gentleman or
noble person in vertuous and gentle discipline," but again the connecting
link is in the Romantic tradition, in Blake's fictive hero, Los, the refiner
in imaginative fire who labors to humanize man, or in Wordsworth's
attempt through poetry to fashion a man in the nobility of a reciprocal
generosity with nature.

Spenser and Milton were Christian humanists and, except for

Wordsworth in his poetic decline, this can scarcely be said of any of their poetic descendants, but the lineage remains not only clear but illuminatingly inevitable in its progression. The Protestant aesthetic, as Malcolm M. Ross has shown, shifts from tradition to innovation in Milton's poetry, but the process can be traced earlier in *The Faerie Queene*, although certainly more ambiguously. Spenser did not allow himself to be inhibited either by the fear that a universal symbolism founded on sacramentalism might betray him into Catholic poetry, or that his own fictive covering might obscure the truths of Scriptural revelation. No one else has so cheerfully and astonishingly compounded pagan mythology, Christian symbolism and personal myth-making while remaining centrally in a main doctrinal tradition of Christianity.

Spenser had the humanist belief that classical thought and poetic form did not conflict with Christian truth; for him all myths merged, as all mirrored a unity of truth. Yet his personal attitude towards mythology is confusing because his sense of history is poetically pragmatic; he seems to seek the relevant, the story he can use, whether it arouses his unrivalled powers for sensuous description or because it might illuminate his allegory of sanctification, and usually because it can do both. The golden world seemed past to him, and although he heralded the greatest single period of English poetry he evidently had as dark a view of his country's immediate literary prospects as any unimaginative moralist might have assumed. Like Sidney, Spenser believed that a poet shared in the creativity of God, and therefore believed also in the poet's responsibility to bring his creation into a meaningful relationship with the moral order of God's creation. Such a belief led Spenser into the writing of allegory, and finally into the ambitious enterprise of his allegorical epic-romance.

Much recent prejudice against *The Faerie Queene* is simply a prejudice against all allegory whatsoever. Works that declare themselves overtly as simple allegories, like *The Pilgrim's Progress*, now tend to go unread, while complex allegorists like Dante, Blake and Melville are studied frequently as if they had not consciously modulated the contexts in which their meanings were to be interpreted. Allegory is now associated for many with mere moralizing, while symbolism has the prestige of the legitimate about it. The Romantic descendants of Spenser, from Blake to Yeats, are partially responsible for this curious confusion. Blake was a great critic, but his distinction between "Allegory & Vision" was not a very happy one: "Fable or Allegory are a totally distinct & inferior kind of Poetry. Vision or Imagination is a Representation of what Eternally Exists, Really & Unchangeably." Indeed, he could not rest in his own distinction, for his own poetry fits his earlier and positive use of the word:

"Allegory address'd to the Intellectual powers, while it is altogether hidden from the Corporeal Understanding, is My Definition of the Most Sublime Poetry." On this definition a proper defence of Spenser's poetry, as well as Blake's can and should be made. The "Corporeal Understanding" is Blake's phrase for any empirical approach that is not open to vision or imaginative apprehension. The unity and, to a good extent, the value of Spenser's masterpiece are certainly hidden from the investigation of much Spenserian scholarship, with its empiricist presuppositions. What Blake means by "the Intellectual powers" is everything the reader's mind is capable of bringing to self-integration as the reader experiences the poem. If the poem falls short of the reader's potential for wholeness the reader will learn it in time, but patience and good will are necessities if the effort is to be made.

Edwin Honig usefully finds "the allegorical quality in a twice-told tale written in rhetorical, or figurative, language and expressing a vital belief." So broad a way of approaching allegory seems the best antidote to the modern suspicion of allegory, a distrust reducing a complex relation between image and idea to the simple deception of an image masking an idea. For allegory in Spenser is neither a discourse in disguised ideas nor a pattern of familiar events deliberately (and momentarily) distorted. Spenser's allegory, in its totality and frequently in its details, reverberates into further meanings by its capability and adequacy as a poem, its strength in self-containment and completeness. *The Faerie Queene* is a more diffuse work than *Paradise Lost* or Blake's *Jerusalem,* more diffuse even than *Finnegan's Wake* (with which it curiously has much in common) but the manner of its metamorphic extension justifies the seeming lack of cohesiveness. For Spenser begins with sustained allegory and ends (he died before conclusion) with an imagined world, a world containing as many of the total possibilities of literature within it as any other professed allegory up to his own time. His apocalyptic Book I may be his masterpiece, but I pass over it here so as to consider the centers of vision elsewhere in his great romance, and in the best of his minor poems.

II

The artistic completeness of Book I compels Spenser to an altogether fresh start in Book II, in which the literary context shifts from the Bible to the classical epic and the theme from experience in the order of grace to experience in the order of nature, a change best analyzed by A. S. P. Woodhouse. Sir Guyon, the quester in Book II, exemplifies heroic virtue more directly and fully than St. George could ever represent sanctification, since the classical virtues are wholly within the natural realm. Though Guyon is spared the fearful purgations of Spenser's first hero, his triumph is necessarily a less definitive one, and the disinterested reader of poetry is rather less likely to be unequivocal in appreciating that triumph, the overthrow of the sensual delights of Acrasia and her Bower of Bliss.

Frequently noted is the clear parallel in narrative structure between the first two books, usefully explained by Woodhouse's frame of reference, the contrast between the two orders, nature and grace. The knight of faith, guided by a veiled but still effectual truth, overcomes his earlier opponents, but falls victim (through his own credulity) to deception and is tempted by an irrevocable despair. The knight of temperance, guided by an invulnerable and moderate wisdom, undergoes temptation but resists it, and falls only through natural exhaustion. Roused again, his awakened nature accomplishes an ethical triumph without direct heavenly aid, unlike the knight of faith who must be rescued by grace, and then refreshed by it in the climactic battle.

Where Book I is dominated by scenes of struggle climaxing in the strife between death and resurrection, the actual battles in Book II are of only secondary importance. The first event in Book I is the Red Cross Knight's victory over Error; the parallel event in Book II is a fight that does not take place, as Guyon recognizes the error of his wrath before fully attacking the Red Cross Knight. Guyon already has the temperate virtues, and needs only to realize them by bringing them into activity in response to a wide range of temptations. By doing so, he becomes the prototype of Milton's Christ in *Paradise Regained*, for his is the task of a Hercules greater than the Herculean heroes of classical epic. Guyon and Milton's Christ must transform a passive consciousness of heroic virtue into an active awareness that knows itself fully because it becomes more itself in the act of confronting temptation. Guyon is of course only a man, and fortunately for the poem he can be tempted, although one sometimes wishes he could be tempted to a greater degree of dramatic indecisiveness as he quests remorselessly on.

The quest of Book II begins with the powerful episode of Amavia and Mortdant, both slain indirectly by the sexual witchery of Acrasia, a Circe-like enchantress. Guyon vows to avenge their death, and begins this process by attempting to care for Ruddymane, the infant abandoned by their self-destructiveness. The ineffectuality of merely natural means to accomplish fully any moral quest is shown immediately by Guyon's inability to wash the babe's hands free of guilty human blood, a frightening symbolic parody of the sacrament of baptism.

The image of the babe's bloody hands haunts the rest of Book II, for the babe's equivocal innocence is an epitome of how closely original sin and the possibility of natural virtue dwell together in the experiential world. The adventures of Guyon are a series of encounters between his temperate affections and the excessive humors leading to "outrageous anger" or lust, or excessive desire of any kind. In these encounters Guyon goes on foot, and his victories are indecisive, for he is more skilled at resisting evils than at abolishing them. Temperance, as Northrop Frye observes, is deliberately displayed as a pedestrian virtue, and Guyon is memorable for what he rightfully declines to do, until the very close of his book when he acts to destroy the Bower of Acrasia.

III

The most remarkable instance of Guyon's passive heroism is Canto VII, the descent into the Cave of Mammon, an episode that renews the archetype of the classical hero's descent to Avernus, as in *Aeneid*, VI. Parted from his moral guide, the prudent Palmer, Guyon undergoes a three day trial in the underworld that seems essentially to be an initiation, a parallel experience to the Red Cross Knight's three day fight with the dragon. This extraordinary myth-making of the Cave of Mammon is partly to be read as the supreme instance in Book II of the negative virtue of temperate endurance, but the invention of Spenser is too absolute to be interpreted only in terms of moral intention.

Charles Lamb noted the dream-atmosphere of the Mammon episode, and praised Spenser for a creation replete with violent transitions and incongruities "and yet the waking judgment ratifies them." The Mammon episode is vision and not dream, for the poetic content is manifest in the images, and not latent in a depth-pattern hidden from the imagination. Milton is the best guide to the Cave of Mammon and Bower of Bliss alike when he writes in *Areopagitica* that Guyon is brought through these places "that he might see and know, and yet abstain." Even Guyon must be purified by trial "and trial is by what is contrary." Guyon must "scout into the regions of sin and falsity," and so it is just and necessary that he accompany Mammon into the depths, even as Christ must undergo the temptations of Satan in *Paradise Regained*.

Mammon offers Guyon the wealth of this world, as well as his daughter Philotime, who is the equivalent of Lucifera in Book I, as Frank Kermode notes. In courteously declining Philotime, Guyon puts from himself all aspiration towards merely worldly honor, as earlier he rejects worldly goods. By passing through the Garden of Proserpina without eating of its fruit, Guyon avoids the fate of Tantalus, who suffers in hell for impiously seeking divinely concealed secrets. The punishment of Tantalus is a demonic parody of the refreshment of St. George by the Tree of Life, just as the punishment of his companion Pilate parodies St. George's being revived by immersion in the Water of Life. (The image of Pilate reminds us also of the Ruddymane episode.) Like Tantalus, the bloody-handed Pilate sinned against the truth, and Guyon, in refusing the fruit of unlawful knowledge, has separated himself from this fundamental consequence of natural depravity.

All through his ordeal Guyon is shadowed by a fiend who would rend him apart at the least yielding to temptation, a persuasive symbol of the spectral self, the dark aspect of nature that must be purged from every man. The silver stool which is Guyon's last temptation, "to rest thy weary person in the shadow coole," was suggestively related by the eighteenth century editor Upten to the forbidden seat in the Eleusinian mysteries, a suggestion elaborated by Kermode as "a punitive chair of oblivion" for those who pervert divine knowledge.

Like Christ in the temptations by Satan, Guyon voluntarily submits to the blandishments of Mammon, and shows his heroism negatively, by a firm resistance. Guyon's is the Miltonic fortitude of patience, the virtue Adam must learn if he is to be saved. As a Christian knight, Guyon does not achieve the revelation granted to St. George, but he does overtake the Homeric and Virgilian heroes by attaining to a perfect control over his own nature through a descent into the underworld. His achieved virtue is heroic but not supernatural; it hesitates on the edge of the world of grace, but does not cross over into the revealed order. At the triumphant end of his ordeal Guyon faints, not because he has been in any way intemperate, but because he has carried his heroism to a verge of the natural condition, and has exhausted nature in doing so. He has not harrowed hell, but he has seen and known the mysteries of hell, and been saved from them by his abstinence. He falls out of his vision back into nature, and as with Keats's Endymion, the first touch of earth again comes nigh to killing him. We are left with the dark splendor of his ordeal, a pattern directly relevant to our society as it was to Spenser's. What Guyon has rejected is what Spenser sought and most men compulsively seek, a glory that shines beautifully because it is surrounded by darkness, a kingdom where the only wealth is death. The moral is an aesthetically powerful dimension of the myth not only because it is universal but because it is observation rather than admonition. Spenser knew himself to be no Hercules, and Guyon's escape is not the victory of an Everyman.

The strength of Spenser's fiction is in its deathly attraction; the reader is not Guyon. A knight of Temperance humanistically fulfills his nature, and faints into the light of every day. The necessarily intemperate reader yields to the imagination, which desires to be indulged. We remain to some extent in the Cave, not because it is the best of places, or even because we are overwhelmingly tempted, but because we are poor; we lack the only wealth which is life.

IV

Probably no section of *The Faerie Queene* so directly identifies its poets as Canto XII of Book II, the account of the voyage towards and the overthrow of Acrasia's Bower of Bliss. Hazlitt praised the "voluptuous pathos" of the Bower, and implied that what was most poetic in Spenser was most at home in the Bower. This is a partial truth and certainly more valuable than the moralistic insistence of many commentators that the Bower is altogether a degraded as well as a degrading place. The Bower is a "horrible enchantment," but an enchantment nevertheless.

The most persuasive modern enemy of the Bower is C. S. Lewis, who has severely insisted that Acrasia's garden is artificial rather than natural, as contrasted to the natural and spontaneous profusion of the Gardens of Adonis. The Bower, again according to Lewis, shows the whole sexual nature in sterile suspension: "There is not a kiss or an embrace in the island: only male prurience and female provocation." To this Lewis again contrasts the Gardens of Adonis, with its teeming sexual life. On this reading, one has got to be something of a *voyeur* to be attracted by the Bower, to be delighted as our "wanton eies do peepe" at Acrasia and her naked damsels.

Lewis is reacting against those critics who have charged Spenser with "actual sensuality and theoretical austerity." Spenser is subtler and more varied in his art than either his moralistic attackers or defenders have been willing to notice. Part of the contrast between the Gardens of Adonis and the Bower of Bliss is certainly due to the element of artifice in the Bower, yet the Bower remains very much within the natural world. Indeed its natural beauty is what we as readers are first asked to notice, and precisely what Guyon must first resist. He wonders much "at the fayre aspect of that sweet place," but does not suffer any delight "to sincke into his sence, nor mind affect." The Bower is nature *mixed* with art, as one might expect of any sophisticated sensuality. Some of its fruits are of burnished gold, yet its boughs hang always heavy with the ripeness of nature. Acrasia and her victim-lover are not caught by Guyon and the Palmer in the act of love, but it will not do to maintain that there are no embraces in the Bower. Acrasia is seen in the "langour of her late sweet toyle," and her spent lover sleeps in her arms in what is intended as a demonic parody of the sleep of Adonis, a vision that would be pointless if it testified only to "male prurience and female provocation." No; whatever the Bower is, it is scarcely a picture of the whole sexual nature in disease. Moral criticism of poetry is self-defeating if it denies Satan his heroic courage, Iago his serpentine insight, or Acrasia her genuine attractiveness, the fierce vigor of her unsanctified sexual nature, presented as its own self-justifying goal. Even the peeping-Tom element in the Bower, which is undeniable, is an equivocal element throughout the poem. Spenser's vision always points us in towards a center in any scene, sexual or otherwise; his is the art of the cynosure, and no poet has yielded so fully to the tyranny of the bodily eye. His heroes long to gaze upon a variety of glories, and to fulfill themselves in that vision. Acrasia's wanton damsels, inviting the gaze of Guyon, are a parody of the Faerie Queene's granting-of-herself in vision to Arthur, and more directly of all Spenser's exposed heroines upon whom we so delightedly spy.

Guyon is not more or less natural than the Bower he overthrows, any more than his resistance to the temptations of Mammon is more or less natural than a surrender to the Cave's wealth would have been. It is because both Guyon and Acrasia are natural possibilities that Spenser is capable of bringing them into an imaginatively meaningful juxtaposition. What Guyon destroys is not evil in itself, but is rather a good that has luxuriated into dangerous excess because it has denied all context. Guyon is faithful to a context in which sexual love can humanize and not merely naturalize, but Acrasia's love robs men of their human nature. If the reader is more inclined towards naturalism than Spenser was, he still need not suspend his disbelief in Guyon's context, for Spenser's poem stands in its own right as a making, rather than as an adornment to a moral order complete without the imaginings of the poet. Acrasia is like Keats's Belle Dame or Blake's maidens of the Crystal Cabinet or the Golden Net, weaving an enchantment horrible only because it pretends to offer a final reality or inmost form within sexual experience alone. The ruined quester becomes a beast of the field, or starves, or enters into a baffled state unable to comprehend his loss. Keats and Blake are more humanistic in their implications as to what a saving context might be, but the mythic pattern they give us is Spenserian.

There is a curious bitterness in the final stanzas of Book II, as Spenser confronts Guyon and the Palmer with the stubborn Gryll, who had been happy as a hog. It was for this Gryll's sake, as for his fellows, that Guyon and the Palmer had surpassed the voyages of Odysseus, had risked the terrors of the sea so magnificently set forth in the earlier stanzas of Canto XII. The temperate voyager has shown the power of a Hercules and the endurance of an Odysseus; with "rigor pittilesse" he has broken down a great work of mixed art and nature, sparing no part of "their goodly workmanship." Part of his immediate reward is the hoggish lament of a Gryll, and the incongruity of this response provokes the abruptness of the canto's end. If there is bitterness here, there is a sour humor as well. Spenser usually spares himself (and us) the Miltonic contempt for "the donghill kinde" of all-too-natural men, but he has something of the Miltonic horror at any forgetfulness of the excellence of man's creation. The Bower is finally seen as a complement to Mammon's cave, as yet another instrumentality for the dehumanization of man. We are asked to believe that the fruit of Acrasia, eaten for its own sake, destroys as surely as the fruit of Proserpina's garden. There is a natural resistance to so harsh a judgment, within Spenser as within ourselves. Gryll is the warning made not to overcome that resistance but to offer a speaking picture that may trouble even the self-indulging imagination.

V

It is in the *Two Cantos of Mutabilitie* that Spenser troubles his own imagination most, by the strongest of his pictures. The *Mutabilitie Cantos* were not published until 1609, a decade after Spenser's death. Though this greatest of poetic fragments was printed as Cantos VI and VII (and two stanzas of Canto VIII) of Book VII of *The Faerie Queene*, one is tempted to read it as a complete unit in itself, a finishing coda to the otherwise unfinished poem. Certainly the fragment's last two stanzas could not have begun anything; what they yearn for is finality, and they proclaim a poet's farewell to his art and his life.

Various commentators have traced (or thought they traced) the effect of Empedocles, of Lucretius and of Bruno on the *Mutabilitie Cantos*, but Spenser is here more than ever inventive, dealing imaginatively with his own obsessional theme of change and decay in the phenomenal world. Probably he owes the debate form of the fragment to Chaucer's *Parlement of Foules*, but *Mutabilitie* is a very un-Chaucerian comedy, with a profound anguish underlying the ebullient surface.

C. S. Lewis has maintained that Spenser's Titaness Mutabilitie "despite her beauty, is an evil force," an enemy of Spenserian health and concord, and indeed an incarnation of corruption and sin, but this is an over-reading through excessive simplification. Part of the immense power of Spenser's fragment is lost if the Titaness is denied all justice, however much of a shudder must accompany the dramatic sympathy. What is poetically most important about Mutabilitie is what we find most surprising—that Spenser had made her beautiful. This is part of our involuntary sympathy with her, and wins even Jove's momentary (and mistaken) indulgence. Another part is in the genesis of the Titanic myth itself; her claim through lineage is better than Jove's. But most crucial is that Mutabilitie is more human than the gods she challenges; if she is tainted by earthly sin, we of course are too, and her mounting up into the sphere of the moon has its Promethean element.

The corruption of Mutabilitie is primarily decay rather than sin, for morality is not very relevant to this fragment. If it were, then Jove might be given power over Mutabilitie, or his ultimate rule over her realm be implied. But Spenser, for once in *The Faerie Queene*, is not giving us a vision of possibility, but a lament of experience, and the phenomenal sway of Mutabilitie is an experiential truth. The beauty of Mutabilitie is part of that truth, as is the virtual identity of Mutabilitie and human existence itself. The charming episode of Faunus and Molanna is an effective digression because the mischief of its natural spirits towards Diana shows a gentler aspect of the revolt against heavenly rule by Mutabilitie. We suffer with poor Faunus, are pleased by Molanna's river-marriage, and are not very edified by Diana's curse on the region around Arlo-hill. On a larger scale, we have some degree of involvement in Mutabilitie's quest against Cynthia, much as we desire the verdict to go against the rebel.

Yet even the verdict is ambiguous, with something of the mythopoeic complexity we have encountered earlier in the Gardens of Adonis. The poetic synthesis of Spenser is indeed conceptually simpler, more sensuous and more passionate than any philosophical resolution of the problem of change and decay could have been. One element in that synthesis is almost a palinode, which emerges most clearly in the two final stanzas, perhaps the most moving Spenser wrote. The close of Chaucer's *Troilus and Criseyde* provides a rough but useful parallel to Spenser's last stanzas, but the heavenly laughter of Troilus is what Spenser seeks, not what he has already found.

The metamorphic land of Faerie is by turns a humanized nature and a demonic labyrinth, but the land of the *Mutabilitie Cantos* is our generative world, neither redeemed nor doomed, but perpetually subject to alteration, some of it cyclic and expected, like that portrayed in the pageant of the months, but some portion totally unexpected, and running generally to the worse. On the simplest and most human level of his subject Spenser is complaining for all men, and the dignity of the universal is deeply invested in his tone. Proud Mutabilitie is unquestioned mistress of all moral things; from her "all living wights have learned to die." When she turns her ambitions to the heavens she projects our deathly desires towards the eternal world, and menaces an orderly alteration with our disorderly and corrupt beauty. Spenser's uniqueness as a poet, which he bequeaths to Keats especially among his descendants, is in the sensuous immediacy of all his imagined worlds. Mutabilitie is descended from chaos and from earth, and so are we. She carries up with her to the moon's sphere the menace of chaos and the beauty of earth, and the supposed right of capability. The relation of poetry to morality has always been a troubled one, but it seems clear that energy and resolution are always poetic virtues, however unlawful or evil their ends may be in actual existence. Spenser's aspiring Titaness has something of the vigor of Milton's greatest creation, the Satan of *Paradise Lost*, and something in consequence, of Satan's aesthetic hold upon us.

Her appeal is made past Jove to "the god of Nature," who appears only through the veiled presence of his surrogate, Nature herself, perhaps suggested to Spenser by the Wisdom of Proverbs 8:22–31, brought forth by God "before his works of old." The judging voice of Spenser's Nature is his version of the voice of the Hebrew God, for Spenser was poetically subtler than Milton, and too involved in the glory of invention to risk a portrayal of God in His proper person. So Spenser's Nature, though a "great goddess" is not to be seen by us as being either man or women, terror or beauty. Yet her shrouding garment burns with the light of the Transfiguration, and her words are to be respected as definitive by Mutabilitie herself.

The Titaness, by her direct appeal to Nature, affords Spenser the opportunity for one of his most brilliant set-pieces, the Cycle of the Seasons and Months. The tone of Spenser in this chant is complex, for much of the alteration he evidences is benevolent towards men. Even Mutabilitie's account of Earth's function is close to that given in the Gardens of Adonis, and her vision of the other elements suggests the lament of Ecclesiastes. When Spenser comes to the seasons, his voice suggests the tragic naturalism of Keats, who must have learned from these stanzas. In the pageant of the months Spenser fuses joyful images of human labor with the dignified and mixed sadness of classicial mythology, as he follows out the course of the vegetative (and Christian) year, till he comes to December, with its Christian paradox of a divine birth in the dead of winter. From this point his stately chant is dominated by dialectical images, with Day and Night, Life and Death, in a creative opposition, preparing the way for the apocalyptic longings of the final stanzas.

The judgment of Nature turns the evidence of Mutabilitie against itself, and makes of phenomenal change and decay an emblem of faith, in reply to the skepticism of the insurgent Titaness: "But what we see not, who shall us perswade?" Everything changes, and yet but dilates being, for natural existence constantly though gradually works towards the revelation of a more human nature. Mutabilitie seeks more palpable sway, yet her desire is self-destructive, for time in Spenser as in Blake or Shelley is the mercy of eternity, and the agent of prophetic redemption. Spenser's humanism is liberated into an imaginative vitalism through Nature's assurances that states of being survive though all things must endure change. The time that shall come, in bringing about the uncovering of all things, will bring also the perfection that reigns over change. Until that time comes, Nature vanishes, leaving Mutabilitie dominant in the lower world beneath the moon, and Jove as ordered change still reigning in the heavens above.

Had Spenser ended there, his fragment would have a curiously cold climax for so turbulent and piercing a work. The poet's voice at its most personal breaks into his poem, weighing the speech of Mutabilitie and desperately granting the pragmatic strength of her claim to all the human world. Renouncing the beauty and pride of the only life we can lead, he turns to the speech of Nature for some comfort, and the urgency of his prayer reverberates strangely against the humanism and love celebrated throughout his poem. Yet even here, as he prays for a sight of the eternal sabbath, he does not allow himself to denigrate the experience of living. All shall rest with God, but meanwhile "all that moveth doth in change *delight.*" The pride of life is "so fading and so fickle" and must yield to "short time," but while it lasts it remains a "*flowring* pride."

VI

Spenser's sonnet sequence, *Amoretti* (1595), is sometimes undervalued because it is read in juxtaposition to Shakespeare's, which it certainly influenced. Even the sequences of Sidney, Daniel and Drayton all have some poems better than any single sonnet in the *Amoretti*, and Sidney's sequence has always had more admirers than Spenser's. Unlike Milton, Spenser does not show himself in his true dimensions in his minor poems (if we except the *Epithalamion*). The Spenserian voice is there, but sometimes we feel it badly needs the mythic atmosphere of Faerie if we are to hear it properly.

The rhyme-scheme (ababbcbccdcdee) of the *Amoretti* may have been invented by Spenser himself; in any case it is characteristic of him in its aural complexity. Characteristic also is the very individual love relationship that the sequence celebrates, a relationship that suggests the ideal portrayed in Books III and IV of *The Faerie Queene*. Spenser, all his deliberate Petrarchism aside, is surely dealing with his own love for Elizabeth Boyle, and the whole sequence moves towards the supreme joy of the *Epithalamion*. Louis Martz usefully notes the "dominant tone of assurance and poise and mutual understanding that controls the series," and so sets it apart from the generality of such sequences. Gentleness and loving esteem on the poet's side, good humor and intelligence on the lady's, are the qualities that overcome the conventional difficulties of courtship. The very sophisticated Spenserian sense of humor, frequently evident in *The Faerie Queene*, is ambiguously involved in this sonnet sequence, although difficult to isolate.

The fifteen sonnets included here are chosen for their intrinsic values, rather than their place in the sequence, and do not in fact give an adequate idea of the sequence's tone. But each has a kind of beauty that is uniquely Spenser's, an *aware* exquisiteness that is marvelously sustained by its urbane self-consciousness and surpassing craftsmanship. Sonnet LXX is, I suppose, not accounted one of the greatest examples of the form in the language, but few poems are as artful in provoking the fine bitterness of a universal nostalgia, and no poem could be more beautiful.

VII

Spenser's *Muiopotmos* or *The Fate of the Butterflie* is a kind of play-poem, like its descendant, Shelley's *The Witch of Atlas*. As an exercise in the mock-heroic, *Muiopotmos* might be expected to echo Chaucer, but the tone of Spenser's charming poem has a mysterious gravity lurking in it, which has attracted many allegorizing commentators of the historical and moralistic varieties. The most convincing allegorization is by D. C. Allen, who reads the poem "as an account of the soul caught in the eternal struggle between reason and sensuality," this account being made through a Christian variation on the myth of Cupid and Psyche.

Spenser's poem is rather more tentative and individual than such a reading might imply it to be, for even its two Ovidian digressions (the stories of Astery, and of Minerva and Arachne) are original myth-makings,

Ovidian only in their borrowings of externals. The strong effect of *Muiopotmos* on Keats and Shelley (and, I suspect, on Blake) testifies to its Romantic quality. Of all Spenser's minor poems *Muiopotmos* is the most prophetic in its sensibility, for it anticipates both the ambiguous tone and the dialectical attitude that the major Romantic myth-makers were to bring to their depictions of the natural world.

In the gay gardens where lavish Nature and contending Art have missed their best effects, the young Clarion enjoys delight with liberty, the greatest felicity that can come to any creature. This Keatsian joy ensues from Clarion's unsundered state; he is lord of everything he sees, and he sees nothing that does not please the eye of Innocence. Although Clarion is the fairest of his kind, he is "unhappie happie," for Jove's own hand weaves a cruel fate against this shining exemplar of "kingly joyaunce." The reference to weaving introduces the Satanic Aragnoll, spider within the Garden of delight. Describing Aragnoll, Spenser invokes the Fall: the spider is "th' author of confusion," and corrupter of paradise. The fault is within the very condition that has produced Clarion's felicity; Aragnoll is "the shame of Nature." We pass from Innocence to destruction without any major image of Experience except for the spider's subtle and deceitful web. The poem's last four stanzas show a startling shift of tone for so playful a work. After two stanzas of very overt mock-heroic, Spenser ends on two nervous and poignant stanzas, with a shocking abruptness in the grisly conclusion. Nothing in the poem suggests that Clarion is actively culpable, that he in any way deserves so terrible a fate. It is the beauty of the natural world, mixed with the spider's art, that deceives Clarion; the soul falls because it must, and the shame is Nature's. The gay gardens offer a vision that they cannot sustain, and no moral is made available to us, unless it be the Romantic one that a more adequate mode of vision is needed, if ever we are to enjoy delight with liberty within a natural context.

VIII

Spenser's hymn for his own marriage, *Epithalamion*, is clearly the finest of his minor poems, and one of the supreme shorter poems in the language, worthy to be considered with *Lycidas* and *Ode, Intimations of Immortality*, for like them it gives in concise form an epic poet's vision of achieved peace. Milton finished *Paradise Lost*, and Wordsworth *The Prelude*, although he did not publish it. Spenser wrote only half of his great poem, leaving us the *Mutabilitie* fragment and the previously published *Epithalamion* as possible indications of how he might have completed the design set forth in his Letter to Raleigh.

Ultimately, any hymn celebrating Christian marriage derives from the Song of Solomon, and from the exaltation of God's marriage to the land and people in Isaiah. The rites of marriage, Mircea Eliade has shown, repeat the archetypes of a divine marriage, in which heaven is united with earth. Spenser takes pains both to associate his own marriage with the union of Jove and Maia, and to dissociate it from the ritual pattern attendant upon other couplings of Jove (with Alcmena, and with night). That pattern (repeated by Dido and Aeneas in *Aeneid*, VI, for instance) is one of bringing together heaven and earth by storm, so as to renew the fertility of earth even as the god takes his human bride. By rejecting storm as the proper setting (lines 326–331) Spenser carefully removes part of the pagan background he has invoked in the reference to Jove and Maia (lines 307–310). From the love of Jove for Maia came the creation of Hermes, cleverest of gods, never violent, bearer of good fortune, god of shepherds and the common people. Of all the gods, Hermes is the most protective, and Spenser may have felt a prophetic need for protection, even as the events gathered that were to lead to his death five years later.

This complexity of mythological reference is vital to the *Epithalamion* for Spenser's poem is more than a joyous celebration, being also a sage and serious vision of human concord and the end of man. The astonishingly beautiful first stanza leads into its refrain by an identification of Spenser and the primal poet Orpheus, who also sang his own marriage hymn, and all but conquered death through song, almost bringing his bride back from darkness into the light. The profound joy that is to come later in the poem, with the poet's descendants seen as overcoming death by joining the company of saints, will be the more triumphant for the dark implications of this first stanza. The Muses have their own mishaps, and Orpheus suffered a tragic *sparagmos*, a fate too possible for Spenser in wild Ireland. Out of these barely hinted anxieties the most beautiful of all refrains rises. Orpheus, bereft of his bride, sang to himself in the woods. Spenser, in expectation of his bride, begins to sing to himself, and the first woodland answer will be only the ringing of his echo. But the isolation ends in the next stanza, and the refrain subtly changes, as the woods now answer in echo to a song of joy and solace, sung to the bride by the companions of the wedding. It is as though the first stanza represented the pre-dawn reflections of the poet-bridegroom, musing in Orphic strain. From the second stanza on the world begins to wake, the morning comes, and with it the greater light of the bride's awakening. Stanza by stanza the world comes to a fuller life, until the bride is described in terms of Solomon's Song, and the temple gates are opened wide for the marriage ceremony.

After the celebration and the moving invocation of night, with its mythological references as mentioned earlier, the poem comes to rest in hushed stanzas of hopefulness and thanksgiving, centering on the rite of marriage as an *imitatio dei*, or renewal of the creation. The integral wholeness of the creation is to be restored, and the bringing-together again of earth and heaven to be accomplished, only through marriage and its progeny. If *The Faerie Queene* had ended with a marriage between Gloriana and Arthur, the hymn at their festival could not have surpassed Spenser's chant for his own bride, and the thematic significance of that hymn would have differed from this *Epithalamion* probably only in degree. The redemption of nature is through the imagination of concord, and that imagination has never expressed itself more definitely than in Spenser's "Song, made in lieu of many ornaments."

IX

The relative coldness of *Prothalamion*, as compared to the warmly personal *Epithalamion*, might cause this lesser and later "Spousall Verse" to be undervalued. The *Prothalamion* is by intention a slighter poem than Spenser's song for his own bride, but its exquisite courtliness and appearance of easy power are unsurpassed in the expression of a deliberate and disciplined joy.

The occasion of the *Prothalamion* is a ceremony of betrothal, the mutually binding promises of human concord. Against the concord of nature at the poem's opening Spenser counterpoints his own "sullein care," the frustration of the courtier and his vain expectations. Walking forth along the Thames, the dejected poet eases his pain by observing the flowers as images of potential concord. The visions of the nymphs and the swans follow, to form the poem's substance, its imminent hope of actual concord, shining more brightly against the perpetually felt but subdued melancholy of the poet. The myth of river-marriage, although a convention, had a personal meaning for Spenser, who returns to it so often in his poetry. The teeming life of the Gardens of Adonis, lavishly freshening human substance, finds its analogue in physical nature in the joining together of rivers, a cyclic renewal that can both suffer mutability and defiantly redeem time. In the *Prothalamion* the dark undersong tells of mutability—the poet's cares; the fall of his patron, "that great lord," Leicester; the decay through pride of the Templars—while the high song dominating the poem joyously acclaims a coming fruition, in the impending marriages, and in the burgeoning greatness of Essex. This emotional counterpoint is resolved in the famous and beautiful refrain, where the first line promises the consummation of joy, and the second hints at a deferred turbulence, the world of troubles soon to come again upon the poetic celebrant of concord.

NORTHROP FRYE

The Structure of Imagery in "The Faerie Queene"

Th{}e *Faerie Queene*, long as it is, is not
nearly as long as the poem that Spenser intended to write, according to
his letter to Raleigh and two of the *Amoretti* sonnets. It therefore at once
raises the problem of whether the poem as it now stands is unfinished or
merely uncompleted. If merely uncompleted, then it still may be a unity,
like a torso in sculpture; if unfinished, then, as in Dickens' *Mystery of
Edwin Drood*, certain essential clues to the total meaning are forever
withheld from us.

Many readers tend to assume that Spenser wrote the poem in the
same way that they read it, starting at the beginning and keeping on until
he collapsed with exhaustion. But while *The Faerie Queene* probably
evolved in a much more complicated way than that, there is no evidence
of exhaustion. In the eightieth *Amoretti* sonnet he sounds winded, but not
bored; and of course he is not the kind of poet who depends on anything
that a Romantic would call inspiration. He is a professional poet, learned
in rhetoric, who approaches his sublime passages with the nonchalance of
a car-driver shifting into second gear. All the purple patches in Spenser—
the temptations of Despair and Acrasia, the praise of Elizabeth in *Colin
Clouts Come Home Again*, the "Bellona" passage in *The Shepheards Calender*—
are deliberate rhetorical exercises. There may be passages in *The Faerie
Queene* that *we* find dull, but there are very few in which Spenser's own
standards are not met. In some cantos of the fifth book, perhaps, he

From *Fables of Identity: Studies in Poetic Mythology*. Copyright © 1963 by Harcourt, Brace &
World, Inc.

sounds tired and irritable, as though he were preoccupied with his anxieties instead of his subject, and in these cantos there are lapses into muddled argument, tasteless imagery, and cacophonous doggerel. But on the whole no poem in English of comparable scope is more evenly sustained. Further, Spenser is not, like Coleridge, a poet of fragments. Just as there is a touch of Pope himself in Pope's admiration for "The spider's touch, how exquisitely fine!," so there is a touch of Spenser himself in Spenser's admiration for the honey bee "Working her formal rooms in wexen frame." He thinks inside regular frameworks—the twelve months, the nine muses, the seven deadly sins—and he goes on filling up his frame even when his scheme is mistaken from the beginning, as it certainly is in *The Tears of the Muses*.

What can be said is that, as one virtue is likely to involve others, Spenser's scheme was bound to foreshorten as he went on. In the historical allegory he still had the Armada to deal with, but in the moral allegory there is already a good deal of inorganic repetition, especially in the symbols of evil (for example, the Occasion-Ate-Sclaunder sequence and the reduplicative foul monsters). In the first book he uses up so much of the structure of Biblical typology that he could hardly have written a second book in the area of revelation; and chastity and justice, each of which is described as the supreme virtue, almost exhaust the sources of plausible compliments to Elizabeth. Spenser may well have ended his sixth book realizing that he might not write any more of it, and designed its conclusion for either possibility. He provides himself, of course, with opportunities for carrying on the story. Apart from Prince Arthur himself, we have a fresh set of characters; a seventh book would doubtless have got some clothes on Serena, who is left nude and shivering at the end of the eighth canto; the poet hints that the baby rescued by Calepine may grow up to be the hero of a future legend; he allows the Blatant Beast to escape again. But there are many such dropped stitches in the plots of the other five books, and they do not interfere with our sense of their unity. At the same time the appearance of Spenser's "signature" in Colin Clout and two other symbols from *The Shepheards Calender*, the four Graces and the envious beast that barks at poets, make the end of the sixth book also a summing up and conclusion for the entire poem and for Spenser's poetic career. There is, at least, nothing in the poem as we now have it that seems to depend for its meaning on anything unwritten.

I shall assume, as a working hypothesis, that the six books we have form a unified epic structure, regardless of how much might have been added that wasn't. There are six books, and Spenser has a curious fondness for mentioning the number six: there are six counsellors of Lucifera, six couples in the masque of Cupid, two groups of six knights fighting Britomart, six judges or Cambell's tournament, six partisans of Marinell at Florimell's tournament, six grooms of Care, and so on. In most of these groups there is a crucial seventh, and perhaps the *Mutabilitie Cantos* have that function in the total scheme of the epic. We shall probably never know on what manuscript evidence the publisher of the Folio numbered the two cantos of this poem six and seven. What we can see is that the *Mutabilitie Cantos* are certainly not a fragment: they constitute a single beautifully shaped poem that could not have had a more logical beginning, development, and end. It is entirely impossible that the last two stanzas could have been the opening stanzas of an eighth unfinished canto, as the rubric suggests. Nor is it possible that in their present form these cantos could have been the "core" of a seventh book, unless that book was inconceivably different in its structure from the existing ones. The poem brings us to the poet's "Sabbath's sight" after his six great efforts of creation, and there is nothing which at any point can be properly described as "unperfite."

To demonstrate a unity in *The Faerie Queene*, we have to examine the imagery of the poem rather than its allegory. It is Spenser's habitual technique, developing as it did out of the emblematic visions he wrote in his nonage, to start with the image, not the allegorical translation of it, and when he says at the beginning of the final canto of Book II:

> Now ginnes this goodly frame of Temperaunce
> Fayrely to rise

one feels that the "frame" is built out of the characters and places that are clearly announced to be what they are, not out of their moral or historical shadows. Spenser prefaces the whole poem with sonnets to possible patrons, telling several of them that they are in the poem somewhere, not specifying where: the implication is that for such readers the allegory is to be read more or less *ad libitum*. Spenser's own language about allegory, "darke conceit," "clowdily enwrapped," emphasizes its deliberate vagueness. We know that Belphoebe refers to Elizabeth: therefore, when Timias speaks of "her, whom the hevens doe serve and sew," is there, as one edition suggests, a reference to the storm that wrecked the Armada? I cite this only as an example of how subjective an allegorical reading can be. Allegory is not only often uncertain, however, but in the work of one of our greatest allegorical poets it can even be addled, as it is in *Mother Hubberds Tale*, where the fox and ape argue over which of them is more like a man, and hence more worthy to wear the skin of a lion. In such episodes as the legal decisions of Artegall, too, we can see that Spenser, unlike Milton, is a poet of very limited conceptual powers, and is helpless without some kind of visualization to start him thinking. I am far from urging that we should "let the allegory go" in reading Spenser, but it is self-evident that the imagery is prior in importance to it. One cannot begin to discuss the allegory without using the imagery, but one could work out an exhaustive analysis of the imagery without ever mentioning the allegory.

Our first step is to find a general structure of imagery in the poem as a whole, and with so public a poet as Spenser we should hardly expect to find this in Spenser's private possession, as we might with Blake or Shelley or Keats. We should be better advised to look for it in the axioms and assumptions which Spenser and his public shared, and which form the basis of its imaginative communication. Perhaps the *Mutabilitie Cantos*, which give us so many clues to the sense of *The Faerie Queene* as a whole, will help us here also.

The action of the *Mutabilitie Cantos* embraces four distinguishable levels of existence. First is that of Mutability herself, the level of death, corruption, and dissolution, which would also be, if this poem were using moral categories, the level of sin. Next comes the world of ordinary experience, the nature of the four elements, over which Mutability is also dominant. Its central symbol is the cycle, the round of days, months, and hours which Mutability brings forth as evidence of her supremacy. In the cycle there are two elements: becoming or change, which is certainly Mutability's, and a principle of order or recurrence within which the change occurs. Hence Mutability's evidence is not conclusive, but could just as easily be turned against her. Above our world is upper nature, the stars in their courses, a world still cyclical but immortal and unchanged in essence. This upper world is all that is now left of nature as God originally created it, the state described in the Biblical story of Eden and the Classical myth of the Golden Age. Its regent is Jove, armed with the power which, in a world struggling against chaos and evil, is "the right hand of justice truly hight." But Jove, however he may bluster and threaten, has no authority over Mutability; that authority belongs to the goddess Nature, whose viceroy he is. If Mutability could be cast out of the world of ordinary experience, lower and upper nature would be reunited, man would re-enter the Golden Age, and the reign of "Saturn's son" would be replaced by that of Saturn. Above Nature is the real God, to whom Mutability appeals when she brushes Jove out of her way, who is invoked in the last stanza of the poem, and who appears in the reference to the Transfiguration of Christ like a mirage behind the assembly of lower gods.

Man is born into the third of these worlds, the order of physical nature which is theologically "fallen" and under the sway of Mutability. But though in this world he is not of it: he really belongs to the upper nature of which he formed part before his fall. The order of physical nature, the world of animals and plants, is morally neutral: man is confronted from his birth with a moral dialectic, and must either sink below it into sin or rise above it into his proper human home. This latter he may reach by the practice of virtue and through education, which includes law, religion, and everything the Elizabethans meant by art. The question whether this "art" included what we mean by art, poetry, painting, and music, was much debated in Spenser's day, and explains why so much of the criticism of the period took the form of apologetic. As a poet, Spenser believed in the moral reality of poetry and in its effectiveness as an educating agent; as a Puritan, he was sensitive to the abuse and perversion of art which had raised the question of its moral value in the first place, and he shows his sense of the importance of the question in his description of the Bower of Bliss.

Spenser means by "Faerie" primarily the world of realized human nature. It is an "antique" world, extending backward to Eden and the Golden Age, and its central figure of Prince Arthur was chosen, Spenser tells us, as "furthest from the daunger of envy, and suspition of present time." It occupies the same space as the ordinary physical world, a fact which makes contemporary allusions possible, but its time sequence is different. It is not timeless: we hear of months or years passing, but time seems curiously foreshortened, as though it followed instead of establishing the rhythm of conscious life. Such foreshortening of time suggests a world of dream and wish-fulfillment, like the fairylands of Shakespeare's comedies. But Spenser, with his uneasy political feeling that the price of authority is eternal vigilance, will hardly allow his virtuous characters even to sleep, much less dream, and the drowsy narcotic passages which have so impressed his imitators are associated with spiritual peril. He tells us that sleep is one of the three divisons of the lowest world, the other two being death and hell; and Prince Arthur's long tirade against night (III, iv) would be out of proportion if night, like its seasonal counterpart winter, did not symbolize a lower world than Faerie. The vision of Faerie may be the *author's* dream, as the pilgrimage of Christian is presented as a dream of Bunyan, but what the poet dreams of is the strenuous effort, physical, mental, and moral, of waking up to one's true humanity.

In the ordinary physical world good and evil are inextricably confused; the use and the abuse of natural energies are hard to distinguish, motives are mixed and behaviour inconsistent. The perspective of Faerie, the achieved quest of virtue, clarifies this view. What we now see is a completed moral dialectic. The mixed-up physical world separates out into a human moral world and a demonic one. In this perspective heroes and villains are purely and simply heroic and villainous; characters are either white or black, for the quest or against it; right always has superior might in the long run, for we are looking at reality from the perspective of man as he was originally made in the image of God, unconfused about the difference between heaven and hell. We can now see that physical nature is a source of energy, but that this energy can run only in either of two opposing directions: towards its own fulfillment or towards its own destruction. Nature says to Mutability: "For thy decay thou seekst by thy desire," and contrasts her with those who, struggling out of the natural cycle, "Doe worke their owne perfection so by fate."

Spenser, in Hamlet's language, has no interest in holding the mirror up to nature unless he can thereby show virtue her own feature and scorn her own image. His evil characters are rarely converted to good, and while there is one virtuous character who comes to a bad end, Sir Terpine in Book V, this exception proves the rule, as his fate makes an allegorical point about justice. Sometimes the fiction writer clashes with the moralist in Spenser, though never for long. When Malbecco offers to take Hellenore back from the satyrs, he becomes a figure of some dignity as well as pathos; but Spenser cannot let his dramatic sympathy with Malbecco evolve. Complicated behaviour, mixed motives, or the kind of driving energy of character which makes moral considerations seem less important, as it does in all Shakespeare's heroes, and even in Milton's Satan—none of this could be contained in Spenser's framework.

The Faerie Queene in consequence is necessarily a romance, for romance is the genre of simplified or black and white characterization. The imagery of this romance is organized on two major principles. One is that of the natural cycle, the progression of days and seasons. The other is that of the moral dialectic, in which symbols of virtue are parodied by their vicious or demonic counterparts. Any symbol may be used ambivalently, and may be virtuous or demonic according to its context, an obvious example being the symbolism of gold. Cyclical symbols are subordinated to dialectical ones; in other words the upward turn from darkness to dawn or from winter to spring usually symbolizes the lift in perspective from physical to human nature. Ordinary experience, the morally neutral world of physical nature, never appears as such in The Faerie Queene, but its place in Spenser's scheme is symbolized by nymphs and other elemental spirits, or by the satyrs, who may be tamed and awed by the sight of Una or more habitually stimulated by the sight of Hellenore. Satyrane, as his name indicates, is, with several puns intended, a good-natured man, and two of the chief heroes, Redcrosse, and Artegall, are explicitly said to be natives of this world and not, like Guyon, natives of Faerie. What this means in practice is that their quests include a good deal of historical allegory.

In the letter to Raleigh Spenser speaks of a possible twenty-four books, twelve to deal with the private virtues of Prince Arthur and the other twelve with the public ones manifested after he was crowned king. But this appalling spectre must have been exorcized very quickly. If we look at the six virtues he did treat, we can see that the first three, holiness, temperance, and chastity, are essentially private virtues, and that the next three, friendship, justice, and courtesy, are public ones. Further, that both sets seem to run in a sort of Hegelian progression. Of all public virtues, friendship is the most private and personal; justice the most public and impersonal, and courtesy seems to combine the two, Calidore being notable for his capacity for friendship and yet able to capture the Blatant Beast that eluded Artegall. Similarly, of all private virtues, holiness is most dependent on grace and revelation, hence the imagery of Book I is Biblical and apocalyptic, and introduces the theological virtues. Temperance, in contrast, is a virtue shared by the enlightened heathen, a prerequisite and somewhat pedestrian virtue (Guyon loses his horse early in the book and does not get it back until Book V), hence the imagery of Book II is classicial, with much drawn from the *Odyssey* and from Platonic and Aristotelian ethics. Chastity, a virtue described by Spenser as "farre above the rest," seems to combine something of both. The encounter of Redcrosse and Guyon is indecisive, but Britomart, by virtue of her enchanted spear, is clearly stronger than Guyon, and hardly seems to need Redcrosse's assistance in Castle Joyeous.

We note that in Spenser, as in Milton's *Comus*, the supreme private virtue appears to be chastity rather than charity. Charity, in the sense of Christian love, does not fit the scheme of *The Faerie Queene*: for Spenser it would primarily mean, not man's love for God, but God's love for man, as depicted in the *Hymn of Heavenly Love*. Charissa appears in Book I, but her main connexions are with the kindliness that we associate with "giving to charity"; Agape appears in Book IV, but is so minor and so dimwitted a character that one wonders whether Spenser knew the connotations of the word. Hence, though Book I is the only book that deals explicitly with Christian imagery, it does not follow that holiness is the supreme virtue. Spenser is not dealing with what God gives to man, but with what man does with his gifts, and Redcrosse's grip on holiness is humanly uncertain.

In one of its aspects *The Faerie Queene* is an educational treatise, based, like other treatises of its time, on the two essential social facts of the Renaissance, the prince and the courtier. The most important person in Renaissance society to educate was the prince, and the next most important was the courtier, the servant of the prince. Spenser's heroes are courtiers who serve the Faerie Queene and who metaphorically make up the body and mind of Prince Arthur. To demonstrate the moral reality of poetry Spenser had to assume a connexion between the educational treatise and the highest forms of literature. For Spenser, as for most Elizabethan writers, the highest form of poetry would be either epic or tragedy, and the epic for him deals essentially with the actions of the heroic prince or leader. The highest form of prose, similarly, would be either a Utopian vision outlined in a Platonic dialogue or in a romance like Sidney's *Arcadia*, or a description of an ideal prince's ideal education, for which the classical model was Xenophon's *Cyropaedia*. Spenser's preference of Xenophon's form to Plato's is explicit in the letter to Raleigh. This high view of education is inseparable from Spenser's view of the relation between nature and art. For Spenser, as for Burke centuries later, art is man's nature. Art is nature on the human plane, or what Sidney calls a second nature, a "golden" world, to use another phrase of Sidney's, because essentially the same world as that of the Golden Age, and in contrast to the "brazen" world of physical nature. Hence art is no less natural than physical nature—the art itself is nature, as Polixenes says in *The Winter's Tale*—but it is the civilized nature appropriate to human life.

Private and public education, then, are the central themes of *The Faerie Queene*. If we had to find a single word for the virtue underlying all private education, the best word would perhaps be fidelity: that unswerving loyalty to an ideal which is virtue, to a single lady which is love, and to the demands of one's calling which is courage. Fidelity on the specifically human plane of endeavour is faith, the vision of holiness by which one lives; on the natural plane it is temperance, or the ability to live humanely in the physical world. The corresponding term for the virtue of public education is, perhaps, concord or harmony. On the physical plane concord is friendship, again the ability to achieve a human community in ordinary life; on the specifically human plane it is justice and equity, the foundation of society.

In the first two books the symbolism comes to a climax in what we may call a "house of recognition," the House of Holiness in Book I and the House of Alma in Book II. In the third the climax is the vision of the order of nature in the Gardens of Adonis. The second part repeats the same scheme: we have houses of recognition in the Temple of Venus in

Book IV and the Palace of Mercilla in Book V, and a second *locus amoenus* vision in the Mount Acidale canto of Book VI, where the poet himself appears with the Graces. The sequence runs roughly as follows: fidelity in the context of human nature; fidelity in the context of physical nature; fidelity in the context of nature as a whole; concord in the context of physical nature; concord in the context of human nature; concord in the context of nature as a whole. Or, abbreviated: human fidelity, natural fidelity, nature; natural concord, human concord, art. Obviously, such a summary is unacceptable as it stands, but it may give some notion of how the books are related and of how the symbolism flows out of one book into the next one.

The conception of the four levels of existence and the symbols used to represent it come from Spenser's cultural tradition in general and from the Bible in particular. The Bible, as Spenser read it for his purposes, describes how man originally inhabited his own human world, the Garden of Eden, and fell out of it into the present physical world, which fell with him. By his fall he lost the tree and water of life. Below him is hell, represented on earth by the kingdoms of bondage, Egypt, Babylon, and Rome, and symbolized by the serpent of Eden, Babylon, and Rome, and symbolized by the serpent of Eden, otherwise Satan, otherwise the huge water-monster called Leviathan or the dragon by the prophets. Man is redeemed by the quest of Christ, who after overcoming the world descended to hell and in three days conquered it too. His descent is usually symbolized in art as walking into the open mouth of a dragon, and when he returns in triumph he carries a banner of a red cross on a white ground, the colours typifying his blood and flesh. At the end of time the dragon of death is finally destroyed, man is restored to Eden, and gets back the water and tree of life. In Christianity these last are symbolized by the two sacraments accepted by the Reformed Church, baptism and the Eucharist.

The quest of the Redcrosse knight in Book I follows the symbolism of the quest of Christ. He carries the same emblem of a red cross on a white ground; the monster he has to kill is "that old dragon" (quatrain to Canto xi; cf. Rev. xii, 9) who is identical with the Biblical Satan, Leviathan, and serpent of Eden, and the object of killing him is to restore Una's parents, who are Adam and Eve, to their kingdom of Eden, which includes the entire world, now usurped by the dragon. The tyranny of Egypt, Babylon, and the Roman Empire continues in the tyranny of the Roman Church, and the Book of Revelation, as Spenser read it, prophesies the future ascendancy of that church and its ultimate defeat in its vision of the dragon and Great Whore, the latter identified with his

Duessa. St. George fights the dragon for three days in the garden of Eden, refreshed by the water and tree of life on the first two days respectively.

But Eden is not heaven: in Spenser, as in Dante, it is rather the summit of purgatory, which St. George goes through in the House of Holiness. It is the world of recovered human nature, as it originally was and still can be when sin is removed. St. George similarly is not Christ, but only the English people trying to be Christian, and the dragon, while he may be part of Satan, is considerably less Satanic than Archimago or Duessa, who survive the book. No monster, however loathsome, can really be evil: for evil there must be a perversion of intelligence, and Spenser drew his dragon with some appreciation of the fact mentioned in an essay of Valéry, that in poetry the most frightful creatures always have something rather childlike about them:

> So dreadfully he towards him did pas,
>   Forelifting up aloft his speckled brest,
> And often bounding on the brused gras,
>   As for great ioyance of his newcome guest.
>   (I, xi, 15)

Hence the theatre of operations in the first book is still a human world. The real heaven appears only in the vision of Jerusalem at the end of the tenth canto and in a few other traces, like the invisible husband of Charissa and the heavenly music heard in the background of the final betrothal. Eden is within the order of nature but it is a new earth turned upward, or sacramentally aligned with a new heaven. The main direction of the imagery is also upward: this upward movement is the theme of the House of Holiness, of the final quest, and of various subordinate themes like the worship of Una by the satyrs.

We have spoken of the principle of symbolic parody, which we meet in all books of *The Faerie Queene*. Virtues are contrasted not only with their vicious opposites, but with vices that have similar names and appearances. Thus the golden mean of temperance is parodied by the golden means provided by Mammon; "That part of justice, which is equity" in Book V is parodied by the anarchistic equality preached by the giant in the second canto, and so on. As the main theme of Book I is really faith, or spiritual fidelity, the sharpest parody of this sort is between Fidelia, or true faith, and Duessa, who calls herself Fidessa. Fidelia holds a golden cup of wine and water (which in other romance patterns would be the Holy Grail, though Spenser's one reference to the Grail shows that he has no interest in it); Duessa holds the golden cup of the Whore of Babylon. Fidelia's cup also contains a serpent (the redeeming brazen serpent of

Moses typifying the Crucifixion); Duessa sits on the dragon of the Apocalypse who is metaphorically the same beast as the serpent of Eden. Fidelia's power to raise the dead is stressed; Duessa raises Sansjoy from the dead by the power of Aesculapius, whose emblem is the serpent. Of all such parodies in the first book the most important for the imagery of the poem as a whole is the parody of the tree and water of life in Eden. These symbols have their demonic counterparts in the paralyzed trees of Fradubio and Fraelissa and in the paralysing fountain from which St. George drinks in the seventh canto.

Thus the first book shows very clearly what we have called the subordinating of cyclical symbols to dialectical ones: the tree and water of life, originally symbols of the rebirth of spring, are here symbols of resurrection, or a permanent change from a life in physical nature above the animals to life in human nature under God. The main interest of the second book is also dialectical, but in the reverse direction, concerned with human life in the ordinary physical world, and with its separation from the demonic world below. The Bower of Bliss is a parody of Eden, and just as the climax of Book I is St. George's three-day battle with the dragon of death, so the narrative climax of Book II is Guyon's three-day endurance in the underworld. It is the climax at least as far as Guyon's heroism is concerned, for it is Arthur who defeats Maleger and it is really the Palmer who catches Acrasia.

We should expect to find in Book II, therefore, many demonic parodies of the symbols in Book I, especially of the tree and water of life and its symbolic relatives. At the beginning we note that Acrasia, like Duessa, has a golden cup of death, filled, like Fidelia's, with wine and water ("Bacchus with the nymph"). There follows Ruddymane, with his bloody hands that cannot be washed. Spenser speaks of Redcrosse's hands as "baptised" after he falls back into the well of life, and the Ruddymane incident is partly a reference to original sin, removable only by baptism or bathing in a "liuing well." The demonic counterparts of both sacraments appear in the hell scene in the cave of Mammon, in connexion with Pilate and Tantalus. Pilate, forever washing his hands in vain, repeats the Ruddymane image in its demonic context, and Tantalus is the corresponding parody of the Eucharist. These figures are preceded by the description of the golden apple tree in the garden of Proserpina and the river Cocytus. Images of trees and water are considerably expanded in the description of the Bower of Bliss.

The fact that the fountain of Diana's nymph refuses to cleanse Ruddymane's hands indicates the rather subordinate role of Diana in Spenser's symbolism. It is clear, if we compare the description of Venus in

Book IV with the description of Nature in the *Mutabilitie Cantos*, that Venus represents the whole order of nature, in its higher human as well as its lower physical aspect. What Diana stands for is the resistance to corruption, as symbolized by unchastity, which is the beginning, and of course always an essential part, of moral realization. Hence Diana in Spenser is a little like the law in Milton, which can discover sin but not remove it. In the *Mutabilitie Cantos* the glimpsing of Diana's nakedness by Faunus is parallel, on a small scale, to the rebellion of the lower against the higher nature which is also represented by Mutability's thrusting herself into heaven at the place of Cynthia, who is another form of Diana. Naturally Elizabeth's virginity compelled Spenser to give a high place to Diana and her protégé Belphoebe, but for symbolic as well as political reasons he preferred to make the Faerie Queene a young woman proceeding toward marriage, like Britomart. Meanwhile it is the virginal Faerie Queene whose picture Guyon carries on his shield, Guyon being in his whole moral complex something of a male Diana.

Temperance in Spenser is a rather negative virtue, being the resistance of consciousness to impulsive action which is necessary in order to know whether the action is going up or down in the moral dialectic. Conscious action is real action, Aristotle's proairesis; impulsive action is really pseudo-action, a passion which increasingly becomes passivity. Human life in the physical world has something of the feeling of an army of occupation about it, symbolized by the beleaguered castle of Alma. The House of Alma possesses two things in particular: wealth, in Ruskin's sense of well-being, and beauty, in the sense of correct proportion and ordering of parts. Its chief enemies are "Beauty, and money," the minions of Acrasia and Mammon, the external or instrumental possessions which the active mind uses and the passive mind thinks of as ends in themselves. Temperance is also good temperament, or the balancing of humours, and Guyon's enemies are mainly humours in the Elizabethan sense, although the humours are usually symbolized by their corresponding elements, as the choleric Pyrochles is associated with fire and the phlegmatic Cymochles with water. The battleground between the active and the passive mind is the area of sensation, the steady rain of impressions and stimuli coming in from the outer world which the active mind organizes and the passive mind merely yields to. Normally the sanguine humour predominates in the active mind; the passive one becomes a victim of melancholy, with its progressive weakening of will and of the power to distinguish reality from illusion. In Spenser's picture of the mind the fancy (Phantastes) is predisposed to melancholy and the influence of "oblique Saturne"; it is not the seat of the poetic imagination, as it would be in a nineteenth-century

Romantic. The title of George Macdonald's *Phantastes*, the author tells us, comes not from Spenser but from Phineas Fletcher, who differs from Spenser in making Phantastes the source of art. Maleger, the leader of the assault on Alma, is a spirit of melancholy, and is sprung from the corresponding element of earth.

Having outlined the dialectical extremes of his imagery, Spenser moves on to consider the order of nature on its two main levels in the remaining books. Temperance steers a middle course between care and carelessness, jealousy and wantonness, miserliness and prodigality, Mammon's cave and Acrasia's bower. Acrasia is a kind of sinister Venus, and her victims, Mordant wallowing in his blood, Cymochles, Verdant, have something of a dead, wasted, or frustrated Adonis about them. Mammon is an old man with a daughter, Philotime. Much of the symbolism of the third book is based on these these two archetypes. The first half leads up to the description of the Gardens of Adonis in Canto vi by at least three repetitions of the theme of Venus and Adonis. First we have the tapestry in the Castle Joyeous representing the story, with a longish description attached. Then comes the wounding of Marinell on his "precious shore" by Britomart (surely the most irritable heroine known to romance), where the sacrificial imagery, the laments of the nymphs, the strewing of flowers on the bier are all conventional images of Adonis. Next is Timias, discovered by Belphoebe wounded in the thigh with a boar-spear. Both Belphoebe and Marinell's mother Cymoent have pleasant retreats closely analogous to the Gardens of Adonis. In the second half of the book we have three examples of the old man and young woman relationship: Malbecco and Hellenore, Proteus and Florimell, Busirane and Amoret. All these are evil: there is no idealized version of this theme. The reason is that the idealized version would be the counterpart to the vision of charity in the *Hymn of Heavenly Love*. That is, it would be the vision of the female Sapience sitting in the bosom of the Diety that we meet at the end of the *Hymn to Heavenly Beauty*, and this would take us outside the scope of *The Faerie Queene*, or at any rate of its third book.

The central figure in the third book and the fourth is Venus, flanked on either side by Cupid and Adonis, or what a modern poet would call Eros and Thantos. Cupid and Venus are gods of natural love, and form, not a demonic parody, but a simple analogy of Christian love, an analogy which is the symbolic basis of the *Fowre Hymnes*. Cupid, like Jesus, is lord of gods and creator of the cosmos, and simultaneously an infant, Venus' relation to him being that of an erotic Madonna, as her relation to Adonis is that of an erotic Pièta. Being androgynous, she brings forth Cupid without male assistance; she loses him and goes in search of him, and he returns in triumph in the great masque at the end as lord of all creation.

The Garden of Adonis, with its Genius and its temperate climate, is so carefully paralled to the Bower of Bliss that it clearly represents the reality of which the Bower is a mirage. It presents the order of nature as a cyclical process of death and renewal, in itself morally innocent, but still within the realm of Mutability, as the presence of Time shows. Like Eden, it is a paradise: it is nature as nature would be if man could live in his proper human world, the "antique" Golden Age. It is a world where substance is constant but where "Forms are variable and decay"; and hence it is closely connected with the theme of metamorphosis, which is the central symbol of divine love as the pagans conceived it.

Such love naturally has its perverted form, represented by the possessive jealousy of Malbecco, Busirane, and Proteus, all of whom enact variants of the myth of Tithonus and Aurora, the aged lover and the struggling dawn. Hellenore escapes into the world of satyrs, a world too "natural" to be wholly sinful. The torturing of Amoret by Busirane, representing the anguish of jealous love, recurs in various images of bleeding, such as the "long bloody river" in the tapestry of Cupid. Painful or not, it is love that makes the world go round, that keeps the cycle of nature turning, and it is particularly the love of Marinell and Florimell, whose names suggest water and vegetation, that seems linked to the natural cycle. Florimell is imprisoned under the sea during a kind of symbolic winter in which a "snowy" Florimell takes her place. Marinell is not cured of his illness until his mother turns from "watry gods" to the sun, and when he sees Florimell he revives

> As withered weed through cruell winters tine,
> That feels the warmth of sunny beam's reflection
> Lifts up his head, that did before decline
> And gins to spread his leaf before the fair sunshine.
>
> (IV, xii, 34)

Book IV is full of images of natural revival, some in very unlikely places, and it comes to a climax with the symbolism of the tree and water of life in their natural context. At the temple of Venus, we are told, "No tree, that is of count . . . But there was planted," and the next canto is a tremendous outburst of water. The wedding of the Thames and the Medway takes place in Proteus' hall, and Proteus, in the mythological handbooks, is the spirit of metamorphosis, the liquid energy of substance driving through endless varieties of form.

The impulse in sexual love is toward union in one flesh, which is part of the symbolism of Christian marriage. The original conclusion to Book III leaves Scudamour and Amoret locked in an embrace which makes them look like a single hermaphrodite. The reason for this curious epithet becomes clear in Book IV, where we learn that Venus herself is hermaphroditic, and of course all embracing lovers are epiphanies of Venus. Naturally this image lends itself to demonic parody, as in the incestuous birth of Oliphant and Argante. Britomart watches Scudamour and Amoret rather enviously, making a mental resolve to get herself into the same position as soon as she can run her Artegall to earth: for Britomart, though as chaste as Belphoebe, is not vowed to virginity. Perhaps it is her accessibility to human emotions that is symbolized by the bleeding wound she receives from an arrow in the first canto of Book III, an image repeated, with a symmetry unusual even in Spenser, in the last canto.

A slight extension of the same symbol of unity through love takes us into the area of social love, or friendship, the theme of the fourth book. Friendship shows, even more clearly than sexual passion, the power of love as a creative force, separating the elements from chaos by the attraction of like to like. The human counterpart of this ordering of elements is concord or harmony, for which Spenser uses various symbols, notably the golden chain, an image introduced into Book I and parodied by the chain of ambition in the cave of Mammon. We also have the image of two (or three) souls united in one body in the extremely tedious account of Priamond, Diamond, and Triamond. It is rather more interesting that Spenser seems to regard the poetic tradition as a community of friendship of a similar kind. In all six books of *The Faerie Queene* it is only in the fourth that Spenser refers *explicitly* to his two great models Chaucer and Ariosto, and his phrase about Chaucer is significant: "thine own spirit, which doth in me survive."

When we move from friendship, an abstract pattern of human community which only noble spirits can form, to justice, in which the base and evil must also be included, we return to historical allegory. Spenser's vision of history (III, ix) focuses on the legend of Troy: the first Troy is recalled by Hellenore and Paridell, and the second, or Rome, by Duessa, who reappears in Books IV and V. The third is of course England itself, which will not collapse in adultery or supersitition if her leading poet can prevent it. In the prophecy of this third Troy we meet an image connected with the wedding of the Thames in Book IV:

> It [sc. London] Troynovant is hight, that with the waves
> Of wealthy Thamis washed is along,
> Upon whose stubborn neck, whereat he raves

> With roaring rage, and sore himself does throng,
> That all men fear to tempt his billows strong,
> She fastened hath her foot, which stands so high
> That it a wonder of the world is sung
> In foreign lands, and all which passen by,
> Beholding it from far, do think it threats the sky.
> (III, ix, 45)

I quote this poetically licentious description of the Thames because it is so closely linked with Spenser's conception of justice as the harnessing of physical power to conquer physical nature. In its lower aspects this power is mechanical, symbolized by the "yron man" Talus, who must be one of the earliest "science fiction" or technological symbols in poetry, and who kills without discrimination for the sake of discrimination, like a South African policeman. In its higher aspects where justice becomes equity, or consideration of circumstances, the central image is this one of the virgin guiding the raging monster. We meet this image very early in the adventures of Una and the lion in Book I, and the same symbolic shape reappears in the Gardens of Adonis, where Venus enjoys Adonis with the boar imprisoned in a cave underneath. Next comes the training of Artegall (who begins his career by taming animals) by Astraea, identified with the constellation Virgo. Next is the vision of Isis, where Osiris and the crocodile correspond to Adonis and the boar earlier, but are here explicitly identified. Finally we have Mercilla and the lion under her throne, where Spenser naturally refrains from speculating on the lion's possible identity with a human lover. It may be the link with London on the Thames that lends such prominence in Book V to the image of the river washing away the filth of injustice. At the same time the virgin who dominates the beast is herself the servant of an invisible male deity, hence the figure of the female rebel is important in the last two books: Radigund the Amazon in Book V, who rebels against justice, and Mirabell in Book VI, who rebels against courtesy. Radigund is associated with the moon because she parodies Isis, and Isis is associated with the moon partly because Queen Elizabeth is, by virtue of Raleigh's name for her, Cynthia.

Just as Book III deals with the secular and natural counterpart of love, so Book VI deals with the secular and natural counterpart of grace. The word grace itself in all its human manifestations is a thematic word in this book, and when the Graces themselves appear on Mount Acidale we find ourselves in a world that transcends the world of Venus:

> These three to men all gifts of grace do graunt,
> And all that Venus in herself doth vaunt
> Is borrowed of them.
> (VI, x, 15)

The Graces, we are told, were begotten by Jove when he returned from the wedding of Peleus and Thetis. This wedding is referred to again in the *Mutabilitie Cantos* as the most festive occasion the gods had held before the lawsuit of Mutability. For it was at this wedding that Jove was originally "confirmed in his imperial see": the marriage to Peleus removed the threat to Jove's power coming from the son of Thetis, a threat the secret of which only Prometheus knew, and which Prometheus was crucified on a rock for not revealing. Thus the wedding also led, though Spenser does not tell us this, to the reconciling of Jove and Prometheus, and it was Prometheus, whose name traditionally means forethought or wisdom, who, according to Book II, was the originator of Elves and Fays—that is, of man's moral and conscious nature. There are still many demonic symbols in Book VI, especially the attempt to sacrifice Serena, where the custom of eating the flesh and giving the blood to the priests has obvious overtones of parody. But the centre of symbolic gravity, so to speak, in Book VI is a pastoral Arcadian world, where we seem almost to be entering into the original home of man where, as in the child's world of Dylan Thomas's *Fern Hill*, it was all Adam and maiden. It is no longer the world of Eros; yet the sixth book is the most erotic, in the best sense, of all the books in the poem, full of innocent nakedness and copulation, the surprising of which is so acid a test of courtesy, and with many symbols of the state of innocence and of possible regeneration like the Salvage Man and the recognition scene in which Pastorella is reunited to her parents.

Such a world is a world in which the distinction between art and nature is disappearing because nature is taking on a human form. In the Bower of Bliss the *mixing* of art and nature is what is stressed: on Mount Acidale the art itself is nature, to quote Polixenes again. Yet art, especially poetry, has a central place in the legend of courtesy. Grace in religion implies revelation by the Word, and human grace depends much on good human words. All through the second part of *The Faerie Queene*, slander is portrayed as the worst enemy of the human community: we have Ate and Sclaunder herself in Book IV, Malfont with his tongue nailed to a post in Mercilla's court, as an allegory of what ought to be done to *other* poets; and finally the Blatant Beast, the voice of rumour full of tongues. The dependence of courtesy on reasonable speech is emphasized at every turn, and just as the legend of justice leads us to the figure of the Queen, as set forth in Mercilla, who manifests the order of society, so the legend of courtesy leads us to the figure of the poet himself, who manifests the order of words.

When Calidore commits his one discourteous act and interrupts

Colin Clout, all the figures dancing to his pipe vanish. In Elizabethan English a common meaning of art was magic, and Spenser's Colin Clout like Shakespeare's Prospero, has the magical power of summoning spirits to enact his present fancies, spirits who disappear if anyone speaks and breaks the spell. Nature similarly vanishes mysteriously at the end of the *Mutabilitie Cantos*, just as the counterpart to Prospero's revels is his subsequent speech on the disappearance of all created things. Colin Clout, understandably annoyed at being suddenly deprived of the company of a hundred and four naked maidens, destroys his pipe, as Prospero drowns his book. Poetry works by suggestion and indirection, and conveys meanings out of all proportion to its words; but in magic the impulse to complete a pattern is very strong. If a spirit is being conjured by the seventy-two names of God as set forth in the *Schemhamphoras*, it will not do if the magician can remember only seventy-one of them. At the end of the sixth book the magician in Spenser had completed half of his gigantic design, and was ready to start on the other half. But the poet in Spenser was satisfied: he had done his work, and his vision was complete.

A. C. HAMILTON

The Structure of Allegory in Books I and II of "The Faerie Queene"

The highest end of the mistres Knowledge, by the Greekes called Architectonike . . . stands, (as I thinke) in the knowledge of a mans selfe, in the Ethicke and politick consideration, with the end of well dooing and not of well knowing onely . . . so that, the ending end of all earthly learning [is] vertuous action.

—SIDNEY

Previously I have treated the '*Idea* or fore-conceite' of *The Faerie Queene*, and the method by which Spenser realizes that Idea as an image in Book I. I wish to consider now his intention which is realized in the end or working of his poem. As the Idea is embodied in an image, the intention is realized in an argument. Though Spenser rightly distinguishes in the letter to Raleigh between his purpose and the poem's end, we may see that they closely correspond: as he labours to deliver the image of a brave knight perfected in the virtues, the poem itself fashions a gentleman or noble person in virtuous and gentle discipline. The image which the poet creates is thus re-created in the reader. Strictly speaking, its Idea is not fulfilled in the writing of the poem—perhaps this is why Sidney, 'in which Architectonical art he was such a

Master', judges a work by its idea—but in the act of reading. Sidney tells us further that the end of the heroical poet who fashions the image of a brave man is accomplished when the reader understands 'why and how that Maker made him'. How Spenser fashioned his image was [previously explored], and we must turn now to the problem of why he made him. In considering the 'doctrine by ensample' which the right poet delivers, we turn, then, from the ensample to the doctrine itself.

The term 'architectonike' suggests both the chief end and also structure. I shall proceed upon the hypothesis which I hope the following pages will support, that Book I is central and unifying within the poem's structure. In the first book the image is rendered for its own sake while the allegorical and tropological levels of significance remain implicit: in the second book that image may be understood in its tropological significance through the parallel structure of the first two books. . . .

I

We may understand the doctrine of Book I by relating the allegory inward to the poem itself, specifically to the parallel structure of the first two books. In paralleling the structure of the first two books, Spenser deliberately points to the *doctrine* of his *ensample*, that is, its tropological significance. And the more precisely we are aware of the nature of that paralleling, the more precisely we may understand the allegory of the whole poem.

It has been commonly observed, of course, that these books are parallel in structure. In each the knight who represents a particular virtue (Holiness, Temperance) leaves the court of the Faery Queen with a guide (Una, the Palmer) and later defeats two chief antagonists (Sansfoy and Sansjoy, Pyrochles and Cymochles); upon being separated from his guide, he enters a place of temptation (the house of Pride, the cave of Mammon), and later falls. Then being rescued by Arthur and united with his guide, he enters a place of instruction (the house of Holiness, the castle of Alma) and finally fulfils his adventure (killing the Dragon, destroying the Bower of Bliss). Such paralleling has been considered part of Spenser's design expressed in the letter to Raleigh, to write twelve books in which twelve knights, as patrons of the twelve virtues, undertake parallel adventures assigned by the Faery Queen. That the later books do not follow this repetitive structure has been variously explained as the need to avoid monotony, to modify the design according to the virtue being treated, or simply—all too simply—as a change of plan. It was left to A. S. P. Woodhouse to explain for the first time the basis of the parallel structure

of the first two books. He suggests that the two orders of nature and grace
which were universally accepted as a frame of reference in the Renaissance
are here carefully differentiated: 'what touches the Redcross Knight bears
primarily upon revealed religion, or belongs to the order of grace,
whatever touches Guyon bears upon natural ethics, or belongs to the
order of nature'. It follows that the parallel structure is designed to bring
into relief differences which depend upon these two orders. He finds that
this difference leaves its mark chiefly upon the education received
by the two knights: the Red Cross Knight shows the bankruptcy of natural
man who must utterly depend upon heavenly grace whereas Guyon shows
how natural man realizes the potentialities of his nature by ruling his
passions through reason. At times he insists more strongly than does
Spenser upon an absolute separation of the two orders: Guyon's reference
to 'the sacred badge of my Redeemers death' confuses the separation, as
does the Palmer's benediction: 'God guide thee, *Guyon*, well to end thy
warke.' Even more confusing is Guyon's invocation to Christ for His
Mercy at the moment when, like Longinus, he levels his spear against the
Cross: 'Mercie Sir knight, and mercie Lord, / For mine offence and
heedlesse hardiment, / That had almost committed crime abhord.' However, thanks to Professor Woodhouse, there seems no doubt now that the
distinction between the two orders of nature and grace provides a necessary frame of reference for understanding the parallel structure of the first
two books.

It does not follow, of course, that Spenser seeks to *illustrate* this
distinction. The two orders of nature and grace provide no more than a
basis upon which Spenser erects his pattern of meaning. Strictly speaking,
they provide an intellectual framework by which the poem may be referred
outwardly to a background of related ideas; as such, they cannot be
identified with that 'antique Image' in its inner syntactic meaning. And it
is the pattern of inner meaning realized by the parallel structure of the first
two books, rather than reducible historical background, which is a key to
the allegory. By my reading, this parallel is more exact than has been
previously observed, and also more significant to our understanding the
poem's doctrine. Further, to read the two books together offers perspective
from which to see the whole poem's unity. Their parallel structure reveals
that such unity would not be found in the projected Book XII, as is
commonly surmised, but is already provided by Book I.

When Spenser writes in the letter to Raleigh that the adventures of
his twelve knights are 'seuerally [that is, differently] handled and dis-
coursed', he prepares the reader for a structure which provides parallel
with contrast. Such structure may be seen in the opening eipsodes of the
first two books. Each begins with a prelude designed to manifest the

knight's nature. Guided by Una, the Red Cross Knight enters the pleasing Wandering Wood where he confronts Error, the female serpent who is an emblem of his twofold enemy later seen as Duessa riding the Dragon; and he triumphs, as he does later, by adding faith (the power of grace) to his force, so proving himself worthy of his armour. At the end, Una blesses her chosen knight as he leaves upon his adventure 'with God to frend'. The opening episode of Book II shows Guyon aroused to wrath by Archimago who seeks through Duessa 'to deceiue good knights, / And draw them from pursuit of praise and fame, / To slug in slouth and sensuall delights, / And end their daies with irrenowmed shame" (II.i.23). The wrathful Guyon so deceived by the enchantress is an emblem of his later foes: his inner foe being the irascible and concupiscent affections embodied in Pyrochles and Cymochles, and his outer foe being Acrasia in her Bower of Bliss. He, too, is led into a Wandering Wood, 'a pleasant dale, that lowly lay / Betwixt two hils, whose high heads ouerplast, / The valley did with coole shade ouercast' (II.i.24), where he attacks the Red Cross Knight. But when he recognizes him and confesses his offence, the Red Cross Knight 'streight way . . . knew / His error' (II.i.28); and Guyon is saved through mercy and the return of reason (the Palmer). At the end he leaves upon his adventure with the Red Cross Knight's blessing and the Palmer's injunction, 'God guide thee'. Being thus parallel, these opening episodes significantly contrast the knights and their adventures. The Red Cross Knight's victory over Error shows his unfallen state: with Una, he enjoys that state of grace within which he may triumph over his enemies. When Una persuades him to 'shew what ye bee', he shows himself to be under her guidance what Sidney calls the poet's image of what 'should be'. Guyon, on the other hand, is an image of what the knight of temperance should not be, when he leaves his guide to be led by Archimago and in intemperate wrath attacks the patron of Holiness. The contrast between them is sharpened by the Red Cross Knight's presence in Book II where they are set apart by the phrases 'that godly knight' and 'a goodly knight' before the opening episode, and the address of 'Saint' and 'Sir' at the end. In Book I the armour is stressed, while the Knight himself remains anonymous, the conventional 'full iolly knight'. In Book II the knight himself is described, demure, temperate, stern, and terrible in sight, and he is named while the arms are conventional: the 'many-folded shield' which is mentioned later is the familiar classical shield in Homer. 'I know your goodly gouernaunce', the Red Cross Knight says to Guyon, but of himself he knows that he is governed by God 'who made my hand the organ of his might'. In the opening episode of Book I the knight is seen in a higher state of righteousness to which he originally and finally belongs. Guyon, on the other hand, is circumscribed by the fallen world of good and evil. The opening line of the book, 'that cunning Architect of cancred guile', and the opening stanzas which describe Archimago's Satanic perversion, 'for to all good he enimy was still', plunge the entire action into the fallen world.

Since Guyon does not belong to any higher state, the opening episode of Book II is patterned upon the Red Cross Knight's next adventure when he falls into the power of Archimago and reverses his former state. Guyon is similarly abused by Archimago disguised as an aged sire, and that enchanter's deception proceeds as before in two stages. First, there is the false tale of the Lady overcome by lust which is told by the wicked spright in Book I, and by Archimago in Book II. Here the Red Cross Knight shows temperance, 'hasty heat tempring with sufferance wise, / He stayde his hand' (I.i.50), while Guyon overcome with 'zealous hast away is quickly gone' (II.i.13). Then in each book follows the false vision of the dishonoured lady shown in the spright who seems to be Una embraced by the lusty Squire, and in Duessa disguised as the virgin who has been raped. Now both knights are overcome by wrath: the one 'pricked with wrath and fiery fierce disdaine' (I.ii.8), the other 'inflam'd with wrathfulnesse' (II.i.25). Wrath leads the Red Cross Knight into lust: after defeating Sansfoy, the sight of the wanton lady now 'did much emmoue his stout heroicke heart' and at her story 'he in great passion all this while did dwell' (I.ii.21,26). Being thus overcome by intemperate affections, his eye of reason blinded, and guided by his will, he falls helplessly into sin. Nothing within himself can restore him to his former state. Guyon, on the other hand, seeks to resist his fall by asserting the power of temperance over his affections. Though at first overcome by intemperance, he begs for Mercy at the sight of the Red Cross. Mercy being freely granted reason returns as his guide, and he becomes 'knit in one consent' with Holiness. This parallel with contrast set up between the Red Cross Knight's deception by Archimago and Guyon's overcoming that deception relates the arguments of the two books. While Book I traces the cycle of events occasioned by man's fall from grace into sin, Book II shows how temperance may prevent that fall.

This relation between the arguments of the two books is illustrated by the succeeding episodes, the story of Fradubio in Book I and the story of Amavia in Book II. These episodes are parallel, each being an allegory of the knight's adventures. After each knight begins his pageant, he travels for a long time with his companion (Duessa, the Palmer) until he seeks shade under a tree from the scorching sun. At the sound of a lamenting voice, he is rapt in astonishment. Then he hears a tragic story of excessive love which brings death: Fradubio's lament, 'my deare loue, / O too deare loue, loue bought with death too deare' (I.ii.31) betrays that same intemperate love expressed in Amavia's lament for Mortdant, 'my Lord my loue; my deare Lord, my deare loue' (II.i.50). Fradubio and Amavia tell a similar story of the witch who so transforms man's weak nature that, when he seeks to escape her power, her charms bring death. Through the witch's enchantment, Fradubio cannot be released until he is bathed in a living well, while the Babe's hands may not be cleansed in the well. We have seen how Fradubio's story contains the Red Cross Knight's adventure: how, like him, he has left his lady for the witch Duessa by whom he is defiled, and may not be restored until he is bathed in the Well of Life. Guyon's purpose, to which he now dedicates himself, is to destroy the witch's enchantment through his own power which, however, must be supplemented by grace. Amavia dressed as the Palmer may cure Mortdant through 'wise handling and faire gouernance', but he is later slain through Acrasia's charms. By this we understand that Guyon needs more than the Palmer's guidance before he may not only cure intemperance but destroy its power. But the present condition of the two knights is contrasted. Guyon, not being involved in the witch's power, may heed Amavia's warning: 'if euer there ye trauell, shonne / The cursed land where many wend amis' (II.i.51). But with powerful tragic irony, the Red Cross Knight is already within the the witch's power. Though Fradubio warns him, 'fly, ah fly far hence away, for feare / Least to you hap, that happened to me heare' (I.ii.31), he cannot escape. Guyon is moved by pity to revenge Amavia 'till guiltie bloud her guerdon doe obtaine'; and though the vow recoils upon him, for he shares that guilty blood, he goes forward to display all heroic virtue. But the Red Cross Knight is far from being the self-reliant hero, such as Guyon, who moves steadily towards final victory. For he is not the hunter, but the hunted; not victor, but the victim; and not hero, but the antagonist of a divine drama which brings him 'in darkesome dungeon, wretched thrall, / Remedilesse, for aie' (I.vii.51). Later Una complains to Arthur that all her knights have failed through 'guilt of sin'. The Red Cross Knight, too, becomes infected with 'guilt of sin' for his hands are imbrued in the guilty blood of Sansfoy. Only at the end of his last adventure may he 'wash [his] hands from guilt of bloudy field' (I.x.60). His guilt is expressed emblematically in Book II by the blood upon the Babe's hands which is interpreted by the Palmer as a token of man's 'bloudguiltinesse'. When Guyon dedicates himself to the task of avenging the bloody-handed Babe, he seeks to avenge the 'guilt of sin' through which man's nature is defiled. The difference between their adventures may be summed up in a word: the Red Cross Knight seeks 'to *redeeme* [Una's] woefull parents head', Guyon '*t'auenge* his Parents death': the aim

of the one is redemptive, and he must submit and suffer in order to free
mankind from a wicked moral order; the aim of the other is retributive, to
assert a just moral order.

Since Guyon seeks to resist man's fall into sin through the power
of Temperance, the occasion of his adventure is given by that moment of
the fall represented by the Red Cross Knight's imprisonment in Orgoglio's
dungeon. Being left, then, to lament, Una rejects life and light, and
in despair wishes for death. But at this nadir of the action, help comes to
her. She is aided first by the Dwarf who lifts her up: 'thrise did she sinke
adowne in deadly swownd, / And thrise he her reviu'd with busie paine',
and then by Arthur who persuades her 'to vnfold the anguish of your hart
. . . [for] found neuer helpe, who neuer would his hurts impart' (I.vii.24,40).
After she tells her story, he vows to redeem her knight. This moment
appears in Book II where Amavia also laments her knight's fall and
lovingly (as is her nature) embraces death: 'come then, come soone, come
sweetest death to mee, / And take away this long lent loathed light.' As
Una laments that Duessa 'with her witchcraft . . . Inueigled [the knight]
to follow her desires vnmeete' (I.vii.50), Amavia laments that 'with words
and weedes of wondrous might', the witch Acrasia 'my lifest Lord she thus
beguiled (II.i.52). (Amavia yields to despair, of course, unlike Una who
later rises to seek her knight.) And in the same manner as help comes to
Una, Guyon lifts Amavia up, 'thrise he her reard, and thrise she sunke
againe', and persuades her 'your grief vnfold. . . . He oft finds present
helpe, who does his griefe impart' (II.i.46). After she tells her story, he
vows vengeance. In relation to the pattern set up in Book I, Book II
begins *in medias res*. The fall is accomplished; the witch has triumphed;
and human nature seen in the Babe is already defiled. At this point Guyon
enters, and he seeks, as does Arthur in Book I, to reverse man's fall.

Throughout his adventure Guyon manifests the power of temperance over those affections through which the Red Cross Knight falls into
the bondage of sin. In Book I we see the knight yield to grief and wrath
when he believes Una disloyal, and then to lust when he meets Duessa. In
Book II we learn how temperance may subdue these affections.

After the opening exemplum of intemperance given by Mortdant
and Amavia, the Palmer declares that through temperance man may avoid
both lust and the fury that drives man to grief:

> temperance (said he) with golden squire
> Betwixt them both can measure out a meane,
> Neither to melt in pleasures whot desire,
> Nor fry in hartlesse griefe and doleful teene.
>   (II.i.58)

The succeeding episode, the story of Phedon, presents in romantic terms the occasion of the Red Cross Knight's leaving Una: each knight believes he sees his lady in wanton lust with a base squire, and through his love, each is overcome by wrath, jealousy, and grief. The Palmer sermonizes upon such intemperate affections which war against 'fort of Reason, it to ouerthrow', and Guyon counsels Phedon that his hurts 'may soone through temperance be easd' (II.iv.33,34). Later Wrath is embodied in Pyrochles in whom wars 'outrageous anger, and woe-working iarre, / Direfull impatience, and hart murdring loue' (II.v.16), and Wrath merging into Lust in his brother Cymochles who 'by kind, / Was giuen all to lust and loose liuing' (II.v.28). Both are subdued by the knight of Temperance. Pyrochles' wrath finally immerses him in the Idle Lake where he seeks vainly to quench his inner flames, while Cymochles' lust confines him to Phaedria's Isle; but Guyon leaves both and proceeds upon his voyage.

The further power of Temperance to resist temptation is displayed by Guyon's descent into Mammon's Cave. This descent clearly parallels the Red Cross Knight's passage through the house of Pride. The house of Richesse corresponds to the house of Pride, both being places of glittering wealth to which the knights are led by a broad beaten highway. Philotime sitting in her 'glistring glory' with the suitors around her throne is an infernal Lucifera: her 'broad beauties beam great brightness threw' (II.vii.45), even as Lucifera's 'bright blazing beautie . . . shone as *Titans* ray' (I.iv.8). Guyon descends to see the damned chained in hell where Tantalus, Pilate, and 'infinite moe [are] tormented in like paine' (II.vii.63), even as the Dwarf sees 'the endlesse routs of wretched thralles' (I.v.51) in the dungeon below the house of Pride. Such parallels only point up the difference between the two knights. The Red Cross Knight chooses at first to remain aloof from the worldlings of the house of Pride, but after his fight with Sansjoy he yields to Lucifera. Guyon, who is explicitly tempted to serve Mammon, must choose by asserting the virtue by which he stands; and this he does throughout triumphantly. (Though the virtue is his own, it is sustained by God: against the lust within the heart which is seen in the fiend who follows Guyon, Spenser prays: 'Eternall God thee saue from such decay.') He resists vigorously the temptations to which the Red Cross Knight finally yields. Though the Red Cross Knight flees the house of Pride in fear, he is readily found by Duessa where he sits resting by a fountain and feeding upon the cool shade. This climactic stage of his fall into Orgoglio's power is reproduced in the culminating episode of Guyon's temptation in the Garden where Mammon seeks 'to doe him deadly fall / In frayle intemperance through sinfull bayt':

Thou fearefull foole,
Why takest not of that same fruit of gold,
Ne sittest downe on that same siluer stoole,
To rest thy wearie person, in the the shadow coole.
(II.vii.63)

But Guyon neither feeds nor rests, and through the power of temperance does not yield.

The relation of Books I and II to the theme of man's fall becomes more explicit when each knight falls into the power of his enemies. Guyon's fall which heralds the coming of Arthur parallels the same mid-point of the narrative in Book I where the Red Cross Knight whose powers are similarly weakened also falls to the ground and is imprisoned until he is rescued by Arthur. As Una is the means by which Arthur intercedes for the Red Cross Knight, the Palmer is the means by which Arthur pledges to aid Guyon. Afterwards the knight praises Una as one 'whose wondrous faith, exceeding earthly race, / Was firmest fixt in mine extremest case', even as Guyon joys to see the Palmer: 'firme is thy faith, whom daunger neuer fro me drew' (I.ix.17; II.viii.53). More important, however, is the the significant contrast which the parallel provides. After his fall to the ground, the Red Cross Knight, being 'disarmd, disgrast, and inwardly dismayde' (I.vii.11), suffers a second fall into Orgoglio's dungeon where 'all his vitall powres / Decayd, and all his flesh shronk vp like withered flowres' (I.viii.41). Since he undergoes spiritual death, Arthur faces a double task: first, to slay Orgoglio, and then to descend into the dungeon. Guyon, however, is only 'dead seeming': his death-like trance renders allegorically an event that happens literally in Book I, as far as the conventions of romance allow. Being so dominated by the affections, he too needs grace: 'for every man with his affects is born, / Not by might master'd, but by special grace.' His foes are prevented by Arthur from disarming and disgracing his fallen body; accordingly, when they are slain, he 'from his traunce awakt. / Life hauing maistered her sencelesse foe.'

Arthur's roles in Book I as the instrument of divine grace, and in Book II as the symbol of magnanimity, appear so different that he has been considered two distinct persons. Yet the parallel between his two roles shows them to be compatible in one person. We have seen how his rescue of the knight in Book I imitates Christ's harrowing of hell. In Book II Spenser uses the same analogue though in terms appropriate to the argument. We see Arthur claim Guyon's fallen body from the Satanic forces represented by Pyrochles and Cymochles. Against the enemies who seek in their wrath to inflict punishment for sin, he sues for pardon. In the debate which follows he is called Guyon's 'dayes-man' (II.viii.28): such was sought by Job to mediate between him and God's wrath. He suffers the symbolic wound in the right side, 'wyde was the wound, and a large lukewarme flood, / Red as the Rose, thence gushed grieuously' (II.viii.39). Finally he slays his foes, and like Christ, claims man's body in the name of Mercy.

Spenser contrasts the scope of each book at certain key points. In Canto X of the first book where the opening stanza sums its argument, the final lines provide a formula for the whole book: 'if any strength we haue, it is to ill, / But all the good is Gods, both power and eke will.' The first line summarizes the knight's moral history during the first half of the book; the second prepares for the second half where the knight under Una is continually sustained by grace until he wields the power to slay the Dragon. 'All the good is Gods', as later in Book II he bears witness: 'his be the praise, that this atchieu'ment wrought, / Who made my hand the organ of his might; / More then goodwill to me attribute nought' (II.i.33). Until this final adventure, he remains the prostrate figure over whom the cosmic forces of light and darkness, represented in Una and Duessa, battle to possess him. In Book II the two opening stanzas of Canto XI sum its argument:

> What warre so cruell, or what siege so sore,
>   As that, which strong affections do apply
>   Against the fort of reason euermore
>   To bring the soule into captiuitie:
>   Their force is fiercer through infirmitie
>   Of the fraile flesh, relenting to their rage,
>   And exercise most bitter tyranny
>   Vpon the parts, brought into their bondage:
> No wretchednesse is like to sinfull vellenage.

> But in a body, which doth freely yeeld
>   His partes to reasons rule obedient,
>   And letteth her that ought the scepter weeld,
>   All happy peace and goodly gouernment
>   Is setled there in sure establishment;
>   There *Alma* like a virgin Queene most bright,
>   Doth florish in all beautie excellent:
>   And to her guestes doth bounteous banket dight,
> Attempred goodly well for health and for delight.

The first stanza repeats the argument of Book I in moral terms, that is, the weakness of human nature; but the second declares the strength of the temperate body. Together they assert the power and limitations of natural virtue. Since Guyon manifests its power throughout his journey, he 'euermore himselfe with comfort feedes, / Of his owne vertues, and prayse-worthy deedes' (II.vii.2). When he sees the damned in Proserpina's garden, he lectures them upon their folly. But the Red Cross Knight whose only strength is to do ill despairs at the memory of 'his deformed crimes, / That all his manly powres it did disperse' (I.ix.48). And when he sees the damned suffering in hell, he sees himself as one of them. But Guyon's display of the power of natural virtue reveals at the same time its limitations. In meeting his enemies, he cannot slay Furor and Disdain; and though he may subdue Pyrochles and Cymochles, he is prevented in the name of temperance from slaying them. Moreover, though the temperate body may resist temptation, it cannot defeat its besiegers. The image of the besieged body given in the first stanza above is the unifying metaphor of the book. It is expressed in Mortdant and Amavia whose 'raging passion with fierce tyrannie / Robs reason of her due regalitie' (II.i.57), in Medina surrounded by her two sisters with their warring suitors, in Phedon whose strong affections 'cruell battry bend / Gainst fort of Reason, it to ouerthrow' (II.iv.34), and culminates in the first half of the book with the image of Pyrochles and Cymochles ready to despoil Guyon's senseless body. The full limitation of natural virtue is seen when Guyon falls, and Arthur must come to rescue him. For though the temperate body is strong, being continually besieged, it stands only by the power of grace.

The significant contrast that we see between the Red Cross Knight's fall and Guyon's, together with the contrast between their rescue by Arthur, defines the scope of each book. The senseless Red Cross Knight dominated by Orgoglio is an emblem of the total depravity of human nature, the death of the spirit. Though he undergoes spiritual death, however, he may be reborn and regenerated through God's grace and finally restored to a higher state. Guyon, prostrate upon the ground under the wrathful Pyrochles and the lustful Cymochles, is an emblem of man's body dominated by the irascible and concupiscent affections. His fall is given in moral, rather than spiritual, terms; and through Arthur's intervention he recovers his natural moral state. He remains, then, upon that natural level which the Red Cross Knight transcends. The cyclical movement of Book I, the spiritual descent and ascent, contrasts with that linear movement upon the natural level described in Book II. In the terms suggested by Professor Woodhouse, we may say that Book I moves upon the level of grace while Book II remains upon the level of nature; but it is important to add that the levels are not exclusive. Though Guyon neither shares the depths of the Red Cross Knight's descent nor rises to his heights, he is not excluded from that knight's regeneration which follows

Arthur's rescue: instead, he enjoys its counterpart upon the natural level. From the parallel structure of the second half of both books, it becomes clear that Book I transcends the natural level explored in Book II by including it.

After being rescued by Arthur, each knight must realize the perfection of his own nature in three stages before completing his adventure. Guided by Una, the Red Cross Knight is first purged of sin in the house of Penance; later in the holy Hospital he is taught to frame his life in holy righteousness; and finally he ascends the hill of Contemplation where through a vision of the New Jerusalem he learns his name and nature. Thus fully prepared for his final adventure, he leaves to slay the Dragon. Guyon is not purged, for he need not learn to cherish himself; instead, 'with rare delight' he enjoys immediately the perfection of the temperate body in the castle of Alma. His delight as he moves through the castle, and his feasting, contrast sharply with the Red Cross Knight's agony in a dark lowly place where he diets with fasting until he 'had past the paines of hell, and long enduring night' (I.x.32). The 'goodly workemanship' of the castle of Alma, its 'wondrous frame' (II.ix.21,44), elaborates at some length matter contained in Book I, that 'wondrous workemanship of Gods owne mould' (I.x.42) which is maintained by the seven bead-men in the holy Hospital. In the final state of his preparation within the castle, Guyon also ascends to see a vision of

> This parts great workmanship, and wondrous powre,
> That all this other worlds worke doth excell,
> And likest is vnto that heauenly towre,
> That God hath built for his owne blessed bowre.
>   (II.ix.47)

What is revealed to the Red Cross Knight as his spiritual nature appears to Guyon as his natural body. The Red Cross Knight is taught his future state as Saint George, his present duty to aid Una, and his past history; Guyon is shown the body's power in the three sages who teach the future, the present, and the past. Heavenly Contemplation teaches the Red Cross Knight his 'name and nation': Eumnestes teaches Guyon his country's ancestry. The episodes are clearly parallel upon different levels, the religious and the secular; but again these levels are not exclusive. Man's spiritual nature which is revealed in Book I is embodied in the second book in the perfection of man's natural body governed by temperance and upheld by divine grace.

The spiritual regeneration of the Red Cross Knight, that continual casting out of sin from the time he regains Una as his guide until he slays the Dragon, provides the pattern for Arthur's fight with Maleger and his troops in Book II. The parallel may help us understand the nature of this fight which has become a crux in the allegory. While Guyon voyages to the Bower of Bliss, Arthur confronts Alma's besiegers who are described earlier as that body so 'distempred through misrule and passions bace: / It growes a Monster, and incontinent / Doth loose his dignitie and natiue grace' (II.ix.1). Maleger is this Monster, the parody of man's body: 'his bodie leane and meagre as a rake, / And skin all withered like a dryed rooke' (II.xi.22). The pattern for his attack upon the castle of Alma, his counterpart, is given in Book I by the Red Cross Knight's spiritual regeneration, the casting-out of his fallen self. When he first emerges from the dungeon, he looks like Maleger with 'bare thin cheekes . . . his rawbone armes . . . were cleane consum'd, and all his vitall powres / Decayd, and all his flesh shronk vp like withered flowres' (I.viii.41), for each manifests that state of sin by which our body is totally depraved. Awareness of his sinful state aroused by Despair so pierces the Red Cross Knight's heart that he seeks to pierce his heart: like Maleger, he tries 'to spoyle the Castle of his health' (I.ix.31). He is saved by Una who leads him to the house of Penance where he undergoes true despair: 'prickt with anguish of his sinnes so sore, . . . he desirde to end his wretched dayes: / So much the dart of sinfull guilt the soule dismayes' (I.x.21). In the end he is purged of 'inward corruption, and infected sin' (I.x.25), further instructed by the cardinal virtues and Mercy, and assoiled by Contemplation. Finally, he is regenerated by the three-day battle with the Dragon: twice he is cast to the ground where he is washed in the Well of Life which can cleanse 'guilt of sinfull crimes', and anointed by the Tree of Life which 'deadly woundes could heale' (I.xi.30,48). In Book II Alma the soul is similarly besieged by the darts of Maleger so that she was 'much dismayed with that dreadfull sight' (II.xi.16). She too is saved by divine grace whose instrument is Arthur. From the parallel with Book I we understand that Maleger is the state of sin, both actual and original; it is that state of sin from which the Red Cross Knight must be purged before he may slay the Dragon, and which must be slain before Guyon may overthrow the power of Acrasia. Spenser uses the myth of Antaeus in both books to describe the overthrow of sin. When the Red Cross Knight falls to the ground apparently slain but rises with greater strength, the Dragon is amazed:

> No wonder if he wondred at the sight,
> And doubted, whether his late enemy
> It were, or other new supplied knight.

> He, now to proue his late renewed might,
> High brandishing his bright deaw-burning blade.
> (I.xi.35)

And on the second day when the knight arises healed of his wounds, again the Dragon is amazed:

> When now he saw himselfe so freshly reare,
> As if late fight had nought him damnifyde,
> He woxe dismayd, and gan his fate to feare.
> (52)

When Maleger is cast to the ground but rises 'much stronger then before', Arthur is amazed:

> Nigh his wits end then woxe th'amazed knight,
> And thought his labour lost and trauell vaine,
> Against this lifelesse shadow so to fight:
> Yet life he saw, and felt his mightie maine,
> That whiles he marueild still, did still him paine:
> For thy he gan some other wayes aduize,
> How to take life from that dead-liuing swaine,
> Whom still he marked freshly to arize
> From th'earth, and from her wombe new spirits to reprize.
> (II.xi.44)

There is no paradox in this contrast between the two books. In Book I the knight is Georgos, or Earth; and the ground upon which he falls, Eden, being watered and nourished by the Well and Tree of Life, sustains him. In Book II we see Guyon fall to the ground and rise 'with so fresh hew' once Arthur slays the affections which dominate his body; but the ground belongs to that fallen nature which perverts man because it was perverted by him at the Fall, and so sustains his enemy. Like the Dragon, Maleger is that terrifying image of the enemy whom man in his own power cannot wound or slay. As the Dragon is slain by the knight's baptized hands wielding his 'deaw-burning blade', Maleger is slain by being cast into the standing lake.

The climax to the two books where the knights arrive at the entrance to Eden offers full parallel with contrast. When the Red Cross Knight marries Una, everything serves his pleasure: the posts sprinkled with wine, the great feast, the precious perfumes, the song of love, the heavenly music of the spheres through which he was 'reft of his sences meet, / And rauished with rare impression in his sprite', and above all, Una whose glorious beauty 'his heart did seeme to melt in pleasures manifold' (I.xii.39,40). These pleasures are parodied in the Bower of

Bliss: the wine offered by its porter, the sweet smells, the song of the rose, the earthly melody of the birds, waters, and wind, enchant man in order to enchain him in Arcasia's bower. Her beauty makes her knight 'quite molten into lust and pleasure lewd' (II.xii.73). The heavenly music which lifts man above himself contrasts with the earthly music which binds him to his senses: the pleasures which fulfil man for further duties contrast with those which put him to sleep. The Red Cross Knight 'swimming in that sea of blisfull ioy', yet who 'nought forgot . . . vnto his Farie Queene backe to returne' (I.xii.41), contrasts with the sleeping Verdant who forgets all honour of arms, 'but in lewd loues, and wastfull luxuree, / His dayes, his goods, his bodie he did spend' (II.xii.80). But the Red Cross Knight's final state is parodied earlier, and it is with this earlier state that the significance of the parallel with Book II may be realized.

Earlier at the mid-point of his adventure, the Red Cross Knight yields all to pleasure: disarming himself, he rests by a fountainside where he feeds upon the cooling shade of the leaves 'wherein the cherefull birds of sundry kind / Do chaunt sweet musick, to delight his mind.' With Duessa in this bower of 'greene boughes decking a gloomy glade', he 'bathe[s] in pleasaunce of the ioyous shade' courting Duessa 'both carelesse of his health, and of his fame'. In just such state is Verdant with the enchantress Acrasia until Guyon frees him. This parallel between the climax of Book II and the mid-point of Book I, and the contrast between the climax of Book II and the climax of Book I, justifies fully the elaborate paralleling of structure which the poet sets up between the two books. By destroying the Bower of Bliss, Guyon overthrows all those forces by which the Red Cross Knight falls into sin. The overpowering sloth, the carnal lust by which he yields to Duessa, the great weakness which leaves him helpless before his enemy: this terrible vision of the noble knight 'forelorne, / And left to losse' now is set against the power of virtue to release man from enshrouding nature, the womb which imprisons man upon the level of nature without possibility of rebirth. In terms of their archetypes which are present at this point, the Red Cross Knight moves toward man's final state in the Heavenly City when he will be fully restored to God, while Guyon turns back to man's original state when he entered Eve's garden and through her enchantments fell from God's grace. The apocalpytic significance of the Red Cross Knight's slaying the Dragon becomes the pattern for Guyon's release of man from imprisonment in the Garden of Eden. As the Red Cross Knight is an image of that second Adam who harrows hell to redeem mankind from Satan's power, Guyon, who runs a like race, imitates him to become a new Adam. He is one who, in Milton's phrase, 'might see and know, and yet abstain'; one who binds Eve and destroys the Garden that man may pass successfully through the world towards his final restoration.

THOMAS GREENE

Mutability and the
Theme of Process

Ⅰn style and structure as well as in
conception, [The Faerie Queene] has to be situated on the far edge of the
Renaissance, at a stage where new forms and ideas and techniques were
still filtered through a late medieval atmosphere. Spenser was stirred by
those intimations of the Renaissance which reached him—doubly removed as he was in Ireland—but we must not attribute to him, as man or
poet, the suavity and self-consciousness of the continental authors he
meant to imitate. He did not share their sharp sense of a gulf between the
enlightened present and the Gothic past, nor did he share the depth of
their veneration for antiquity. If he sometimes echoed Homer and alluded
to Virgil, he paid warmest homage to Chaucer. Even his irony—for
Spenser was quite capable of irony—is blurred for us by its unclassical
temper. All this being so, one must not look to him for the classical
virtues of poise, clarity, economy, and shapeliness. His poetry rather is
penetrated by other virtues whose names one scarcely knows, virtues
which take their definition from his placid, earnest, ceremonious voice.
One grasps those virtues, and all the charm and profundity they bring into
being, only by accepting Spenser's poetic mode—a mode whose obvious
attributes are quaintness and naïveté. Naïve perhaps Spenser is, but you
must be careful not to apply the word unguardedly, lest it return to mock your
wisdom. For heading the list of Spenser's insidious virtues are his intractability
to useful categories and his impermeability to worldly condescension. . . .

To arrive at a [sound] approach we had better look at the text itself. The one conventional example of a celestial messenger's descent in *The Faerie Queene* is a brief, transitional passage, not truly representative of the poem's poetic richness. But the larger unit in which the descent appears—The Cantos of Mutabilitie—forms one of the great dense nexuses of the whole work, as well as its (unintended) conclusion. These two cantos (with two stanzas of a third) are concerned with the rebellion of the Titaness Mutabilitie against the rule of Jove. Having established her dominion on earth, she ascends to the circle of the moon, there to claim the throne of Cynthia. When she attempts to secure the throne by violence, the earth and sky are deprived of light, and their inhabitants brought into consternation:

> Fearing least Chaos broken had his chaine,
> And brought againe on them eternall night . . .
> (VII.6.14.6–7)

Mercury, whose planet lies closest to the moon, is particularly alarmed, but all the gods together call upon Jove for an explanation:

> All ran together with a great out-cry,
> To Joves faire Palace, fixt in heavens hight;
> And beating at his gates full earnestly,
> Gan call to him aloud with all their might,
> To know what meant that suddaine lack of light.
> The father of the Gods when this he heard,
> Was troubled much at their so strange affright,
> Doubting least Typhon were againe uprear'd,
> Or other his old foes, that once him sorely fear'd.

> Eftsoones the sonne of Maia forth he sent
> Downe to the Circle of the Moone, to knowe
> The cause of this so strange astonishment,
> And why shee did her wonted course forslowe;
> And if that any were on earth belowe
> That did with charmes or Magick her molest,
> Him to attache, and downe to hell to throwe:
> But, if from heaven it were, then to arrest
> The Author, and him bring before his presence prest.

> The winged-foot God, so fast his plumes did beat,
> That soone he came where-as the Titanesse
> Was striving with faire Cynthia for her seat:
> At whose strange sight, and haughty hardinesse,
> He wondred much, and feared her no lesse.
> Yet laying feare aside to doe his charge,

At last, he bade her (with bold stedfastnesse)
Ceasse to molest the Moone to walke at large,
Or come before high Jove, her dooings to discharge.

And there-with-all, he on her shoulder laid
His snaky-wreathed Mace, whose awfull power
Doth make both Gods and hellish fiends affraid:
Where-at the Titanesse did sternely lower,
And stoutly answer'd, that in evill hower
He bid her leave faire Cynthias silver bower;
Sith shee his Jove and him esteemed nought,
No more then Cynthia's selfe; but all their kingdoms sought.

The Heavens Herald staid not to reply,
But past away, his doings to relate
Unto his Lord; who now in th'highest sky,
Was placed in his principall Estate,
With all the Gods about him congregate . . .

(VII.6.15–19)

The divine council is presently interrupted by the presumptuous entrance
of the rebel herself, who astonishes the gods with her beauty, her disdain-
ful rejection of their authority, and her appeal for a higher judge to
arbitrate the quarrel:

. . . To the highest him, that is behight
Father of Gods and men by equall might;
To weet, the God of Nature, I appeale.

(VII.6.35)

Jove seems forced to agree, and on the appointed day Nature appears (of
indeterminate sex, but now called a goddess), introduced by the poet with
fervent veneration and esoteric symbolism. The Titaness discourses at
length upon the extent of her dominion, but her plea is rejected in a
momentous and celebrated judgment:

I well consider all that ye have sayd,
And find that all things stedfastnes doe hate
And changed be: yet being rightly wayd
They are not changed from their first estate;
But by their change their being doe dilate:
And turning to themselves at length againe,
Do worke their owne perfection so by fate:
Then over them Change doth not rule and raigne;
But they raigne over change, and doe their states maintaine.

(VII.7.58)

In the Cantos of Mutabilitie Spenser treats most conclusively and explicitly that theme of process which unceasingly obsessed him and which was also the commonest and greatest of Elizabethan themes. Its philosophical formulation here makes so skilful and eclectic a blending of earlier systems that a host of commentators have failed to agree on its "sources." The Cantos keep their freshness—and more, their enigmatic elusiveness—in spite of their theme's familiarity, in spite of exhaustive research and a crushing burden of interpretation. They remain intrinsically difficult and, in their conclusion, characteristically ambivalent.

They are difficult in part because the debate they present hinges on *two* areas of dispute, upon both of which collectively *two* distinct judgments are made—by Nature and by the poet. It seems to me that the former of these dualities has not been sufficiently stressed. The two areas disputed by Mutabilitie and Jove are the terrestrial and celestial worlds, areas which Spenser carefully distinguishes throughout the fragment. At the opening of the action, Mutabilitie is already *de facto* suzerain on earth. From the outset of her enterprise, she has planned to subdue the whole universe (VII.6.4.1–4), but as yet she has succeeded only in the lower world:

> At first, *on earth* she sought it to obtaine;
> Where she such proofe and sad examples shewed
> Of her great power, to many ones great paine,
> That not men onely (whom she soone subdewed)
> But eke all other creatures, her bad dooings rewed.

> For, she the face of earthly things so changed,
> That all which Nature had establisht first
> In good estate, and in meet order ranged,
> She did pervert, and all their statutes burst:
> And all the worlds faire frame (which none yet durst
> Of Gods or men to alter or misguide)
> She alter'd quite, and made them all accurst
> That God has blest; and did at first provide
> In that still happy state for ever to abide.

> . . . O pittious worke of MUTABILITIE!
> By which, we all are subject to that curse,
> And death in stead of life have sucked from our Nurse.
>
> (VII.6.4–6)

Whatever the moral or legal rights of this conquest, no one is inclined to dispute it; the quarrel arises only when Mutabilitie attempts to extend it into heaven:

> And now, when all the earth she thus had brought
> To her behest, and thralled to her might,
> She gan to cast in her ambitious thought,
> T'attempt the empire of the heavens hight,
> And Jove himselfe to shoulder from his right.
>
> (VII.6.7)

The immediate point at issue is control of heaven, and thus Jove defines the quarrel in terms of an encroachment into *his* realm by an earthly power:

> Harken to mee awhile yee heavenly Powers;
> Ye may remember since th'Earths cursed seed
> Sought to assaile the heavens eternall towers,
> And to us all exceeding feare did breed:
> But how we then defeated all their deed,
> Yee all doe knowe, and them destroied quite;
> Yet not so quite, but that there did succeed
> An off-spring of their bloud, which did alite
> Upon the fruitfull earth, which doth us yet despite.
>
> Of that bad seed is this bold woman bred,
> That now with bold presumption doth aspire
> To thrust faire Phoebe from her silver bed,
> And eke our selves from heavens high Empire . . .
>
> (VII.6.20–21)

There is no question at this stage of Jove's power on earth. Earth, it would seem, has little to do with 'heavens high Empire," and exists for Jove chiefly as a source of upstart nuisances. When presently the upstart makes her appearance, Jove immediately asks his uppermost question:

> What idle errand hast thou, earths mansion to forsake:

Mutabilitie answers by reference to her mixed parentage: although her mother is Earth, her father is Titan, rightful ruler of heaven. Thus she inherits the government of both realms. But Jove denies the claims of Titan and continues to speak of Mutabilitie as a creature of earth:

> Will never mortall thoughts ceasse to aspire,
> In this bold sort, to Heaven claime to make,
> And touch celestiall seates with earthly mire?
>
> (VII.6.29)

Whereupon Mutabilitie appeals to the God of Nature, whose authority embraces *both* mortal and immortal, earth and heaven:

> Father of Gods and men by equall might.

The trial moreover is to be attended by the inhabitants of both realms:

> . . . All, both heavenly Powers, and earthly wights,
> Before great Natures presence should appeare . . .
>
> (VII.6.36)

> As well those that are sprung of heavenly seed,
> As those that all the other world doe fill . . .
>
> (VII.7.3)

Thus throughout these preliminary scenes Spenser repeatedly distinguishes the two realms concerned and focuses the dispute only upon the higher.

This focus is enlarged once Mutabilitie begins to plead at the opening of the trial. Now for the first time she imputes to Jove a claim to the entire universe:

> To thee therefore of this same Jove I plaine,
> And of his fellow gods that faine to be,
> That challenge to themselves the whole worlds raign . . .
>
> (VII.7.15)

only to enter her own rival claim and to assert that the two realms are actually one:

> For, heaven and earth I both alike do deeme,
> Sith heaven and earth are both alike to thee;
> And, gods no more then men thou doest esteeme:
> For, even the gods to thee, as men to gods do seeme.
>
> (VII.7.15)

From what precedes and follows, this argument would appear to be specious. Ultimately, continues Mutabilitie, the universe is Nature's, but each "principality" belongs to her. Her ensuing demonstration of her right—i.e. of vicissitude as a universal principle—falls not surprisingly into two parts. The first, devoted to the earth . . .

> And first, the Earth (great mother of us all) . . .
>
> (VII.7.17)

contains an analysis of the ever-changing elements and a procession of the personified seasons, the Hours, Day and Night, and Life and Death—all creatures of this terrestrial realm. Mutabilitie concludes this first part of her discourse (VII.7.14–47) by summing up:

> . . . Wherefore, this lower world who can deny
> But to be subject still to Mutabilitie?
>
> (VII.7.47)

Jove interposes an objection here, revealing for the first time that he does lay claim to a kind of hegemony over earth at two removes. But he is quickly answered, and Mutabilitie proceeds to the second part of her discourse by turning upon him with the crucial question:

> Yet what if I can prove, that even yee
> Yourselves are likewise chang'd, and subject unto mee?
> (VII.7.49)

Her argument is now based on the inconstancy of the planetary courses, and secondarily on the earthly birth of Jove and Cynthia. This second part is much shorter than the first (thirty-four stanzas to six), although it is this part alone which seemingly touches upon the original point at issue. Having concluded this argument, she turns to the goddess-judge to make her final plea:

> Now judge then (O thou greatest goddesse trew!)
> According as thy selfe doest see and heare,
> And unto me addoom that is my dew;
> This is the rule of all, all being rul'd by you.
> (VII.7.56)

Nature proceeds to her verdict that all things reign over change by employing change to perfect themselves. She then addresses Mutabilitie:

> Cease therefore daughter further to aspire,
> And thee content thus to be rul'd by me:
> For thy decay thou seekst by thy desire;
> But time shall come that all shall changed bee,
> And from thenceforth, none no more change shall see.
> (VII.7.59)

The upshot of the debate hinges on the word *further*. Does Nature mean: "No longer aspire to overthrow my rule?" Nominally, Mutabilitie has never so aspired but has rather repeatedly acknowledged Nature's superior power ("That is onely dew unto thy might . . ."; ". . . all being ruled by you"). Does Nature mean that Mutabilitie aspires to overthrow her, as the embodiment of order, without realizing that this is the ultimate result of her enterprise? Or does she mean, laying stress on *thus*: "Aspire no higher than earth. Be content to remain my viceroy *here*?" Or again: "Remain on earth. Be content to accept my verdict." The latter two alternatives would accord better with what follows. Perhaps in this passage, as in so many of Spenser's, we must accept a certain vagueness which permits the synthesis of several meanings.

In any case there is no doubt about the poet's own resolution in

the following stanza, the first of the unfinished eighth canto, the penulti-
mate stanza of the poem. The rueful melancholy of that resolution is too
frequently passed over for the concluding prayer, and yet without it the
prayer loses its terrible pathos. The poet is unconvinced by Mutabilitie's
claim to, or rather her fitness for the celestial throne, but he is sadly
convinced of her rule on earth:

> When I bethinke me on that speech whyleare,
> Of Mutability, and well it way:
> Me seemes, that though she all unworthy were
> Of the Heav'ns Rule; yet very sooth to say,
> In all things else she beares the grestest sway.
>
> (VII.8.1)

The first part of her discourse may have been irrelevant to the legal issue,
but it is only too relevant to the poem. The metaphysical reply of Nature
is little consolation to the individual in the existential desolation of his
contemptus mundi:

> . . . Which makes me loath this state of life so tickle,
> And love of things so vaine to cast away;
> Whose flowring pride, so fading and so fickle,
> Short Time shall soon cut down with his consuming sickle.
>
> (VII.8.1)

At the very end of his immense poem, Spenser can no longer "find the
mortal world enough," and the slow, familiar, meditative voice breaks
with unwonted poignance into a final cry for deliverance:

> Then gin I thinke on that which Nature sayd,
> Of that same time when no more Change shall be,
> But stedfast rest of all things firmely stayd
> Upon the pillours of Eternity,
> That is contrayr to Mutabilitie:
> For, all that moveth, doth in Change delight:
> But thence-forth all shall rest eternally
> With Him that is the God of Sabbaoth hight:
> O that great Sabbaoth God, graunt me that Sabaoths sight.
>
> (VII.8.2)

Professor Bush writes: "In Mutability . . . the philosophic assertion of permanence behind the flux is not enough for a poet who is
Christian and medieval. He turns from such cold consolation to the refuge
of faith . . . In a moment of intense revulsion and spiritual insight, all
things seem dross except God." If faith is indeed a refuge here, it is a lonely
and bitter one. For the poet has no sight of God or of that hearsay

Sabbath. He invokes and he waits, but he affirms only the reality of the Titaness. If she has been checked in heaven, she never dreams of surrendering earth, and the whole fragment breathes with the energy of her vital being. Even if she aspires no *further*, her present dominion is sufficiently awesome.

Although the *Cantos* differ sharply from the rest of the poem, they also epitomize it. The authority of the title assigned to the fragmentary seventh book by its first publisher—*Of Constancy*—is uncertain. But in a larger sense this title might be assigned to each of the foregoing six books, whose nominal virtues—Holiness, Temperance, Chastity, Friendship, Justice and Courtesy—are all interpreted in terms of constancy. Underlying the fairy tale adventures against a dragon, an enchantress, a wizard, a tyrant, a monster—adventures in which good and evil are comfortably separated—underlying these is the profounder, darker, wearier conflict with vicissitude, which contains all adventures and engulfs them. That mightier antagonist is the stronger for its invisible ubiquity—like Nature, "unseene of any, yet of all beheld." It is to be found in the self, in history, in nature, in the cosmos. Against vicissitude little is achieved of true permanence: Red Cross and Arthur continue to wander; Artegall is recalled to face detraction; Calidore's Beast regains its freedom; Britomart awaits her marriage and the loss soon to follow. The motif of human insecurity is reiterated with obsessive insistence:

> Blisse may not abide in state of mortall men.
> (I.8.44)

> Nothing is sure, that growes on earthly ground.
> (I.9.11)

> No earthly thing is sure.
> (II.9.21)

> But what on earth can alwayes happie stand?
> (V.3.9)

> So feeble is mans state, and life unsound,
> That in assurance it may never stand,
> Till it dissolved be from earthly band.
> (II.11.30)

Moreover the drama of each principal hero hinges upon the insecurity of his dedication. Of these six heroes (Cambell and Triamond do not merit to be ranked with them) only Britomart and Arthur remain unambiguously constant, and even Arthur's constancy is momentarily questioned (III.1.19.1–2).

By thus setting his nominal fable, with its somewhat obvious victories, against the muted but fundamental conflict with flux, Spenser resembled a poet whose work he may or not not have understood—the poet of the *Iliad*. But as a Christian Platonist he was not disposed to resolve that conflict with the heroic tragedy of the *Iliad's* conclusion. His own resolution is presented in the Mutabilitie Cantos with significant ambivalence; a succincter, perhaps a clearer resolution might be isolated in such a stanza as the following, even though its apparent purpose is simply to indicate the hour:

> By this the Northerne wagoner had set
> His sevenfold teme behind the stedfast starre,
> That was in Ocean waves yet never wet,
> But firme is fixt, and sendeth light from farre
> To all, that in the wide deepe wandring arre:
> And chearefull Chaunticlere with his note shrill
> Had warned once, that Phebus fiery carre
> In hast was climbing up the Easterne hill,
> Full envious that night so long his roome did fill.
>
>   (I.2.1)

By repeating certain images throughout the poem, Spenser endows them with accretions of meaning. A chapter could be written about each of the five great images in this stanza—the star, the ocean, the wanderer, day, and night. In particular, the image of the wanderer guided by a celestial light is so common in Spenser's poetry as to become archetypal. But a very summary paradigm of these images' interrelations must suffice here. The stanza quoted presents sunrise as a reassuring, "chearefull" occurrence, instinct with the jocund bustle of Protestant zeal. But the sun in itself can neither maintain its advantage over night nor guide the wanderers. Rather the ocean and the "deepe"consist precisely of that flux which alternates day and night, good and evil, joy and sorrow, endlessly. This particular sun rises on an action which is anything but auspicious—Red Cross' misguided abandonment of Una. This day will see the beginning of his moral and literal wandering. But even when hero and heroine are reunited, when Red Cross is purged, and the dragon slain, he must continue to wander in a universe ostensibly Manichean. The dark principle of that universe is personified by Night, who appears three cantos later as a Satanically regal and awesome divinity, the "most auncient Grandmother of all." She is addressed, in a memorable phrase, as one who

> . . . sawst the secrets of the world unmade

and she is altogether magnificently sinister. In Book Three Arthur apostrophizes her in his great hymn (III.4.55–60) as the source of all suffering, evil, and death. Only the star is capable of piercing night and guiding the errant mortal, that star so firmly fixed that it remains above flux and is "in Ocean waves yet never wet." The star is the Platonic Good and the Christian God of Sabbaoth, that which dwells apart and transcends the good or evil of this world. Red Cross on the Mount of Contemplation is permitted a vision of that transcendent sphere, but not the experience of it; he must wait, as the poet waits and the reader waits. On earth he can hope at best for the sunlight of grace, the sunlight of Arthur's shield.

Thus *The Faerie Queene* is set in a divided world, a dualistic world waiting to be monistic. The poem itself alternately celebrates and grieves the vicissitude it represents. But the burden of the whole is too somber to permit heroism its unwithering garland of enduring achievement. The one momentous event which the present withholds is out of human hands. The Day of Judgment, which d'Aubigné and Milton regarded as a settling of moral scores, meant to Spenser a period to vicissitude, a release from wandering, the advent of the star. Until that day, until "the stedfast rest of all things firmly stayd Upon the pillours of Eternity," all victories will appear as pseudo-victories, for they stand to evil as morning stands to evening. Despite appearances and the scholastic verdict of Nature, the mongrel Titaness is the true victress of the poem, and the time of her fall is not yet.

II

The stanza form which Spenser contrived, and which has earned him deserved praise, influenced inevitably the syntax and the style of his poem. In three obvious ways his stanza differs from the *ottava rima* of his models: it is longer; its rhyme scheme is more intricate; its last line is a foot longer than the others, and so more final. The effect of these innovations is first of all to isolate the stanza, to make of it much more of a separate, self-contained thing. The *ottava rima*, by its very flexibility and simplicity, its failure to call attention to itself, is far better adapted to narrative. It adjusts itself to two sentences as well as to one, and if the poet chooses to continue a sentence into the following stanza (as Ariosto and Tasso do, to say nothing of Pulci) that liberty does not really violate the form. But in Spenser the syntactic unit—the sentence—tends to be fitted to the prosodic unit—the stanza. Occasionally Spenser fits two sentences into a single stanza, but he is invariable in ending the stanza with a full stop. I should say also that he places some other mark of punctuation after many more lines than the Italians do.

The effect of these changes is to render Spenser's syntax more complex and more sinuous, to slow the reader's pace as he moves through a maze of clauses, and to create a faint sense of release when he finds his way to the last line's tranquil resolution. The slowness and sinuosity of his style, and the soft melancholy of his falling rhythms, suggest that image of wandering which is almost essential to romance and certainly to *The Faerie Queene*. But the last line, which is often syntactically independent or partly independent, and prosodically distinct, seems to re-establish a momentary order. The syntax is quite different from the "improvisational" syntax of d'Aubigné, who was confined by no stanza form at all, because Spenser's sentences must always be rounded off neatly at the foreseen moment. But before that end, his syntax is likely to be open, loose, asymmetrical, and repetitive.

Consider for example the stanza in which Jove despatches Mercury:

> Eftsoones the sonne of Maia forth he sent
> Downe to the Circle of the Moone, to knowe
> The cause of this so strange astonishment,
> And why shee did her wonted course forslowe;
> And if that any were on earth belowe
> That did with charmes or Magick her molest,
> Him to attache, and downe to hell to throwe:
> But, if from heaven it were, then to arrest
> The Author, and him bring before his presence prest.
>
> (VII.6.16)

The main verb is *sent*, but five other verbs depend upon it as vague infinitives of purpose—*knowe, attache, throwe, arrest, bring*. Of these the last four appear in the closing three lines of the stanza, separated from the main verb by six or more lines, and by the semicolon in line four. A second semicolon in line seven separates off the last two infinitives still further. The objects of the infinitive *to knowe*—a noun and a clause—are related in an awkward, nonparallel coupling, to say nothing of their redundancy. Moreover the *if* clause in the following line is briefly confusing because one expects it to be parallel to the *why* clause above it (instead of modifying *attache*). The *if* clause contains a further subordinate clause (line six) which increases the complexity. Finally the reference of the pronoun *it* in line seven is a little mystifying, given the use of *him* in line six; *it* must probably be referred to *cause* in line three, but the reader is unlikely to grasp the reference immediately. Spenser's use of pronouns is repeatedly vague. Of course he was in part reflecting the looser syntax of his age, but he is consistently and outstandingly loose even among his contemporaries.

These features of Spenser's style influence his poem in two important ways. First of all the tangled and circular sentence structure, together with the melancholy and deliberation of his manner, deprive his language of that puissant energy which is common to most epic poetry. To say this is not to disparage Spenser, but it is to limit the kind of experience his poem affords. Subtle and seductive his language is, but it lacks the virile directness and natural force which inform even those great epics born of artificial, aristocratic tradition. This lack modifies whatever heroic achievement *The Faerie Queene* contains.

The second influence is more difficult to describe, but it leads to a quality which is basic to the poem and which is insidiously ubiquitous. This is the *blurring* of Spenser's language and even of his mind. To demonstrate it, I would begin by pointing to his use of the conjunction *and*. We have already seen how, in the stanza quoted above, the *and* in the fourth line connects two nonparallel elements, and in the fifth appears to connect clauses while in fact it connects infinitives. Analogously, in the line

> At whose strange sight and haughty hardinesse

the *and* connects two nouns which do not quite fit one another. *Hardinesse*, meaning *effrontery*, is a moral quality. But by "strange sight" Spenser means something altogether different—not simply "strange appearance," because Mutabilitie is later described as beautiful; her very being there is strange, and her untoward set-to with Cynthia. Thus *sight* and *hardinesse* are not coupled without wrenching. But the coupling does not lack a certain logic. The strangeness and the hardiness make up a single experience of Mercury, muddled together in his mind as they are in the reader's. Nothing is more typical of Spenser—in treating large elements as well as these minuscule ones—than the muddling together of the slightly unlike, the dissolution of contours, the blurring of meaning, the sacrifice of precision to the larger, vaguer aura. Today such a sacrifice is unfashionable, but I fear it cannot better be defended than by pointing to such an example as *The Faerie Queene*. If it seems to you unpardonable, then you had better give Spenser up.

We have already encountered an analogous sort of blurring in the ambiguity of the Mutability Cantos' conclusion. But in other respects it operates from their opening—for example in the associations we are led to attach to the major figures. Jove is partly the god of Homer and Hesiod, partly the planet, partly the principle of order in the celestial universe, and perhaps a little bit the Christian God. But then that God also appears as a separate power—the God of Sabbaoth—in the final stanza. He also enters into the figure of Nature through a simile (VII.7.7) which compares her to the transfigured Christ. God "enters into" the conception of Nature, but she cannot be equated with Him as simply as C. S. Lewis suggests; the imagery connects her with the great Venus of Book Four, and thus with Lucretius' Venus; she has something of Concord as well, and the Nature of Alanus ab Insulis, whom Spenser names, and perhaps the Nature of Cicero. In the neo-Platonic scheme she is equivalent to the Anima, the World-Soul, which imparts form and being to matter. Her most recent incarnation is in Joyce's ALP, the "Annyma" of *Finnegans Wake*. But above and beyond all these equivalences, she is the great mythical divinity of Spenser's own seventh book, evoking now one and now another of her counterparts, but remaining her own integral self through the continuity of her name and presence in the action.

The most distinctive, the most original and inimitable quality of the whole poem lies in this perpetual *becoming* of its characters. Just as the associations of Nature shift, just as Mutabilitie is partly the Titaness daughter of Earth, partly Mary Stuart challenging Cynthia-Elizabeth, partly the Christian Satan who introduced original sin, partly a natural principle, partly a philosophic doctrine, so the status and meaning and concreteness of all the manifold figures of the poem shift and fade and recombine. The Red Cross Knight is now Holiness, now simply a holy man, now Leicester, now Saint George, now Everyman, now the typical errant Christian, now Christ himself, or most commonly some fusion of several of these, so that one needs perpetually to take a cross-section in order to apprehend him. Elsewhere, moreover, he is none of these; he is merely the individual, Red Cross, whom we know as we know any other individual in fiction.

The Faerie Queene is a ballet of images, motifs, situations, allusions, and characters woven and interwoven in ever-changing patterns, never altogether constant and never altogether new, "eterne in mutabilitie."

. . . . The new form edges out the old one. Similarly the ultimate reality on the highest level is blurred and faint before one reaches it. Wherever one stands upon the ladder, the levels above one are indistinct, and the things below are too contemptible to matter much as distinct entities. They never disappear altogether but they fade, fall out of focus, or are subsumed. Spenser's allegory is far from closed to the orthodox conception, but it is deeply influenced by the neo-Platonic. As it rises and falls from one level to another, the other levels tend to hover, as it were, a little out of focus.

It is hard to ascribe Spenser's technique either to artistic naïveté alone or to a subtle self-consciousness. Both perhaps contribute to his profound but easily overlooked originality. For of all the great poems which achieve epic amplitude, *The Faerie Queene* is one of the freest of convention. It contains scores of conventional passages, but it is superbly untrammeled by them. This freedom is precisely the opposite of the reader's first impression, because the poem first *looks* as though it were rigidly conventional. But in this respect too it is Protean; it moves boldly up and down the hierarchy of genres. It requires a bit of reading to discover that Spenser's bow to decorum is the emptiest of rituals; he makes his rules and chooses his modes, altering them as suits his absolute pleasure. Thus *The Faerie Queene* is a much more unpredictable poem than one expects, and so much more delightful. With familiarity one becomes attuned to Spenser's fancy and grasps the harmony beneath the apparent disorder. But the principle of continuity is a living, internal force, scarcely to be articulated. The Mutabilitie Cantos are a quintessence of all of Spenser, but they also constitute an abruptly new beginning.

The only literary work whose organization remotely resembles *The Faerie Queene*'s is that whose heroine I have already called Spenserian—*Finnegans Wake*. Joyce, like Spenser, wrote a dream vision of history, fitting the techniques of metamorphosis and transvaluation and fragmentation of the operations of the liberated fancy, liberated in the one case by allegory as in the other by sleep. Both heightened the vision with experimentally evocative and unfamiliar language. Joyce's theme was identical with Spenser's—the nature of historical process, and each treated it with that mingling of courage and resignation which imitates the profoundest responses to life. Each sweetened his orthodox Aristotelian heritage with a measure of Plato or of Plato's wayward stepchild, Giordano Bruno. The one had had a lover's quarrel with Ireland and the other felt for her an enemy's affection. Both made parables of the simplest things: earth, water, and sky, day and night, seasons, years, and generations, drawing their evasive wisdom from the gnomic circles of nature. Both celebrated a marriage of waters, and the sweet joy of the Medway's bridal day anticipates the Liffey's wearier union, "rolling down the lea" to her perpetual and renewing death. Only their tone is different: the tragic gaiety of *Finnegans Wake* in its roguish astringency sounds in harsher consonance than Spenser's untremulous serenity.

THOMAS P. ROCHE, JR.

The Marriage of the Thames and Medway

The sea lifts, also, reliquary hands.
—CRANE, *Voyages III*

The marriage of the Thames and the
Medway occupies a climactic position in Book IV. From a purely structural point of view it is contrasted to the House of Busyrane in Book III.
As Amoret, imprisoned by a wall of flame, is rescued by Britomart; so
Florimell, imprisoned by walls of waves, is rescued from Proteus through
the occasion of this marriage of rivers. Within its own book the reluctant
consent of the Medway (4.11.7) recapitulates Scudamour's winning of
Amoret in the preceding canto and anticipates the awakening of Marinell
in the next. The marriage is both a commentary and analogue of reluc-
tance transformed to consent in a young lady and a young man—one more
example of the theme of *discordia concors*. In another sense it is a cosmic
symbol of the power of the Temple of Venus and on the social level is
paralleled by Marinell's sudden love for Florimell.

Although these structural parallels are important in pointing out a
significance for the marriage greater than the usual praise of its descriptive
beauty, although they direct the reader's attention to the marriage as a
symbolic statement of the meaning of the Temple of Venus and the love
of Marinell and Florimell, they do not tell why Spenser chose the river

From *The Kindly Flame: A Study of the Third and Fourth Books of Spenser's "Faerie Queene."*
Copyright © 1964 by Princeton University Press.

marriage to express these parallels. To do that we must study with some care the structure and symbolism of the canto and relate Spenser's marriage to the concept of river marriages and their literary precedents.

A little more than a century after Spenser published *The Faerie Queene* Daniel Defoe writes in a rather characteristic vein: "I shall sing you no Songs here of the River in the first Person of a Water Nymph, a Goddess (and I know not what) according to the Humour of the ancient Poets. I shall talk nothing of the Marriage of old *Isis*, the Male River, with beautiful *Thame*, the Female River, a Whimsy as simple as the Subject was empty, but I shall speak of the River as Occasion presents, as it really is *made glorious* by the Splendor of its shores. . . ." One can begin to understand Defoe's irritation with the convention of the river marriage as it is exemplified by Drayton's great unread classic, *Poly-Olbion*, and in a sense there is something artificial and merely poetical about the conception. Two rivers join and flow to meet the ocean. And yet to dismiss the river marriage as a legitimate device for poetry is to ignore its significance in the history of English literature.

The river marriage, which must be carefully distinguished from the Ovidian metamorphosis of a nymph into a stream, is a subject peculiar to the Renaissance in England, where it was first used as a formal device by antiquarian scholar-poets, culminating in Drayton's monumental work. The nineteenth century gives us such examples as Shelley's delightful *Arethusa* and Peacock's laborious *The Genius of the Thames*. In the twentieth century there has been a resurgence of interest, especially among the more symbolic or mythic writers. One has only to think of the lyrical "riverrun" in *Finnegans Wake*, or Hart Crane's description of the Mississippi in *The Bridge*, or Eliot's allusions to Spenser's river marriages in "The Fire Sermon" to be convinced that the river marriage has once more become an important poetic device.

These disparate works of art have two characteristics in common. They describe actual rivers, and these descriptions are used symbolically. The all but endless enumeration of English rivers in *Poly-Olbion* builds up a marvellous picture of England, its history and geography. As Douglas Bush reminds us, "The best translation of the title is simply 'Merry England.'" *Poly-Olbion* creates unity from diversity and evokes a symbol of England by amassing minute particulars. The modern writers have reversed the situation. Whereas Drayton's patternless enumeration of rivers eventually creates a symbol of unity, the modern writer starts with a pattern that can best be symbolized by the marriage of rivers. The river marriage becomes for the modern writer a symbol of one part of the eternal pattern of flux in time. Northrop Frye has described this pattern of process in treating *The Waste Land*: ". . . although there is a fire sermon and a thunder sermon, both with apocalyptic overtones, the natural cycle of water, the Thames flowing into the sea and returning through death by water in the spring rains, is the containing form of the poem." The "Doublends Jined" of *Finnegans Wake* repeat the same pattern in the endless Viconian cycle of Anna Livia Plurabelle.

Spenser stands somewhere between these two types and is in many ways the progenitor of both. The marriage of the Thames and the Medway leads to Drayton through its enumeration of river names and to Joyce and Eliot through its symbolism. Spenser is the great poet of mutability in English. Blake and Shelley, Yeats and Joyce and Eliot have all learned from him. They are all intensely aware of the tension between the temporal and the eternal and the ultimate resolution of this tension in some kind of Apocalypse. . . .

After the publication of this second installment and before the publication of *Poly-Olbion* there are more numerous allusions to river marriages, always basically symbolic. . . . Whether it is a case of direct Spenserian influence or simply an historical coincidence, rivers and river symbolism became an important part of pageants about this time, and it is almost impossible to decide how responsible Spenser is for the fashion of river symbolism. This is the best answer Hilda Taylor could give in her interesting thesis on topographical poetry in the Renaissance: "The influence of the pageants upon Drayton's *Poly-Olbion* is unquestionable; the case of Leland, Vallans, and Spenser is less clear, since recorded examples of the particular kind of allegory in question in English pageants of the earlier date are neither so numerous nor so striking as in these later pageants which may conceivably have been affected by the poems." It would be rash to go beyond this statement in assessing Spenser's influence on later river symbolism. In light of the slim evidence it will be better to turn to the examples of river marriages in Spenser, for like the general subject of river marriages they have received hardly any critical attention.

Spenser first mentions the Thames and the Medway in the July eclogue of *The Shepheardes Calender*:

> Here has the salt Medway his sourse,
>   wherein the Nymphes doe bathe.
> The salt Medway, that trickling stremis
>   adowne the dales of Kent:
> Till with his elder brother Themis
>   his brackish waues be meynt.
>   (79–84)

. . . All Spenser's river marriages deal with the problem of mutability. The context of the passage from the July eclogue in a speech by

Morrell the goatherd, who represents the forces of pride and modernity in the Church. In his rebuke to the humble Thomalin he justifies his sitting on a hill with the assertion that hills are holy places to saints, that the muses dwell on a hill and that Christ himself sanctified Mount Olivet.

> Besyde, as holy fathers sayne,
>   there is a hyllye place,
> Where *Titan* ryseth from the mayne,
>   to renne hys dayly race.
> Vpon whose toppe the starres bene stayed,
>   and all the skie doth leane,
> There is the caue, where *Phebe* layed,
>   the shepheard long to dreame.
> Whilome there vsed shepheards all
>   to feede theyr flocks at will,
> Till by his foly one did fall,
>   that all the rest did spill.
>
> (57–68)

This passage, which comes just before the Thames-Medway reference, contains in embryonic form all the elements of Spenser's Irish river myths. Titan running "hys dayly race" calls to mind Spenser's constant concern with passing time, the cyclical repetition of day and night, spring and fall, summer and winter. The same impulse draws him to the "natural cycle of water" where rivers are constantly changing and ever the same. The physical cycle describes a perfect circle: Ocean to cloud to rain to river and back to Ocean—"eterne in mutability." The ocean is the girdle of the earth, the analogue to eternity. The tension between this temporal cycle and eternity is evoked by the cave where Diana, the Titan's twin, laid Endymion "long to dreame." We need hardly be reminded that Arlo Hill is the favorite haunt of Diana until the folly of Faunus brings "an heauy haplesse curse" and Diana deserts the hill forever. The result of this fall is the marriage of Fanchin and Molanna. If the consequence of the Fall seems slight, we must remember that even Milton allowed that his First Transgressors "hand in hand with wandring steps and slow/ through Eden took thir solitarie way." Mulla and Bregog, Molanna and Fanchin, Medway and Thames—all Spenser's river marriages—with differing emphasis, are myths about love in a fallen world. The pattern is the same: Eden—the Fall—love in marriage. Spenser is trying to show that the only way to retain the vestiges of our pre-Fall Eden is through the union of lovers, of friends, of rivers. Robert Frost's comment in another poem about the Fall is appropriate to Spenser.

> The question that he frames in all but words
> Is what to make of a diminished thing.

With this in mind we may turn to the structure and symbolism of the marriage of the Thames and Medway to see how Spenser varies the mythic pattern and how he relates this marriage to the structure of Book IV.

Spenser begins by reminding the reader that he has left Florimell languishing in a dungeon since Book III, canto 8, and that Marinell's mother is still searching for a cure of the wound inflicted by Britomart in Book III, canto 4. The marriage is the occasion for bringing these two threads of the narrative together.

> It fortun'd then, a solemne feast was there
>   To all the Sea-gods and their fruitfull seede,
>   In honour of the spousalls, which then were
>   Betwixt the *Medway* and the *Thames* agreed. . . .
>
> So both agreed, that this their bridale feast
>   Should for the Gods in *Proteus* house be made;
>   (4.11.8–9)

With this apparently tenuous connection between his main narrative and this episode Spenser invokes the aid of the muse and begins the procession.

The procession has been compared to the masque because of its pageant-like descriptions, but the effect is not that of a masque—it can hardly be called a procession, for the main effect is that of a static picture. The participants do not move. The poet describing the procession moves through his description in the same way that one "reads" a medieval painting, moving from scene to scene within the frame of one picture.

The actual description is 43 stanzas long and orderly in the extreme. Neptune and Amphitrite, preceded by Triton (11–12), are followed by their offspring, the sea-gods (13–14) and the founders of nations (15–16). Next come Ocean and Tethys, preceded by Nereus (18–19) and followed by the famous rivers of the world (20–21). After a brief digression in praise of women (22) Arion (23) leads in the procession of the bridegroom (24–44), including his parents Tame and Isis with their "grooms" (24–26), his tributaries (29), his "neighbour floods" (30–39), and the Irish rivers (40–44). Last comes the procession of the bride attended by her two pages and handmaids (40–42) and followed by the fifty Nereids (43–51), of whom one is Cymoent (Cymodoce), Marinell's mother.

It should be evident that the procession is really composed of four smaller processions, each with its own focal point: Neptune-Amphitrite, Ocean-Tethys, the bridegroom Thames, and the bride Medway. The first three of these are preceded by mythical figures, which are clues to the meaning of that particular procession. Within each procession the order of names is dependent on many factors, of which rhyme and meter is not the least important. In the case of the English rivers Spenser names the tributaries of the Thames, and then follows a counter-clockwise order, beginning with the Severne and ending with the Lindus; P. W. Joyce contributes a slightly more complicated order for the Irish rivers. Order there is, and order implies design and meaning, and the meaning of this orderly structure is our next concern.

The first of the sub-processions is that of the sea-gods and founders of nations. It is led by Triton, half-man and half-fish. He represents that part of the sea that is fertile and brings prosperity and concord to the land. He is Neptune's trumpeter, and when he blows his trumpet, "it is a signe of calme and fayre weather." He is the appropriate symbol of the lawful and orderly aspects of the sea, ruled by Neptune, who has the power over the foundations of buildings. He leads in those gods who govern the sea and those who have established order on the land. This group is followed by the older generation of sea-gods represented by Nereus, the old man of the sea, and Oceanus and Tethys, who represent the fertility of the sea and the primary substance that eventually leads to the law and order preceding them in the procession. Lotspeich cites Natalis Comes, 8.1, as the source of Spenser's conception of Ocean: "Oceanus, qui fluviorum et animantium omnium et Deorum pater vocatus est ab antiquis, . . . quippe cum omnia priusquam oriantur aut intercidant, indigeant humore: sine quo nihil neque corrumpi potest, neque gigni."

These two great principles of the symbolism of the sea bring in their wake Arion, the herald of the wedding party. He represents the power of order and harmony to curb the cruel and unlawful aspects of the sea. As Spenser writes in *Amoretti* 38:

> *Arion,* when through tempests cruel wracke,
> He forth was thrown into the greedy seas:
> through the sweet musick which his harp did make
> allu'rd a Dolphin him from death to ease.

Arion reintroduces the theme of *discordia concors* and precedes the bride and groom, who have been united after an initial disharmony.

The essential purpose of this procession is to show the unity underlying the multiplicity of life, as symbolized by the world of the sea. After the emergence of Tame and Isis instead of the expected geographical descriptions in the manner of the antiquarian poets Spenser asserts his independence, abandoning the usual iconographical attributes of rivers:

> But he their sonne full fresh and iolly was,
> All decked in a robe of watchet hew,
> On which the waues, glittering like Christall glas,
> So cunningly enwouen were, that few

Could weenen, whether they were false or trew.
And on his head like to a Coronet
He wore, that seemed strange to common vew,
In which were many towres and castels set,
That it encompast round as with a golden fret.

Like as the mother of the Gods, they say,
In her great iron charet wonts to ride,
When to *Ioues* pallace she doth take her way;
Old *Cybele*, arayd with pompous pride,
Wearing a Diademe embattild wide
With hundred turrets, like a Turribant.
With such an one was Thamis beautifide;
That was to weet the famous Troynouant,
In which her kingdomes throne is chiefly resiant.

(4.11.27–28)

Two aspects of these stanzas demand special comment, the more obvious of the two being the comparison to Cybele. She is the great mother of the gods and first taught men to fortify cities. This is why she wears a turreted crown. Spenser describes her in the sixth sonnet of *The Ruines of Rome*, a sonnet translated from du Bellay, which ultimately owes its source to Virgil. The principles of law and order and ancient fertility represented by the first two groups in the procession are drawn together in this simile. Cybele is a symbol of ancient civilization and fertility, of which Troynouant is the latest example. Spenser is going beyond the patriotic zeal of the antiquarian poets to show that his nation partakes of the ancient order of civilization, that its youthful fertility, symbolized by the Thames, is the inheritance of the beginning of civilization, of Troy and Rome, and thus generalizes the Trojan imagery woven into the third and fourth books. This brief simile implies his belief in the destiny of Britain and its ultimate roots in the glories of the past.

To emphasize this point he etherealizes the substance of his river: "few Could weenen, whether they [the waves] were false or trew." And similarly the description of the Medway makes her something more than a river:

Then came the Bride, the louely *Medua* came,
Clad in a vesture of vnknowen geare,
And vncouth fashion, yet her well became;
That seem'd like siluer, sprinckled here and theare
With glittering spangs, that did like starres appeare,
And wau'd vpon, like water Chamelot,
To hide the metall, which yet euery where
Bewrayd it selfe, to let men planely wot,
It was no mortall worke, that seem'd and yet was not.

(4.11.45)

The two rivers are described as that curious state where sunlight and waves become nothing and everything all at once, where things are just about to become ideas—the realm of mythic vision. The most commonly known analogue to this state is Shelley's *To a Skylark*.

> Keen as are the arrows
> Of that silver sphere
> Whose intense lamp narrows
> In the white dawn clear,
> Until we hardly see, we feel that it is there.

Just at that point where the day star becomes invisible its significance becomes clear. The pageant of the Thames and Medway is the highest expression of the joy and fullness of Spenser's conception of marriage. The reader is, as it were, enveloped in the vision along with the poet until he too can feel the significance of the unifying power of love and can return shortly to the complete concord and unity of the prelapsarian world where man is most himself when he has given most of himself. Unity has momentarily emerged from the diversity of mutability.

This is the significance of the marriage of the Thames and Medway for Spenser, for Book IV, and for the reader who is attuned to the subtle power of his symbols. Their subtlety is not derived from picayune differences; rather it is always a rich and vibrant variation on some basic theme—in this case the theme of mutability and the relation of order to chaos, of time and eternity. Although it is not stated in the poem, the reader knows that this marriage must dissolve itself in the multiplicity of the sea and that this act of union will occur and dissolve again and again, and ultimately from his knowledge of the physical world that the act of union and dissolution are the same and inseparable. Like the paradox of the procession of Mutabilitie, whose apparent multiplicity is the expression of the principle of universal order Spenser's river marriage ends abruptly with the incantatory effect of the names of the Nereids, the individualized spirits of fertility, among whom is Cymodoce. The reader is once more in the world of Marinell and Florimell, although in reality— the reality of the mythic vision—he has never left it, for Spenser's canto of the marriage of the Thames and the Medway is simply a universal expression of the love that moves the universe and lovers alike.

DONALD CHENEY

Gardens of Adonis

In its present state, *The Faerie Queene* contains no direct presentation of Cleopolis. The poem's action takes place in the undefined, neutral terrain familiar to chivalric legend: a series of open spaces serving as battlefields, bounded by wilderness and linked by devious and perilous paths. The heroes are far from home, in that other country of challenge and response. If the various palaces, cottages, and caves scattered over this terrain are sometimes presented as miniature social units, they refer specifically and primarily to the concerns of the poem's action at the time of their appearance. At most these microcosmic societies may demonstrate the ideal working of an individual virtue; but they do not pretend to be total images of the societal impulse, as does the perpetually offstage court of Gloriana.

Similarly, the "natural" settings found in the poem—the gardens, groves, and other images of retreat—offer a picture of the natural order which is always relative to the persons visiting them: they cannot be abstracted from their narrative contexts. [This essay] will examine these settings in an effort to define the images of nature and the natural order which they imply, but it will be ultimately concerned with the relevance of these images to the poem's larger purpose: a presentation of human responsibility in a world where the Golden Age is at most a distant memory of a society that can never be literally restored, one in which mankind enjoyed an easy communion with the rhythm of a friendly nature. For fallen and redeemed man, Love has taken on a new meaning beyond that attributed to it in the scheme of nature. In its more complex

From *Spenser's Image of Nature: Wild Man and Shepherd in "The Faerie Queene."* Copyright © 1966 by Yale University Press.

role as an organizing principle of society and the central factor in man's search for divine enlightenment, the physical aspects of love will be of assistance only in proportion as the individual succeeds in recognizing the place of nature in the Christian order of values.

Of the various natural settings described in *The Faerie Queene*, the Garden of Adonis offers the most prolonged and comprehensive meditation on the natural order. Consequently, the following discussion will consist chiefly of an examination of the Garden and its relevance to the contrast between Belphoebe and Amoret in Book III. But it is not enough to consider the description in its narrative context alone. The passage itself (III.vi.29ff.) focuses on the narrator's conflicting attitudes toward Nature. Readers who have regarded it as a conveniently quotable statement of Spenser's philosophy may have been guilty of critical fallacies, and they have usually been indiscreet in exposing themselves to the challenge of opposing statements drawn from other passages in the poem; but they have been responding to an undeniable mode of personal reference visible in the shifting tones of the description. The narrator is trying to "locate" the Gardens with reference to his own, human experience, and in his attempts to be true to their sympathetic and unsympathetic aspects alike (their "hard" and "soft" aspects, in the terms used by Lovejoy and Boas), he describes what amounts on the visual level to no single garden but to a series of Gardens of Adonis. The very discontinuity of the topography—the problems which it raises as to Time's presence or the meaning of "in" and "out" in stanza 32, for example—suggests that the passage is dialectical rather than descriptive in its structure. It also suggests one reason for the especial futility in this instance of the conventional source study that tries to identify Spenser's point of view: the poet is trying to assimilate the full range of possible attitudes toward the seasonal cycle of generation.

One expression of the paradox under examination here is seen in the very title given to these gardens. The phrase in antiquity refers to a potted plant or forcing bed in which the brevity of the seasonal cycle is accentuated:

> *Socrates:* . . . Now tell me this. Would a sensible husbandman, who has seeds which he cares for and which he wishes to bear fruit, plant them with serious purpose in the heat of summer in some garden of Adonis, and delight in seeing them appear in beauty in eight days, or would he do that sort of thing, when he did it at all, only in play and for amusement? Would he not, when he was in earnest, follow the rules of husbandry, plant his seeds in fitting ground, and be pleased when those seeds which he had sowed reached their perfection in the eighth month?
>
> (Plato, *Phaedrus*)

"What do you mean . . . by gardens of Adonis?" "I mean," said Silenus, "those what women plant in pots, in honour of the lover of Aphrodite, by scraping together a little earth for a garden bed. They bloom for a little space and fade forthwith."

(Julian, *The Caesars*)

Spenser's Garden would seem at first to have little in common with these ephemeral plants. On the contrary, the principal force of the description as a whole is toward a celebration of permanence in the midst of and through the mutability of individual flowers: the climax, and the most memorable lines of the passage, assert triumphantly that "There is continuall spring, and haruest there/ Continuall." The negative view of Adonis as flower seems more adequately suited to the Tassesque melancholy of the singer at the Bower of Bliss, whose apostrophe to the rose similarly stresses its mortality. Yet an identical ambiguity is inherent to both gardens, Spenser's and those of the celebrants of Adonis. For in proportion as a flower's characteristic life-span is shortened it becomes a more convenient symbol not only of the brevity of human life but also of its capacity for a racial immortality through successive generations. Or to put it differently, the chief hindrance to an acceptance of human mortality lies in the relative length of the individual life: a perspective in which the cycle is accelerated reduces the significance of the individual biography and hence neutralizes the threat of time to man's sense of value. It is toward such a perspective that the poet is working in his description of the Gardens, struggling against a pessimism like that urged by Acrasia, who can only see futility in heroic endeavor when confronted with the example of vegetable nature. In Book II, it may be recalled, Acrasia's rose translates into tones of despair the more lighthearted dalliance with which Phaedria perversely invokes the lilies of the field in her appeal to Guyon (II.vi.16).

It may be useful, therefore, to note the negative connotations of the Gardens of Adonis as they emerge from the classical sources quoted above, for Spenser's gardens are contrasted, explicitly or implicitly, with a number of other settings in the poem. In terms of the action of Book III, the Gardens are challenged by the House of Busyrane. The fact that Amoret is educated in one and menaced in the other, together with the location of the two descriptions, one at the middle of the book and the other at its end, should make this comparison inevitable. Secondly, as the terrestrial abode of Venus, the Garden is opposed to the wilderness where Diana and her nymphs roam, the environment in which Amoret's twin sister, Belphoebe, is educated. And as a natural setting that celebrates physical love, it is further contrasted with the incitements offered in Book II by Acrasia's bower and Phaedria's isle. Readers have frequently mentioned this last contrast, though they have debated the problems of comparing scenes which occur in different books and are consequently directed to different emphases. And finally, as an evocation of a pre-lapsarian Paradise to which the Faeries enjoy a ready access denied to fallen mortals, the Garden of Adonis must be compared with the poem's more limited versions of pastoral, the groves and humble bowers that refresh the flagging spirits of those visitors to Fairyland who are bound to the responsibilities of their historical roles. In the light of these comparisons, Spenser's Garden of Adonis will be shown to have retained some of the connotations which were traditionally associated with its name, even before it was expanded to denote a full-scale mythological garden. The cycle of seasonal birth, death, and rebirth celebrated in the worship of Adonis finds an expression in both kinds of garden, in the forcing-beds scorned for their ephemeral products as well as in the terrestrial paradise envisioned in *The Faerie Queene*. The present chapter will discuss the relationship between love and the natural order as it is expressed through the four areas of comparison mentioned above, and will explore the concept of "chaste affection" which directs the poem's complex of attitudes toward nature.

Although Socrates' objection to the precocious development fostered by gardens of Adonis is not precisely that implied by Spenser, the very fact of Busyrane's ability to kidnap and transfix Amoret does suggest an inadequacy of some sort in her education. In Book III Spenser is dealing freely with the material of romance, material that affords extensive precedent for rather hazily or ambiguously motivated erotic quandaries; and his account of Amoret's difficulties manages to be generally credible without providing much specific ethical definition. Readers continue to debate the precise label to attach to Busyrane's challenge. But instead of attempting to decide, for example, whether he represents Amoret's lust, or Scudamour's, or that of some third party, it is more profitable to begin by taking him simply as a vile enchanter in his own right, like Archimago, and to ask in what way Amoret's training has been so one-sided as to have left her unable to break free from his enchantments, at the same time that it has given her the strength to resist his temptations. The answer to this question concerns the inadequacy of the natural order in itself—the "course of kynde"—to account for the role played by courtly love in the organization of human impulses. Amoret is educated in a place where Cupid is thoroughly domesticated, subordinated to the reproductive goals of Nature, and himself a family man. It is not until she has left the Garden and come to the Fairy court that she learns of his role as a source of civil strife, a force for disorder which is at variance with his role in the Garden. Busyrane introduces her to this new picture of Cupid, through the "mask of loue" which he brings in at her bridal feast and employs as a device to kidnap her while her companions are "Surcharg'd with wine" and assume that what they are watching is "By way of sport, as oft in maskes in knowen"(IV.i.3). On the one hand this incident provides a dramatic illustration of the dangers inherent in the situation of the banquet, where the drinking of wine is both a means to social integration and a potential cause of disorder. At the same time, it is specifically Amoret who is unprepared for these images of love which constitute the currency of a courtly society; she has been trained to a love which is natural, purposeful, monogamous (and hence chaste in Spenser's sense of a chaste marriage), but by the same token physical.

In the Garden of Adonis love has no meaning apart from this physical context. The frankness of love there, its freedom from rancor or envy (III.vi.41), is accompanied by a similar freedom from the stratagems by which the erotic impulse is made a means to power. Busyrane is not simply introducing Amoret to the discovery that Cupid is no respecter of marriage bonds (and hence indicating that adultery is implicit in the language of the court); he is also capitalizing on the fact that as the darling of Venus she has been deprived of those defenses which enable her twin sister to enjoy all the social dominance characteristic of the Petrarchan mistress. Amoret's naïveté takes the form of an inability to handle the abstracted language of courtly love in isolation from the physical context in which she has been educated, and toward which she is destined through her marriage with Scudamour, whose name significantly is as reminiscent of Cupid as her own. Busyrane may be seen as offering the knowledge of Good and Evil to one who has till now led her life in a Paradise free from such knowledge; but both the names of the principal characters and the nature of the action make clear that a specific area of knowledge is involved.

The image of Cupid is central to Spenser's presentation of this problem, and it is within the context of erotic mythology that Amoret's history is contained. Just as it is in love's wound ("her dying hart,/ Seeming transfixed with a cruell dart," III.xii.31) that Busyrane will dip his pen, so it is as a result of a fruitless search for Cupid that Venus comes to adopt Amoret in the first place. Cupid is generally associated with the goadings of sexual desire, and with the physical and emotional appetites which inspire to love. Venus is closer to the figure of Mother Nature, and represents the larger natural principles of generation which lie behind the sexual desires of animals and humans: she is appropriately the "mother" of Cupid. If Cupid embodies the erotic appetite, Venus is concerned with actual fruition: as she remarks to Diana, "my delight is all in ioyfulnesse,/

In beds, in bowres, in banckets, and in feasts" (III.vi.22). Ideally, mother and son live together in harmony, and Cupid's "wanton parts" are accessory and instigatory to the enactment of Venus' rites. But when he runs away from home, irked by his mother's chidings, his actions cease to be subordinated to the demands of the natural order, and become instigations to chaos.

This runaway Cupid may be described in the terms of Latin poetry as a capricious and undisciplined boy whose indiscriminate sport wreaks havoc on all levels of society: this is the presentation found in the description of Venus' search for him (III.vi.11ff.). Or he may take on the attributes found in medieval love poetry, where he is a full-scale deity, presiding over the courts of love and enforcing submission to the principles of courtly love. He is most clearly seen in this latter role in the description of Mirabella's trial (VI.viii.32ff.); but the tapestries at the House of Busyrane and more importantly the Masque of Cupid there (III.xii.1ff.) show him in this context as well. In one sense these two roles are not strictly distinguishable, since both are expressions of his traditional function and differ only in the degree of seriousness attached to his disruption of the harmonious and rationally controlled relationships between individuals. But it is inevitable that a view of human society which sees love as the central organizing principle—as is true in different senses of both courtly and Christian love—should tend to regard Cupid in a much more serious light than had the antique tradition. The relatively lighthearted treatment of Cupid's ravages as they are seen by Venus in her searches through court, city, country, and wilderness is symptomatic of his classical role: the fact that his ravages are viewed in order of descending importance—ranging from the woeful Ladies and Lords and the view of him as "the disturber of all ciuill life," to the plaints of shepherds which provoke only smiles from Venus, to the apparently untouched haunts of Diana—reinforces the sense that Cupid is little more than a naughty child. Venus' selection of Amoret to serve as his replacement ("in her litle loues stead, which was strayd,/ Her *Amoretta* cald, to comfort her dismayd") stresses his diminutive status, and suggests at the same time that this change in domestic arrangements cannot fail to represent an improvement.

Most noteworthy in the entire scene leading up to Spenser's presentation of the Gardens of Adonis is its suggestion of apparent triviality. Its idyllic and playful tone, the hearsay quality of all its evidence for Cupid's misbehavior, the tact with which Venus quickly placates Diana's annoyance, all work against any suggestion of a basic opposition between the principles of Love and Chastity. As Venus is quick to point out, she and Diana are no more than civil servants, heads of their respective departments but by no means autonomous: "We both are bound to follow heauens beheasts,/ And tend our charges with obeisance meeke" (III.vi.22). Spenser's imitation of Moschus' idyll, with its relaxed narrative and absence of intricate allusion, gives overtones of a social harmony that is actually at odds with the situation being described. Later incidents will demonstrate the significance of Cupid's behavior, and of the distinction between "perfect Maydenhed" and "goodly womanhed," the goals which Diana and Venus establish for their respective charges. But for the moment all is calm. The poet alludes to Cupid with complaisance, and in describing the Gardens of Adonis his immediate concern is with the problem of mutability. The Cupid who reappears at the end of the canto has (as least temporarily) set aside his "sad darts" to play the role of husband and father. The problem of love's wounds (the subject of so much of Book III) has been adroitly, if ominously, repressed.

The richness and compression of Spenser's treatment of the Gardens, beginning with stanza 29, contrast with the looseness of this preceding scene; but there is no interruption of the continuing sense of a natural order which is thoroughly under control. The logical inconsistencies in the description cannot be explained away. But the fluent transitions minimize one's awareness of them, by continually diverting the reader's attention away from the physical, topographical status of the garden itself, toward an emphasis on the narrator's reactions. Actually, several distinct attitudes to Garden-of-Adonis myths are presented in succession; the overriding notion of Permanence in Mutability embraces them all and lends them the appearance of compatibility. First there is the myth of the Garden as a kind of conservatory,

> . . . the first seminarie
> Of all things, that are borne to liue and die,
> According to their kindes.
>
> (III.vi.30)

This Garden is a place distinct from the actual world, set off from it by gold and iron walls. "All that to come into the world desire" are fitted with "sinfull mire" and sent out to live in the world, returning after death to the Garden, via the "hinder gate." "All" of what, though? To equate Spenser's "naked babes" with human souls is to overlook the fact that animals and fishes are sent out as well (stanza 35). And the infinitely varied shapes of creatures bred here include among them "Some fit for reasonable soules t'indew": the inference is that the shapes are themselves something apart from the souls.

Yet these stanzas do seem, at least to a modern reader, to suggest that the image of birth represented by the passage of the naked babes from the Garden into the world is in some sense an image of the body-soul relationship. There is much talk of the union of the immortal part and the mortal. But even more importantly, one senses throughout that as a generation myth, purporting to describe the way in which God's creatures come into the world and leave it, obeying the command to increase and multiply, this description must be a complete one; and to be complete it must at some point contain an image of the human soul.

Actually, however, it does not. Spenser is concerned here with a portrayal of the *natural* order; to emphasize the absence of the soul from this order would be neither necessary nor consonant with the sense of the completeness and integrity of this order, considered in itself. Probably the Elizabethan reader would not have been tempted to confuse natural and supernatural, and to expect to find the soul in this context. For him the allusion to "reasonable soules" cited above would be readily understood as indicating the precise point—man—at which the natural world accommodates a supernatural element derived elsewhere.

Recognition of the fact that the Garden of Adonis is an expression of the natural order helps to clear away much of the confusion which has resulted from attempts to reconcile its distinctions between forms and substance with the transcendent, Platonic senses of these terms. The stumbling block has been that Spenser's forms are transitory and his substances permanent, where in Platonic terms the opposite would have been expected:

> The substance is not chaunged, or altered,
>   But th'only forme and outward fashion;
>   For euery substance is conditioned
>   To change her hew, and sundry formes to don,
>   Meet for her temper and complexion:
>   For formes are variable and decay,
>   By course of kind, and by occasion;
>   And that faire flowre of beautie fades away,
> As doth the lilly fresh before the sunny ray.
>   (III. vi. 38)

Confronted with this statement, the reader who has taken the Garden of Adonis as an otherworldly abode of souls and "Platonic forms" must judge either that Spenser has unaccountably reversed his terms, or that the Garden is ambidextrous, growing both souls and at the same time the mortal "forms of other things." To reject both of these alternatives is to reject as well the notion that the Garden contains any suggestion of personal immortality. What is immortal in nature is the "huge eternall

Chaos" where the substance is unchanging precisely because it is undifferentiated. In the hothouse atmosphere of the Garden, with its sundry beds
each devoted to a different kind of being, the Sun/Adonis (the parallels
between the description of Adonis here and the preceding description of
the Sun's impregnation of Chrysogone make this identification unavoidable) begets forms in the recipient substance of the Earth.

Since these forms—aptly imaged as flowers, the commonest of all
emblems of mortality—are themselves destined to die, it is logically
appropriate that they should be menaced by the figure of Time with his
scythe. What does seem inconsistent, however, even when we recognize
the impermanence of these flowers, is that Time should be actively
present in a Garden described as a nursery or "seminarie" whose walls set
it apart from the "mortal state" of the world outside. Surely the wicked
Time described in stanza 39 is a full-scale image of mortality: he represents
a force more inclusive than Abortion or Infant Mortality or Unscientific
Gardening; and he cuts down plants which are already flowering and in
their full glory. The image of the Garden of Adonis would be blurred
indeed if we were being asked to imagine Venus as producing her vast
array of forms for export at the same time that she retained some of these
forms as a part of her private landscaping plans. But Spenser does not
superimpose one image on another: rather, the earlier image fades away
and no further mention is made of Genius, the outer walls of the Garden,
or the endless ranks of flowerbeds.

The poet's first presentation of the Garden has stressed the immu-
tability of the physical substance which supplies the endless round of
generation and decay. From the first union of form and substance in the
womb of the earth (and there is surely an image of the womb in the walls
of this first Garden), the life history of the creatures is followed as they
emerge into the world and reach maturity. At this point, beginning with
stanza 39, the first garden-of-Adonis image is supplanted by another,
by which the Garden is an image of the natural world itself. This
Paradise bears a striking resemblance to Eden: it is a place in which
the natural order is wholly observed, so that the only hindrance to
"immortall blis" is the fact that mortality is a necessary factor in that
order:

> But were it not that *Time* their troubler is,
>   All that in this delightful Gardin growes,
>   Should happie be, and haue immortall blis:
>   For here all plentie, and all pleasure flowes,
>   And sweet loue gentle fits emongst them throwes,
>   Without fell rancor, or fond gealosie;

Franckly each paramour his leman knowes,
Each bird his mate, ne any does enuie
Their goodly meriment, and gay felicitie.

There is continuall spring, and haruest there
Continuall, both meeting at one time:
For both the boughes doe laughing blossomes beare,
And with fresh colours decke the wanton Prime,
And eke attonce the heauy trees they clime,
Which seeme to labour vnder their fruits lode:
The whiles the ioyous birdes make their pastime
Emongst the shadie leaues, their sweet abode,
And their true loues without suspition tell abrode.
(III.vi.41–42)

These two stanzas describe the society to which Amoret is educated in the Garden. The contrast between this natural society and the civilized world represented by the fairy court is indicative of the weaknesses in her upbringing, which leave her unable to combat the enchantments of Busyrane. In the Garden of Adonis love is sweet, and throws gentle fits; merriment is unconstrained, unenvied, freely admitted, and fruitful. Spring and harvest are simultaneous and continual: love is not dissociated from its generative goal. The "true feminitee" to which Amoret is educated in this environment is radically defenseless; for it participates spontaneously in the cycle of life without fear of any challenge to personal identity. In this natural order love is so wholly a part of generation that marriage rites are as superfluous as any other intrusion of Art: it is only in a less innocent world which has learned good and evil that human community is no longer natural and becomes a perilous and fleeting achievement.

It is in the middle of this Paradise, so conceived, that a third Garden of Adonis is found: a grove located on the top of a "stately Mount," representing Nature on a higher level of abstraction, the allegorical and mythological focus of Spenser's presentation of the Garden. This third image is an inclusive one, in the sense that it assumes the two preceding views of nature—its permanence in the midst of mutability, and its spontaneous assimilation of love to this larger rhythm. But it is also detached from Time in a way that the two preceding Gardens had not been: its concern is with the permanence of the generative principle, which is something quite different from the permanence of undifferentiated substance asserted at the beginning of the presentation of the Garden. Here the union of Venus and Adonis is described as an everlasting moment, transcending the inevitable mortality of the forms which it begets. It is important to recognize the progression of imagery leading up to this passage.

In the first vision of the Garden the basic image is that of the flower, which is sown in the ground, fertilized by the Sun, brought to maturity, and then cut down by Time. Not surprisingly, the imagery of the second view of the Garden is concerned with forms of life which have a more conspicuous sexuality: the birds playing among the shady leaves, the trees with their combination of colorful blossoms and heavy fruit. The third view of the Garden combines these two strands of imagery. First there are described the myrtle trees which enclose the grove and perfume the ground with their sweet gum:

> And in the thickest couert of that shade,
>   There was a pleasant arbour, not by art,
>   But of the trees owne inclination made,
>   Which knitting their rancke braunches part to part,
>   With wanton yuie twyne entrayld athwart,
>   And Eglantine, and Caprifole emong,
>   Fashiond aboue within their inmost part,
>   That neither *Phoebus* beams could through them throng,
> Nor *Aeolus* sharp blast could worke them any wrong.
>
> (III.vi.44)

This natural arbor affords protection against the extremes of sun and wind, ensuring a temperate climate suitable for the unhampered enjoyment of love. Curiously enough, the language of this description echoes an earlier stanza describing the care with which Belphoebe protects the "faire flowre" of her "chastity and vertue virginall":

> That dainty Rose, the daughter of her Morne,
>   More deare then life she tendered, whose flowre
>   The girlond of her honour did adorne:
>   Ne suffred she the Middayes scorching powre,
>   Ne the sharp Northerne wind thereon to showre,
>   But lapped vp her silken leaues most chaire,
>   When so the froward skye began to lowre:
>   But soone as calmed was the Christall aire.
> She did it faire dispred, and let to florish faire.
>
> (III.v.51)

Belphoebe has been trained to protect herself against the elements. Amoret, on the other hand, has been brought up in an environment where nature has taken care of this matter for her. Small wonder, then, that she is unprepared for the intemperate weather outside the Garden. . . .

The Gardens of Adonis are accessible only to the Fairy race. As a terrestrial paradise, an expression of a kindly Nature where the weather is always temperate and the living easy, they can be no more than a nostalgic daydream for the fallen Christian. But as an ideal they continue to hold a powerful appeal which requires serious scrutiny. In presenting the stories of Belphoebe and Amoret, Spenser is describing a classical educational experiment, of the sort that begins: Take two identical twins, A and B; separate them at birth. . . . In this case, the variable to be tested is the element of protectiveness. The twins, born under virtual laboratory conditions, are raised in atmospheres of "hard" and "soft" primitivism, respectively: Belphoebe is trained by Diana and her nymphs to the rigors of the chase, while Amoret is sheltered from the elements and trained to a passive femininity. The contrast is not unlike that developed by Socrates, in the lines from the *Phaedrus* cited at the beginning of this chapter. The results obtained by Spenser's experiment suggest a similar conclusion. The question has been the relative durability of the "flowers" cultivated by these two horticultural techniques; and it is seen that Amoret's goodly womanhood can be seriously menaced in the outside world, and requires the assistance of the hardier bloom of one trained to the sterner ideal of chastity.

Since *The Faerie Queene* is concerned with portraying the education of a prince—or more specifically, of a Queen—it may be that the education of Belphoebe and Amoret has a topical relevance as well. Elizabeth's rigorous training had served her well in the masculine role to which she was called; and in Ascham's boast of her, that "Her mind has no womanly weakness," it is easy to see a parallel to Spenser's emphasis on Belphoebe's invulnerability. In any event, Spenser's concept of chastity demands the qualification provided by Amoret's history. There is no question of evil or falsehood in the Gardens of Adonis and the natural principles which they represent. What is at stake is the question of the adequacy of those principles to prepare an individual for the perils of human society. Before comparing the Gardens with any other pastoral setting in *The Faerie Queene*, two facts should be borne in mind: first, that it is presented as a training ground, in which an individual is prepared for life in the actual world; and secondly, that it is a woman who is to be educated in it. Neither of these conditions applies to the Bower of Bliss, for instance. The celebration of sexual intercourse in the Gardens is informed by an awareness of its role in the cycle of birth and death, whereas Acrasia's Bower celebrates it for its own sake, unreasoningly. But the main difference between the two settings lies in their roles: one as an image of natural order, the other as an image of human irresponsibility. The myth of Mars and Venus, which lies behind the picture of Acrasia and Verdant in the Bower, relates to the truancy of the irascible instinct, the subordination of one motive to another; in the context of Book II it is expressive of a disruption of that ordering of values which gives the individual an impetus toward his goal in life. In its less serious form, this disruption may simply delay the hero from his quest, as Guyon's Phaedria or Odysseus' Calypso seek to do; more seriously, it may subvert the reason so completely as to destroy the hero's human qualities, to enchant him as Acrasia or Circe seek to do. Acrasia's Bower presents Nature as an image of the human condition, and pretends that it is a complete picture. To do so is to deny man's superiority to the beast; and for this reason the acceptance of Acrasia's image of life leads toward an animal metamorphosis.

Any discussion of Spenser's pastoral settings must be careful, therefore, to distinguish among the various roles which they may perform. They may be designed as a preparation for human life, as is true of the Gardens of Adonis and of the forests where Belphoebe and Artegall are educated. They may be temptations to a truancy from the responsibilities of life, as with Acrasia's Bower. Or, finally, they may be places of retirement from the confusion of this life, where men who have fulfilled their duties in this world may prepare themselves for the life to come. In this case, the pastoral settings are not directly concerned with presenting images of the natural order, true or false, but offer a simple contrast to the abodes of human society, providing an individual with a humble setting where nature fulfills his barest needs and where he is free to contemplate heavenly matters without distraction. This kind of setting is seen most clearly in the home of the Hermit who cures Serena and Timias in Book VI:

> . . .towards night they came vnto a plaine,
> By which a little Hermitage there lay,
> Far from all neighbourhood, the which annoy it may.
>
> And nigh thereto a little Chappell stoode,
> Which being all with Yuy ouerspred,
> Deckt all the roofe, and shadowing the roode,
> Seem'd like a groue faire braunched ouer hed:
> Therein the Hermite, which his life here led
> In streight obseruaunce of religious vow,
> Was wont his howres and holy things to bed . . .
>
> (VI.v.34–35)

This Hermit, who is described as a retired warrior of great renown, recalls the later career predicted for Redcross, when Contemplation tells him that true holiness is to be won ultimately by prayer and meditation rather than by glorious actions. He also recalls the disguise adopted by Archimago repeatedly in Book I. He is reminiscent, on a very different level, of Sir

Henry Lee, whose Retirement Tilt of 1590, with its farewell to a life of involvement in Elizabethan pageantry, carries the cult of Elizabeth to its logical conclusion, in his promise to the sovereign "To be your Beadsman now, that was your Knight":

> My helmet now shall make a hive for bees,
> And lover's songs shall turn to holy psalms:
> A man at arms must now sit on his knees,
> And feed on prayers that are old age's alms.
> And so from court to cottage I depart,
> My Saint is sure of mine unspotted heart.

An awareness of the pageantry which attended Elizabeth will help to restrain the reader of *The Faerie Queene* from an undue emphasis on the explicitly Christian implications of such a character as the Hermit. The mixture of flattery and genuine religious fervor found in this quasi-sacred imagery of Elizabethan compliment is difficult to analyze; but it is as clearly present in Spenser's poem as in the more ephemeral entertainments of the period. Pastoral motifs are predictably dominant in the entertainments presented to Elizabeth during her progresses: a contrast between her glorious court and the rural abodes of her nobles is inevitably a major theme under such circumstances. She is saluted by the semicivilized genii of these places: nymphs, wild men, and even on occasion a Fairy Queen, all pay homage to her divine radiance. In ways that can seldom be precisely and persuasively identified, the unique character of Elizabethan society, with its opposition of Town and Country in a sense unknown on the Continent, is reflected in the pastoral settings of *The Faerie Queene*.

The literally pastoral world of Pastorella and the shepherds to which Calidore retreats in Canto x of Book VI combines aspects of all the settings enumerated above. It represents a temptation to avoid the responsibilities of the quest, and is therefore a world which Calidore cannot adopt permanently: his pastoral garb is only a temporary disguise. Like the Hermit's Ivy-church, it is a world in which Nature readily yields man the bare necessities of his existence, and in which Meliboeus' contempt for wealth predicates the simple life as the basis of true contentment. Like the Gardens of Adonis, it is the setting for an education—that provided by the vision of the Graces, whose dance illuminates the action of Courtesy in human society. And like Redcross and Adonis and the Hermit, the poet is able to find in this pastoral milieu a fitting if paradoxical conclusion to his heroic quest. These pastoral episodes of Book VI depend for their full meaning, however, on the "antique image" of Artegall's Justice as it is presented in Book V. By demonstrating the distance between an ideal, spontaneously ordered natural society as it is envisioned in the myth of the Golden Age, and the harsher reality of a savagely repressive order as it is found in the fallen world of man, Spenser gives a new meaning to the pastoral impulse, and suggests the more tentative, partial and even illusory victory to be won against the forces of disorder that challenge the social unit. The patron of Courtesy is no dragon-killer; the "Grace" with which he is endowed is of a far different kind than that of Redcross. But together with Artegall, he betokens the poem's shifting frame of reference, from the individual's search for personal identity toward an increasing emphasis on the bonds by which society is defined. The natural world in its harsher and gentler aspects becomes now less an object of meditation than a setting within which man constructs his world.

A. BARTLETT GIAMATTI

The Bower of Bliss

In Book II, the garden of Proserpina
gives us a perverted Eden where the consequences of intemperance echo
far beyond the limits of a simple temptation to indulge in the goods of the
material world. From both Phaedria and Proserpina's gardens, Guyon has
learned of the various types of temptations in and of the material world,
and he has learned how both imply the inversion of the values of God.
Guyon has seen both these versions of the evil garden, and now he is
ready, or will be after his sojourn at Alma's, for the grand garden of Book
II, which sums up all the gardens and all the temptations—the Bower of
Bliss.

At Alma's, Guyon learns that if the body submits to "reasons rule
obedient," there is a place for pleasure in a temperate man's constitution.
The banquet Alma serves to her guests—"attempred goodly well for
health and for delight" (xi, 2)—is indicative of Spenser's ability to conceive of pleasure and virtue existing in harmony. This is a very important
consideration for the virtue of Temperance in Book II, especially for the
Bower of Bliss, and it marks the essential difference between Spenser's
treatment of the Bower and Tasso's of the garden of Armida.

> Now ginnes this goodly frame of Temperaunce
> Fayrely to rise. . . .
>
> (xii, 1)

Guyon is ready to complete his quest.

Guyon's odyssey to Acrasia's Bower has been fully treated by others

---

From *The Earthly Paradise and the Renaissance Epic*. Copyright © 1966 by Princeton University Press.

in regard to its allegorical significance and literary sources. I would like only to notice several ways in which themes from the gardens in Cantos v and vi are recapitulated in the journey to the Bower. As they go farther across the ocean toward Acrasia's, Guyon, the Palmer and the boatman are suddenly assailed by horrible sea monsters "Such as Dame Nature selfe mote feare to see," and these unnatural creatures are called "All dreadfull pourtraicts of deformitee" (23). The unnatural is conveyed through an "art"-image, and both unnatural and "artistic" are, through the Palmer's words, linked to

> that same wicked witch, to worke us dreed,
> And draw from on this journey to proceed.
>
> (26)

Magic, art, the unnatural—all are associated again.

At stanza 28, we have a variation on these themes. A siren sings, and Guyon is momentarily tempted to listen, but the Palmer advises him that her plaint is

> onely womanish fine forgery,
> Your stubborne hart t'affect with fraile infirmity.
>
> (28)

The seductive power of illusion is, as it was before, related to evil. Then the temptation of the mermaids, who are really sirens (30–32), occurs, and many of these motifs are summed up in those creatures Comes said represented "nothing other than voluptuous desire." They are first seen in a little bay which the poet compares to "an halfe theatre" (30), an image he took from Ariosto (*Orlando Furioso*, XIX, 64) and one which emphasizes the artificiality, the cunningly contrived quality, of the ensuing scene and siren song (32–33). The reference to their bathing in "deceiptfull shade" completes the implication of their false and illusory characteristics. Then in a story which has no precedent in classical mythology, Spenser tells how the mermaids attained their present, unnatural forms. They are the results of having "striv'd" with the Muses for "maystery" (31). Thus the theme of strife between art and nature is here foreshadowed in this struggle between the usurping sirens and the natural masters of art, the Muses. The siren-mermaids' skill, like their bodies, is perverted and serves only to seduce travelers so they may be killed. The fatal, powerful attraction of sexuality is embodied in this small embellishment upon traditional figures and old themes.

The Bower of Bliss itself is approached at stanza 42. From 42 to 49 we enter the garden at one stage; from 50 to 57 we pass through another stage, and repeat the same process again—another gate, another porter. Stanzas 58 to 61 then take us deeper into the garden. In all of these movements, Spenser is showing us how the very beauty of the place is the result of its evil nature. In different ways, he is—from the premise of the analogy between Acrasia's magic and her character as sexual indulgence and depravity—demonstrating how the elements of art and nature, and the theme of illusion, lead to a conclusion concerning the garden's corrupt and corrupting character. The first sight of the Bower is that of

> A place pickt out by choyce of best alyve,
> That Natures worke by art can imitate.
> (42)

I think this must refer to Acrasia, she who could be counterfeit Nature, and thus produce the overlavish scene which the rest of the stanza describes. Having established art and nature as one of his indices to the garden's character, as it was in Tasso, Spenser now adapts and develops (in stanza 44) that distinguishing feature of Ariosto's island-garden, the motif of the life of sensual indulgence as a debilitating illusion. There Guyon and the Palmer pass through the walls of the Bower by way of a gate. Much has been made of the scene above the gate, which depicts the love of Jason and Medea (44–46). However, one searches in vain for any comment on the gate itself. Yet it is most significant, for

> Yt framed was of precious ivory . . .
> (44)

which is an obvious reminiscence of the gate of ivory in *Odyssey*, XIX, 562–567 and *Aeneid*, VI, 893–896, through which pass the false or evil dreams. (Good, truthful dreams pass by the gate of horn.) It seems to me Spenser is subtly bringing us into the Bower as a false state of mind, a self-imposed illusion. This was certainly the implication of Cymochles' dreams at Canto v, 37, and vi, 27. The knight and his Palmer now approach a figure on the porch under the gate. Spenser says that this was not the good genius, Adgistes, who protects every man,

> But this same was to that quite contrary,
> The foe of life, that good envyes to all,
> That secretly doth us procure to fall,
> Through guilefull semblants, which he makes us see.
> (48)

He is "Pleasures porter" and has been much discussed; for our purposes it is interesting to note that he seems to embody the two themes we have traced thus far. He is "pleasing, more than naturall," and daintily "deckt"

(49) with flowers; that is, he is superficially (and artificially) lovely, and essentially effeminate. He is not only not what he seems (his name is even misleading), but he is something of a magician himself. He has the power to manipulate illusions, and when Guyon rejects his bowl of wine, the knight also breaks the "staffe, with which he charmed semblants sly" (49). The porter is the "genius" of the garden in one true sense, however; he embodies the essence of the place's corrupt compound of unnatural beauty and fraudulent appearances which is meant to ruin a man. He tempts us, as the poet says, "to fall," and in that statement Spenser reestablishes the ultimate religious context and terms of the episode. For in that simple infinitive, the poet makes his first suggestion that this is not only a dangerous place, but indeed a false garden of Eden.

At stanza 50, the knight and his companion recommence their view of the place, and once again the poet tells us art did "decke" (like the porter) nature and "too lavishly adorne" her. Again art makes nature seem "more than naturall"; and the unnatural is the result. Stanza 51 seems a conventional passage describing perpetual springtime, lack of frost, storms, winds, etc., in short, the usual perfect climate of the garden of delight. But this stanza, presented with no comment, is itself an instance of unnatural Nature. We know from Book I (viii, 44; ix, 11, 16) and Book II, in the description of Alma's castle:

> O great pitty that no lenger time
> So goodly workemanship should not endure!
> Soone it must turne to earth: no earthly thing is
> sure
>
> (ix, 21)

that the only thing on earth which is constant is decay and change. Thus this plain of Acrasia's which seems immutable and unchangeable is in the deepest sense unnatural and illusory. Nothing which obeys the Creator's law could ever make the same claim. In stanza 52 the garden is compared to the loveliest places of the ancient world—Tempe, Ida, Parnassus—and is said to be more beautiful than all. Indeed, it is more lovely than

> Eden selfe, if ought with Eden mote compayre.

The delicacy of the poet must not be taken as simply a means for describing the garden; it must also be understood as Spenser's way of condemning the garden. The Bower of Bliss in fact wants to be compared to the garden of Eden; and it wants to be a new Eden, inhabited by a depraved Eve, where all mankind can be induced "to fall." To create this false Eden, the witch's art has embellished Nature, has improved on God, and has created a blasphemous imitation of the true earthly paradise. Like the poets before him, Spenser conveys the garden's beauty and attraction in the same terms which reveal its falsity and dangers. Here the terms are the most inclusive, for beyond temperance and intemperance, reason and delight, nature and art, are the suggestions of the divine and the demonic, good and evil.

Guyon "wondred" at the sight before him (as he had in Mammon's cave, viii, 24) but like Carlo and Ubaldo (*Gerusalemme Liberata*, XV, 57) he passes by "Brydling his will, and maystering his might" (53). Then again we go through the cycle of illusion and artificial nature; Guyon sees another gate, then "no gate, but like one" made of branches whose arms "fashioned" a porch (5). This is art in action, that is, nature as she enlisted into art's cause which is seduction. From the vine come bunches which

> seemd to entice
> All passers by to taste their lushious wine, . . .
> Some deepe empurpled as the hyacine,
> Some as the rubine laughing sweetly red,
> Some like faire emeraudes, not yet well ripened.
> (54)

> And then amongst, some were of burnisht gold,
> So made by art, to beautify the rest. . . .
> (55)

The artificial, which has made no effort to pass for the real, nevertheless infects all around it with its artificiality. The real grapes, compared to gems, suddenly acquire an artificial quality which is increased when they are juxtaposed with the truly artificial gold grapes. Art and nature are beginning to blur; the false and the real commence to merge as we go deeper into Pleasure's realm. In short, we are being seduced by the landscape, and at the same time shown through the landscape the false state of mind we are being seduced into: a state of mind where the distinction between good and evil is potentially obliterated. To go into the Bower of Bliss is to lose the power of one's reason. To lose the power of reason is to become a beast, which is, of course, the literal fate of so many of Acrasia's lovers. But it is also, more subtly, to live a prisoner of one's appetites and passions, in a state of Hell, and this too is a constant undercurrent in Spenser's treatment of the Bower. For the place is often associated with the demonic and hellish, one instance of which occurs in stanza 55. Here the boughs, laden with golden as well as real grapes, lean down just as the branches did in Proserpina's garden, vii, 54. The echo of that Eden in Hell serves to strengthen the suggestions of the Bower as a blasphemous, evil imitation-Eden.

Once again, Guyon passes a porter, this time Excess "Clad in fayre weedes, but fowle disordered" (55), and again he repulses an offer of wine; now he rejects the cup "violently" (57) where before it was "disdainfully" (49). The greater the implied danger, and the temptation, the more violently it is rejected. At stanza 58, as at stanzas 42 and 50, we seem to recapitulate again the vista and its implications:

> There the most daintie paradise on ground
> It selfe doth offer to his sober eye.

Now these lines sum up all the accumulated significances of the preceding passages. Because of the suggestions of this place as a parody of Eden, the first words about "paradise" denote a sinister as well as beautiful land-scape. Then from the *Gerusalemme Liberata*, XVI, 9–10 Spenser adapts stanzas 58 and 59 and, like Tasso, he defines the relationship of art and nature:

> One would have thought, (so cunningly the rude
> And scorned partes were mingled with the fine,)
> That Nature had for wantonesse ensude
> Art, and that Art at Nature did repine;
> So striving each th'other to undermine,
> Each did the others worke more beautify.
>
> (59)

And then, for the last time, Spenser follows up his generalized statement about art and nature with an illustration of art's relation to illusion and the role of sexuality. In stanzas 60 and 61 we see a fountain decorated with art.

> [It] with curious ymageree
> Was overwrought, and shapes of naked boyes,

and the art presents an illusion as they

> seemd with lively jollitee
> To fly about playing their wanton toyes.
> (60)

Over the scene on the fountain is a trail of golden ivy, so cleverly made that he

> who did not well avis'd it vew,
> Would surely deeme it to be yvie trew.
> (61)

We have entered the Bower in three stages (42–49, 50–57, 58–61), and three times Spenser has shown us the relation of art to nature, and then art as it was further identified with illusion and the theme of the Bower as a deceptive state of mind. Ultimately the poet has brought all these themes to bear on the garden as a place of sexual temptation and depraved behavior. Essentially, however, Spenser has been defining the garden through the roles of art and nature in it.

What exactly is the result? Is Spenser's conception of the Bower the same as Tasso's of Armida's garden, which Spenser imitates and whence the art-nature opposition immediately derives? No indeed, though the superficial parallels are valuable for a general comparison of the two, a comparison which, for broad purposes, Spenser surely wanted us to make. But substantially the roles of art and nature, like the two gardens, like the poems themselves, are very different. In Tasso, the whole landscape was a product of art, because all that Armida represented, her way of life and values, was false. Tasso saw nothing redeeming in Armida's world (though he tried desperately to redeem Armida), and therefore he pictured her garden as completely artificial. There was no room in the good life for the senses. Spenser has no such view. Delight and pleasure are not at all necessarily incompatible with duty and honor; the senses are not automatically the enemies of the spirit, if the rational—ultimately Christian—mean is maintained. Thus art and nature function not as indistinguishable worlds, both opposed to Truth, as in Tasso, but rather as emblems of the good and the bad. There is real, as well as artificial, nature in the Bower. What Spenser does is show art as "striving" with Nature, undermining nature, and in this he means us to see an allegory of the good, natural, healthy instinct as it is perverted and infected by lust and overindulgence. Acrasia's art seeks to make nature incontinent, i.e. overabundant, just as her sexuality seeks to make human nature self-indulgent and depraved. Art and lust do not try to pass for what is "natural"; rather, they lurk beneath the natural, inherent, as it were, in the natural. They seek to infect what surrounds them and bend it to their will, as the golden grapes infect the real grapes and bend the bough, as the pleasure that "secretly doth us procure to fall" insidiously hopes to render us helpless and finally dead. Basically Spenser sees a deadly enmity between self-indulgence and temperance, or the unnatural and the norm; he sees Acrasia and what she represents as the "foe of life" (as the porter was called in stanza 48), because the very basic, necessary and vital principle of life is threatened by her. As her art perverts the natural creation of God, so lust perverts, through self-indulgence, the natural creative act. And as the art which enhances nature issues in the unnatural, the radically unfruitful, so self-indulgence in sexuality is finally sterile and thus in this sense unnatural. Acrasia is a false god who kills, not creates, life; her Bower is a false Eden which produces pain and degradation instead of harmonious bliss. Spenser has a more difficult task than Tasso; for instead of condemning all of nature and all of the senses, he must show us the mean. He must allow us to see how the fair and the foul have a common origin, and how that which abides by the norm of the natural (in the sight of God) is fair, while that which violates the natural for its own end is foul.

The rest of the canto shows us Guyon passing through the Bower as viewed in these terms. What the first 25 stanzas (37 to 61) defined, the second 25 (62–87) exemplify. We see the knight, who within himself contains the normal, natural amount of pleasure in the senses, gradually fall prey to the artifice of the maidens, to the inherent susceptibility of the senses to take pleasure only in themselves. As this process takes place, Spenser shows us how sensuality in fact leads finally to sterility. Guyon sees the two maidens naked in a stream. They "wrestle wantonly" and do not bother to conceal their bodies from "any which them eyd" (63). The sensuality of the garden, here displayed in maidens, as it was in Tasso, is immediately associated with voyeurism, with the sterility of sex by the eyes. This is again emphasized in the last line of stanza 64 as the girls "th'amarous sweet spoiles to greedy eyes revele." Like Carlo and Ubaldo before him, Guyon slows down to watch, and "His stubborne brest gan secret pleasaunce to embrace" (65). The maidens see him, and like Tasso's "donzelle," they entice him through their false modesty and calculated coyness, their seemingly innocent displays (66–68). At this point, Guyon's "melting" heart (66) is sufficiently inflamed so that in his face

> The secrete signes of kindled lust appeare.
> (68)

Both here and above in stanza 65 "secrete" is the word for the onset of lust; and it echoes that false genius who

> secretly doth us procure to fall.
> (48)

The commencement of incontinence is insidious, covert, *inner*—because it begins by subtly assaulting and undermining that natural delight in pleasure and appetite which, checked by reason, is natural, indeed necessary, to a man. Lust secretly undermines reason as art undermined nature (59); and lust's signs begin to appear on Guyon's "sparkling face" (68) just as the golden grapes

> did themselves emongst the leaves enfold,
> As lurking from the vew of covetous guest.
>
> (55)

We see happening in Guyon what the earlier landscape defined as man's general inner condition in the Bower—the insidious perversion of natural means to unnatural ends. That such a process only leads to sterility is emphasized by the reaction of the Palmer:

> He much rebukt those wandring eyes of his.
>
> (69)

Guyon is neither the *exemplum* of rigid morality, like Carlo and Ubaldo, nor the completely susceptible pawn, like Ruggiero or Rinaldo. Guyon is the man, like all men, who contains within him the natural appetites and desires, and, thus, in this fallen world, also the potentialities for depravity.

Spenser now shows us one who *did* succumb. Again we have a hint of the Bower as a false Eden in the suggestion of "paradise" (70); we hear lovely music, and then we, the readers, see

> the faire witch, her selfe now solacing
> With a new lover, whom, through sorceree
> And witchcraft, she from farre did thether bring.
>
> (72)

Like the first view of her Bower (v, 27ff.), this first view of Acrasia is for us. Guyon will come upon her after we have realized her full significance.

Her lover is asleep. As we see later (76), his head is in her lap, that "grembo molle" of the *Gerusalemme Liberata*, XVI, 18. She leans over the sleeping form,

> her false eyes fast fixed in his sight,
> As seeking medicine whence she was strong,
> Or greedily depasturing delight.
>
> (73)

Though the man is asleep, Acrasia nonetheless fixes her eyes on his, and not only the sterility but the Narcissism of the *Gerusalemme Liberata* comes back to us. Indeed, this is the traditional pose of Venus and Mars, and "depasturing" is a literal translation of the Italian "pascendo," first applied to Venus and Mars in *Le Stanze*, I, 121, and then to Armida and Rinaldo in the *Gerusalemme Liberata*, XVI, 19. Yet here Acrasia completely dominates the man in a way Armida, for instance, never did. Rinaldo was at least conscious in Armida's garden; this young man is not, and thus a sinister quality pervades the place which was lacking in the previous poems. Where Rinaldo sighed *as if* his soul were going into Armida, here Acrasia

> through his humid eyes did sucke his spright.
> Quite molten into lust and pleasure lewd.
>
> (73)

The imagery of liquid connected with lust (I, vii, 7; II, v, 28) is summed up in her sucking up his molten soul. But even more, the traditional passivity of the male, usually compared to an infantile state, is here made even more arresting. The male seems dead and there is a vampirish quality about Acrasia. Venus, who usually is the animating spirit of this kind of tableau, seems to have given way to some ghastly, demonic female. There seems to be a violation of the male's essence here, which is much more profound than that suffered by the knights in the Italian poems; for at the center of this garden we have come not to the source of simple illusion or immorality, but rather to the image of death—a love which is almost necrophilia, a woman whose kiss brings death. Proserpina haunts the figure of Acrasia, as her hellish Eden underlies, perhaps literally, this blasphemous Eden.

When, after an adaptation of the song of the Rose, Guyon and the Palmer creep forward, they finally see her: like Aleina, she seems to have on a "vele of silke and silver thin" (77), and like Armida, her breasts are exposed, and perspiration stands out on her face (78). And again, as in the Italian epics, much is made of the sterility (and implied Narcissism) of such a love by the emphasis on her as "spoyle/Of hungry eies" and on her own eyes which inflame but do not satisfy (78). There is only one touch which makes her different from her predecessors, and that occurs at the beginning of the witch's description: she is reclining on bed of roses

> As faint through heat, or dight to pleasant sin.
>
> (77)

Sin. Let us not be misled by that "pleasant," for that would be to fall into the Bower's trap. "Sin" functions here as that "sinfull bayt" (vii, 64) of Mammon's did in the garden of Proserpina. It reveals the ultimate consequences of succumbing to temptation in this world; it implies the ultimate, religious, standards by which men are judged and against which this garden (and Proserpina's) have set themselves. "Sin" finally establishes the norms by which men must live and from which these false Edens tempt them to fall.

Briefly, we see the man who is her beloved; he is young, handsome, and his arms, now abandoned, betray the signs ("old moniments") of many warlike and noble encounters (79–80). Though the theme that the life of self-indulgence deters one from the pursuit of honor is explicit here, we also see in his "nobility" (79) which is so disgraced an *exemplum* of what the garden's landscape and Guyon's momentary lapse taught us: that inherent in the natural good is the potential for unnatural evil; latent in the continent or temperate man is the incontinent, intemperate man. As the world is full of tests and trials, one of them is to maintain "continence/In joyous pleasure" (vii, 1) and keep, through "goodly government," the body "attempred . . . for health and for delight" (xi, 2). This is, after all, the point of the quest and the lesson of the Bower canto.

After Guyon and the Palmer have caught the pair in the Palmer's "subtile net," and have bound them, Guyon destroys the Bower (83). His thorough and complete job has been questioned by many commentators who profess to see the Puritan conscience of the poet at work here. Such comments are misled and misleading. Not only did the earthly paradise convention in the Renaissance epics demand the destruction of the delightful, evil place (the realms of Alcina, Acrasia and Armida were all reduced in one way or another), but the whole thrust of Book II demands it. This act is evidence of Puritanism only if a recognition of the proper role of the senses and a *restoration* of them to that role are Puritanical. Here Guyon becomes an elemental force; it is, in this man who has been learning temperance, the "tempest of his wrathfulnesse" that asserts itself. It is his native, righteous, proper indignation, and the Palmer makes no move to check him. Guyon is not destroying Pleasure in its best sense here; he is restoring it. He becomes a tempest in stanza 83 because he is like the cleansing force of Nature herself as she restores what is good to its true place in the scheme of things. It may seem paradoxical that in destroying the Bower Guyon is restoring anything; but it is Acrasia who manufactured the first paradox as she perverted nature and rendered the most creative act the most sterile and dehumanizing. Guyon turns the Bower upside down to put things right side up again. He restores the proper balance of beauty and truth when he now makes "of the fayrest late" the "fowlest place" (83). As he asserts the power of the reason over appetite, he restores the proper distinctions between fair and foul, good and evil.

The last stanzas of Canto xii clearly make this point. The beasts which charge up to the knight and his guide are only those reduced by Acrasia's lust

> into figures hideous,
> According to their mindes like monstruous.
> (85)

Here all the early associations of the Bower as a false state of mind, and of art as an analogue for lust and the unnatural, are tightened by the Palmer's revelation of these bestial men. And what does Guyon reply to his companion's words?

> Sad end, quoth he, of life intemperate,
> And mournefull meed of joyes delicious!
>
> (85)

This last line is the most revealing. Spenser, in a way Tasso never could, does not deny pleasure or the senses; he only denies unchecked and total indulgence. As Guyon says these words, the allegory of the Bower seems to become completed, and the "frame of Temperaunce" begins to be fulfilled.

But, as there is in all men the potential for incontinence, so within mankind there are those who prefer the bestial state. Such a man is Gryll, who complains when the Palmer restores him to "naturall" (86). He prefers his "hoggish forme," and the words of scorn which Guyon now speaks make amply clear what Gryll chooses when he chooses to live in his former state of mind:

> See the mind of beastly man,
> That hath so soone forgot the excellence
> Of his creation, when he life began,
> That now he chooseth, with vile difference,
> To be a beast, and lacks intelligence.
>
> (87)

Some modern commentators have professed admiration for Gryll's stubbornness, his refusal to submit. Every man to his own deepest dreams. However, what Gryll has chosen is Hell. Spenser does not deny him the right to choose, but the poet makes it clear that such a life is contrary to the "naturall" in its finest sense, that which most resembles the "excellence/Of his creation." Man is fallen, but he can be saved, if he uses what he retains of his innocent nature—"when he life began"—to serve his Creator. To do otherwise is to deny the image and hope of that first garden for the specious joys of a false Eden; it is to substitute for the possibility of redemption a horrible parody of innocence in a mire of self-indulgence. Such a life is to "lacke intelligence," to be among those, as Virgil said to Dante,

> C'hanno perduto il ben de l'intelletto.

> (who have lost the good of the intellect.)
>
> (Inferno, III, 18)

Spenser's garden vision includes much more than the earthly paradises of the Italians. He sees not only the illusory quality, the immoral dimension, of the life of sexual indulgence; he sees its horror precisely because he can see the goods which are being wasted. He is neither the total skeptic nor the exclusive moralist. Spenser sees proper pleasure compatible with honor and duty, and he sees how the senses can be made to exist in harmony with the spirit. Because he has a broader vision of the joys of life, he is able to give us a more ghastly vision of their perversions and a deeper warning of the profound consequences of sin. Thus his earthly paradise presents the most striking Renaissance version of man's search for peace in a garden, and the dangers and terrors of mistaking some earthly bliss for that bliss which is found only, and finally, in God.

HARRY BERGER, JR.

The "Mutabilitie Cantos": Archaism and Evolution in Retrospect

The view of experience expressed in and as Spenser's poetry is shaped by a radically historical consciousness. It is historical in two reciprocal aspects: the objective character of Spenser's vision is *evolutionary*; its subjective mode is *retrospective*. The present essay will explore these terms in the specific context of the *Mutabilitie Cantos*, but I shall preface my interpretation with some remarks of a more general nature in order to clarify my use of these terms. By evolutionary I mean that we may find in Spenser's poetry an overall developmental pattern in which three vectors coalesce: from lower to higher, from simpler to more complex and, of course, from earlier to later. These vectors run parallel courses in the history of the individual psyche and in that of culture or civilization. The relation between these two courses is reciprocal. Haeckel's discredited biogenetic formula, "ontogeny recapitulates phylogeny," covers one side of it: the individual organism (the microcosm, the human or physic *discordia concors*) manifests in compressed form the development of culture from its earlier childhood phases to its later more sophisticated phases. The normal and normative growth of human consciousness and conscience is from a relatively narrow, simplistic or elementally "pure" perspective to a broader, more complex and comprehensive perspective. In early or in regressive stages, for example, distinguishable areas tend to

From *Spenser: A Collection of Critical Essays*, edited by Harry Berger, Jr. Copyright © 1968 by Prentice-Hall, Inc.

blur or overlap, as when the mind fails to perceive or respect the boundaries between itself and the world, man and God, self and other, love and hate, heaven and earth, the divine and the chaotic or natural sources of energy. The other side of the reciprocity between psyche and culture is the effect of the microcosm on any phase of the larger order: here Spenser agrees with Plato, Virgil, and others in depicting the institutions and products of "early" culture as dominated by, expressive of, those tendencies of the psyche which are usually described as childlike, austistic, superstitious, sensuous.

The subjective mode of Spenser's historical vision is restrospective: he looks back into the past from his own *here and now*. In his early or archaic world, action is caused for the most part by the large-scale play of forces which, though psychic as well as cosmic, operate outside of any individual will or consciousness. Book III of *The Faerie Queene* is especially ordered to suggest how entirely independent actions and episodes, occurring in widely separated places and moments of the Spenserian world, are triggered in such a way as to produce a meaningful coalescence whose import could not possibly be grasped by any of the figures involved, except perhaps for gods and prophets (and even their perspectives are limited in ways to be discussed below). The driving purpose of this organic system of forces is beyond its conscious members because both system and purpose are retrospectively fashioned by the poet, and only tentatively, temporarily, fulfilled in his own time. The possibility of prophecy is founded on deterministic presuppositions, and a leading characteristic of Spenser's "primitive" age is the manifest domination of behavior by extra-human forces whose influence tends toward the conservation or restoration of an archaic state of affairs. As psyche and culture develop, this collective and determined mode of behavior gradually yields to the more active and original assertions of individual souls. When the center of will, decision, and activity is located in the individual consciousness, archaic determinism gives way to retrospective determinism as the dominant organizing mode.

When cosmic and primitive influences dominate, the forms of existence tend to be at once unstable and universal (i.e., recurrent, generic or archetypal). When psychic and rational influences dominate, the forms tend to be personal, unique and potentially more stable; at the same time, the forms of discord, evil, danger and temptation are subtler, therefore less easily located and contained. Fundamental to this model is Spenser's conviction that no moment of union or reconciliation, of relief or triumph, is to be construed as absolute—absolute either in the sense of being final, or in the sense of being totally one-sided. Every triumph or resolution at a lower level of existence or an earlier phase of experience releases new and different problems at a higher level or a later phase. This will be oddly demonstrated in the *Mutabilitie Cantos*, where the vision of cosmic harmony which triumphantly concludes canto vii in the medieval mode triggers a new brief lyric moment of anxiety in the closing stanzas.

The full vision of the pattern I have been describing is seldom attained by characters within the Spenserian world, while its complex and articulated unity is a condition attained by soul, state, or culture only in relatively advanced phases of its career. And only in such phases does the imagination double back to activate the tacit or latent elements—the primitive and palingenetic factors—of experience in order to set the present moment within its developmental context. As I suggested before, Spenser presents the latest form of experience both *in* his work and *as* his work. The historical sense which is the defining mark of that work asserts itself in his effort to locate the various elements of his poetic *discordia concors* at their proper temporal distances from the present. His poetry thus represents in its complex form all the phases which preceded it and which it, in effect, supersedes. This representation is achieved by means of the technique of *conspicuous allusion*: the depiction of stock literary motifs, characters, and genres in a manner which emphasizes their conventionality, displaying at once their debt to and their existence in a conventional climate—classical, medieval, romance, etc.—which is archaic when seen from Spenser's retrospective viewpoint.

The *Mutabilitie Cantos* provide the most concise and complete embodiment of Spenser's historical consciousness. Explicitly lyric or self-referential in mode, the poem not only directs our attention toward the "modern" narrator, it also reveals the effect of his retrospective narrative on his own feelings. Spenser uses conspicuous allusion to organize the poem along evolutionary lines: its three sections—canto vi, canto vii, and the final two stanzas—develop what is in effect an ontogenetic recapitulation of the phases of experience from pagan through medieval modes of imagination to the lyric (and renaissance) present. Canto vii, the medieval phase, includes, infolds, and transcends the two simple pagan modes (epic and pastoral) of the comic sixth canto. The later moment is a more complex, more finely articulated revision of the earlier moment, which it redirects and transforms; but it is itself distanced and superseded in the poem's concluding stanzas.

If we look carefully at six-stanza poem we shall see that all the themes, attitudes and problems to be displayed throughout the work are present here in a special and temporary form, i.e., dominated by a limited viewpoint which will change as Spenser moves through the poem:

What man that sees the ever-whirling wheele
 Of Change, the which all mortall things doth sway,
 But that therby doth find, and plainly feele,
 How MUTABILITY in them doth play
 Her cruell sports, to many mens decay?
 Which that to all may better yet appeare,
 I will rehearse that whylome I heard say,
 How she at first her selfe began to reare,
Gainst all the Gods, and th'empire sought from them to beare.

But first, here falleth, fittest to unfold
 Her antique race and linage ancient,
 As I have found it registred of old,
 In Faery Land mongst records permanent:
 She was, to weet, a daughter by descent
 Of those old Titans, that did whylome strive
 With Saturnes sonne for heavens regiment.
 Whom, though high Jove of kingdome did deprive,
Yet many of their steeme long after did survive.

And many of them, afterwards obtain'd
 Great power of Jove, and high authority;
 As Hecate, in whose almighty hand,
 He plac't all rule and principality,
 To be by her disposed diversly,
 To Gods, and men, as she them list divide:
 And drad Bellona, that doth sound on hie
 Warres and allarums unto Nations wide,
That makes both heaven and earth to tremble at her pride.

So likewise did this Titanesse aspire,
 Rule and dominion to her selfe to gaine;
 That as a Goddesse, men might her admire,
 And heavenly honours yield, as to them twaine.
 At first, on earth she sought it to obtaine;
 Where she such proofe and sad examples shewed
 Of her great power, to many ones great paine,
 That not men onely (whom she soone subdewed)
But eke all other creatures, her bad doings rewed.

For, she the face of earthly things so changed,
 That all which Nature had establisht first
 In good estate, and in meet order ranged,
 She did pervert, and all their statues burst:
 And all the worlds faire frame (which none yet durst
 Of Gods or men to alter or misguide)
 She alter'd quite, and made them all accurst
 That God had blest; and did at first provide
In that still happy state for ever to abide.

Ne shee the lawes of Nature onely brake
   But eke of Justice, and of Policie;
   And wrong of right, and bad of good did make,
   And death for life exchanged foolishlie:
   Since which, all living wights have learn'd to die,
   And all this world is woxen daily worse.
   O pittious worke of MUTABILITIE!
   By which, we all are subject to that curse,
And death in stead of life have sucked from our Nurse.

By the end of the poem Spenser will stand before us as a *man* in meditation, responding personally to what he has made and seen. But here he introduces himself in a more detached stance as a *poet* who will use an old story to exemplify and embellish the power of mutability. At first he separates himself from the audience ("What man . . .") whose concern he will delineate in fiction. His attention moves back to the pagan genealogy and its sources, mentioning not only Mutabilitie's ancient lineage, but also the antique account of the lineage. "Faery Land" seems to have two references: to his own literary world or imagination, the myths and fictions devised by the poet of *The Faerie Queene*; and to the "antique rolles" in the "everlasting scryne" (I.Pr.2) of the Muses, the fictions, myths, and legends recorded throughout history. The association of the everlasting *scryne* (from *scrinium*, a chest or casket for manuscripts) with antique rolls and of "records permanent" with "registered of old" suggests something fixed early in culture, therefore permanent but not necessarily adequate. This kind of permanence sets itself over against that of "the ever-whirling wheele," and it therefore embodies the wish to resist inevitable change, to memorialize for all time a particular vision or solution that arose in response to a particular situation. As the ever-whirling wheel is an early and defective view of the dynamic recurrence that yields the constancy of Nature, so this archaic permanence is a defective prevision or imitation of that on which Nature and the poet meditate at poem's end. In the second and third sections, these simple opposites—whirl and permanence—will converge and interpenetrate, will move forward and inward from the reconciling cosmic symbolism of the medieval mind to the lyric present in which the poet stands, altered yet still unreconciled—even more deeply divided, in fact, by what he has envisaged.

Something like this larger pattern of movement is condensed in the proem, though it takes a different direction. Stanzas 2–4 comprise a relatively matter-of-fact rehearsal in the antique pagan mode of canto vi. Stanza 5 anticipates canto vii by introducing Nature and allowing Judaeo-

Christian echoes to filter in. As the poet lists Mutabilitie's evil effects in stanzas 5 and 6, the rhythm and feeling of his rhetoric build toward the exclamation—"O pittious worke of MUTABILITY!"—and toward the final couplet that at once generalizes the curse and draws it close by the use of the first person plural. Like the blatant beast at the end of Book VI, Mutabilitie seems to rush from the remote past into the poet's present as her influence spreads throughout the universe and into the human domain where Justice and Policy have been abused. The proem thus ends at a nadir. Having moved from the position of detached narrator, the poet now joins his mortal audience, plainly feels the effect of what he has found or invented, and actualizes the grimmest possibilities of the opening lines.

These lines imply a limitation of vision and response most explicitly glossed by the proem to Book V, which the sentiments expressed in stanza 6 echo in more condensed form. The man that sees the everwhirling wheel may not see beyond it, and as a result he *plainly* feels mutability as entirely evil. In addition to *clearly* or *vividly*, the word *plainly* carries the sense of *directly, flatly, simply*. Spenser here depicts an objective attitude, a general frame of mind, and then adopts it as his own. It is nevertheless adopted with a degree of detachment as the *wrong* attitude, one that affects his view of life, that will affect his poem, and that is modified in the course of narration. In Book V and the *Mutabilitie Cantos*, he locates this attitude in the poetic first person in order to dramatize it, give it play, and put it to the test. The attitude is the basic problem—the enemy, as it were—with which both poems deal. It is an attitude that in one form Spenser stated directly at the beginning of *A View of the Present State of Ireland*. Irenius reports the received opinion that it is Ireland's "fatall destinie" that no purposes "mente for her good" can succeed in reforming that miserable nation, perhaps because of "the *very Genius* of the soile, or influence of the starres, or that Allmighty god hath not yeat Appointed the tyme of her reformacion or that he reserveth her in this unquiet state still, for some secrete skourge, which shall by her Come into Englande." Eudoxus pooh-poohs this opinion as the "vaine Conceipt of simple men" and attributes the trouble rather to "the unsoundnes of . . . Counsells and Plottes." He then offers the commonplace criticism, perhaps most familiar to us in Edmund's famous soliloquy on Gloucester's self-deception, that "it is the manner of men that when they are fallen into anye Absurditye or theire accions succede not as they woulde they are ready allwaies to impute the blame theareof unto the heavens, soe to excuse their owne follies and imperfeccions. . . . it is the manner . . . of desperate men farre driven to wishe the utter ruine of that which they Cannot redresse. . . ."—

the manner not only of the egalitarian giant of *The Faerie Queene* (V.ii), for example, but also of the justice of Talus and Artegal and, to some extent, of Spenser's own vision of actuality in that book.

When Spenser dramatizes this "vaine Conceipt" at the beginning of the *Mutabilitie Cantos*, he immediately connects it with the "records permanent" of antiquity. It is the response "of simple men," the pessimistic fatalism of the vulgar mind "farre driven." At the same time it is characterized as regressive by being "historically" located in an archaic framework of pagan conceptions and images. The essence of this framework lies in the polarity between Mutabilitie and Nature as Spenser initially presents it—*initially*, that is, because the idea of nature in vi.5–6 will be radically altered in the figure of Natura who dominates canto vii. Nature in vi.5–6 has already succumbed to mutability, who *brake* her laws, *changed, did pervert*, and *alter'd quite* her original estate and the world's fair frame. Stanza 5 tends to push Nature back into Eden and identify the reign of her enemy with the whole history of fallen man, though the general pagan context diffuses the Edenic reference so that it is suggestive of any conception of the first golden age. This idea of nature has already been outmoded because it projects unrealistic expectations; it is based on a longing for too perfect and fixed a state of nature. Under the pressure of actual life, so unguardedly sanguine a hope dialectically produces its opposite, that is, the despairing acceptance of negative mutability as life's ruling principle, which in turn generates the wish to escape back into the paradisaic state of nature. Wish-fulfillment and nightmare are simple contraries, twinned and mutually intensifying impulses, neither of which is more realistic than the other. We may thus translate the fabled triumph of mutability over sublunary nature into its psychological equivalent: it is the triumph of a view of earthly life that "sees the ever-whirling wheele" of entropic change as the nature of things, having succeeded an inadequate and fragile view of nature as a pleasure garden where all things endure forever just as they were when "establisht first / In good estate, and in meet order ranged." In terms of the mythology of Book V, this radical counterswing from the golden to the iron age, from Saturn to Jove, is signified by the departure from earth of Astraea, whose virginity symbolizes classical disdain and self-withholding exclusiveness. Her desire to resist change, to retain in its purity her ruthlessly idealistic and aprioristic justice, is related to the feeling that the present decay of justice, politics, and ethics may have been determined from creation by the mechanics of physical change:

Me seemes the world is runne quite out of square,
From the first point of his appointed sourse,
And being once amisse growes daily wourse and wourse.
(V.Pr.1)

This is archaic determinism, whose premise of irreversible decline dissipates the possibility of second thoughts and second chances, of rebirth, redemption, and revision. It encourages the violent repressiveness of iron-age justice in Jove, Hercules, Artegal, Talus, and the stoic censors.

The opposed visions of the ever-whirling wheel and the ever-abiding happy state are permanent possibilities for the mind, but they represent an archaic mode of seeing and feeling. Therefore they "may better yet appeare" in the *whylome* form recorded early in man's psycho-cultural history. In signalling his return to this mode, the poet dramatically enacts the urge to escape time, change, and history. During the remainder of the sixth canto this assumption of the archaic perspective is comically sustained by a number of parodistic devices that I shall now discuss:

1. To attribute all evil to mutability, "to impute . . . unto the heavens" the blame for human follies and sins and failures, is the first stage of a time-honored mode of evasion. The next stage is to devise a way of producing an Ultimate Solution in a single encounter, and this is accomplished by condensing all evils into an allegorical or mythological scapegoat who may then be defeated by a more powerful divine embodiment of order. Helpless man may thus surrender both his responsibility and his power, may relieve himself of moral efficacy and effort, consigning the good fight to the cosmic forces of Darkness and Light. This is a return not only to primitive, but also to childlike, sensibility—thus the appropriateness of Spenser's recourse to an old fairytale. From the total evil plaintively delineated in the first six stanzas he withdraws into a purely recreative world of ancient fable and into a comic portrait of the way in which antique genres—the high and low styles of heroic bombast and pastoral homeliness—render and cope with the problem of mutability.

2. The opposition between simple change and simple permanence, black mutability and golden nature, plaintive and recreative attitudes, high and low styles, points toward an attempt stylistically to imitate an archaic pattern mentioned in the beginning of this essay—the separation of elements into pure and mutually exclusive contraries. Such divisiveness is already the essence of the fable action in this canto, from the first mention of Mutabilities's antique lineage through the facing-off with Cynthia and Jove in the new arrangement of these contraries in the

pastoral digression. The action of the canto is so disposed as to emphasize the catabolic process of fragmentation, the breaking down of primeval and unstable compounds: chaos/earth/heaven; Uranus/Titan/Saturn and Saturn/ Jove; Jove/Hecate/Bellona (the latter two being opposed principles of order and disorder); male and female, old and young, separating off from the primal family matrix; the members of the ruling Olympian pantheon set at odds among themselves by Mutabilitie's assault (vi.23); the hints of a composite goddess splitting into Hecate, Cynthia, and Diana; Mutabilitie by implication dividing into Faunus and Diana, the lustful voyeur and the Astraean destroyer of Ireland's "first . . . good estate"; the uneasy pastoral alliance between Ovidian mythic and Irish actual landscapes.

This pattern penetrates the division of the canto into high and low styles. The inherent contrariety between epic and pastoral perspectives is intensified by Spenser's comic exaggerations of the devices which characterize each mode: in the former, bombastic rhetoric, heroic vaunting and "flyting," Homeric formulas, cosmic muscularity, panoramic vistas, and in general the fusty, expansive, and broad-planed way of at once magnifying and simplifying problems; in the latter, the problems reduced, lightened, dissipated in homely analogies, rustic minutiae, buffoonery, sylvan diversions, minor woodland metamorphoses, and echoes of Spenser's own early literary play.

The pastoral episode is not comic relief, for the simple reason that it is no less serious than the heroic episode, in which the inflated presentation is continually punctured. The conflict between Mutabilitie and Cynthia, for example, is little more than a scuffle between oversized schoolgirls (vi.13), and Jove ends five thundering stanzas in a wheedle: "ceasse thy idle claime thou foolish gerle" (vi.34). Both episodes are equally comic and recreative, equally acts of withdrawal into ancient fairyland from the grimmer vision of the opening stanzas. The more intricate and pressing human issues, the problems of justice and polity, are introduced at the beginning and conspicuously ignored. Early epic and pastoral are portrayed from the standpoint of the present as pure contraries that fall on either side of real life; the poet climbs upward and backward to Jove's heaven until Jove is about to be passed by (vi.35–36), at which point he runs downward to make a new beginning in Cynthia's unfallen wood.

3. In canto vi, Mutabilitie, Cynthia, Mercury, Arlo Hill, and to some extent the other gods, including Jove, all suffer the same ignominious fate at the hands of their author; they are *desymbolized*, for they are more cosmic, portentous, and epic at the beginning of the canto than at the end. Spenser first flashes the full range of symbolic references while converting the referents to mythic or allegorical personifications, then

conspicuously ignores or abandons these references for the literal play of his story. Withdrawal into the recreative now of storytelling is heightened by the fact that most of the symbolic references that are present-as-excluded are plaintive. Mutabilitie begins as the ever-whirling wheel of entropic change, is personified before being blamed for the sum total of human vicissitudes, and, immediately after the proem, drops off these first two stages to become merely a very large, aggressive, and upward-mobile woman with some of the qualities of Britomart and Radegund. Spenser's obvious relish in heroic parody, the enjoyment with which he gratuitously elaborates details of dialogue and description, produce something like a cartoon-strip world whose heroine is a version of Superwoman; but it is a world seen through the eyes of *Mad* magazine.

This recreative desymbolizing is historical in its implications, because Spenser directs us to the more recent identities of the gods as planetary forces before he moves back to animate their older mythological images as Ovidian dramatis personae. Cynthia and Mercury are introduced in astronomical guise (vi.8,14), but are immediately converted to emblematic or mythological figures. Mutabilitie climbs to the "Circle of the Moone" and Cynthia's "bright shining palace,"

> All fairely deckt with heavens goodly *story*;
> Whose silver gates (by which there sate an *hory*
> Old aged Sire, with hower-glasse in hand,
> Hight Tyme) she entred, were he liefe or sory:
> Ne staide till she the highest *stage* had scand,
> Where Cynthia did sit, that never still did stand.
>
> Her sitting on an Ivory throne shee found,
> Drawne of two steeds, th'one black, the other white,
> Environd with tenne thousand starres around,
> That duly her attended day and night;
> And by her side there ran her Page, that hight
> Vesper, whom we the Evening-starre intend:
> That with his Torche, still twinkling like twylight,
> Her lightened all the way where she should wend,
> And joy to weary wandring travailers did lend. . . .
>
> (vi.8–9, italics mine)

The italicized puns pivot the scene from astronomical space and function to theatrical or emblematic fiction, and this process is completed in the symbolic reversal whereby Vesper's torch becomes the subject, and his twilight only the comparison, of the simile. By the time Mutabilitie has laid hold of Cynthia—"raught forth her hand / To pluck her downe perforce from off her chaire" and threatened to club her with "her golden

wand" (vi.13)—the hieratic emblems have themselves given way to physical action that on the one hand is heightened by epic scale and rhetoric
and on the other hand is comic, even pastoral, in its inconsequence. A
multi-level stage set replaces the spheres, embellishing an action invented
and controlled by the myth-making mind. This frames the foreground
artifice—the reduction to purely visual and spatial terms of a subject
whose essential meaning is temporal.

Desymbolizing is a contrastive technique that, while dividing the
surface narrative from its significant background, keeps both before us. We
are encouraged to feel that the narrative obscures the themes that generate and organize the plot of the fable. We learn at the beginning of the
canto that the superlunary world is about to be threatened by mutability.
The heroine's ascent through the spheres therefore acts out some contemporary commonplaces in a pessimistic or apocalyptic vein. Perhaps it also
alludes to current changes in astronomical and cosmological theory.
Toward the end of the epic section, we are given glimpses of the hidden
order that will emerge in canto vii. Jove begins to use legal jargon (vi.33).
Mutabilitie, whose ultimate ambition was presented earlier as a martial
attempt to displace "highest Jove" from his palace in the "highest sky,"
aims beyond Jove (vi. 34–36) and wants to plead her case before "the highest
him," the "God of Nature." Jove is grudgingly forced to accede, and bids
"Dan Phoebus Scribe her Appellation seale." By this time Mutabilitie has
become more beautiful, or at least her physical stature and beauty are
noted by Spenser, the gods, and Jove (vi.28, 31–34) for the first time only
after she has ascended to Jove's palace. This alteration will be clarified in
the next canto, when the beauty of change is emphasized, but here it
seems a purely gratuitous and *ad hoc* touch.

4. All this points toward a purposeful disjunction between the
underlying order apparent to the medieval Christian imagination of canto
vii, and the misguided, obscure anticipations of the pagan mythopoesis
that dominates canto vi. This disjunction, the fourth and final aspect of
canto vi to be discussed, reinforces the conspicuously digressive quality of
the narrative. It sets off the instability of the characters and, occasionally,
of the narrative. It heightens the comic effect of inflatedness and irrele-
vance that attends the posturing of the gods. For, looking back from
stanzas 33–36, we see the episode in an entirely new light. Mutabilitie's
real problem is procedural and falls within the legal domain of Right, not
the martial domain of Might: she wants a hearing and apparently has to go
through channels and attract the attention of the proper authorities to get
one. This lends her previous wranglings the air of legalistic maneuvers.
Her transactions with Cynthia, Mercury, and Jove retrospectively assume

this character, whereas Jove's feeble effort at seduction (vi.34) seems motivated not solely by lust, but also, as she points out, by his desire to keep her from putting her case before the court. As the plot action moves closer to the higher and later system of forces disclosed in the next canto, it reveals the influence of that system with increasing clarity.

From this standpoint, the heroic pagan gestures are at once more meaningless in themselves and more signficant as expressions of limited responses. There is very little real action or conflict in the episode, and even this is continually interrupted or deflected: the tussle with Cynthia, the interchange with Mercury, the military council of gods, the assault on heaven, and the interview with Jove are all broken off (vi.17, 19, 24ff., 35–36) for apparently arbitrary reasons before they produce any serious consequences. Plot and narrative therefore seem ruled by contingency and whim, by unforeseen occurrences and unexpected reactions. Against this pattern, such resounding passages as the following are faintly ridiculous, especially the final example, in which the advent of mutability reduces the ancient psycho-pomp to his Lord's legman:

> Eftsoones she cast by force and tortious might,
> Her [Cynthia] to displace. . . .
>
> (vi.10)

> Fearing least Chaos broken had his chaine,
> And brought againe on them eternall night. . . .
>
> (vi.14)

>   Doubting least Typhon were againe uprear'd,
> Or other his old foes, that once him sorely fear'd
>
> (vi.15)

> And there-with-all, he on her shoulder laid
>   His snaky-wreathed Mace, whose awfull power
>   Doth make both Gods and hellish fiends affraid:
>   Where-at the Titanesse did sternely lower,
>   And stoutly answer'd, that in evill hower
>   He from his Jove such message to her brought,
>   To bid her leave faire Cynthias silver bower;
>   Sith shee his Jove and him esteemed nought,
> No more then Cynthia's self; but all their kingdoms sought.

> The heavens Herald staid not to reply,
>   But past away, his doings to relate
>   Unto his Lord. . . .
>
> (vi.18–19)

The antique thunder, the fear of the recurrence of old catastrophes, the portentous gesture with the caduceus—these items, all futile or beside the point, contribute to Spenser's image of the archaic mind. Together with the emergent influence of the medieval *concordia discors*—the process of gradual, ordered change silently moving and modifying these *antickes*—they suggest that mind's inflated self-image, its tendency toward violent and headlong yet easily deflected impulses, its backward-looking reliance upon ancient precedents, and its consequent ignorance of or resistance to Nature's message that all things "by their change their being doe dilate."

Thomas M. Greene has described the "perpetual *becoming*" of Spenser's characters while their "status and meaning and concreteness . . . shift and fade and recombine," and this is exemplified in a pointedly contrapuntal manner by the *Two Cantos of Mutabilitie*. What unfolds in the seventh canto as cyclical and developmental change, appears at the surface of canto vi as random motion and instability. The gods not only shift from planets to characters, they suffer sudden changes of quality and whim, as when the stern titaness becomes beautiful and Jove is moved from anger to desire. Both Mutabilitie and Mercury experience, then *boldly* overcome, unexpected impulses of fear (vi.17–18; 25–26). When Mutabilitie and Cynthia face off, the latter is momentarily infected with her enemy's nature ("sterne countenaunce and disdainfull cheare," vi.12). Cynthia's demotion to her earthly domain, in the pastoral digression, seems to intensify this influence. She destroys her *locus amoenus* just as the titaness had destroyed golden nature. As if in reaction to her closer involvement with mutable earth and lustful males, she waxes Astraean in her self-withholding disdain (vi.42) and her anger at folly and weakness (vi.51, 54–55).

The pastoral digression is the most interesting example of instability, because it is the speaker himself who is affected: Spenser introduces Arlo Hill as a place of revelation "Where all, both heavenly Powers, and earthly wights, / Before great Natures presence should appeare," but presents himself as distracted immediately after by the thought of his own earlier pastoral portrait of that region of Munster ("my old father Mole, whom Shepheards quill / Renowmed hath with hymnes fit for a rurall skill," vi.36). He spends the next stanza vacillating:

> And, were it not ill fitting for this file,
>   To sing of hilles and woods, mongst warres and Knights,
> I would abate the sternenesse of my stile,
> Mongst these sterne stounds to mingle soft delights;
> And tell how Arlo through Dianaes spights
> (Beeing of old the best and fairest Hill

That was in all this holy-Islands hights)
Was made the most unpleasant, and most ill.
Meane while, O Clio, lend Calliope thy quill.
(vi.37)

The fact that the conditional is negative in force, and that Calliope is more appropriate for great Nature's trial than for Faunus' minor tribulations, suggests that Spenser has controlled the impulse to digress. But this only accentuates the about-face of the next lines, in which he appears to yield to his caprice in spite of himself.

As an alternative to the prospective trial, the pastoral episode may strike us even more sharply as reversion and diversion—reversion to an obviously fanciful mixture of outmoded Spenserian, Irish, and classical myths of the permanence-mutability conflict, and diversion from the glimpse of cosmic order to a playful explanation of the entropic change that still prevails on earth. The problems raised in the opening stanzas of canto vi re-enter in much diminished and localized form. Well-known metamorphic catastrophes are alluded to but averted. The canto concludes with a kind of black joke upon Ireland—Diana's "heavy haplesse curse" that specifies that wolves should

all those Woods deface,
And Thieves should rob and spoile that Coast around.
Since which, those Woods, and all that goodly Chase,
Doth to this day with Wolves and Thieves abound:
Which too-too true that lands in-dwellers since have found.
(vi.55)

Having looked through the archaic or youthful mind's anthropomorphic window on the world, Spenser ends on a Eudoxian note that makes light of that whole realm of explanation: "men fallen into any Absurditye . . . are ready allwaies to impute blame theareof unto the heavens, soe to excuse their owne follies and imperfections." It is the explanation, not the problem, that is parodied, for the canto, like the six-stanza proem, ends with a sudden return to the present and to the nearness, the actuality, of the dark "state of present time" in Ireland. It ends, furthermore, upon a more intensely pessimistic note: "desperate men farre driven . . . wishe the utter ruine of that which they Cannot redresse." The destructive wish flashing forth in the final stanza makes the Ovidian *pourquoi* story and "the image of the antique world" seem frivolous by contrast—a flight into the recreative mode of imagination, with its focus upon the pleasures of fancy and the ornaments of verse. It is the mode most appropriate to the poet in his youthful phase, but when revived in its pure form in a later stage, it is a function of the escape impulse.

This conclusion frames the next canto within the motivational context that will lead ultimately to the concluding two stanzas. For if things are still bad on earth, maybe they will work out more happily in heaven. If a grasshopper flight over Ireland touches down on bumpy terrain, maybe a higher flight, a more panoramic view, an increase in distance, an Astraean remoteness, will resolve the discords and ugliness into a satisfying pattern. I think it is important to keep this context in mind when reading canto vii. Otherwise the more obviously positive and triumphant aspects of the vision of order may appear to solve all problems in a real and unqualified manner, which certainly is not the case so far as Spenser is concerned. The opening stanzas of canto vii register with some delicacy the degree and kind of resolution we may expect, and they also stand dramatically as a reaction to the pastoral interlude.

> Ah! whither doost thou now thou greater Muse
>   Me from these woods and pleasing forests bring?
> And my fraile spirit (that dooth oft refuse
>   This too high flight, unfit for her weake wing)
> Lift up aloft, to tell of heavens King
>   (Thy soveraine Sire) his fortunate successe,
>   And victory, in bigger noates to sing,
>   Which he obtain'd against that Titanesse,
> That him of heavens Empire sought to dispossesse.
>
> Yet sith I needs must follow thy behest,
>   Doe thou my weaker wit with skill inspire,
> Fit for this turne; and in my feeble brest
>   Kindle fresh sparks of that immortall fire,
> Which learned minds inflameth with desire
>   Of heavenly things: for, who but thou alone,
>   That art yborne of heaven and heavenly Sire,
>   Can tell things doen in heaven so long ygone;
> So farre past memory of man that may be knowne.

Except to classify the digression under a new and more general category (the mortal poet's insufficiency), he speaks as if it had not occurred and the woods had not been defaced. Looking forward, he describes Jove's prospective victory as much more complete than it in fact will be. The language of the second stanza promotes a momentary blurring of pagan and Christian muses and divinities, but insofar as we feel the presence of the pagan muse, we are allowed to suspect that she is capable of nepotism. The final couplet fills out the chronological relations in the poem. The happening on Arlo Hill occurred too long ago to be remembered by man; the contemporary poet must woo a muse whose usefulness arises not only from her transcendence but also from her antiquity. "So farre past memory of man" refers to both and leaves temporarily unresolved the location of the event; as a vision of pagan-Christian concord, it is culturally "later" than the vision of canto vi, yet Nature's trial and judgment are pushed very far back into the past and /or very high up in heaven. We may feel that it is the image of a wished-for stabilization of order that occurred at the beginning of time, and this may lead us to see in canto vi an inadequate pagan version, in canto vii a more adequate medieval version, of the same mythical event.

The medieval account reflects more accurately than its predecessor the essential feature of that mythical event, namely, its promise of a cyclical natural order whose processes recur throughout the course of time. This superiority is made evident in a number of ways, though space does not permit more than a brief itemization.

First, canto vii reconciles the antique contraries of epic and pastoral, contracting the expansive and relatively vacant regions of canto vi into the narrow, densely packed confines of its middle ground (vii.3–4). In canto vi, the poet's eye ranged through the ancient heaven and earth, going where the action was. In canto vii, the action and characters come to Arlo Hill.

Second, the desymbolized figures are, so to speak, resymbolized. The gods resume their planetary functions, and their influence is felt not only on earth but also in the zodiac. The literal reaches of the two-level pagan cosmos are infolded in Arlo Hill, which, desymbolized by the poet and Diana in canto vi, now regains its symbolic value as an apocalyptic height. Mutabilitie cannot be contained within her own personification; she stands for processes that are beyond her not only because they are diffused throughout the natural universe, but also because they have values diametrically opposed to those the titaness affirms. Although she is conveniently defeated and *whist* in the single action of the trial, this is the classic Spenserian feint: the defeat of an externalized and localized enemy diverts attention from the continuing and deepening effectiveness of the enemy within; Mutabilitie is limited mainly by the rigid qualities and archaic personification to which "she" lays claim, and the disappearance of the titaness corresponds to the infiltration of all nature by mutability.

In this connection, it is significant that Mutabilitie talks so much. She is a real windbag, and Spenser's judgment upon Faunus is surely meant to rub off on her:

He could him not containe in silent rest;
But breaking forth in laughter, loud profest
His foolish thought. A foolish Faune indeed,
That couldst not hold thy selfe so hidden blest,
But wouldest needs thine owne conceit areed.
Babblers unworthy been of so divine a meed.

(vi.46)

Had Faunus followed the example of the goddess Natura—stayed hidden and kept as still as possible—he would have seen what he wanted to see. The more Mutabilitie speaks, the more she imposes and expresses herself as a personality, the clearer her limitations become; if she only gets what she, as a titaness, claims, it will be much less than what mutability, as a process, covers. Her prosopopoia is thus itself a primitive form of self-seeking and self-deceiving arrogance, as Nature points out: "thy decay thou seekst by thy desire" (vii.59). The ultimate stage of resymbolization would be *depersonification*, in which the referent breaks free from its containing symbolic form. Thus released, it is open to new forms and to new life in later times. This process is already under way as we move from the aggressive pagan individuals of canto vi to the impersonal concord of forces and functions shining more clearly through the figures and emblems of canto vii. More retrograde and stubborn than the others, Mutabilitie is almost the last to get the word.

Third, the organization of Nature's concord in canto vii is dominated by the form of the cycle, or round. This form appears not only in the obvious pageant of seasons and months, but also in the stanzas of Nature (vii.5–13), discussed below, and in the larger unit of the canto as a whole, which moves from benign Christian Nature through Mutabilitie's older vision of negative elemental change (vii.17–26) and back to a benign nature that had dilated to assimilate mutability's influence. Both cantos together may also be viewed on this cyclical model in terms of the semantic pattern, symbolizing—desymbolizing—resymbolizing, which binds the movement of the whole poem into a single action.

Fourth, the cyclical pattern is not one of simple recurrence, but rather one in which recurrence is part of a larger evolutionary movement. In this movement, the older and simpler elements are at once negated and upheld (*aufgehoben*, Hegel's term for the one process divided into these two contrary moments). Mutabilitie and the gods persist in the same attitudes they held before, even while debating planetary influence. In his one stanza of rebuttal, Jove cites that influence as evidence for his previous claim: it is true, he admits, that all things under heaven are changed by Time,

> who doth them all disseise
> Of being: but, who is it (to me tell)
> That Time himselfe doth move and still compell
> To keepe his course? Is that not namely wee
> Which poure that vertue from our heavenly cell,
> That moves them all, and makes them changed be?
> So them we gods doe rule, and in them also thee.
>
> (vii.48)

His language is purged of the old heroic thunder, but the archaic resistance to change lurks in the legalism, *disseise*, which usually connotes *wrongful* or forcible dispossession. Mutabilitie's discourse on the elements is similarly located between the old and the new: it is related to the mock-heroic business of canto vi very much as the "philosophical" discourse in *Metamorphoses* XV is related to the metamorphoses of Ovid's first fourteen books; and as a piece of Lucretian materialism, it aims at demythologizing the elemental processes, for example,

> So, in them all raignes Mutabilitie;
> How-ever these, *that Gods themselves do call,*
> Of them doe claime the rule and soverainty. . . .
>
> (vii.26, italics mine)

At the same time, the argument reveals its proponent's antique and limited viewpoint in reducing the principle of life to "unsteady ayre" (vii.22) and in selectively dwelling upon changes that reveal only instability, unpredictability, hostility, or decline. Her summation concisely recapitulates that early vision and early state of world order that the medieval concord passes by and upholds *as* early, as fulfilling necessary yet partial functions in an evolving universe of whose real nature those functionaries are scarcely aware:

> Thus, all these fower (the which the ground-work bee
> Of all the world, and of all living wights)
> To thousand sorts of Change we subject see:
> Yet are they chang'd (by other wondrous slights)
> Into themselves, and lose their native mights;
> The Fire to Aire, and th'Ayre to Water sheere,
> And Water into Earth: yet Water fights
> With Fire, and Aire with Earth approaching neere:
> Yet all are in one body, and as one appeare.
>
> (vii.25)

Echoing this stanza at the end, Nature corrects and reinterprets the process, thus emphasizing Spenser's evolutionary view that things sustain and enrich themselves through self-surrender to the fated influences of time—fated because communicated from whole to part. Nature finds

> that all things stedfastnes doe hate
> And changed be: yet being rightly wayd
> They are not changed from their first estate;
> But by their change their being doe dilate:
> And turning to themselves at length againe,
> Doe worke their owne perfection so by fate. . . .
>
> (vii.58)

At once dynamic and organic, cyclical and developmental, this explanation is in direct contrast to Mutabilitie's image (emphasized by her jaggedly disjunctive "Yet . . . yet . . . yet" construction) of the elements fighting each other, becoming each other, and finally falling into the undifferentiated "one body."

In a rough way, the process of reinterpretation affects all the large-scale relations between the two cantos. The discourse on elemental flux may be linked to the earlier myth of the revolt of the titans by reference to Natalis Conti's reading of that myth as a symbol of *elementorum mutationes*. Mutabilitie's ascent to the house of Jove is translated from image to argument (vii.49–55) when she describes, in Ptolemaic order, changes in the planetary gods. Her beauty appears as the beauty of change in Nature's pageant. Jove's attempt to make her his mistress finds a parallel in his statement (vii.48) that although time and change rule in the lower world, they are controlled by the *vertue* poured "from our heavenly cell." The references to Astraea and Diana in the cycle of months (vii.37,39) allude glancingly to the rigor and questionable justice of the golden-age sensibility that dominated canto vi. All these parallels dramatically exhibit Nature's message that things—in this case, conceptions or interpretations—"by their change their being doe dilate." The continuity of cultural ideas is guaranteed by demythologizing the older pagan version and resymbolizing it in the newer medieval context.

The various characteristics of canto vii are vividly present in the set of stanzas devoted to Nature—not only those, noted above, that make its vision "later" and more positive than that of canto vi, but also those that arise from its deliberately imposed limits and exclusions. The latter are suggested by the sorting-out process that occupies the following stanzas:

> Now, at the time that was before agreed,
>   The Gods assembled all on Arlo Hill;
> As well those that are sprung of heavenly seed,

As those that all the other world doe fill,
And rule both sea and land unto their will:
Onely th'infernall Powers might not appear;
Aswell for horror of their count'naunce ill,
As for th'unruly fiends which they did feare;
Yet Pluto and Proserpino were present there.

And thither also came all other creatures,
    What-ever life or motion doe retaine,
    According to their sundry kinds of features;
    That Arlo scarsly could them all containe;
    So full they filled every hill and Plaine:
    And had not Natures Sergeant (that is Order)
    Them well disposed by his busie paine,
    And raunged farre abroad in every border,
They would have caused much confusion and disorder.

Then forth issewed (great goddesse) great dame Nature,
    With goodly port and gracious Majesty;
    Being far greater and more tall of stature
    Then any of the gods or Powers on hie:
    Yet certes by her face and physnomy,
    Whether she man or woman inly were,
    That could not any creature well descry:
    For, with a veile that wimpled every where,
Her head and face was hid, that mote to none appeare.

That some doe say was so by skill devised,
    To hide the terror of her uncouth hew,
    From mortall eyes that should be sore agrized;
    For that her face did like a Lion shew,
    That eye of wight could not indure to view:
    But others tell that it so beautious was,
    And round about such beames of splendor threw,
    That it the Sunne a thousand times did pass,
Ne could be seene, but like an image in a glass.

That well may seemen true: for, well I weene
    That this same day, when she on Arlo sat,
    Her garment was so bright and wondrous sheene,
    That my fraile wit cannot devize to what
    It to compare, nor finde like stuffe to that,
    As those three sacred Saints, though else most wise,
    Yet on mount Thabor quite their wits forgat,
    When they their glorious Lord in strange disguise
Transfigur'd sawe; his garments so did daze their eyes.

(vii.3–7)

As Spenser's earlier tongue-in-cheek reference (vi.36) to Arlo—
"Who knowes not Arlo-Hill?"—may have suggested, it is hardly a mythic
or literary landmark, and the contraction of the natural universe to a
somewhat eccentric locale works like a signature. Whatever vision we are
about to see will fit the modest scope of this poet's purposes and may be
expected to answer the previous episode. The visionary place must not
again be allowed to decline into a figure of contemporary actuality at its
worst. The polarity between recreative and plaintive modes, like that
between epic and pastoral genres, must be reconciled in the synthesis of
the later moral mode, as in the vision on Mount Acidale. Thus Spenser
begins by reversing the pattern of decline and instability that marked
the previous canto and by opposing to the sad-brow complaint of vi.1–6, a
creative sequence that depicts something like an accelerated cosmogony
and theogony: first, the sharing out of the universe among heavenly,
earthly, and infernal gods and powers, described in descending order and
logically followed by Pluto and Proserpina—logically, because they carry
us back from the depths to vernal earth and are admitted not only as
seasonal gods, but perhaps also as pagan divinities sustained and revised
by subsequent allegorization; next, the multitude of natural kinds and
creatures on whom order must be imposed just as, in other Spenserian
contexts, *eros* aligns the elements emergent from chaos (HL 71–91); third,
the appearance not of the fecund source itself, but of its personification.
Nature is described first as a goddess and then as greater than the gods,
first as possibly mortal (male or female) and then as a transcendent
mystery, first as the primitive form of Venus (the Magna Mater, goddess
of lions and the law of the claw) then as a later conception, the symbol of
heavenly beauty (Sapience). The image takes on added richness if seen to
include and develop Spenser's own earlier images, especially the veiled
Venus of IV.x–xi:

> So fertile be the flouds in generation,
> So huge their numbers, and so numberlesse their nation.
>
> Therefore the antique wisards well invented,
> That Venus of the fomy sea was bred. . . .

In rejecting the lion-headed figure, preferring the sun-headed figure, and comparing himself to the biblical observers of the Transfiguration, Spenser at once moves Nature more definitely toward a Christian
context and affirms his own selective and retrospective presence. His
reference to Chaucer and Alanus two stanzas later specifies the Christian
context as medieval, but also as secular and literary: Chaucer, the "pure
well head of Poesie" did not dare describe such radiance,

But it transferd to Alane, who he thought
Had in his Plaint of kindes describ'd it well:
Which who will read set forth so as it ought,
Go seek he out that Alane where he may be sought.

(vii.9)

In following his *auctor's* example, he fixes the image at a certain historical distance from the present. At the same time, in stanzas 8 and 10, he establishes Nature in a *locus amoenus* reminiscent of the *Foules parley* as well as of his own ideal gardens: the earth "her self of her owne motion" produced a pavilion of trees that seemed to do homage to Nature and "like a throne did shew"—"Not such as Craftes-men by their idle skill / Are wont for Princes states to fashion"; flowers "voluntary grew / Out of the ground," and seemed richer "then any tapestry, / That Princes bowres adorne with painted imagery." Human art and government are together excluded from this idyllic order whose ease and security are guaranteed by a transcendent power of nature. It is typical of this familiar pastoral logic that it blends subhuman and superhuman nature together to produce a model of sure spontaneous behavior in which the subjects (*natura naturata*) both automatically and voluntarily express the will of the ruler (*natura naturans*)—a model free of the pride and weakness of fallen human nature.

The infernal powers, the "confusion and disorder" that call forth the "busie paine" of Nature's Sergeant, the lion-headed goddess, the prideful luxury of princes—these are mentioned in order to be excluded. After a glance at his own earlier pastoral (the vernal renewal of Mole in vii.11), Spenser circles back to the epic marriage of Peleus and Thetis "On Haemus hill"(vii.12), a pagan prevision of "the *paradis terrestre* in which man lived before the apple thrown by Discord, that *diable d'enfer*, began our woe." From the unfallen nature on Haemus to the resurrected nature on Thabor and Arlo, and from the archaic god's-eye view of Phoebus ("that god of Poets hight" who, they say, "did sing the spousall hymn" of Peleus and Thetis) to the saintly vision and its analogues in the redactions of later poets, Spenser overleaps the valleys of fallen nature, synoptically compressing into Arlo's middle height a history of apocalyptic moments, summits of redeemed time and purged vision. Present-as-excluded are those socio-political problems that lead to the breaking of the laws "of Justice and of Policie." The prohibition of the infernal powers who administer the irreversible doom of Hell is a logical consequence of this exclusion.

The creatures on Arlo are specified in terms of "life or motion"; man, if he is included, is present only as a member of this organic domain. Later, when the pageant of seasons and months reaches out to embrace human activities, love, recreation, procreation, and labor—it absorbs them into the securely determined cycles of "the lawes of Nature," cycles whose upward thrust from winter to spring and death to life is carefully emphasized. This benign pattern of continuity, positive change, and birth and rebirth is condensed into the familiar paradoxes of the brief concluding description of Nature:

> This great Grandmother of all creatures bred
> Great Nature, ever young yet full of eld,
> Still mooving, yet unmoved from her sted;
> Unseene of any, yet of all beheld. . . .
>
> (vii.13)

The antithesis "unseene/beheld" is blunted by the fact that the latter term may mean "possessed." Nature is possessed by, held in the forms of, all its creatures, and is therefore visible to its creatures, perhaps also is viewed mentally as in a vision. This is a more dynamic, powerful, and beneficent figure than the goddess described at vii.5–6, and Spenser's circling back to the second passage from the first gives the effect of an advance, for he has shifted attention from her garments and visual presence to her operations and inner nature. The paradoxes are interpreted by the preceding stanzas in such a way as to infold both the cyclical and developmental patterns, since the renewal is cultural and linear as well as seasonal and recurrent. The underlying matrix, "full of eld," gives rise not only to various living kinds but also to various human conceptions of nature. Thus great Nature may be the effect as well as the cause of all creatures—"of all creatures bred."

The ideal and idyllic qualities of this medieval vision derive from its dialectical relation to canto vi; it is *an* improvement over the pagan viewpoint, but not *the* final improvement. As a reaction to the golden-age pessimism underlying canto vi, it swings a little too far in the opposite direction, providing not a tentative *discordia concors*, but a carefully purified *concordia discors* whose climax is the cycle of seasons and months. In its elliptically emblematic reference to—and coordination of—human, seasonal, and zodiacal phenomena, this pageant attains to a cosmic synthesis sufficiently panoranic in scale to minimize the subtle yet fundamental problems of social life and human relations. The vast network of psycho-social and psycho-cultural problems considered throughout *The Faerie Queene*, and especially in its last three complete books, is admitted in allusion, echoes, and oblique references. But it is present-as-excluded; it is either resolved into the limited context of nature's round, or muffled, pushed into the background, by the hieratic quality of the pageant. What the poet stresses, especially in the more vivid genre-life details, are natural problems—hunger, age, heat, and cold—and these are so closely observed that they tend to divert our attention from the symbols of the other, less simple, evils. By these devices, the poet reminds us of the fact that his vision of nature has been selectively refined and idealized.

This is why we must not confuse Spenser's picture of the medieval mind with what are often thought of as Spenser's medieval habits of mind. Commentators frequently have noted the medieval texture of the canto in term of the sources and traditions behind it, for example,

> for such images as the signs of the zodiac, the personification of the seasons and the months, the council of the gods, and the allegorical debate, dozens of analogues in medieval plastic and literary art make source hunting unnecessary.

> For centuries the months and their labors appeared over and over again in calendars and books of hours, above the portals of cathedrals, in handbooks and encyclopedias, signifying that the divisions of time . . . are part of the divine plan, and that by labor man works out his own place in it. The medieval man who paused to contemplate the great stone calendar over a church door found various meanings there, . . . and all of them apply to Spenser's Calendar.

If this vision is particularly attractive to Spenser, it is not because he is uncritically traditional or unconsciously medieval. The medieval mind may have believed in this vision as a divine and providential work, a panoramic picture of God's real order of nature. But Spenser employs the technique of conspicuous allusion in this canto not only to distance that vision in terms of cultural time, but also to emphasize its artistic and artificial quality. The essence of the order is so clearly dependent upon and communicated by its artistic organization, the whole harmony of the natural universe is so dramatically foreshortened and its rhythms condensed by Spenser's symbolic shorthand, that we are impressed primarily by the synoptic power of the human poet's imagination. This impression is heightened by the forms that comprise the network of allusion: literature, pageantry, emblematic imagery, ancient cosmological speculation, the arts of relief and illumination, judicial process, and debate.

The two cantos I have just discussed develop a cosmic rather than a microcosmic vision; their subject is the harmonious order of the physical and organic universe; the domain of the human psyche and society as such is not included as an object in that field; human attitudes have been externalized into pagan and medieval world views. The concluding stanzas move beyond the vision into the mind that has unfolded it and into the lyric moment evoked by that unfolding:

When I bethinke me on that speech whyleare,
  Of Mutability, and well it way:
  Me seemes, that though she all unworthy were
  Of the Heav'ns Rule; yet very sooth to say,
  In all things else she beares the greatest sway,
  Which makes me loath this state of life so tickle,
  And love of things so vaine to cast away;
  Whose flowring pride, so fading and so fickle,
Short Time shall soon cut down with his consuming sickle.

Then gin I thinke on that which Nature sayd,
  Of that same time when no more Change shall be,
  But stedfast rest of all things firmely stayd
  Upon the pillours of Eternity,
  That is contrayr to Mutabilitie:
  For, all that moveth, doth in change delight:
  But thence-forth all shall rest eternally
  With Him that is the God of Sabbaoth hight:
Of that great Sabbaoth God, graunt me that Sabbaoths sight.

There is an uncertainty of tone reflected especially in the ambiguous syntax of the first stanza, lines six and seven: (1) "This thought makes me loathe this unstable life, and makes me (to) cast away the love of things"; (2) "I am loth to cast away this state of life and this love of things." As an adjective, *vaine* could modify either *love* or *things*: the love may be vain not because things are vanity, but because all such attachments are doomed; things are loved because they flower into brief beauty, perhaps in vain. In the adverbial position, *vaine* enforces the second alternative: the state of life and love of things may be vainly put off if no experience or vision can attain to what lies beyond the mutable whirl. Similarly, the often noted doubt about *Sabbaoth* (meaning either rest or host) carries the unresolved feeling through to the end: (1) "Grant me the vision of that final rest"—or, more forcefully, "Grant me its prospect, put it within reach"; (2) "Grant me a vision of that Host"—the armies of the saved, the children of the spirit, the Host assembled at the end of time. He wants to get beyond the clutches of change, and the first emphasis is simply upon escape. But he also wants to carry the variety up with him—"all things firmely stayd." The doubts of the first stanza suggest the added possibility that he may be asking to see this vision *now*, while alive, since he cannot be certain of what is to come. And though these stanzas have been described as moments of prayer, they express, as Watkins has put it, "desire rather than affirmation." The final line is not a great leap through faith; it is a slow and guarded turning *toward* prayer and faith, moving from mere indication ("Him that is . . .") through half-apostrophe

("O *that* great Sabbaoth God") to the final direct exhortation. It is as if, should he turn too quickly, too hopefully, too unguardedly, nothing would be there.

Though the conclusion may be called plaintive, this does not mean that—in Greene's words—if Spenser's faith "is indeed a refuge here, it is a lonely and bitter one." For we have moved, through the two cantos, from one sort of complaint to another, and from a plaintive attitude dramatically, impersonally, given play by the man-as-poet, to a plaintive attitude affecting the poet-as-man as he considers what he has made. The first complaint is based upon rejection, upon fear of life, upon disillusionment with the world, upon the desire to escape from the world as it is and return to some pristine mythical state that the mind locates before time and change. The final complaint arises from so strong an involvement in and attachment to, such utter delight in the changing world, that the poet bemoans its fragility. "Spenser . . . has made the inevitable confession, that he loves all changing, mortal things too much, and they are betraying him. . . . the commitments to mortality have gone too deep to allow [the renunciation of earthly love]." Having oscillated between the elemental divisions of pagan pessimism and the organic harmony of medieval optimism, he attains to a more complicated and dynamic equilibrium at the end, still looking backward, still thrusting forward, still revolving doubts.

Cheney has described as follows the "mixture of opposing attitudes with which Mutabilitie is being viewed":

> One pole of this opposition is the Christian *contemptus mundi*, the feeling of exhaustion and disdain for this world and intense longing for the combination of absolute delight and absolute rest to be found through death in the "Sabaoths sight" hinted by nature. At the other pole is the artist's delight in the inexhaustible variety of his creation. . . .

The first sentence needs some modification; the attitudes described here resemble those that reciprocally reinforce each other in canto vi and that are overcome by the shift in canto vii to the variety of natural and artistic creation. What is required after canto vi is a redistribution of values and a redirection of longing; earthly life must be enhanced, the absolute must be distanced or veiled, and the distinction between the mundane and the transcendent more rigorously honored. This theme is touched upon in two passages: At vi.32 Jove criticizes Mutabilitie for wanting "Through some vaine errour or inducement light, / To see that mortall eyes have never seene"; and at vi.46 Spenser chides Faunus for breaking out into laughter because he cannot contain his "great joy of some-what he did spy"—

"Babblers unworthy been of so divine a meed." These are comic images of the "intense longing for . . . absolute delight" and vision, for the unveiled nearness of divinity, and for possession of the god's-eye view—a longing entailed by "disdain for this world."

The poem as a whole enacts a turning away from these conjoined opposites. Thus in canto vi the "highest heaven" is identified with Jove, whereas in canto vii we find a higher celestial region (the zodiacal sphere of the fixed stars) and clues to the very different spiritual heaven clearly disclosed only in the final stanza of the poem. The contrast of genres in canto vi intensifies the pastoral insignificance of the earthly episode; the perspective on both episodes, visually or qualitatively, is that of the gods (Mutabilitie, Jove, Diana), whereas their burden centers on the departure of a goddess from an unworthy and ruined earth, an earth seen by the uncomfortable ruling pantheon as the chief source of danger. The poet's initial gesture in canto vii is to move higher up for a more panoramic and harmonious view, then to settle into the middle region of Christian pastoral on Arlo. By the time he has described Arlo and Nature, this view has been further defined and "lowered"—located in terms of a particular cultural moment, a literary tradition, and his own limited, selective vision (his reliance on sources, his effort to make adequate comparisons, the weakness of mortal sight). This "descent" of viewpoint and desire is traced in the sequence of summits and seers: first, the easy mixture of mortal and immortal elements in the marriage of Haemus, whose singer was the god of poets himself; second, the more miraculous moment of transfiguration, seen by saintly mortals, symbolizing both the absolute transcendence of Christ, and his promise to resurrect earthly nature; third, the literary vision on Arlo, a fable invented by the humanistic poet who gives it historical distance by looking through medieval eyes and through a variety of traditional modes of expression.

This psychological movement of the point of view and of desire down into earth and history appears in other details. The second description of Nature is "lower" than the first, and though Mutabilitie calls her "Goddess" after this, the poet himself does not. The two specific references to Christian belief are both to Christ—his transfiguration and incarnation (vii.41). The pageant itself is centered on earthly activities as the focus of cosmic motions. In all these ways, then, the seventh canto reverses the upward- and outward-bound thrust of the pagan sensibility with its unguardedly childlike anthropomorphism. Canto vii places in high relief the archaic impulse to unify heaven and earth on earthly terms that presume to raise men closer to gods while actually lowering heaven to put it within the finite reach of man. The Christian answer to this centers on the paradigm of the Incarnation. Whereas the pagans envisaged their deities as human in form and behavior but remote from man in attitude, the three-personed God is mysterious and remote from man in terms of behavior, much closer to man in the manifestations of his love. The unbridgeable gap between man and a God who is Wholly Other requires God to descend. The descent, in enhancing fallen nature by expressing God's love for it, urges man to cherish not disdain it.

But from the standpoint of the sixteenth-century poet, this good news, along with its medieval edition, was delivered long ago; man's problems and attitudes were changed, but not automatically resolved thereby. Although Spenser opens himself to the consoling harmony of the medieval world view, his stylized presentation is itself a way of lowering and limiting that view, since it declares its origins in the mind and art and culture of man. The Nature of canto vii is less easily identifiable with those aspects of divine providence to which it ostensibly refers than with the creative process of poetic imagination. This is suggested by Cheney's phrase, "the artist's delight in the unexhaustible variety of *his* creation" (italics mine). The organization, emblems, images, *topoi*, and personifications (including Nature herself) are generated by the intercourse between nature as underlying matrix and the poet's mind. Toward the end of the canto, after the processes of nature have been unfolded in the discourse on elements, the pageant, and the passage on planetary gods, Natura is even more closely linked to the poet. Firmly personified at vii.57, she speaks for the first time, then vanishes "whither no man wist," concurrently with the canto's last words. "Her doome" sets forth in a plain statement what the entire canto has already enacted: The poet's moral or argument is simply placed in her mouth, and immediately after, he gives the phrase "turning to themselves at length againe" a new direction by turning to consider his own state of mind as affected by the argument.

Such an identification of nature with art places a heavy burden and a high value upon the work of the human mind and the function of man's art and vision. For where else if not here is the summit and fulfillment of created nature to be found? If, as many Renaissance and Reformation thinkers suspected, the forces of reality both transcend and differ in character from their equivalent forms in the mind, how else can they be even obscurely adumbrated? If God makes the world, it is His collaborator, man, who makes world views. However insubstantial the pageant of human forms in nature, culture, art, and play, it may yet be the only token, the only record and impress of a power that may not find expression after man has had his day: "If it be now, 'tis not to come; if it be not to come, it will be now." But the poet cherishes at the end of the poem the hope that "if it be not now, yet it will come; the readiness is all. Since no man has aught of what he leaves, what is't to leave betimes? Let be."

Yet these assertions of man's shaping power can be taken seriously only if they do not claim too much, only if made tentatively and experimentally, placed in quotation marks, or in the presumptive fiction of play and poem. The magic and triumph of art resides in its ability to indicate the reality before which all art fails. When this happens, make-believe becomes "unrealistic," its tissue grows artificial, diaphanous to the point of vanishing. To be closed within the poet's secure second nature, to substitute *a world view* for *the world*, to long for solutions and resolutions not found in life, is to confuse the true *contemptus mundi* with "the feeling of exhaustion and disdain for this world." Thus Spenser shifts and opens his prospect throughout the poem, discloses new depths and distances continually emerging and continually receding. In the final moment the furthest depth is touched, but only lightly touched, for the poet's long brooding, his slow turning, his tone of reaching and beseeching, express a Sabbaoth God still moving away from man approaching.

ISABEL G. MacCAFFREY

Allegory and Pastoral
in "The Shepheardes Calender"

To read the large-scale masterpieces of Elizabethan literature with something of the agility they assume and demand is an art which must be self-consciously cultivated by us today. *The Shepheardes Calender*, an early, relatively brief essay in a complex mode, provides exercise for our wit in smaller compass. We ought, I believe, to bring to it something of the same resources that we bring to Spenser's larger work. As Ernest de Selincourt wrote, "It lies along the high-road that leads him to Faery land." It is the product of the same sensibility, and in it we can discern the special proclivities of the poet's imagination: the preference for radical allegory and "iconographical ambiguity"; the search for a form that will contain variety and unify it without violating its subtle life-patterns; the exploitation of a setting that can also serve as a complex controlling metaphor. The great invention of Faerie Land is anticipated by Spenser's evocation of the archetypal hills, valleys, woods, and pastures of the *Calender*.

Early critics tended to read the work as a kind of anthology, a series of experiments in various verse-forms; Spenser's themes, conceived as subordinate to his forms, could be subsumed under E. K.'s categories, plaintive, moral, and recreative. The poem's reputation has taken an upward turn in the past few years, accompanied by a critical tendency to stress the unifying power of its metaphors, and there have been several attempts to reduce its pattern to a single thematic statement. The reconstruction of the poem's composition by Paul McLane suggests the difficul-

From *English Literary History* 1, vol. 36 (March 1969). Copyright © 1969 by The Johns Hopkins University Press.

ties of determining the history of Spenser's intention; but McLane's conclusion supports the inclination of modern readers to see the *Calender* as the product of a unified design, eventually more or less explicit in the poet's imagination.

While it is, I believe, essential to assume that *The Shepheardes Calender* makes sense as a whole, many readings of it, though subtly argued, in the end ignore certain of its elements that may not conform to the proposed pattern. A. C. Hamilton's discussion of the poet's "effort to find himself," R. A. Durr's distinction "between the flesh and the spirit, *amor carnis* and *amor spiritus*," M. C. Bradbrook's thesis that Spenser deals with "the pursuit of honour, surveyed from what was traditionally the lowest of human occupations"—all of these accounts, and others, offer us valuable perspectives on Spenser's themes. But all underestimate the power of the poet's imagination, its world-making energy, its drive toward comprehensiveness, its urge to include rather than to exclude meanings.

This energy is visible at the start in Spenser's very choice of forms. His "originality" lay in combining a group of eclogues with a calendar framework, that is, variety with unity. It is a typically Spenserian invention: the two forms neutralize each other's disadvantages and cooperate to produce a structure that uniquely combines symbolic range and resonance with the most fundamental ordering pattern in our experience, the life-cycle itself. The etymology of *eclogue* encourages us to view the separate poems as independent "selections"; the calendar offers the limitation of a circumscribing frame at once linear and cyclical. In consequence, the *Calender* already exhibits the formal paradoxes that confront us in infinite recombination in *The Faerie Queene*: discontinuous continuity, multiple reference, analogical relationships that point simultaneously to likeness and to unlikeness.

These paradoxes are set in motion and contained by the pastoral paradigm, which is to some degree implied by both of the poem's formal components, eclogue and calendar. Development of the implications of pastoral in the early Renaissance had brought it to a point of relative sophistication which was exploited and then notably extended in Spenser's poem. It is important to realize that by the 1570's, the paradigm was not confined exclusively to idyllic themes. Originating in the impulse to criticize artificial and corrupt urban civilization, the pastoral "world" itself was soon infected by that corruption and became in turn the object of critical scrutiny. In the eclogues of Mantuan and Barnabe Googe, the pastoral metaphor is microcosmic, and the preoccupations of fallen man, as well as his vision of unfallen bliss, can be accommodated within it. So, in the *Calender*, Spenser's imagined world includes storms and sunshine, friendly and hostile landscapes, benevolent and ravenous animals, good and bad shepherds, high and low personages. The poet has chosen not to limit himself to the merely idyllic version of pastoral. This choice is reflected in the formal range of the *Calender*. The decorum of the convention dictated that it move, stylistically, in a temperate zone between the heights of epic and tragedy, and the depths of satirical comedy; the range was wide enough, however, to permit excursions into both these extreme borderlands, as the *Maye* and *October* eclogues demonstrate. The twin concepts of the calendar, with its changing seasons and months, and of the eclogue-group, with its changing metrical and tonal patterns, thus combine with the multiple references of sophisticated pastoral to compose a design of rich potentiality. Above all, this complex literary paradigm offers a context hospitable to allegory: as A. C. Hamilton has said, "the most obvious parallel between the *Calender* and [*The Faerie Queene*] is that each is radically allegorical."

We have to ask, then, what the nature and concern of the allegory may be; and the answer must resemble the answers we devise in commenting on the much more complex allegory of the later poem. Paul McLane has observed that Colin Clout's career is like that of "the main characters of the *Faerie Queene*, most of whom lead a double or triple life on the various levels of the poem." Though the metaphor of "levels" is, I believe, one that we ought to discard in speaking of allegory, McLane's point concerning the multiple life of Colin can be extended to all the major images of the *Calender*. An obvious example is provided by the avatars of Pan, who figures as Henry VIII, as the "God of shepheards all," and as Christ, "the onely and very Pan, then suffering for his flock." These meanings are not equally valid or ultimate, metaphysically, but they are equally potent in the poem, and they imply each other. We lose something by insisting on any single meaning of a Spenserian image, for the reason that all the meanings are related to and shed light on each other. The "statement" incarnate in each thus includes a comment on the relationship of a particular imagining to congruent ones. The *Calender*, like *The Faerie Queene*, is encyclopedic in its design, for Spenser's imagination (like Milton's) is most at home when it is working in a context that can include, or at least allude to, the entire cosmic order. The poem's concern is the nature of human life—our life's shape and quality, its form, its content or "feel," and ultimately its relation to the one life outside and beyond it.

It is this effort at comprehensiveness that makes us uneasy with any single formula for the *Calender*'s meaning, whether religious, social, or metaphysical. Boccaccio's defense of the poet's fictions includes the remark that images are used to "make truths . . . the object of strong intellectual effort and various interpretation." Pope, who thought *The Shepheardes Calender* "sometimes too allegorical," praised the poems basic metaphor because it allowed Spenser to expose "to his readers a view of the great and little worlds, and their various changes and aspects." He is speaking of the pastoral which, like the calendar frame, encourages, indeed demands, variety of reference; in Puttenham's famous phrase, it was devised "to insinuate and glaunce at greater matters," which, as W. L. Renwick pointed out in the commentary to his edition, could refer to several kinds of subject. "Since all personal and contemporary affairs were proper subject for Pastoral, the interpretation of the simple allegory is various: the shepherds are poets, scholars, governors, ecclesiastics, by a series of easy allusions." All of these matters, in Spenser's imagination, involved each other; each area of "meaning" overlaps with the others, and each alone can offer only an incomplete statement concerning human life.

Renaissance and medieval ontology provided, of course, a rationale for a literature of multiple significances. In a world of concentric realities, a single metaphor could touch several circumferences in one trajectory; intersecting a number of different but analogous worlds, it could speak of church, of state, of poetry, of the individual soul's destiny, of divine providence as manifested in the cosmic pattern. It is well to remind ourselves of this relationship between the literature and the "world picture" of the Elizabethans, for although it has now become a cliché, it lends point to the choice of allegory as the vehicle for major works by Spenser and others, as well as to the development of a drama with broad symbolic resources. For Spenser, the interlocking complexities of reality could only be rendered accurately in a sequence of metaphors susceptible of simultaneous reference—that is, the continued metaphor of allegory.

The Shepheardes Calender, then, as Spenser's first attempt to devise a "visionary geography," must be read as an anticipation of his greatest work. The formal differences between the two poems are, of course, obvious. The continuousness of the metaphor in the *Calender* is not that of narrative; the poem "has a situation but no plot." The ground-metaphor of *The Faerie Queene* is the chivalric world of Faerie Land, a place where lives unfold and journeys are traced. Time dominates the *Calender* not as the medium of narrative, but as a geometric pattern which may be described schematically as a circle intersected by linear tracks. The space of the poem is an imagined space whose emblematic features conform to the particular circumstances of each eclogue and are related to those of other eclogues, both adjacent and remote. All of them are drawn from the body of images loosely contained within the pastoral paradigm, but spatial continuity, like narrative line, is not to be insisted upon. The description of the structure by W. W. Greg is still the most comprehensive and objective:

> The architectonic basis of Spenser's design consists of the three Colin eclogues standing respectively at the beginning, in the middle, and at the close of the year. These are symmetrically arranged . . . [and supported] by two subsidiary eclogues, those of April and August, in both of which another shepherd sings one of Colin's lays. . . . It is upon this framework that are woven the various moral, polemical, and idyllic themes which Spenser introduces.

In this geometrical structure, the poem's meaning is figured. As almost every recent critic has said, that meaning somehow concerns man's relation to the cycle of nature. Spenser is considering the degree to which "natural" terms must enter into a definition of what man is; we are made aware of the pattern of human life as biologically cyclical, but also as spiritually transcendent in various directions: hence the design of linear or vertically oriented images intersecting the circular ground-plan. [As the critic Kathleen Williams notes,] "Man is part of nature, but this world's brief beauty gives him less than he asks, and though he loves it he needs to look beyond it. . . . For us the natural cycle is in itself the way of death, and we will gain life only by looking to the cycle's source."

The character whose life is defined by these patterns, as Greg's description properly points out, is Colin Clout. Yet exclusive concentration on Colin may obscure Spenser's purpose; if this hero is a pilgrim, he never attains the Heavenly City, and it is left to other voices to define for us the alternatives to the life within "nature" figured by Colin's career. His life is congruent with the circle's movement toward "experience" and imminent death. He is an anti-hero, his unredeemed existence tracing a movement which defines the failure of man to realize his *own* nature. Colin recognizes that submission to the seasonal round has led only to death: "So now my yeare drawes to his latter terme" (*Dec.* 127); his life has passed like a dream, and bidding adieu to the "delightes, that lulled me asleepe" (151), he is left alone in a winter landscape.

Colin's uncompleted quest for understanding is expressed in the poem by a sequence of changes in the relationship between nature and man, devised with a good deal of subtlety by Spenser to provide simultaneously a commentary upon a critique of the macrocosm / microcosm analogy at the root of the pastoral paradigm. The *Calender* begins in January, principally so that Spenser may stress the circular pattern by framing his poem with "winter" eclogues. Since *Januarye* is also the first stage in Spenser's critique of his analogical base, we must see man and nature in it as congruent. Hence, when the poem begins, the protagonist has already suffered disillusionment as the result of love-longing; "his carefull case" resembles "the sadde season of the yeare," as the Argument painstakingly indicates. In fact, we are to see Colin in unwounded innocence only through the reminiscences of other shepherds. The Colin of *Januarye*, however, is still a *literary* innocent; in making his comparison between careful case and sad season, he uses the metaphor of the mirror, indicating that for him the macrocosm still reflects accurately the little world of man, offering valid analogies for his inner state:

> And from mine eyes the drizling teares descend,
> As on your boughes the ysicles depend.
>
> (41–42)

In *Iune*, however, as Greg points out, Spenser devises "a specific inversion of the 'pathetic fallacy' " in order to express Colin's literary disillusionment. The insights of experience include the recognition that a naive version of the pastoral metaphor inadequately expresses reality. It is no accident that in *Iune* Colin explicitly renounces the "rymes and roundelayes" of his youth, thus described by Hobbinol:

> Whose Echo made the neyghbour groues to ring,
> And taught the byrds, which in the lower spring
> Did shroude in shady leaues from sonny rayes,
> Frame to thy songe their chereful cheriping.
>
> (52–5)

The relationship of sound to echo, a version of the mirror-image of *Januarye*, is shown to be invalid in June when the harmonies of nature clash with the disharmony of Colin's suffering. He is exiled from Paradise, and those songs now seem to him "weary wanton toyes" (48).

In *December*, Colin reflects on life and death, finally recognizing, and despairingly accepting, the fundamental incongruity of man and nature. His Muse is "hoarse and weary"; his pipe is hung up on a tree (140–41).

> And I, that whilome wont to frame my pype,
> Vnto the shifting of the shepheards foote:
> Sike follies nowe haue gathered as too ripe
> And cast hem out, as rotten and vnsoote.
>
> (115–18)

Those aspects of his life which indicate its congruence with nature are unsatisfying or inadequate to the demands made upon them. The old

Colin is wise in nature's ways; he has learned "the soothe of byrds" and "the power of herbs," yet this knowledge is of no avail in curing his "ranckling wound."

> But ah vnwise and witlesse *Colin cloute*,
> That kydst the hidden kinds of many a wede:
> Yet kydst not ene to cure thy sore hart roote,
> Whose ranckling wound as yet does rifelye bleede.
>
> (91–4)

The metaphor of unripeness, which Milton was later to develop in the opening lines of *Lycidas*, insists that fulfilment for man cannot be looked for within the cycle.

> The flatring fruite is fallen to grownd before,
> And rotted, ere they were halfe mellow ripe.
>
> (106–7)

The life of Colin Clout, then, traces for us the line of human life as it diverges psychologically from the life of nature, while remaining physically bound to it. The event which allows this divergence to manifest itself is a familiar one in pastoral poetry from Theocritus to Marvell. It is love, the disturber of pastoral harmony, a metaphor for the troubling of human life which we call sin—that is, the dominance of passion. It is, as Colin says, the result of pride: "But ah such pryde at length was ill repayde" by Cupid (*Dec.* 49). In consequence the orderly cycle of human life is turned awry, its promise blasted. This melancholy situation is depicted in Theocritus' eighth Idyll, as rendered by an anonymous translator of 1588:

> A tempest marreth trees; and drought, a spring:
> Snares unto foules, to beastes, netts are a smarte;
> Love spoiles a man.

Mantuan's *Eclogue II* (Turberville's translation) describes the pains of the "unlucky lad" Amyntas:

> Forgetful he of former flocke, and damage done with knaves,
> Was all inraged with this flash; at night he nought but raves.
> The season that for quiet sleepe by nature poynted was,
> In bitter plaintes and cruell cries, this burning Boy did passe.

And Marvell's Mower, in the century after Spenser, complains of the "unusual Heats" that accompany Juliana:

> This heat the Sun could never raise,
> Nor Dog-star so inflame's the dayes.

It from an higher Beauty grow'th,
Which burns the Fields and Mower both:
Which mads the Dog, and makes the Sun
Hotter than his own *Phaeton*.
Not *July* causeth these extremes,
But *Juliana's* scorching beams.

The interesting feature of all these descriptions of love lies in their stress on the disruption of macrocosmic harmony. Images of tempest, drought, insomnia, and withered grass became appropriate figures for man's fallen state, the seasons' difference that signifies the penalty of Adam. In the Argument to *December* Colin's "summer"is meteorologically described: "which he sayth, was consumed with greate heate and excessiue drouth caused throughe a Comet or blasinge starre, by which he meaneth loue, which passion is comenly compared to such flames and immoderate heate." Colin himself repeats the point:

A comett stird vp that vnkindly heate,
That reigned (as men sayd) in *Venus seate*.
(59–60)

The congruence between man's nature and external nature is violently reestablished in a baleful conjunction of planets and passions; the analogy becomes a kind of parody upon the harmonious prelapsarian unity.

The pastoral metaphor is further developed in *Iulye*, in which Colin does not figure and where Spenser sophisticates the man / nature relationship with specific reference to the Fall of Man and the loss of the eternal spring of Paradise. This eclogue, like *Damon the Mower*, identifies unusual heats with a higher cause, but theological rather than amorous. In an astrological passage, the shepherd Thomalin deplores the weather of the dog days and declines to ascend the hills where he will be exposed to it.

And now the Sonne hath reared vp
  his fyrie footed teme.
Making his way betweene the Cuppe,
  and golden Diademe:
The rampant Lyon hunts he fast,
  with Dogge of noysome breath,
Whose balefull barking bringes in hast
  pyne, plagues, and dreery death.
Agaynst his cruell scortching heate
  where hast thou couerture?
(17–26)

The hills have been unsafe for man, Spenser goes on to say, ever since "by his foly one did fall," to make us all exiles. Sin thus condemns man to live in an unsheltered world, hostile and uncongenial, characterized by unhappy love, alienation from God, and finally, the despair of *December*.

Spenser develops the theme of exposure to a hostile environment in several of the eclogues, and in varying tones. In *Iune*, the outcast Colin "Can nowhere fynd, to shroude my lucklesse pate" (16). In the quaint fable at the end of *Iulye*, the good Algrin meets the fate of Aeschylus. His "bared scalpe" has been the target for a shellfish dropped by an eagle, and he now "lyes in lingring peyne" (221, 228), a warning against exposure to the rigors of the heights. A different sort of exposure, another kind of hostility, are displayed in the "recreative" mood of *March*. In this eclogue, the shepherd Thomalin, like Colin when we first meet him, is already love-wounded. Spenser recounts the process by which the wounding occurred, the surprising of Cupid "within an Yuie todde" and the god's mocking revenge for having been hunted. *March* is playful, even trivial, but it is integrated into the scheme of the *Calender*, obliquely through the analogue with Colin, and more directly as one of Spenser's presentations of the dangers that attend our lives. Willye's account of his father's adventure with Cupid extends the relevance of the little incident.

> For once I heard my father say,
> How he him caught vpon a day,
> (Whereof he wilbe wroken)
> Entangled in a fowling net,
> Which he for carrion Crowes had set,
> That in our Peeretree haunted.
> (106–11)

It is an experience that recurs in each generation, indeed in almost every human life. In the spring of all our years, "lustie Loue" awakens and makes sport of us; the paradox of the huntsman ensnared expresses a characteristic experience. No shepherd, "wandring vp and downe the lande" (64), is safe, the darts of love will penetrate his presumption, as the shellfish punished the innocent aspiration of Algrin in *Iulye*.

The notion of an environment that is hostile to man is, of course, one of the insights of experience, which moves from "soft" to "hard" pastoral. Spenser traces this process in the dialogue between youth and age in *Februarie*; and it is figuratively reiterated by Colin, looking back over his life:

> Where I was wont to seeke the honey Bee,
> Working her formall rowmes in Wexen frame:
> The grieslie Todestoole growne there mought I see

> And loathed Paddocks lording on the same.
>   And where the chaunting birds luld me a sleepe,
>   The ghastlie Owle her grieuous ynne doth keepe.
>   (Dec. 67–72)

The emblem of an orderly nature that offers a model for man gives way to the *décor* of death. In fact, Nature is a threat to man, who must assume with respect to it an attitude of constant vigilance. The darkest eclogue of *The Shepheardes Calendar* is *September* where the theme of the watchful shepherd is presented in the fable of Roffyn and the wolf. Diggon Davie anticipates Colin's figure of the sleep of illusion as he points the moral:

> How, but with heede and watchfulnesse,
> Forstallen hem of their wilinesse?
> For thy with shepheard sittes not playe,
> Or sleepe, as some doen, all the long day.
>   (230–33)

It is a harsher version of the austere message of Piers in *Maye*. Hobbinol's protesting reply to Diggon conveys, beneath the speaker's hedonism, despair and a sense of inevitable decay.

> Ah Diggon, thilke same rule were too straight,
> All the cold season to wach and waite.
> We bene of fleshe, men as other bee.
> Why should we be bound to such miseree?
> What euer thing lacketh chaungeable rest,
> Mought needes decay, when it is at best.
>   (236–41)

At the end, in answer to Diggon's question, "what way shall I wend, / My piteous plight and losse to amend?" he can offer only stoic retirement to his cottage until "fayrer Fortune" shall prevail (244–5, 257). Blindfolded, fickle Fortune, Milton's "blind Fury," was the favorite Renaissance emblem for the random, meaningless condition of earthly life. Hobbinol's solution sounds naive, and is meant to; Colin in *Iune* admired him as a model of pastoral harmony, but *September* may be read as an ironic commentary on that vision of regained Paradise. Hobbinol could not, then, cure Colin, nor can he now evade the fact that men of flesh are "bound to . . . miseree." Diggon is being punished for his foolhardiness in seeking an "vncouth" fortune outside his pastoral homeland; but this exile is the fate of each of us and should not be construed as merely another critique of "ambition." Diggon is not a "worldes childe" in the sense that Spenser uses that phrase of Palinode in *Maye*. His comments on life's bleakness are generalized in the fable of *September*. Roffyn, Colin Clout's master, is clearly a virtuous shepherd, "meeke, wise, and merciable" (174), as well as "Argus eyed" (203); his misfortune, and his vigilance, express the eclogue's theme: "God shield man, he should so ill haue thriue" (226).

Immediately following the nadir of *September*, the *Calender* takes an upward turn. If we look at the structure as a whole, not merely at the Colin "plot," we can observe Spenser causing his form to cooperate with his theme. As E. K. observes, *October* and *Nouember* are in a higher mood than any of the eclogues that preceded them (with the exception of the *Aprill* lay). We ought to take seriously his epithet for October, "loftye"; high flight is the motif of both these poems, "vertical" imagery prevails, and both anticipate escape from that wheel of "miseree" to which *September* saw men bound. Yet both poems belong to "the cold season," and thus mark, structurally, a divergence between the declining seasonal round and the uplifting powers of the human imagination. Though both include laments—for the decay of poetry and the death of Dido—both also show the means of transcendence and escape from these disasters. Within "nature," spring follows the cold season; within human life, there is a movement not identical, but analogous. In *Nouember*, the pattern is familiar, inevitable in a Christian pastoral elegy: *La mort ny mord*, death is "the grene path way to lyfe." In *October*, the solution is secular and less final, but it turns on a similar paradox: love, the source of human distress and a figure for man's fall into sin, is at the same time the pathway to regained Paradise. The design of the two poems is the same—out of suffering springs joy and release—and both are thus "answers" to Diggon's question, "What shall I doe?" in *September*; both demonstrate that escape from the wheel is possible. The impeccable poetic logic supports E. K.'s description of the *Calender* as "finely framed, and strongly trussed vp together."

The poem's final movement, then, as Durr has said, "declares that man cannot, like the other creatures, live his life in accordance with the seasonal round." But Spenser's analysis of human life involves neither an ascetic disdain for the pleasures of the temporal world, nor a "rejection" of pastoral. Rather, those pleasures are defined and confirmed with relation to an ultimately religious sanction; and the power of the pastoral paradigm is reaffirmed as having *metaphorical* validity. Like Milton in *Lycidas*, Spenser forces upon us the unwilling recognition that we can never regain Paradise literally. Hobbinol's idyll in *Iune* is threatened by all the hostile forces loose in the poem, including death, which enters *Iune* itself in the lament for Tityrus. Just so, the singer of *Lycidas* must recognize that the idyllic world of "Rural ditties" has been lost forever, that the dead shepherd can never return in his old form. But he will undergo a sea-change into "the Genius of the shore." So Dido, in *Nouember*, lives again, transformed:

> The honor now of highest gods she is,
>   That whilome was poore shepheards pryde.
>   (197–98)

The meaning of both *Lycidas* and *The Shepheardes Calender* concerns the need for us to accept a nonliteral, invisible reality as the one most relevant to us as human beings. This reality, in both poems, is defined in the Christian terms conventional for pastoral elegy; in *October*, it is accessible, as well, to the poetic imagination. Awareness of a nonliteral realm of experience can be made to enlighten our *earthly* lives. We must follow the permutations of this theme through several eclogues, to demonstrate how, within the paradigm of the pastoral, Spenser creates his interrelated meanings.

  Iulye lies at the center of the *Calender* and in many respects is its pivot. In both *Iune* and *Iulye* the Fall of Man is mentioned explicitly; and an awareness of our fallen state is crucial to an understanding of both eclogues. *Iulye* can also be read as an affirmation of the pastoral life understood in terms of biblical metaphor, rather than in the literal terms of Hobbinol's stanzas in *Iune*—upon which, in fact, it serves as a commentary. The two Emblems of *Iulye* clash and cooperate to make Spenser's point. *In medio virtus*, says Thomalin; *In summo felicitas*, says Morrell. The moral seems plain: virtue and happiness are incompatible in this life, since one cannot be *in medio* and *in summo* at the same time. Or rather, one cannot unless one is aware of the figurative ranges of meaning for these terms, which support the Christian paradox of the exaltation of the lowly. Spenser presents his shepherd and goatherd in a *paysage moralisé* which one of them interprets correctly (that is, figuratively) and the other presumptuously (that is, literally), Morrell supports his claim that hills are the healthiest habitat for man with references to saints, to the vision of Endymion, and to Christ on Mount Olivet; but none of these parallels is relevant to his own condition. Finally, he insists:

> Hereto, the hills bene nigher heauen,
>   And thence the passage ethe.
> As well can proue the piercing leuin,
>   that seeldome falls bynethe.
>   (89–92)

His image is a dangerous one; and his method is that of "a lewde lorrell," as Thomalin scornfully points out, demanding that the emblems of nature be read with a less literal mind.

> Alsoone may shepheard clymbe to skye,
> that leades in lowly dales,
> As Goteherd prowd that sitting hye,
> vpon the Mountaine sayles.
> (101–4)

E. K. enforces the point: "Note the shepheards simplenesse, which supposeth that from the hylls is nearer ways to heauen." What emerges from *Iulye* is a definition of two versions of "shepheards simpleness"—simple-mindedness, and a sophisticated awareness of the true meaning of simplicity. The analogue adduced by Thomalin is Abel, the first shepherd; we remember that he was a type of Christ, and the implications are finally elaborated in E. K.'s lengthy gloss of the Emblems. He admits that Morrell's Emblem is "most true," Thomalin's being obviously "true" as well; both have the sanction of "olde Philosophers." They can be reconciled only when we see that for man their truth must be understood figuratively; they are literally reconciled only in the Christian godhead where all paradoxes are resolved. E. K. approves of both interlocutors in his last sentence, the "great doctour" who offers as a model *Christus humillimus*, and the "gentle man" who responds with an allusion to *Deus altissimus*. We must follow both, remembering that, at last, they are one.

Leading a retired life in anticipation of the reward achieved by Dido in *Nouember*, the good shepherds of *Iulye* exemplify one way in which pastoral can provide us with a model. They are early versions of characters in *The Faerie Queene*: Heavenly Contemplation who instructs the Red Cross Knight, and the Hermit who heals Serena and Timias in Book VI. Yet allusion to these characters can help us to see that "religious" solutions to the human predicament must be augmented by models for virtuous life in the world. Heavenly Contemplation sends the Knight back to the world to complete his quest, and the Hermit has himself been a knight, "proued oft in many perillous fight" (VI.vi.4). There is no question but that Spenser in the *Calender* was recommending to the clerics of his day the life of lowly retirement that imitates the apostles. The allusion to the shepherd of Ida in *Iulye* (145–48), to say nothing of Piers' overt moralizing in *Maye*, brings home to us the incompatibility of pastoral virtue and fallen human history.

"But shepheard must walke another way" from children of the world (*Maye*, 81); for those in secular life there must be other solutions.

Some of the possibilities for a virtuous life within society are explored in *August,* in *Aprill,* and in the discussion of imagination in *October* and its gloss. *August* and *October* provide Spenser's readers with a comprehension of the significance of "pleasaunt layes" that passes beyond the complaints of Colin Clout. In *Iune,* he laments because poetry is not magic. Tityrus' songs could not save him from the outrage of death; and as the eclogue ends, Colin is recognizing his own impotence: "I am not, as I wish I were" (105), that is, capable of piercing Rosalind's stony heart. Had he inherited Tityrus' powers, he says, "I soone would learne these woods, to wayle my woe" (95). The argument ignores the earlier awareness that Tityrus had been unable to salvage his own "skill" from death's ruin; but in one line, Colin glances at a source of solace that Spenser will develop later. Poetic skill is as "passing" as its human possessors, but its memory survives in the "workes of learned wits," "The fame whereof doth dayly greater growe" (92). The growth of Colin's own fame is signified, in the action of the *Calender,* by the presence of three of his songs, performed by his friends and betokening the true power of art. It cannot effect literal changes in the world of nature; but in its imagined worlds, perfect harmony can reign, to be recreated each time the song is sung for our instruction and delight. The sestina of *August,* whose power and sophistication contrast notably with the naive rhymes of Perigot and Willye, is an "answer" to the harsh insights of *Iune.* It is "a doolefull verse / Of Rosalend," the record of suffering, of passion, but ere transformed into a fictive action that reproduces the dolorous harmonies envisaged in *Iune.* There, the literal woods hard-heartedly refused to wail; but here, "wild woddes" resound Colin's sorrows, "banefull byrds" accompany his complaint, and a "gastfull groue" offers appropriate *décor* for the melancholy scene. The poem is a kind of charm, evoking in imagination the correspondence of microcosm and macrocosm, accidentally but temporarily visible in *Ianuarye,* and unobtainable in the literal "nature" of *Iune.* The effect of the song on the other shepherds is insisted on; though it is a "heauy laye," Willye eagerly anticipates its performance:

> For neuer thing on earth so pleaseth me,
> As him to heare, or matter of his deede.
> (147–8)

At the end, both song and performance are praised.

> O *Colin, Colin,* the shepheards ioye,
>   How I admire ech turning of thy verse:
> And *Cuddie,* fresh *Cuddie* the liefest boye,
>   How dolefully his doole thou didst rehearse.
> (190–3)

"Doole" becomes a source of delight as it is transmuted into art; though it cannot "cure" its maker, it can confer on him an immortality of fame, for "monuments of Poetry abide for euer."

These are E. K.'s last words; they are augmented by his gloss for *October*, where Spenser makes explicit the two aspects of his definition of art, obliquely rendered in *August*. Poetry is a nonliteral action, and a source of immortality. Though the poet does not make a logical connection between these two ideas, we may see them as related: *because* poetry's mode of being is outside the world of nature, it can defy natural decay. E. K.'s explication of the Emblem is a definition of imagination which suggests that this relationship was present in Spenser's mind: "Poetry is a diuine instinct and vnnatural rage passing the reache of comen reason." Like the divine furor of love, it can provide a ladder that will take us out of the foul rag-and-bone shop of nature's cycles. Piers' exhortation to Cuddie to summon up his poetic powers uses the same figure to describe love's power:

> Lyft vp thy selfe out of the lowly dust
>
> (38)

> loue does teach him climbe so hie,
> And lyftes him vp out of the loathsome myre.
> (91–2)

As a consequence of this "lifting up," love itself is immortalized, as it was in *August*; and immortality can be conferred, as well, on others. A familiar Renaissance solace appears in E. K.'s gloss: poets achieve eternity of fame not only for themselves, but for their subjects, whose "worthines and valor shold through theyr famous Posies be commended to all posterities."

The vertical perspectives offered by these two "ladders"—poetic inspiration, and love—are extended and consummated in the elegy sung in *Nouember*, where a vision of Dido's immortality consoles its lamenting audience:

> Ay francke shepheard, how bene thy verses meint
> With doolful pleasaunce, so as I ne wotte,
> Whether reioyce or weepe for great constrainte?
> (203–5)

The paradoxes expressed in these lines are neither exclusively theological, nor exclusively aesthetic; they are both at once, the point being that art is the most exact mirror of ultimate mysteries. As every alert reader of the *Calender* observes, *Nouember* provides the source and end for all lesser visions. The transposition of pastoral imagery into a transcendental key, deriving as it ultimately does from *Revelation*, confers upon this mode of imagining the sanction of the divine artist. "Fayre fieldes and pleasaunt layes there bene" in Heaven (188); as a result, fields and lays are reinvigorated for us as metaphorical anticipations of bliss.

But the elegy is also an object lesson in the limits of poetry's power; it cannot alter things as they are by reviving Dido and reversing the calendar. She was "the fayrest May . . . that euer went" (39), but this is November, and remains November within the literal action. In "the trustlesse state of earthly things" (153), no springtime lasts, and man has only one springtime. Spenser enforces this implied statement of poetry's powers and limits in his allusion to Orpheus in *October*. Piers is praising Cuddie's songs:

> Soone as thou gynst to sette thy notes in frame
> O how the rurall routes to thee doe cleaue:
> Seemeth thou dost their soule of sence bereaue,
> All as the shepheard, that did fetch his dame
> From Plutoes baleful bowre withouten leaue:
> His musicks might the hellish hound did tame.
> (25–30)

In spite of his "musicks might," Orpheus did not succeed, finally, in reversing the course of nature, and Eurydice's ultimate fate would, one imagines, have been present in the minds of Spenser's readers. What is not in question, however, is poetry's power to tame Cerberus and to ravish the sense of its human audience.

What emerges, then, from the climactic eclogues of *The Shepheardes Calender* is a balance of attitudes held in equilibrium, intensifying the complex point of view visible in the work as a whole. Man must suffer inevitable outrage from the forces released in nature at the Fall, and against these forces there is no remedy within nature itself, or within the power of mere "natural man." Poetry cannot provide a talisman against death, nor heal the wounds of love, nor recreate the state of innocence. Yet the power of imagination in man is a real power, if rightly understood as "an vnnatural rage"; it gives us access to a transnatural realm of being where our ultimate destiny lies.

The lay of *Aprill*, the third of Colin's songs, is designed, like those in *August* and *Nouember*, to confirm Piers' claim in *October* that love, seconded by imagination, can lift us out of the cycle of death. All three poems offer visions of a world in which reality corresponds to human desires. All are elaborate in form, their higher mood surpassing the reach of ordinary shepherds' wit. In celebrating Eliza, Rosalind, and Dido, Colin must keep decorum with themes that transcend the natural order as he observes it in "reality" in many of the other eclogues. The fox of *Maye*, the wolf of *September*, the "Ambitious brere" of *Februarye*, the lowly pastors of *Iulye*, the disharmonies of *Iune*—all these manifest the nature of fallen being. But *Aprill* and *August* offer visions of possibility, and *Nouember* a glimpse of actuality that transcends all human potentiality. Bacon was later to disparage poets for submitting "the shows of things to the desires of the mind," but as both Sidney and Spencer affirm, those desires themselves bear witness to the presence of a realm of being inadequately figured by the shows of things.

All three of Colin Clout's songs are monuments of wit and demonstrations of its capacities; the *Aprill* lay is, in addition, Spenser's most eloquent depiction of a monument of power, a model that refers to our life on earth. It is a vision of perfection within fallen nature that can be effected by exercising another kind of art. Once our world has become the prey of sin, nature can be restored to something like its original purity only with the aid of civilization, that "nurture" regularly opposed in Elizabethan debates to unaltered "nature." The arts of government can unite antagonists and create another Eden, at least a demi-paradise—the garden of the world, as Elizabeth's poets were fond of calling her kingdom. This world is presented in *Aprill*, where the lay's formal artifice can be taken as a symbol of all the artful patterns that bring order out of chaos. *Aprill* speaks of the work of art, be it a commonwealth, a dance, or a poem; *October* speaks of the maker, "the perfect paterne of Poete." He can create on earth a mirror, fragile but exact, of the world not as it is but as it might be. The making of golden worlds is the chief function assigned to poetry by Sidney; and it lies behind Piers' description of the poet's heavenly goal in *October*:

> Then make thee winges of thine aspyring wit,
> And, whence thou camst, flye backe to heaven apace.
> (83–4)

In *Nouember* we contemplate the true heavenly garden; in *Aprill* we see a fictive version of its earthly counterpart, transient but potent, created by poet and queen. Colin's art cooperates with that of "our most gracious souereigne" to produce a golden world in imagination; and this world is capable, as the Envoy to the *Calender* insists, of surviving every catastrophe except the final one: "It shall continewe till the worlds disolution."

The microcosmic character of the lay of *Aprill* hardly requires elaboration. The images create a comprehensive harmony that extends from the flowers on the green to golden Phoebus and silver Cynthia, removed from their "natural" orbits, like the Sun in Donne's *The Sunne Rising*, to circle this little cosmos and do homage to its sustaining power. Here, as in Eden, spring and autumn dance hand in hand and flowers of all seasons blossom together to deck Eliza, whose complexion predictably unites "the Redde rose medled with the White yfere" (68). Joining classical and native strains, as later they were to be joined in *Epithalamion*, nymphs of Helicon dance beside Ladies of the Lake and "shepheards daughters, that dwell on the greene" (127)—the two latter groups figuring, it has been suggested, a union of the spirits of water and land. The "chiefest Nymph" brings the final tribute: a coronal of olive branches, signifying the surcease of war, Eliza's establishment of the Peaceable Kingdom, the Golden Age restored. The *Aprill* lay, though not composed in the heroic mode prescribed by Piers in *October*, speaks of the subjects there recommended, and is presided over by Calliope (100). The epic poet is to turn to

> those, that weld the awful crowne,
> To doubted Knights, whose woundlesse armour rusts,
> And helmes vnbruzed wexen dayly browne.
>
> (Oct., 40–42)

Another incarnation of Elizabeth, Mercilla in *Faerie Queene* V, is also a peaceable ruler; at her feet is a sword "Whose long rest rusted the bright steely brand" (V.ix.30). The sterner style of epic demands images like those of the rusted armour or sword; and those images, too, remind us that epic treats of life in a harsh and threatened fallen world, where the sword may at any moment be drawn. For the homely yet courtly vision of high pastoral, the coronal of olive is more decorous. Yet both images project an ideal that was often referred to by writers on the arts of government. Spenser's version of it in *Aprill* is a world of possibility created by poetry; Castiglione celebrates princely virtue in *The Courtier* in a congruent allusion:

> That vertue, which perhaps among all the matters that belong unto man is the chiefest and rarest, that is to say, the manner and way to rule and to raigne in the right kinde. Which alone were sufficient to make men happie, and to bring once againe into the world the golden age, which is written to have beene when Saturnus raigned in the olde time.

Pastoral imagery finds a new sanction in figuring this happy state, as in *Nouember* its validity was to be confirmed in another direction. The more one reads *The Shepheardes Calender*, the more one is struck by the force of Hallett Smith's judgment that "the pastoral idea, in its various ramifications, *is* the *Calender*." The pastoral paradigm, in the service of a potent and resourceful imagination, proves itself to be a flexible expressive instrument. The serious use of pastoral in the Renaissance, by Spenser and others, received, of course, support from its presence in the Bible and from the central paradox of Christianity where low degree is exalted. So the humblest genre can figure the highest matters. This paradox is exploited by Spenser in a secular context in *Aprill*, where the greatest personage of the land enters the shepherds' country world and hallows it. In turn, that world itself provides emblems supremely apt for figuring the special graces of her reign. There is a union of estates, a little mirror of Gloriana's England—appropriately enough, if we recall that on the twenty-third of the month was celebrated the feast of England's patron saint.

Having tested for himself the resources of one of the basic metaphors of his tradition, Spenser laid aside his pastoral pipe for a time. Already, the queen of shepherds was being metamorphosed into the queen of faerie. Yet pastoral was not abandoned for good; it is absorbed into Faerie Land itself, making an essential contribution to the vast landscape of *The Faerie Queene*.

ANGUS FLETCHER

Imagery and Prophecy in "The Faerie Queene"

As the author of a romantic epic in which, as Richard Hurd claimed in the *Letters on Chivalry and Romance*, a complex design orders an even more complex action, Spenser depends heavily on two cardinal images for his prophetic structure: the temple and the labyrinth. These two archetypes organize the overall shaping of *The Faerie Queene*, and while other archetypal images play a part throughout the poem, the temple and the labyrinth, as "poetic universals," are sufficiently large and powerful images to organize an immense variety of secondary imagery, leading thereby to an equally varied narrative.

Temples and labyrinths have a singular advantage to the poet, in that they both imply special layout and a typical activity within that layout. Furthermore, while both images suggest man-made structures— men have built temples and labyrinths—they each have a set of natural equivalents. Temples may rise out of the earth in the form of sacred groves, while labyrinths may grow up as a tangle of vegetation. The cardinal dichotomy of the two archetypes will permit the typical Renaissance interplay of art and nature. For both images the idea of design is crucial, and their stress on pattern as such gives Spenser's intricate poem a certain stability.

Yet design itself may play an ambiguous role when the two great images are set in counterpoint against each other, because whereas the image of a temple is strictly formalized, to frame the highest degree of

From *The Prophetic Moment: An Essay on Spenser.* Copyright © 1971 by The University of Chicago Press.

order, the idea of a labyrinth leads in the opposite direction. The labyrinth allows a place, and would appear to create a structure, for the notable indeterminacy of the textural surface of *The Faerie Queene*. Labyrinthine imageries and actions yield "the appearance, so necessary to the poem's quality, of pathless wandering," which, as Lewis continued, "is largely a work of deliberate and successful illusion."

The image of the temple is probably the dominant recurring archetype in *The Faerie Queene*. Major visions in each of the six books are presented as temples: the House of Holiness, the Castle of Alma, the Garden of Adonis, the Temple of Venus, the Temple of Isis, the sacred round-dance on the top of Mount Acidale. Even the Mutabilitie Cantos display this "symbolism of the center," as the trial convenes at the pastoral *templum* of Diana, Arlo Hill. In many respects the chief allegorical problems of each book can most easily be unwrapped if the reader attends closely to the iconography of such temples, and for that reason Lewis referred to them as "allegorical cores," while Frye calls them "houses of recognition."

Together the temple and the labyrinth encompass the archetypal universe of *The Faerie Queene* and in that sense their meaning is more than allegorical. It is a narrative reality within the epic. Heroes come to temples, which they may enter and leave, and they pass through a labyrinthine faerieland. This archetypal scene of heroic action is not Spenser's own invention, though he develops it with great ingenuity. As Frye argued in the *Anatomy of Criticism*, apocalyptic and demonic imagery polarize the structures of a truly vast number of literary works. On the other hand, for English poetry *The Faerie Queene* occupies a special place, since it is the "wel-head" of English romantic vision. Since it is romance, and not pure myth, it modulates the images of shrine and maze, to fit the scheme of romantic *entrelacement* and its chivalric manner.

In essence the temple is the image of gratified desire, the labyrinth the image of terror and panic. While in its originating form myth is "undisplaced," here the images of temple and labyrinth may be rendered in a more "realistic" or romantic guise, so that, for example, the purity of the temple is represented as the chivalric equivalent, a noble and chaste prowess. Spenser "romanticizes" the apocalyptic temple. Similarly he romanticizes the demonic labyrinth, which he does not hesitate to represent in undisplaced myth, as a twining monster of shape-shifting demon, but which he more often displaces into more romantic forms which better suit the romantic level of his mythography.

The archetypal and the displaced treatment of the temple and the labyrinth lead to a rich tapestry. Critics have done much to illuminate the interaction of the two archetypes, but in the following account I shall try chiefly to bring out the fact that when the dichotomy is narrowed, or forced into visionary union, prophecy results. This vatic nexus will be seen to imply a mode of visionary history, which keeps *The Faerie Queene* close to reality even when it seems to be reaching out to a distant world of spirit.

THE TEMPLE

A *templum* is a sacred, separated space. It may assume various geometric outlines (four- or five-sided, for example), but ideally it is round. The circularity of the horizon is borrowed, to create the archetypal form of the shrine: "*templum* designates the spatial, *tempus* the temporal aspect of the motion of the horizon in space and time. Within the temple space is said to become "sacred space," or "hallowed ground." One result of the establishment of the sacred space of the temple is that man can thereby exclude the profane world. Generally, in its extreme form, this is an exclusion of chaos. Thus the temple is always a microcosm, or, in the case of a city like ancient Rome, a *mundus*—a cosmos marked out by a sacred line dug or drawn around the edges of the city, within which all is ordered and theoretically indestructible."

The temple, like any major archetype, has a rich iconography. Drawn out of nature and reflecting the original creative powers of God, the temple may be an enclosed garden, a sacred grove of trees, a sacred mountain top, or any other natural eminence. Book I, Canto X of *The Faerie Queene* shows the Redcrosse Knight led to the summit of "the highest mount" after he has done penance in the House of Holiness. There an old man named Heavenly Contemplation shows the knight a vision of the ultimate temple, the City of the New Jerusalem. The quality of sacred centeredness strengthens when the poet, in an aside, compares the "highest mount" with the three other sacred mountains essential to Spenserian myth, Mount Sinai, the Mount of Olives,

> . . . that sacred hill whose head full hie,
> Adorned with fruitfull Olives all arownd,
> Is, as it were for endlesse memory
> Of that deare Lord, who ofte thereon was fownd,
> For ever with a flowring girlond crownd,

and thirdly Mount Parnassus, "on which the thrise three learned Ladies play / Their heavenly notes." The knowledge gained from such a vantage point is too dazzling for mortal eyes, and when Redcrosse comes away from it, he cannot see: "dazed were his eyne, / Through passing brightnesse."

The sacred mountain finds a Renaissance imitation in the works of artful gardeners who, not content with planting gardens, trees and shrubbery, raise at the center of the planting a "mount," an artificial eminence capped, like Belphoebe's "stately theatre," with a pavilion or summer house. In poetry the Ovidian genre of the erotic epyllion gives a free play to such fancies, perhaps most richly exemplified in Drayton's image of Diana's paradise, atop Mount Latmus, in *Endimion and Phoebe*. Drayton first elaborates on the "stately grove" climbing the sides of the mountain, calling it, at one point, a "stately gallery." Though its trees are in the traditional Ovidian order of a catalogue, the grove is also watered by "straying channels dauncing sundry wayes, / With often turnes, like to a curious Maze." Then above the grove there rise steps, or "degrees" of "milk-white Marble," and finally "Upon a top, a Paradise was found." The natural paradise is a model of articulate form. The same tendency toward hierarchic structure appears in the artificial *templum*.

Architecturally the temple may be a palace, a church, a tabernacle, a shrine, a sanctuary, any sacred building built on the plan of a *mundus*. While perhaps originally all such buildings were approximations of the circle, their imaginative extension took innumerable forms in later historical development: the spiral, the square, the polyhedral, the cube, the pyramid, the cross, and so on. Sometimes temples and castles are confused, and for the trench or wall of the *mundus* there is exchanged a "moat defensive." Sometimes, on the model of the Eternal City, the *templum* expands to become a large and complicated urban structure, *urbs* being the microcosmic form of the celestial *orb*. Or, turning back from large to small, the whole vast macrocosm can be reduced to a miniature of itself, first to an emblematic shield, like those of Achilles or Aeneas in the *Iliad* and *Aeneid*, then, even smaller, to a sacred *nodus* or knot. The range of magnitude is truly enormous. It may stretch from Herrick's amber bead ("The urn was little, but the room / More rich than Cleopatra's tomb") to the universe itself—"the temple represents the image of the world." John of Gaunt's prophecy in *Richard II* makes the whole realm of England into a temple.

Experientially the temple provides the perfect model for the creation of a home. As such the temple is the resting place of man, the center, the *omphalos*, of his world. The hieratic center of this central place is the hearth fire. The temple is the house of life.

In stressing the vital radiance of the templar form, we should not forget what may be the more basic fact, that through the vision of the temple the hero finds a place, as distinct from the indefinable and largely empty space which is excluded by the *mundus*. Among the various attributes of the temple, it may be used to emphasize the concept of limit, edge, margin, boundary or closure. Not only does each *templum* have set boundaries, closing it off from the profane empty space, but it also will usually have reticulated subdivisions which, like the interior arrangement of a cathedral or like the Stations of the Cross, permit secondary closures within the larger closure of the whole templar cosmos. Closure is present at all levels of templar form. Within the Spenserian Garden of Adonis, a true *hortus conclusus*, the "seminal reasons" are sown in distinct orders: "And every sort is in a sundry bed / Set by it Selfe, and ranckt in comely rew." *The Garden of Cyrus* (1658) perhaps marks the culmination of what Browne himself called "inexcusable Pythagorisme," but we should note that its principal method is the analysis of the "net-work plantation" into its mirroring subsections, until the whole templar form of the garden yields a "law of reflexion." During the Renaissance and Baroque periods, Browne and others like him are not so much eccentrics, as extremists in a profession of mystical "analysis" and anatomizing which is in fact a widely common practice. Closure is structurally powerful here, even though the simple outside wall of the temple is suggestively complicated (reticulated) by the intricacy of innumerable inner walls.

Among Spenserian examples the House of Alma may best illustrate this reticulation of the templar form, and it readily suggests the sort of action that typifies the templar scene. Whatever happens to Sir Guyon when he enters this shrine, the structure itself is guarded and tended by ministers of a cult. Their guardianship is an integral aspect of the structure, so that when, in the allegory of the digestive system, there is a "stately hall," there is also a ministering steward, Diet, who takes charge of the menu, while a maître d'hôtel, Appetite, walks up and down, bestowing "both guests and meat." With its complete and also comical ordering of its mythic materials, this temple is indeed a "goodly frame of temperance." Similarly with other temples, we find that structure implies a ministry of some kind. When Redcrosse does penance, he is helped or instructed by the servants of the House of Holiness, its angelic ministers. Faith, Hope, and Charity guide and support the hero's confirmation in the sacramental role of *microchristus*. From them and from their temple he acquires the sanctity that will make him Saint George of Merry England.

Because such a strong sense of ritual informs the life of the temple, it is important, with Spenser, not to identify the high degree of structure with a merely external cult. Spenser is a Reformation poet, and during this period the Christian frame of reference alters, bringing the Church and its authority into a closer union with the self of man. By reducing the legitimate scope of the *ecclesia* in its secular establishment, the Reformation opened the way to what must have seemed a new and radically *expanded* individual selfhood. The externally visible temple of Mother Church and her institutionalized cult is in part replaced by an interior shrine, whose great monument in English poetry comes after Spenser, in *The Temple* of George Herbert. The range of human action occurring outside the temple may have seemed to the pious Catholic to have greatly extended, to his distress. The Protestant poet (and later the Counter-reformation poet, as a kind of orthodox Protestant) would insist, on the other hand, that by interiorizing his faith he had made it much finer. Herbert's poem "The Window" catches this exalted and expanded sense of a redeeming selfhood.

> Yet in thy temple thou dost him afford
> This glorious and transcendent place,
> To be a window, through thy grace.

Windows open out onto a scene, allowing light to pass through. Rivalries of faith and works cannot obscure the abiding reality of the cardinal image itself: the temple is a place of enlightenment. Argument then follows only over the mystical place and placement of the temple. Its essence remains unchanged, even in Reformation imagery, though it now has a new relation to human consciousness.

Enlightenment is an almost magical access to the truth, and in the temple the ritual ministrations of the priest and beadman, guardian and servant, create an expectant air of teleological form. Every temple subordinates its own rather rigid structure to the promise of a lively flow of energy. This promise it embodies in ceremonial festivity. Thus Herbert, for example, ends *The Temple* with the image of the love feast: "So I did sit and eat." We find that templar rituals often culminate in a ceremony of truth. It has the effect of binding the hero to a fortunate, if strenuous, destiny. It may take many forms, but all are types of betrothal, of the kind that inspired Spenser in his two marriage odes, both of which, we might add, display the templar aspiration in their stanzaic forms. The "arithmological stanza" (II. ix, 22) reduces the marriage trope to its absolute microcosm, by fusing masculine and feminine principles in the one theoretical frame of the human body—"O work divine." The conclusion to Book I establishes the ceremony of truth within the narrative form of the whole epic: "Fair Una to the Red Cross Knight / Betrothed is with joy." Truth in the Spenserian setting is always a consequence of betrothal, and at the moment of most intense vision truth *is* betrothal, not merely its consequent. Truth and troth meet at the restoration of Eden, and their meeting generalizes to the scope of a national drama when the monarch, as in Book V, undertakes to protect and judge her people.

Prophecy requires the verbal or visionary expression of this contractual trust based on a betrothal. Because the betrothal is truly mutual, it accords with the dictates of conscience and it expresses the conscious choice, the deliberate wish, of the parties to the marriage. By its ceremonies of truth the prophetic poem shows that human bonds—the "bonds of society"—will have generative power. Troth is blessed by the benign providence of a higher favoring Being. This favor appears gratuitously in the pleasures of the season, the warmth, light and songs of springtime, the festivity and dancing of a harvest home.

The temporal connotations of the original Latin *templum* suggest this holiday air. Through its roots *templum* grows into a cluster of related terms, "temper," "temperate," and "contemplate" (with their antitype, the "tempest"). The temporal property of the temple resides in the fact that, within it, time, as well as space, is sacred. Thus the name for temple crosses back and forth between the two dimensions of time and space. Spatially the temple breaks into and organizes the endless extension of the labyrinth. Temporally it arrests the ordinary unbroken duration of temporal flow. Inside the temple time shares with space the immutable closure of the perfect circle.

Religious vision sees the temple permitting a perfected symbolic action, as man engages in the ancient rituals of his faith, so that life takes on holiness with the church walls. This we can test easily enough—the feeling of both space and time, when we enter the shrine, is one of removal from the ordinary world we live in, into a life beyond the clock and the marketplace. The temple is quiet, if not silent. Its perfect song is the Sanctus. It gets its temporal name from the fact that a given ground may be chosen, cut off, structured and consecrated in such fashion that through a sacred blessing (a logos) man isolates time, which then acquires a dimension of stillness. The temple is the still point of the turning world.

Action here is bound to be largely symbolic, as in the Mass. Once within the sacred confines of the church, man is free to reenact the symbolic myths of origin from which his faith springs. Thus the Christian communion reenacts the first giving of the sacrament. (Repetition plays a central role in this, and we find that drama itself seems to have been born in the temple.) The principles enunciated by the inner forms of the templar structure, the "articles of faith," the mysteries of the faith, tend to be associated with the immemorially distant beginnings of a spiritual history. To derive his unchanging principles man goes back to the stage of "once upon a time," *in illo tempore*. Having done so, he can then build up a system of liturgical repetitions of that *arche*, the archetypal beginning. To reinforce the periodic aspect of time in the temple, most religions cele-brate hierophanic rituals arranged according to the forms of the liturgical year. The experience of these recurrent rituals (the Easter Week services, for example) collapses ordinary time. The believer feels himself caught up in an "eternal present," a fulfilling contemporaneity. The phenomenology of this collapsed time is entirely paradoxical—emptied of business, it is full; quieted and stilled, it is a breathing, hovering kind of time, the hierophany of stillness in motion.

THE LABYRINTH

The opposite of the ideal templar form is the "perplexed circle" which a metaphysical poet, Henry King, described in his poem "The Labyrinth"

> Life is a crooked Labyrinth, and wee
> Are dayly lost in that Obliquity.
> 'Tis a perplexed Circle, in whose round
> Nothing but Sorrowes and new Sins abound.

Christian dogma blamed this bewilderment on a blindness beginning with the Fall. Thus Raleigh's *History of the World* speaks of men who, having "fallen away from undoubted truth, do then after wander for evermore in vices unknown." Orthodoxy held that Christ alone could save men from this "home-bred tyranny."

> Thou canst reverse this Labyrinth of Sinne
> My wild Affects and Actions wander in.

Beginning his epic with a Christian version of the classical *in medias res*, Spenser makes a labyrinth crucial to the first episode of *The Faerie Queene*. Redcrosse, the Lady Una, and the Dwarf are caught by a "hideous storme of raine," a tempest, as Spenser twice calls it.

> Enforst to seeke some covert nigh at hand,
>   A shadie grove not far away they spide,
>   That promist ayde the tempest to withstand:
>   Whose loftie trees yclad with sommers pride,
>   Did spred so broad, that heavens light did hide,
>   Not perceable with power of any starre:
>   And all within were pathes and alleies wide,
>   With footing worne, and leading inward farre:
> Faire harbour that them seemes; so in they entred arre.

> And forth they passe, with pleasure forward led,
>   Joying to heare the birdes sweete harmony,
>   Which therein shrouded from the tempest dred,
>   Seemd in their song to scorne the cruell sky.
> (I, i, 7 and 8)

There follows the famous Ovidian catalogue of trees, each given its proper use and therefore brought into line with a human culture. The catalogue is an epitome of order and syntax, and Spenser projects its systematic character by a strict procession of anaphoras and exemplary appositives. If we were not alerted to the overtones of "loftie" and "sommers pride," the rich leafage darkening the light of heaven, we might notice nothing untoward until the last line of the catalogue: "the maple seldom inward sound." Otherwise this would appear a fine plantation. If the forest misleads, it does so in spite of something the travelers can praise, that is, in spite of its mere *nature*. Spenser, however, is playing on the old proverb about not being able to see the forest for the trees. His exceedingly strict stanzaic game disguises the spiritual danger inherent in the darkness of the forest, the *selva oscura*. Instead the stanza becomes an agency in the deception, providing a fine instance, I would think, of the "rhetorical" function of verbal formulas, which Paul Alpers has recently stressed in *The Poetry of "The Faerie Queene."* The deception is gradual.

> Led with delight, they thus beguile the way,
>   Untill the blustring storme is overblowne;
>   When weening to returne, whence they did stray,
>   They cannot finde that path, which first was showne,
>   But wander to and fro in wayes unknowne,
>   Furthest from end then, when they neerest weene,
>   That makes them doubt, their wits be not their owne:
>   So many pathes, so many turnings seene,
> That which of them to take, in diverse doubt they been.
>
> At last resolving forward still to fare,
>   Till that some end they finde or in or out,
>   That path they take, that beaten seemd most bare,
>   And like to lead the labyrinth about;
>   Which when by tract they hunted had throughout,
>   At length it brought them to a hollow cave,
>   Amid the thickest woods.
> (I, i, 10 and 11)

Una, the embodiment of Truth, at once recognizes the labyrinth for what it is: "This is the wandring wood, this *Errours* den, / A monster vile, whom God and man does hate." The turbulence of the "hideous storme of raine" persists in the description of the monster Errour. Like the tempest that wrapped itself around the travelers, the dragon would surround them in natural or unnatural fury. Spenser gains something at once by making his first antagonist a dragon whose "huge long taile" is a grotesque incarnation of the twists and turns of the maze: "God helpe the man so wrapt in *Errours* endlesse traine." Errour can so tie herself in knots that she creates her own "desert darknesse."

The encounter with the dragon links the ideas of error and wandering, suddenly fixing the malevolent aspect of the maze. This forest is ominous, threatening, and should produce a wise, dwarfish panic. Seen in this light the labyrinth is a purely demonic image, the natural cause of terror. So strong is the aftertaste of this terror that the reader may at once forget how pleasantly the forest had beguiled the unwary travelers. This is our first introduction to an ambivalence that colors almost every episode in the poem. As to the baffling form of the maze there can be no doubt, once one is "in" it. Though all avenues are promising, none ever gets anywhere. While some winding passages enter upon others, those others turn into dead ends, or twist back to return the seeker to his starting point. In the garden of forking paths an opening is often the barrier to an openness.

The artist of the maze may, reversing the idea of a temple, grow high and formal walls of hedge, or he may baffle the quester by thickening and complicating a natural outgrowth of trees, plants, rocks or streams. Spenser is aware of both the artificial and the natural maze, both of which are models in *The Faerie Queene* for a rich iconography of motion. The sinuous lines of the maze can be reduced to a mythic essence, with such characters as Pyrochles or Cymocholes, whose names and behaviour imply the motion of waves and furious, redundant turbulence. (This Milton later chose as a metonymy for both Eve and Satan.) More largely, when the maze provides a perverse map, the hero finds himself following the antitype of the direct and narrow "way" of salvation. In the phrase of Spenser's early *Tears of the Muses*, the blinded hero deserves Urania's complaint, since he has gone astray: "Then wandreth he in error and in doubt." Even Truth itself, as Una, is forced to wander.

> Now when broad day the world discovered has,
> Up *Una* rose, up rose the Lyon eke,
> And on their former journey forward pas,
> In wayes unknowne, her wandring knight to seeke,
> With paines farre passing that long wandring *Greeke*,
> That for his love refused deitie:
> Such were the labours of this Lady meeke,

Still seeking him, that from her still did flie,
Then furthest from her hope, when most she weened nie.
(I, iii, 21)

The allusion to Odysseus sets two kinds of wandering against each other, the erroneous wandering of Redcrosse against the "true" wandering of Una, who is patterned partly on the hero who refused immortal life with Calypso ("the hider"). The *Odyssey*, with its inset tales of utopian vision, joins the idea of wandering with the idea of a finally targeted quest, the return home. Thus wandering may satisfy a benign form of nostalgia.

More usually Spenser associates the state of wandering with the idea of blank extension—words that typically accompany wandering are "wide," "deep," "long," and "endless." Wandering may also be "vain." To wander is to live in a state of continuous becoming (if such a paradox can be imagined), so that Spenser keeps errantry and error in process, by preferring the present participle, "wandering," to other grammatical forms. Like Hobbinol in the June Eclogue, the hero suffers from a "wandring mynde," and he must govern his "wandering eyes." The strange and the monstrous, like blindness and vanity, are further associations of the image of errantry, and it is not long before the reader forges a yet larger associative link with this wandering motif: resemblances met in this meandering life often strike the hero as uncanny, *unheimlich*.

By dramatizing the "image of lost direction," as Frye has named this archetypal cluster, Spenser is following long centuries of traditional iconography. Besides the dense forest, where the labyrinth is all tangle, mythology can pursue this sinister logic to its conclusion, where it discovers the image Eliot used for his microcosmic epic of the modern world, the wasteland. If the labyrinth is the archetypal order of things outside the temple, if it is the basic image of profane space, then its form is to be defined not so much as a material setting (trees, rocks, streams, etc.) as a general condition of unmapped disorder. The poet born into a Christian world will often suggest that outside the temple lies the desert, the place of inevitable wandering. Without a guide, like a Guyon without his Palmer, man appears destined to wander forever. In the desert he may die horribly, alone, or he may fade away in gradual exhaustion. The wasteland is an unmarked wilderness. The Children of Israel would surely have been lost but that "the Lord went before them by day in a pillar of a cloud, to lead them the way; and by night in a pillar of fire, to give them light; to go by day and night." Without such signs a man deserted cannot choose but lose his way, and wandering becomes his destiny.

Common to these images of the deserted profane space, with their burning sands and feeble, inadequate shade "under the red rock," is a cosmic emptiness, a terror that man and god have withdrawn from the evil represented by the unbounded horizon. When the sea is depicted as an element of chaos, it too shares in this iconography of cosmic desertion, for then sailors wander over its "pathless wastes." In a somewhat comic vein Spenser suggests this sea-born confusion in his myth of Phaedria, who pilots her "wandring ship" over the Idle Lake until she reaches the floating island. How much more fearful is the waste sea that imprisons Florimell, or the mythologized Irish Sea crossed by the shepherd in *Colin Clouts Come Home Again*.

> And is the sea (quoth *Coridon*) so fearfull?
> Fearful much more (quoth he) than hart can fear:
> Thousand wyld beasts with deep mouthes gaping direfull
> Therein stil wait poore passangers to teare.
> Who life doth loath, and longs death to behold,
> Before he die, alreadie dead with feare,
> And yet would live with heart halfe stonie cold,
> Let him to sea, and he shall see it there.
> And yet as ghastly dreadfull, as it seemes,
> Bold men presuming life for gaine to sell,
> Dare tempt that gulf, and in those wandring stremes
> Seek waies unknowne, waies leading down to hell.
>
> (200–211)

If the terror of infinite space may be realized on land and sea during the Renaissance, an even wider sense of the vastness of outer space grows apace, and poets may now envision the receding horizon through the yet larger forms of space travel, as in *Paradise Lost*. During the Renaissance material horizons were rapidly expanding, notably those of the tiny island power into a world explorer and world trader. In *The Merchant of Venice* the profane world is mapped by an inversion of the stillness of a perfect Belmont—the wandering of lost merchant ships.

The Spenserian meditation might be expected to come down heavily on a pessimistic note, but it does not. The poet opposes his own demonic imagery. Because the labyrinth comes to be his dominant image for the profane space lying outside the temple, the labyrinth becomes the largest image for faerieland as a whole. Logically then, if we except the final apocalypse of the New Jerusalem, the heavenly City, the sacred temple space will always be found *inside* the labyrinth. The human temple assumes the existence of the labyrinth, where it finds itself. The labyrinth specifies the large and open extensions of faerieland, the temple its perfect enclosures. As in a Western, without the desert there can be no stockade, no Fort Bravo, not even a Dodge City.

In principle, therefore, the profane world is simply the world outside, or before, the temple; it is *pro-fanum*. It thus has a neutral aspect, into which we must briefly inquire. On this level the profane world appears to be the arena of business, of mundane commerce, of the Rialto, the marketplace, the undistinguished, ordinary, everyday scene of man's mortal life. News here means largely the ups and downs of gain and loss. Such was the "profit and loss" of Eliot's drowned Phoenician sailor, and such "the motive of action" in *East Coker*. On the whole, on this level, life simply goes on, with the individual and the species seeking its own survival, if not its fortune.

The truth is complicated here, as with other archetypal clusters. What emerges from *The Faerie Queene*, as from *The Wasteland* and the *Four Quartets*, is a labyrinth imagery which is only apparently dualistic. As a picturesque beauty may be intricate so may the beauty of this poetic maze called faerieland. Edward Dowden wrote that *"The Faerie Queene*, if nothing else, is at least a labyrinth of beauty, a forest of old romance in which it is possible to lose oneself more irrecoverably amid the tangled luxury of loveliness than elsewhere in English poetry." Loveliness is not the whole story, but the tangle and luxury are truly Spenserian, and their form is mazelike. They are basic Spenserian facts chiefly because the labyrinth itself permits an ambivalence. The temple may perhaps be unreservedly benign and desirable. The labyrinth is, by contrast, suspended between contraries.

The labyrinth is not a polarity, but a continuum joining two poles. It might be constructed according to the formula: Terror—Neutrality (Indifference?)—Delight. The terrifying is readily understandable as one pole. The delightful is less easy to account for. But even here the poet is traditional. Military defenses had been early transformed into the fanciful form of magical protections thrown up around a sacred spot. Hostile beings and influences cannot penetrate the web of mazed spells cast by the medicine man. Such visionary defenses are understandable enough, since the defenders of a real city surrounded by an intricate outwork, would know its turns and twists intimately, while the attackers would not. Eliade has observed that frequently the labyrinth protected the temple by providing a trial of initiatory access to the sacred world within. Perhaps on this analogy it could be argued that the "delightful land of faerie" is a maze surrounding the series of temples which comprise the heart of each successive book, and that in this sense faerieland "protects" each temple. The labyrinth implies a rite of passage. [As Mircea Eliade points out], "The labyrinth, like any other trial of initiation, is a difficult trial in which not all are fitted to triumph. In a sense, the trials of Theseus in the labyrinth of Crete were of equal significance with the expedition to get the golden apples from the garden of Hesperides, or to get the golden fleece of Colchis. Each of these trials is basically a victorious entry into a place hard of access, and well defended, where there is to be found a more or less obvious symbol of power, sacredness and immortality." This perspective on the continuum gives faerieland a double value which Spenser's readers have often observed, that while its lack of structure is threatening to the hero, he still persists in his quest, as if delighted by his good fortune in being awarded the heroic trial. Though each quest moves ambiguously "forward" in the manner of Redcrosse and Una ("at last resolving forward still to fare"), each quest also assumes the goal of a homecoming. Not surprisingly we find that the most Spenserian of the Metaphysicals, Andrew Marvell, is fascinated by the idea of the protective labyrinth. This image governs the form of "The Garden" and makes it a lyric temple never fully detached from the profane world, where men, amazed, wander about, seeking fame and fortune. The truly green nature that surrounds one in England lends substance to this mythography.

In a revealing passage of his autobiography C. S. Lewis caught this natural perspective on the problem of the protective labyrinth. He was talking about youthful walks in Surrey, which he contrasted with walks in Ireland, his homeland. "What delighted me in Surrey was its intricacy. My Irish walks commanded large horizons and the general lie of land and sea could be taken in at a glance; I will try to speak of them later. But in Surrey the contours were so tortuous, the little valleys so narrow, there was so much timber, so many villages concealed in woods or hollows, so many field paths, sunk lanes, dingles, copses, such an unpredictable variety of cottage, farmhouse, villa, and country seat, that the whole thing could never be clearly in my mind, and to walk in it daily gave me the same sort of pleasure that there is in the labyrinthine complexity of Malory or *The Faerie Queene*." Physical perambulation here provides a model for reading Spenser.

Such walking tours of *The Faerie Queene* will generate a growing atmosphere of centeredness, as each picture of the picturesque scene is framed in the mind's eye, becoming a momentary symbol of the center. At such times the essential emptiness of Faerieland fills with structured shapes, and the reader will feel the presence of the temple as the tempering harmony of order in disorder.

PARODIC TRANSFORMATIONS

The ambivalence of the labyrinth is a prominent case of the mythological "parody" whereby, for example, a demonic image provides a travesty of an apocalyptic image. The wasteland is the demonic parody of the delightful maze. Similarly with the temple: the Bower of Bliss and the House of Busirane are demonic parodies of temples of pleasure and love. The Caves of Despair and Mammon are demonic parodies of the temples of Holiness and Temperance. In such "waste houses," as Lewis called them, one often finds "no living creature," and in that case the hero has Britomart's experience of "wastefull emptinesse." Demonic parody is a fully developed Spenserian technique. The narrative consequence of this technique is a continuous creation of ambiguous choices for the hero. Everywhere the hero must decide whether he is looking at the real thing, or at a double of the real thing. He is rarely given a choice between flatly different things. He can never take the forms of being for granted. He can only hope that, with his memory of principles holding firm and his love of the good remaining strong, he will continue in the process of discovery.

Parody is, however, a symmetrical effect. The parodic process enters the poem as the testing of good by evil, but it may be reversed. The neutralizing of the labyrinth is a case of a benign, if not exactly apocalyptic, parody. A certain amount of comedy will arise out of the apocalyptic transformation of the fearsome labyrinth. And with a poetic imagery thus loosened up, the reader will have to look for the means of knowing the direction of parody. Whatever means it is, it will be an emergent attitude, a superordinate.

The key to the direction of parodic change will be the hero's freedom to continue his quest. If he is free to go forward, for him at that moment the labyrinth is benign or at least neutral. If he is held or trapped in place, like the lovers in Busirane's palace or like the obsessed Furor, then he is a creature of the sinister maze. Similarly, if a "paradise" like the Bower of Bliss prevents free exit to its denizens, then it is a demonic parody of a true paradise. The defining principle is freedom to enter and leave. The demonic parody of the temple, that is, the sinister form of the labyrinth, is thus always a prison.

Again the genre of romantic epic makes it easy to narrate the testing of mythic parodies. The freedom of entry and departure is an issue as soon as the hero begins to move about in faerieland. The labyrinth assumes the function of a necessary medium through which the hero must pass in his life of continuous initiation. "The supreme rite of initiation is to enter a labyrinth and return from it, and yet every life, even the least eventful, can be taken as the journey through a labyrinth. The sufferings and trials undergone by Ulysses were fabulous, and yet any man's return home has the value of Ulysses' return to Ithaca"—a value on which Joyce placed considerable stress. There is no completely Odyssean hero in *The Faerie Queene*, but there is a little of Odysseus in many of Spenser's protagonists, especially insofar as they are seeking to respond to the transformations of an endlessly shape-shifting scene. Held in the maze, the hero emerges from it suddenly in the middle of the way. Suddenly he gets a perspective on the perspectiveless tangle. Daedalus, who made the inescapable labyrinth, in which even he might get lost, was not accidentally a mythic inventor of human flight. With Proteus, he is the master of transformations. He invents wings, the parody of a bird's wings, and he invents the maze. It seems important that Daedalus is thus the inventor of the original prison, which he could redeem or transform by his parodic invention of the means of freedom. Something of the equivocal nature of this double achievement inheres in the rich overtones of the terms "daedal" and "daedalian," with their implication of endless but slightly sinister prolixity.

PROPHECY AND HISTORY IN "THE FAERIE QUEENE"

Prophecy is a visionary interpretation of the life of the spirit. A vocation rather than a job, prophecy gives the poet an inspired voice, and with this voice he utters, not words, but the Word, the Logos. A divine spirit speaks through him, informing his human speech with a rare self-possession. The prophetic poet is uniquely sure of himself, and this he shows by allowing his utterance to be enigmatic and obscure on its surface, knowing that the immediate surface of the riddle is supported by an underlying clarity. The prophet seeks to be the clear medium of the divine wisdom—Blake held that he wrote his poem by "dictation." His task is literally a calling. In *The Faerie Queene* the strangely automated ritualism of the verse is one familiar sign of this vocation. In general such "dictated" speech displays a freedom from material reference. The prophet seeks "the liberation of a word of God, which becomes objectively powerful far beyond the personal range of the prophet's activity. Once spoken and current, his word is, as we might almost say, depersonalized, and enters upon its own independent history. . . . The word will be more or less detached from its human speaker, and become an independent event." Even though the Old Testament prophets are highly individual in their styles of utterance, their prophetic speech abandons the typical aims of personal communications (self-expression) and takes on the role of a communal and, if need be, impersonal eloquence.

The prophet may be opposed to the futurist predictor, but he is even more unlike the mystic, whose passive, quietistic, contemplative resignation and removal from the hurly burly of life are expressed as a strong distrust of history. The mystic shuns the life of man in time, seeking a withdrawn perfection. Prophets reject withdrawal. "Their inspiration did not make the prophets [of the Old Testament] independent of the historical conditions of their time. They did not desire or conceive any such independence. The notion of them as mystical dreamers brooding in a realm above space and time, and forecasting the remote future in riddles to be deciphered by an amazed posterity, is wholly misleading. They were intensely men of the hour. . . . Their interests were particular and not general, concrete and not abstract." And yet, as Dodd goes on to say, "they spoke eternal truth." The paradox may be resolved if we think that the prophet utters an eternal truth that is immanent in the daily affairs of men. This daily life is contained in the notion of history.

With Spenser the varieties of history are threefold, but only one of these has major force in his poetry. There is, to begin with, the cyclical historiography of the ancient Greeks, which tends to discern a periodic order in "the spectacle of incessant change." Great men perform great actions, and these are complete, like the plots of plays. But history in this view has no overall structure or unity that can be conceived developmentally. During the Renaissance this historiographic mode persists in longer poems like *Albion's England* and the *Mirror for Magistrates*, and we find that the periodic image of life gives the poet an arsenal of cyclical images. Samuel Daniel catches this tone of inevitable cycle in his valedictory couplet addressed to the "great men," Essex and Mountjoy: "And therefore leave, sad muse, th'imagined good./For we must now return again to blood." Doom is almost casual, and destiny automatic.

A second, more tentative historiographic style, that of modern historical study, is beginning to gain momentum during the period when Spenser wrote. According to such a model—and it remains very much an infant discipline—the historian's interest attaches, not to vast and impressive mythographic structures, but to the statement of limited chains of causal connection. The mapping, the surveying, the anatomizing of contemporary Elizabethan Britain and furthermore of English overseas voyaging play a major part in this development. Speculations on the growth of law and justice, we shall discover, share this same interest in record and research, and here too the concern for historical *conditions* will undermine belief in mere cyclical repetition. Nevertheless, although Spenser reflects this critical outlook in his *Vewe of the Present State of Ireland*, it exerts only a secondary influence on his poetry, giving it a Machiavellian hardness of attitude toward the pieties of mythographic history.

The third shape of history, somewhat misleadingly called "linear," finds its remoter origins in the Old Testament. [As Lewis observes] "The Hebrews saw their whole past as a revelation of the purposes of Jahweh. Christianity, going on from there, makes world-history in its entirety a single, transcendentally significant story with a well-defined plot pivoted on Creation, Fall, Redemption, and Judgment." Seemingly chaotic and unrelated events are shown to have a progressive character; history appears to move in a certain direction. Because wandering bulks large in this story, the form of history in this tradition should be called "linear" only with the express understanding that with it the line is not a very straight line. Lewis and others have referred to this mode of thought as "historicism," by which is meant "the belief that by studying the past we can learn not only historical but also metahistorical or transcendental truth." The governing drive in this historicist view seems to be the desire for a sense of direction.

The Old Testament shows how the Children of Israel are chosen to enact the central role in a providential drama. During the reign of Elizabeth this shaping view of a "linear" history would characterize the thinking of most Puritans, and Englishmen generally to the extent that they imagined England was chosen in a manner similar to the election of Israel. Prophecy arises out of such soil almost automatically. The prophet confronts a heterogeneous mass of deviations from a straight line—which come about in the nature of almost any personal or corporate existence. He gives these deviations a meaning. Moses shows how the errors, wanderings, trials of the Exodus demand a reduction to order, and he achieves this reduction by demonstrating that the apparently random omens of the desert are the natural signs of a divine ordinance. By showing that the wanderings of the chosen ones are momentously linked to the all-known but veiled design, the prophet "straightens" the twisting, labyrinthine shapes of profane time. When the children are lost, he unveils his prophetic gift, an inspired sense of direction.

Spenser is a Christian poet and he subordinates the insights of cyclical and scientific history to the Christian revelation of a prophetic historicism. When Coleridge remarked that *The Faerie Queene* showed "a marvellous independence and true imaginative absence of all particular space or time," he was only partly right. Like *The Shepheardes Calender* the epic may allude to topical events, but it does so in a universalizing way, so that allusions to current happenings tend to go *through* their historical particularity, till they reach a level of transcendent meaning. From each ephemeral contact with history there emerges a larger pattern, a providential British destiny. Emergency here has the intentionality of the Logos. Each particular crisis advances a single great argument.

The poet's "acceptance of history—this reduction of dream to providential event" is uttered as prophecy. The stories told in *The Faerie Queene* have their natural narrative form, each to its own, but the larger mythos of the poem as a whole acquires the providential form of an historicist dream. Romantic narrative aids this development. Each temple holds out an intermediate promise of final recognition. All intermediate errantry becomes a metaphor for the search for structure in a disordered world. Errantry modulates into cognitive error, which in turn may extend into theology, as in Book I, where error is from time to time lack of faith, of law, of joy. Una, "representing" the Temple, stands for that special "oneness with" which is the mark of a transcendental faith in the true God. Error denotes a mistaken deviation from a right line of thought or conduct, and in this broader sense of deviation from correct judgments error is the symbolic action that typically occurs in the labyrinth. In addition, although error permits the wildest wandering once the deviation has started, the radical assumption of error is always a way (the *via* of the *homo viator*) from which the deviation departs. When judgment corrects an error, the symbolic act of correction is a return to the right way. These spatial metaphors are standard in the imagery of prophetic historicism.

Spenserian heroes are always learning something, and sometimes they gain corrected visions of their lives, when they receive enshrined wisdom. Sir Guyon and Prince Arthur, for example, are given a short course in history. Redcrosse learns who he is, Saint George, when Heavenly Contemplation leads him to reflect on the difference between the City of God and the City of Man. This reflection divides and yet also unites the temple with the labyrinth. Such recognitions are the basis of the internal prophetic structure of the poem at large. Even so, it is also possible to call *The Faerie Queene* a prophetic poem because it goes beyond these periodic visions vouchsafed to the hero. It does include these moments of truth. But *The Faerie Queene*, like all legitimate prophecy, is a larger unity. It is a "constitutive" vision. It builds "the constant incorporation of past, present, and future events into that which claims to be a word of the everlasting God." The constitutive aim of prophecy amounts to an inbuilding function, an assimilation of the poetic narrative to a steadily emerging vision of a final, guiding Logos. Each episode of knight errantry adds its material substance to the accumulated argument of a higher truth, the revelation of a providential will. Because Spenser is a

Christian poet, writing in the tradition laid down by the Old and New Testaments, this higher revelation usually ends up as a vision of justice.

Poetically the superordinate vista is revealed as the gradual marriage of the poem with its message. *The Faerie Queene* may at first appear a random collection of heroic quests—we have six Legends, but we might as well have twelve, ten, or twenty-four. The poem, looked at "from a distance," itself finally becomes a heroic quest, the poet's myth of prophetic historicism. Berger has shown this in some detail, as a property of Book VI. But of Book I he has given a similar account: "We might approach the first Book in this light as a dialectic between hero and poet: the knight, through weakness of will and mis-placed confidence in self, permits the evil to grow and to dominate the poem; the poet illuminates the growing evil, catches and controls it as image, through the widening network of allusion, the delicate modulations of symbolic reference. What happens to the knight becomes clearer as well as more more critical. It even seems that Redcrosse gets well *in order to* make the evil luxuriate, tempt it to assert itself and so expose its true nature." Some readers may object that this process would contaminate Spenser's muse. But reflexive virtuosity is the natural condition of prophetic utterance. The more reticulated the poem becomes, the more it reflects the poet's exuberant involvement with his own genius and freedom. Orpheus, rather than Narcissus, the suicidal beauty, is the spirit of this poetry. An Orphic enthusiasm lends grace and a kind of permanence to the ephemeral glory of the native ground marked out by the temple and the labyrinth.

PATRICIA A. PARKER

The Romance of Romance

Readers frequently have sensed, in reading Book VI [of *The Faerie Queene*], that the poem, if not demonstrably ending, is beginning, retrospectively, to explore its own implications. Humphrey Tonkin finely remarks in it a tension between two types of romance—the chivalric and pastoral—which is finally a tension between *The Faerie Queene*'s two archtypes, quest and circle, forward movement towards end or accomplishment, and the bower, or embowered moment, along the way. The task of the knight of Courtesy is the accomplishment of the end Artegall does not reach—the subduing of the Blatant Beast. But just as in the Legend of Friendship the resolution of end, conflict, or "travail" is suspended in favor of a *discordia concors*, so in the Legend of Courtesy, the emphasis falls not only on the completion of the quest but on the delights—and discoveries—of the "way." The opening stanzas of the Proem extend this dwelling upon, or dilation of, that middle space to the delightful "wanderings" of the poem itself:

> The waies, through which my weary steps I guyde,
>> In this delightfull land of Faery,
>> Are so exceeding spacious and wyde,
>> And sprinckled with such sweet variety,
>> Of all that pleasant is to eare or eye,
>> That I nigh rauisht with rare thoughts delight,
>> My tedious trauell doe forget thereby;
>> And when I gin to feele decay of might,
> It strength to me supplies, and chears my dulled spright.
>> (VI. Pro. 1)

From *Inescapable Romance: Studies in the Poetics of a Mode.* Copyright © 1979 by Princeton University Press.

This stanza seems to gather up and remove the sting from images and phrases which earlier in the poem suggested more dangerous kinds of delay. The "delightfull land" of Faery echoes the solace of the Wood of Errour ("Led with delight, they thus beguile the way"), while "Exceeding spacious and wyde" inevitably recalls the Bower of Excess and its more suspect dilation. "Rauisht," if it picks up echoes of Arthur's dream of the Faerie Queene ("Was neuer hart so rauisht with delight," I. ix. 14.6), also recalls the false Una brought to Red Cross ("So liuely, and so like in all mens sight, / That weaker sence it could haue rauisht quight," I. i. 45. 4–5).

Similarly, the bowers encountered as this Legend proceeds seem now to be not dangerous temptations, but rather part of the inwardness of the Virtue itself. The first enclosed space is that "siluer bowre" which, "hidden" from "view of men, and wicked worlds disdaine" (Pro. 3. 3–4), is "the sacred noursery / Of vertue" (3.1–2), the growing place of Courtesy. And this bower anticipates the proliferation of desirable *tempes* which, after the social and political concerns of Book V, seem manifestly a form of retreat, and yet one whose leading "inward farre" (I. i. 7. 8) is now not *in malo* but *in bono*. Young Tristram dwells in seclusion "amongst the woodie Gods" (VI. ii. 26. 3), the Salvage Man "Farre in the forrest by a hollow glade" where "foot of liuing creature neuer trode" (iv. 13. 5–8). Priscilla is discovered with Aladine, as Serena with Calepine, in secret "shade" (ii. 43. 2; iii. 20. 3). The Hermit shuns "this worlds vnquiet waies" (vi. 4. 7) and Meliboe the "vainenesse" of the court (ix. 24. 9). The three Graces were begotten in a "pleasant groue" (x. 22. 3), and Courtesy itself seems linked with the honoring of privacy, as Calidore apologizes for intruding upon the bower of Calepine and Serena (iii. 21). *Tempe* indeed proves, as the Book progresses, to be only temporary, and the bower a fragile defense against more threatening intrusions, but the sense which accompanies its loss, in this Legend, is frequently a sense of regret, and not the sense of the priority of the questing or forward movement which overturns the dangerous embowered spaces and suspect "shades" of earlier Books.

From the perspective of a retreat not suspect but delightful, the linear thrust of the quest itself becomes a kind of intrusion, a movement which if it involves the accomplishment of a goal, also breaks up the pastoral *tempe*. The mention of Calidore's armor as he doffs it for "shepheards weed" (ix. 36. 3–4) seems almost inevitably to provoke the comparison to Paris and Oenone (36. 7), to an entry into a retreat which finally meant its doom. The potentially problematic nature of questing is raised earlier in the poem, in the elemental questers of Book II and the end-stopped or possessive pursuits of Books III and IV. But here it seems curiously to be reflected in the Blatant Beast itself—both the quest's ostensible object and a monster which like Malory's Questing Beast seems at least partly to embody the restlessness of questing, a pursuit whose "toile" (x. 2. 2) anticipates that rejected in Marvell's very Spenserian "Garden." Calidore's choice of the "perfect pleasures, which doe grow / Amongst poore hyndes" (x. 3. 5–6) is a retreat from his primary objective, and yet is praised by the poet in contrast with the hunt after "courtly fauour" and its "shadowes vaine" (x. 2). Indeed, the folly of exclusive focus on an end or goal is perhaps most evident in the case of "Courtesy," which must not only follow the quest laid upon the knight by the Queene (x. 1. 4), but have the leisure, and occasion, to "shew" what it professes (xii. 2. 4).

Yet this contrasting of desirable retreat and intruding "pursuit" is only one aspect of the complexities of this Legend. The bower and its cognates, the closed circle and the centripetal gaze, participate in an ambivalence which is created, as so often in Spenser, by a network of internal echoings, the unsettling repetition of the same words in several dissonant contexts. The motif of the cynosure or closed visual circle links the sight of Pastorella on her "litle hillocke" (ix. 8. 1) with the vision of the Graces on Mt. Acidale, but it also includes the cannibals staring at the nakedness of Serena (viii. 43) and the merchants' "greedy" gaze (xi. 13. 8). The description of Calidore's "hungry eye" (ix. 26. 7) as he gazes upon Pastorella may be simply part of the vocabulary of love, but it is disturbing as well, coming as it does only one canto after the cannibals' "feeding," and may be a reminder that the cynosure is always at least potentially a visual gluttony or embowered fix, a variant of the enchantress feeding her eyes upon the paralyzed youth (II. xii. 73).

Similarly, the inwardness of the bower may provide the privileged site of vision, but it also involves, in this Book, the ambivalence of what Wallace Stevens later called "evasion," the impulse of "retreat" in both senses. Echoes of Phaedria's bower in the opening stanzas and beyond seem to be presenting the positive side of its appeal, the pastoral retreat where to take no thought for the morrow is to be open to the grace of God as well as of nature. Yet Meliboe's honeyed words in praise of the retired life (ix. 26) have the same effect as Despair's (I. ix. 31), and the success of the brigands is at least partly enabled by the passivity of an attitude, or retreat, which neglects to prepare for them. Even at the climax of the pastoral interlude and of the Book itself—the vision upon Mt. Acidale in canto x—the curious juxtaposition within the motto which precedes it suggests that vision itself may be a form of evasion, and in this respect, this center of several concentric rings only intensifies the problematic inwardness of the retreat:

> Calidore sees the Graces daunce,
>   To Colins melody:
> The whiles his Pastorell is led,
>   Into captiuity.

The juxtaposition—however fortuitous—implies that "Pastorell" may be ravished *because* Calidore is rapt in vision, a fixation which, like an earlier one, leaves him without "any will . . . thence to moue away" (ix. 12. 2), at the same time as the destruction of the "pastoral" by the brigands leaves a sense of the melancholy of intrusion, of the sacrifice of circle to line.

   This interrogation of both embowered space and that which intrudes upon, or supersedes it, heightens the poem's earlier exploration of both questing and retreat to the point where the Book's subject seems to be becoming the ambivalences of romance itself. In a Legend which seems on the surface so simple, so many contradictions remain as contradictions juxtaposed but not resolved into any higher meaning. Some of the Book's most important passages are irreducibly ambiguous, capable of saying at least two things at once, and manage simultaneously to suggest both the possible connection and potential conflict between its principal concerns—bower and quest, inward and outward, origin and issue. Several of its passages explore the possibility that the enclosed bower and forward quest might not be antagonists—either in the sense of Resolved Soul and Created Pleasure in Book II or in the sense of the fragile *tempe* violated by intruders—but rather complements, enabling the knight to emerge from the refreshment of retreat while still drawing from its "well" (Pro. 2. 5). Yet the very lines which suggest this fruitful dependence also contain the alternative—conflict rather than complementarity between the Legend's several opposites.

   In the Proem itself, the possibility of continuity between inner and outer, bower and emergence, is expressed in the metaphor of "ripenesse," of the "heauenly seedes" in the hidden "bowre" which burst forth into "honour" (Pro. 3). The sense here of a fruitful connection is continued in the imagery of fruition or pregnancy—the process of bringing to birth—which links the "noursery" of "vertue" with the nurture of the Legend's several children, from Tristram whose "bud" of courtesy "At length breakes forth" (ii. 35. 8–9) to the secret pregnancy of Claribell and the final emergence of Pastorella. The Proem, however, also presents a relation of inward and outward which is not continuity, but conflict. The several "buts" of stanza 5 ("But vertues seat is deepe within the mynd, /

And not in outward shows, but inward thoughts defynd," 8–9) reflect a tension between the "hidden" (3. 3) and the manifest, between "true curtesie" (5. 1) and the "forgerie" fashioned only "to please the eies of them, that pas" (5. 3–4).

Lewis, Tuve, and others have consistently argued that the eternal in Spenser is the ground as well as the goal of the temporal, that which enables divagation or wandering to be a species of "play." Yet Book VI, for all its happy endings, recovered origins, and miraculous coincidences, seems to admit of some radical doubt, a doubt which involves the questioning of its most central images. The Proem invokes a fruitful or natural connection between origin and issue, in the image of seeds grown to ripeness or of rivers returned to their "King" (7. 4–5), and seems to align with these the "bloosme of comely courtesie" which "brancheth forth in braue nobilitie" (4. 2–4). Yet Courtesy, if it has its hidden origin "deepe within the mynd" (5. 8), may also emerge as mere *bel sembiante*, a contrast to the nakedness of the Graces (x. 24). "Grace" itself embodies a tension between the uncontrollable (the Graces appear and disappear; grace either strikes or does not) and the art of control: there is both continuity and distance between its various meanings. Calidore is the knight through which the hidden virtue is to be made manifest, but the showing forth of his courteous arts is often indistinguishable from calculation. The "kind courtesies" which he "inuents" (ix. 34. 6) for Pastorella echo the too artful courtesy of Blandina in canto vi, and his adaptation of "manner" to occasion (ix. 36. 2) curiously resembles her ability to temper "words and lookes" (vi. 41. 9). His "queint vsage" (ix. 35. 2) and its contrast with the "lowly things" (35. 5) of Pastorell reflect the tension throughout the Book between the virtue nurtured on a "lowly stalke" (Pro. 4. 3) and the "Courtesie" derived from "Court."

This suggestion of both a continuity and a potential gap or "shade" between origin and issue, inward grace and outward sign, also extends to the more general preoccupation of the Book with origins and sources. The poem itself seems to be returning to its beginnings, as Serena recalls Una, Acidale the House of Holiness, the Hermit Contemplation, and the "harrowing" of the brigands' cave the recovery of Eden. The Legend is even generically in touch with origins, in its return to pastoral, a traditional and, for Spenser, actual early mode. But the Book which asks to be shown the source of its own virtue also calls into question the return to origins or the possibility of their recovery, emphasizing the gap as often as the link between origin and issue, including the "origin" which is etymology ("Of Court it *seemes*, men Courtesie doe call . . ." i. 1. 1, my italics). Courtesy itself is not always traceable to a particular source or "birth," and the examples of the gentle Salvage Man and the savage Sir Terpine both question the predictability of its origin and undercut the singularity of its possible "nourseries." Both continuity and discontinuity with origins are suggested through the copresence in this Legend of real and supposed foundlings. Pastorella is returned to, and recognized by, her natural parents, but the bear baby is *"gotten, not begotten"* of Sir Bruin (iv. 32. 7), and the teasing coincidence of names leaves it comically uncertain whether or not an actual homecoming is involved.

This complication of the return to origins also finally extends to the origins of romance itself. Countless readers have recorded the sense in this Book of returning to the roots of the genre, in a Legend whose anthology of romance motifs runs the gamut from Wild Men, faery rings, and secret cells to brigands, mysterious foundlings, and the reunion of parents and children. But there is a sense in which this rehearsal of romance motifs also distances them, these origins like other origins in the Legend both sought and seen as retreating. The Book multiplies its tales of the unexpected or miraculous end, and the venerable romance *topos* of conversion is reflected in the unexpected changes of heart in Briana and Crudor, in Sir Enias, and perhaps in Mirabella. The revelation of Pastorella's birthmark is the romance tale of recognition and restoration in its purest form. But it might also be said that Spenser is deliberately distancing these images. The seeming contradiction between the romance of infinite delay and the romance of happy endings dissolves in this Legend, where the happy ending is itself a form of retreat. A sense of miraculous fortune hovers over Calepine's coming upon the cannibals just in time to save Serena. But "fortune" is here, as in Ariosto, the poet himself, and Spenser seems uncharacteristically at pains in this Book to point to the resultant artifice of its transitions:

> The which discourse as now I must delay,
> Till *Mirabellaes* fortunes I doe further say.
> (vii. 50. 8–9)

> But first it falleth me by course to tell
> Of faire *Serena*, who as earst you heard . . .
> (viii. 31. 1–2)

> But day, that doth discouer bad and good,
> Ensewing, made her knowen to him at last:
> The end whereof Ile keepe vntill another cast.
> (vii. 51. 7–9)

Both the marking of transitions and the careful interweaving of episodes throughout Book VI contribute to this sense of artifice, an impression which Spenser usually mutes. Calidore disappears in canto iii and does not reappear until canto ix, a digression which calls forth another of the narrator's metaphors for his own activity (ix. 1). The happy endings, by their very nature, seem contrived. The story of the foundling Calepine saves is virtually a parody of the fortunate coincidence. The baby who begins as the prey of a "cruell Beare" (iv. 17. 8), is borne by Calepine, and finally, in answer to a prophecy, becomes the heir of "Sir Bruin," seems a *reductio ad absurdum* of the romance tale and its almost perfect circular form. Each of the Legend's images of refuge—of the closed or embowered circle or the fortunate ending—is shrouded by a simultaneous sense of distance and contingency. The happy ending whereby Sir Bruin gets his heir is specifically said to be a miraculous forestalling of a fiend called "Cormoraunt": it is, that is to say, a tale told against time. But canto xi—the canto of the carnage in the brigands' cave—opens with a reflection on the possibility of any "sure happinesse," "on earth too great a blessednesse" to last.

This sense of the fragility of the enclosed space and happy ending extends finally to the status of words and the power of poetry itself. Book VI is a highly literary legend: "Meliboe" is a name taken from both Virgil and Chaucer; Aladine suggests the printers Aldine; "Colin Clout" is an allusion both to Skelton and to Spenser. "Turning all to game" (IV. iv. 13. 1) is a frequent image, in Book IV, for the *concordia* of gracious speech, its crucial element of "play," and this "play" reaches its climax upon Mt. Acidale. But if words too are part of making outward what is inward, and thus part of this Legend's reflections on the *form* of emergence, there is a sense in this literary legend that words alone are by no means certain good. The "glas" of the Proem (5.5, "Which see not perfect things but in a glas . . .") is both that which separates inward and outward (5.6, "that glasse so gay, that it can blynd . . .") and the shadowy *speculum* of mediation. The vision of Mt. Acidale has to do not only with vision—as in the episode of Contemplation in Book I—but with poetic mediation, as Colin Clout's "dilation" (x. 21. 1: "Tho gan that shepheard thus for to dilate . . .") fills in the gap left by the disappearance of the Graces. This "dilation" is itself a form of emergence or coming-out: it has a Hermes or hermeneutic function in relation to its source, like the "meantime" of procession between origin and end in the Neo-Platonic *dilatio* of Mutabilitie. But it also a sign of absence, and it is a tribute to the complexity of Spenser's double vision—of the limitation or loss signalled by this "dilation" and yet also of its worth—that readers have tended to stress one *or* the other.

Courtesy, like poetry, depends upon the art of words: Calidore is, for Spenser's knights, untypically short on weaponry and the implication is that words are his substitute. But when, in the fight against the brigands, Calidore finds a "sword of better say" (xi. 47. 5), the suggestion in the *double entendre* is that words have failed him, that the humanist Hercules Gallicus has reverted to the more purely physical hero. His "harrowing" of the brigands' den recalls the descent of Orpheus to regain Eurydice, and Pastorella's restoration seems to be a successful version of that myth. But the happy ending of Pastorella's return is specifically put before the pursuit of the Blatant Beast, and Calidore's victory is only temporary.

Spenser's own claim to be the "Bryttane Orpheus" sounds implicitly through the *Shepheardes Calender* and *The Faerie Queene*: Orpheus in the "October" eclogue (28–30) is the legendary tamer of Cerberus and in the Legend of Friendship (IV. ii. 1) the civilization hero of Comes' description, the singer who calmed the discord of the Argonauts. Spenser's image of himself as an Orpheus draws at least partly on that portion of the myth which celebrates the poet's triumph over time; but the Orpheus of Book VI is more the dismembered and unsuccessful one. The Graces can no more be recalled than can Eurydice. And the descendant of Cerberus, the "fearefull dog" (xii. 36. 9) Calidore leads "in bondage" through "all Faery land" (37. 1–5), escapes to attack even the "gentle Poets rime" (40. 8). The Book in which the possible complementarity of withdrawal and emergence is figured by the simultaneous advance and retreat of the dancing Graces, ends instead with a splitting apart or distancing of directions. The happy romance ending of Pastorella's return retreats from view as the narrator leaves mother and daughter to a joy whose privacy he cannot describe (xii. 20–22), while the Blatant Beast seems in the final stanzas ("So now . . . now . . . of late") to be advancing towards us, breaking through the circle of the poem into the harsh world of the present.

Book VI opens with a petition to be guided in the "strange waies" (Pro. 2. 8) of the "delightfull land of Faery" (1. 2), which "none can find, but who was taught them by the Muse" (2. 9), and the poet asks to have revealed, and to be led into, a "siluer bowre" far from "wicked worlds disdaine" (3. 4). But the gap between hidden bower and the poet's world seems to be widening in the final lines, as "Pastorell" is left behind and Calidore's victory (xii. 38–39) recedes into the past of a Faery Land forlorn. The suggestion through the Legend is that to inquire too closely into origins—or to penetrate a secret "shade"—would be to intrude upon a privacy, like that of a grace which cannot be forced or the Graces who disappear when Calidore determines to question their identity. But here this circumspection seems to be yielding to its other aspect, a sense of being ineluctably excluded from this bower, or unable to find the "way." The shadow which falls between origin and issue, bower and emergence, may finally be that of a retreat whose shade is impenetrable and a "noursery" whose location cannot be "revealed" (Pro. 3), not even by the "Muse."

The duality of judgment surrounding Calidore's pastoral retreat— seen both as a deviation from his "first quest" ("Vnmyndfull of his vow and high beheast," "entrapt of loue, which him betrayd," x. 1. 3, 7) and as refusal to "hunt still after shadowes vaine" (x. 2 .7)—has provoked a critical controversy which seeks to settle what Spenser leaves in ambiguous suspension, and this ambiguity extends to the stanzas which treat of the "staying" or "straying" of the poem itself. The same opening to canto xii which defends Calidore's delay offers a defense of the poet's own digression or wandering ("Right so it fares with me in this long way, / Whose course is often stayd, yet neuer is astray," 1. 8–9). Yet, in the *topos* which connects poetic and actual "feet," the "spacious" ways and ravishing "delight" of the Book's opening stanza suggest the possibility that poetry itself may be a siren song, an invitation to oblivion ("forget thereby") as persuasive as Phaedria's; and this voice in Spenser anticipates Romantics and Romantic critics since who note that *accidia*, the poem's moral evil, is also part of its poetic vagrancy, or "charm."

Spenser's sixth and last completed Book thus carries a resonance which provides not only a retrospect on romance but a sense of its prospects, the fortunes of the form from Milton to the Romantics, and beyond. Coleridge observed in a lecture "the marvelous independence and true imaginative absence of all particular space or time" in Spenser's poem, adding "it is truly in land of Faery, that is, of mental space. The poet has placed you in a dream, a charmed sleep, and you neither wish, nor have the power, to inquire where you are, or how you got there." His remark, however revealing of later conceptions of romance, falls short of Spenser's fine distinction between placed and unplaced, history and "faerie." But it does carry further a suggestion already implicit in the poem's final Legend, that romance itself is a bower, charm, or region of wandering, an evasion, and yet one perhaps necessary to the life of poetry, the only chance for creation in a Mammon world. If the displaced "faerie" at the opening of Book II anticipates the delights of Wallace Stevens' "Description without Place," the questioning here of both bower and questing, shady retreat and the demands of the "waking" world, leads in later versions of romance to a more anxious opposition. To emphasize the sense in Book VI of romance reflecting upon itself is not to substitute a

Romantic reading of *The Faerie Queene* for a more sensitively historical one, but simply to suggest what in the poem itself was to make it the romance poet's poem. Spenser's final Legend seems to privilege neither the overturning of the bower by actuality nor its own impulse to retreat; yet if it explores the possibility of a fruitful connection between the two, it also acknowledges its failure, the apprehension of a distance not diminishing but widening. The "end" of the embowered space in Book VI is as often catastrophe or loss as it is fulfillment, and the simultaneously suspect and protective "staying" of such spaces, including the poem itself, intensifies an element already in the poem and transforms it. *The Faerie Queene* is imbued with a sense of the doubleness of all things, the perception that "some virtues and some vices are so nicely distinguished, and so resembling each other as they are often confounded." But the ambiguities and unresolved contradictions of Book VI seem to participate less in the poem's network of parody doubles and real and counterfeit forms than in a genuine ambivalence, what may be finally not a doubleness of vision but a doubleness of mind.

The sense of both the desirability and the danger of delay or wandering remains in this Book in suspension, just as the final stanzas of the *Mutabilitie Cantos* leave the question open, impenetrable to a critical controversy whose very assumption of a definitive or final reading may not be appropriate to the deliberate, or perhaps, as one reader suggests, simply fortuitous, ambiguity of the closing lines. In the speaker's last reflections on the "doome" of Nature and the extent of Mutability, the ambiguity of "loath" ("Which makes me loath this state of life so tickle, / And loue of things so vaine to cast away," VII. viii. 1. 6–7) leaves finally uncertain which is prized, "mutability" or its ending. The movement of the syntax is not, as so often in Milton, a *correction* of the first line by the second, but, characteristically for Spenser, a *complication* of it. And the closing lines— both the prayer for the final "Sabbath" and the claim that "all that moueth, doth in *Change* delight" (vii. 2. 6–9)—leave finally open the question of which is uppermost, the dilation of a creation he would be "loath" to leave or the precipitation of the fall of all that stands between him and the promised "Eternity."

LAWRENCE MANLEY

Spenser and the City:
The Minor Poems

The historical significance of Renais-
sance cities is inseparable from their status as ideas. Burckhardt implied as
much when he began his *Civilization of the Renaissance in Italy* with a
chapter on "The State as a Work of Art"; and a recent work on the urban
culture of Renaissance Italy has enshrined the implication in its title:
Power and Imagination. Not just in Italy, but at different times and in
different ways throughout Europe, the life of Renaissance cities was shaped
not only by evolving economic forces and civic forms, but also by a
growth in civic awareness, a consciously novel effort to frame an urban
ideology. Because its chief architects were often literary humanists, that
ideology embodied as a major theme the role of literary culture in the
structure of power. According to the Ciceronian myth fostered by humanists, the arts of speech lay at the very roots of civic order. "The highest
science with which to govern the city," Brunetto Latini explained, "is the
science of language; without language there would be no cities, nor could
we establish justice and human community. And as Lord Berners similarly
remarked in the preface to his translation of Froissart's *Chroniques* (1523–25),
political power flows from literary sources: "So thus, through the monumentes
of writynge, . . . many men have ben moved, some to bylde cytes, some
to devyse and establisshe lawes right profitable, necessarie, and behovefull
for the humayne lyfe. . . ."

Mythographical commonplace had bestowed on poets a distin-

From *Modern Language Quarterly* 3, vol. 43 (September 1982). Copyright © 1983 by
University of Washington.

guished role in this process, for the figures of Orpheus and Amphion were said to exemplify the basic truth that the life of the city was coeval with the life of poetry. Boccaccio said of Amphion that

> his moving stones with his cythara to construct the walls of Thebes was none other than that by sweet speech he persuaded ignorant and savage men, living scattered about, to come together in one place, to live in civilized fashion, and to enclose the city with walls for public defense.

And Natalis Comes similarly claimed that when Orpheus

> had met with people still savage, who were living without any inkling of manners and without laws, and who were wandering through the fields after the manner of beasts, having built no shelter, he carried so much weight by speaking and by the smoothness of his speech, that he brought them over to a gentler kind of life, called them together in one place, and taught them to build cities, to obey the laws of cities, and to preserve the rites of marriage.

Orpheus and Amphion appear frequently in the mayoral pageants of Tudor London, and as part of the royal entertainment of Henry II in Paris in 1558, Orpheus led forth a ship carried by the Argonauts to express the city's support of the king. When Sidney defended poetry for its contribution to "the ethic and politic consideration," he instanced the story that "Amphion was said to move stones with his poetry to build Thebes," and Thomas Lodge demonstrated the almost literal authority of the myth when he flatly declared, "Poetes were the first raysors of cities. . . ."

Critics have remarked that "no poet has less to say about great cities" than Spenser, and that even in his epic poem "there is a surprising absence of cities." For Spenser, the Orphic voice—at least in its urban, Amphionic mode—is intertwined with others as part of a complex poetic career. The "Bryttane *Orpheus*," as one encomiast called him, was also the poet "whose Muse whilome did maske, / As time her taught, in lowly Shepheards weeds." Indeed, the Vergilian program that provides the basic shape for Spenser's career seems to overshadow the Orphic model; to begin as Vergil is to begin late, not early, in the history of culture, with a sophisticated literary pose or "maske," a "timely" pastoral voice whose plaint—already weary of the city—is in cultural terms a second start rather than a true beginning: "Resort of people doth my greefs augment, / The walled townes do worke my greater woe" ("August," 157–58), *The Shepheardes Calender*). As a literary point of departure, Cuddie's plaint, like the plaints of Colin Clout, presages a poetic career whose orientation toward the city will be complex and oblique, and whose epic culmination will embrace its pastoral beginnings in a *discordia concors*, deferring the progress toward Cleopolis with counterthrusts like Calidore's, when

> from the citties to the townes him prest,
> And from the townes into the countrie forsed,
> And from the country back to priuate farmes he scorsed.

> From thence into the open fields he fled. . . .
> (*The Faerie Queene*, 6.9.3–4)

But in Spenser's poetry, the sense of pastoral as a flight or a second beginning stems from a cultural priority attached to the city. The traditional *otium* of pastoral—always defined by shifting oppositions to urban *negotium*—is for Spenser an especially impermanent state. In cultural terms an exile, it is neither a true beginning nor end; in poetic terms a "maske" or role, it is a temporary, transitional strategy. If it seems unclear to Colin Clout, when he comes home again, just where home really is, that is because he leads the life of an exile, "banisht . . . like wight forlore, / Into that waste, where I was quite forgot" (*Colin Clouts Come Home Againe*, 182–83). As Gabriel Harvey observed, Colin Clout "is not euery body," but a sophisticate; not so rustic as Cuddie or Thomalin, he speaks for a poet who was, in crucial ways, a Londoner.

Born in Smithfield, probably the son of a journeyman clothworker, Spenser was educated, through the civic philanthropy of a major London guild, as a "poor boy" at the Merchant Taylors' School. Taught by Richard Mulcaster, a contributor to London's street pageants who once wrote that he loved Rome, but London more, he received a gown and a shilling to represent his school at the funeral of Robert Nowell, a wealthy London citizen whose family later contributed to Spenser's support as a sizar (or poor scholar) at Cambridge. His first appointment as secretary to the bishop of Rochester brought him several times to London, on at least one occasion dressed, Gabriel Harvey suggests, as a "yunge Italianate Seignior and French Monsieur." By 1579 in the service of Leicester, Spenser proudly addressed his letters to Harvey from Leicester House, and he married his first wife at St. Margaret's in Westminster that same year. Spenser's final eighteen years of service in Ireland were punctuated, toward the end, by several returns to London, on the last of which, if Jonson could be believed, he "died for lake of bread in King Street."

This career, like the city to which it was anchored, encompasses a remarkable range of social influences—mercantile, learned, ecclesiastical, and courtly. What the bare events and rumors may suggest in the way of personal experience—aspiration, success, disappointment—seems inseparable from the central setting, a city rich in promise and in perils. Though

Spenser's literary education would in any case have inclined him to adopt the public stance of classical poets, personal experience may also explain why Spenser's self-understanding as a poet is so closely tied to his assessment of the city as an index to his culture's viability. That assessment is a mixed one. If, as I believe, Spenser's career demonstrates a "growth of the poet's mind," a developing confidence in both the powers of poetry and the possible endurance of his culture, the context of this growth is always a fundamental ambivalence, in which the city may at different times express vice, vanity, imperial grandeur, political virtue, concord, prosperity, mutability, or cultural longevity. The range of symbolic possibilities indeed runs parallel to the generic variety in Spenser's corpus, sometimes actually motivating genre, sometimes serving as a point of reference, but always underlining the extent to which, for Spenser, the city can be a literary as well as a cultural microcosm.

In his approach to the city, then, Spenser expands the Vergilian capacity for paradox. The epic celebrant of a renascent civilization, Spenser is simultaneously its chief poet of mutability, and in his poetry the symbolic glory of the city is rarely separable from a sense of its corruptible mortality. When the Orphic voice sounds so remotely in the October eclogue, it announces a cultural as well as a poetic belatedness. There is no honor in attempting "to restraine / The lust of lawlesse youth" or "their trayned willes entice" where no "brest of baser birth doth thee embrace" (21–22, 24, 82). In Orphic terms, poets and cities are culturally symbiotic; ever since ancient "vertue gan for age to stoupe" (67), the decline of the one has meant the decline of the other. The death of Roman glory has bereaved the world of song: "And all the worthies liggen wrapt in leade, / That matter made for Poets on to play" (63–64). Spenser's struggle to recover the Orphic power in the *Ruines of Rome* is thus an effort to reverse the historical corruption of civic culture, to restore the dead to life:

> O that I had the *Thracian* Poets harpe,
> For to awake out of th'infernall shade
> Those antique *Caesars*, sleeping long in darke,
> The which this auncient Citie whilome made:
> Or that I had *Amphions* instrument,
> To quicken with his vitall notes accord,
> The stonie ioynts of these old walls now rent,
> By which th'*Ausonian* light might be restor'd:
> Or that at least I could with pencill fine,
> Fashion the pourtraicts of these Palacis,
> By paterne of great *Virgils* spirit diuine. . . .
> (25.337–47)

On the one hand, history presents the poet with a terrible challenge, for his situation, late in the history of culture, seemingly precludes a ready assumption of the Orphic role, the civic voice. The dreary record of history more readily elicits mourning for the city's passing than hopes for its renewal. On the other hand, this very situation, by analogy with that of Vergil, a poet who built one city from the ashes of another, holds forth the promise of a circuitous route through which the Orphic power may be eventually recovered. Spenser's assumption of a Vergilian career in the eclogues, which postdate at least some of his reflections on urban ruins, thus anticipates a later phase in which the Vergilian and Orphic roles will roughly coincide—in celebration of the city. Calliope, the Muse of epic poetry whom Spenser invokes in *The Faerie Queene* to culminate his Vergilian progress, is the mother of Orpheus; in the April eclogue it is she who leads forth the Muses in a pastoral celebration that foreshadows the epic praise of Gloriana and her city, Cleopolis. In the light of this promise, Spenser's pastoral beginning appears, not as a flight from the city, but as a hopeful step toward its reedification. The pastoral role initiates a process of *translatio* by which Spenser, in assuming the Vergilian mantle, prepares for the rebirth of Orpheus in himself and of the city for his time.

The true beginning of this process—indeed of Spenser's career—lies not in Arcadia but in the urban ruins of antiquity. For Spenser, these ruins form the poetic foundation for a larger fabric of reflection on the city. In their earliest appearance—in the "Sonets" Spenser translated for the English edition of Jan Van der Noot's *Theatre for Voluptuous Worldlings* (1569)—the ruins evoke a civic grandeur overshadowed but not effaced by the greater glory of "The holy Citie of the Lorde" (15.3). The first eleven of the fifteen "Sonets" are drawn from Du Bellay's *Songe*, in which the poet meditates on emblems of fallen Roman glory. The passing of Rome, mourned by Du Bellay, is offered by Van der Noot as support for the purpose of the *Theatre* as a whole, which is "to shewe how vaine, transitorie, deceitfull, vnprofitable, and vncertain worldly things be." In the apocalyptic perspective created by Van der Noot's addition of four original sonnets based on Revelation, Rome's ruin fulfills a typological promise: "Now for a truth great Babylon is fallen" (13.14). Placed after Du Bellay's sonnets, those by Van der Noot culminate with St. John's view of the New Jerusalem and thus conclude a sequential order whose vision of the city proclaims that "all is nought but flying vanitie" (1.11).

Set against this sequence, however, stands a spatial order, a ring structure, whose central element, in the eighth sonnet, is not St. John but a wailing nymph, "Hard by a riuers side" (8.1). As the only sonnet in which the genius of Rome speaks for itself, the nymph's lament was already unique in Du Bellay's cycle; by moving it from the tenth to the central eighth position, Van der Noot highlights a pointed conflict between the Earthly City and the New Jerusalem. The nymph's lament divides a diptych on either half of which lie three emblems of Roman glory fallen (5–7 and 9–11) and four symmetrically opposed visions, Du Bellay's of Rome 1–4) and Van der Noot's from Revelation (12–15). The sequential order tips the balance in this structure of counterpoised tensions, but the awesome visions from Revelation contend for their eventual mastery against an Earthly City whose imposing grandeur is made compelling by a temple of "an hundred pillers" (2.2), a "sharped spire / Of diamant" (3.1–2), and a "triumphall arke" of "Alabaster" (4.3–4). St. John's final vision offers consolation for the destruction of these monuments and the worldly vanity—the "auncient glorie of the Romane lordes" (4.8)—they symbolize. The Roman civic context remains an important element in the sequence, however, and in his gloss Van der Noot explains how the Roman "sumptuousnesse and superfluitie hathe oftentymes thoroughe dissention, discorde and sedition amongst them selues . . . ben to their great hinderaunce and damage."

In this very gloss, as in the sequence, there sounds a humanistic note, a concern for civic virtue, that runs in counterpoint with both the disillusionment of Du Bellay and the otherworldly thrust of Van der Noot and Spenser. Indeed, the central complaint of the nymph embodies an essential ambiguity of the Calvinist theology that informs the *Theatre*. On the one hand, she evokes the biblical image of the Psalmist when "By the riuers of Babel we sate, and there we wept, when we remembered Zion" (Ps.137:1) or the desolate Jerusalem of Lamentations: "How doeth the citie remaine solitarie that was ful of people? She is a widdow: she that was great among the nacions and princesse among the prouinces, is made tributarie. She wepeth continually in the night, & her teares *runne downe* by her chekes" (Lam.1:1–2). On the other hand, however, she speaks also as the noble civic conscience of Rome, lamenting both the "ciuile bate" that "Made me the spoile and bootie of the world" and the "Neroes and Caligulaes," the rapacious prelates, she has since brought forth (8.9–10,14). The culminating apocalyptic voice of St. John supersedes but never wholly silences her responsible voice. Hers is but the frail voice of human impotence, but one that speaks for an Earthly City whose human, civic glory adds poignance to an ultimate doom. The *Theatre* is erected on humanist foundations still visible beneath the Calvinist superstructure. And, significantly, when Spenser revised the "Sonets" as *The Visions of Bellay*, he excised the four Revelation sonnets of Van der Noot, replaced them with the four missing sonnets of Du Bellay, and thus restored the cycle to its original and more secular shape as a humanist meditation on ruins. This restoration, itself a humanist's archaeological labor, shares with the "Two Cantos of Mutabilitie" in that larger revision through which Spenser moves with increasing confidence toward an acceptance of historic change, purged of his more youthful apocalyptic hysteria.

The early "Sonets" nevertheless remain a shadowy presence throughout that revision, for they provide the basic iconography—the contrast of city and river—through which Spenser continues to explore the meaning of the Earthly City. In the "Sonets," the contrast of nymph and river, Rome and Tiber, places the city in a temporal context that in turn gives way to an eternal parallel in the New Jerusalem, where "A liuely streame, more cleere than Christall is, / Ranne through the mid" (15.12–13). The two versions establish a thematic pattern, subdued but implicit in the sequence: the city may be swept away before the flow of time or stand in triumph as the eternal order through which time flows. Polarized in the *Theatre* by an impassable gulf between the temporal and the eternal, these alternatives nevertheless share a common iconic structure. And though, as a poet of great patience, Spenser always stops short of a premature or millenarian conflation of this polar structure, as a citizen and humanist he must perforce allow that in their symbolic resemblance these poles define a range of human potential along which the Earthly City, in its relation to time, may aspire to the condition of the eternal.

In the *Ruines of Rome*, a translation of the *Antiquitez de Rome* to which Du Bellay had appended the *Songe*, this symbolic range of potential reemerges as a distinctly human continuum. Rome represents the fullest extent of worldly achievement, good as well as bad: "*Rome* was th'whole world, and al the world was *Rome*" (26.359). The *mundus* or macrocosmic *orbis*, the entire civilized world, reduces to the microcosmic *urbs*, to "one sole Cities strength" (8.100). This strength combines the temporal and the transcendent. "The lowest earth ioin'd to the heauen hie" (8.106). From a purely temporal perspective, the river triumphs over the city, and only "*Tyber* hastning to his fall / Remaines of all" (3.39–40). As "The pray of time, which all things doth deuoure" (3.36). Rome's ruin supports the potentially apocalyptic point that "all this whole shall one day come to nought" (9.126). Unlike the *Theatre*, however, the *Ruines* ultimately averts apocalypse, for in this city the people's "vertue yet so fruitfull was"(8.103) that though her empire falls,

> And that though time doth Commonwealths deuowre,
> Yet no time should so low embase their hight,

> That her head earth'd in her foundations deep,
> Should not her name and endles honour keep.
>   (8.109–12)

The Roman *urbs* so epitomizes the Roman *orbis*, and civic virtue so pervades Roman achievement, that their joint failure is presented as the true cause of Rome's fall. Alone against the world, Rome "Sustein'd the shocke of common enmitie" (21.284) and sailed successfully on the high seas of fortune and history.

> But when the obiect of her vertue failed,
> Her power it selfe against it selfe did arme;
> As he that hauing long in tempest sailed,
> Faine would ariue, but cannot for the storme,
>   If too great winde against the port him driue,
>   Doth in the port it selfe his vessell riue.
>   (21.289–94)

This version traces Rome's fall to the city itself, and thereby echoes Isidore's distinction between *urbs* and *civitas* (*Etymol.* 15.2.1), between the city that, defined by its walls, falls to enemies without, and the city that, defined by civic harmony, falls to the enmity within. Du Bellay's emphasis on the latter—on "Ciuill furie" (31.429)—as the cause of Rome's fall defines the city, rather than the empire, as the center and archetype of political destiny.

Moreover, when Du Bellay confronts the city with the accusation "Your blades in your owne bowels you embrew'd" (24.330), he echoes a key passage from the *Aeneid*, in which Vergil, with fresh memories of civil war, anchors Rome's imperial destiny to its civic virtue. As Anchises unfolds before his son the future of empire, he recurs frequently to the themes of civic order and discord that will unite and divide the city. Through such figures as Numa, "first king of Rome to found the city's laws," Tullus, the Tarquin kings, and Brutus, Anchises leads up to the civil wars and delivers the following exhortation:

> My sons, do not
> let such great wars be native to your minds,
> or turn your force against your homeland's vitals.

The failure to heed this exhortation, Du Bellay's whole cycle implies, only underlines the extent to which the order of the city shapes historic destiny. "Romane courage" builds the city, but it is a city that can "turne to ciuill rage, / And be her selfe the matter of her fires" (23.313, 315–16). As a symbol for all human potential, the city, now a ghost, has fallen to the river running through her heart. The formlessness and flux to which the order of the city capitulates lie as near to hand as the Tiber. And so the poet, like the wailing nymph of the *Songe,* traces Rome's fall, not to the fury of other civilizations, but to an inner demon that Roman order has failed to hold in check:

> No blame to thee, whosoeuer dost abide
> By *Nyle,* or *Gange,* or *Tygre,* or *Euphrate,* . . .
> Nor the bolde people by the *Thamis* brincks, . . .
> Nor the borne Souldier which *Rhine* running drinks:
> Thou onely cause, O Ciuill furie, art. . . .
>
> (31.423–29)

Spenser returns to the same configuration of river and city in *The Ruines of Time,* but in order to establish, in a native context, a new significance for ancient ruins. Unlike the earlier "Sonets" of the *Theatre* or the *Ruines of Rome,* works of humanist apprenticeship in which Spenser is less an imitator than a faithful translator, *The Ruines of Time,* an original work, allows Spenser to reflect more freely on his own civic setting and thus to assert his independence from the Continental mode of ruins poetry. Though he announces this independence by choosing as the object of his meditations Verulamium, a great town of Roman Britain which enjoyed the privileged status of *municipium,* Spenser actually begins his poem by seeming to adhere closely to the earlier models. Walking "beside the shore / Of siluer streaming *Thamesis*" (1–2), the poet beholds at the site of Verulam "A Woman sitting sorrowfullie wailing" (9); she is "th'auncient *Genius* of that Citie brent" (19). Once "that Citie, which the garland wore / Of *Britaines* pride" (36–37), she has now, like Rome, "in mine owne bowels made my graue" (26). In her ruin she has become the symbol of the "vaine worlds glorie" (43), and the changeful river that once ran by her side evokes the utter vanity of human desire. But against the river stands her recollection of a former grandeur:

> High towers, faire temples, goodly theaters,
> Strong walls, rich porches, princelie pallaces,
> Large streetes, braue houses, sacred sepulchers,
> Sure gates, sweete gardens, stately galleries,
> Wrought with faire pillours, and fine imageries. . . .
>
> (92–96)

This grand synathroismus pays tribute to the cultural significance of cities, and in the later elegiac praise of Walsingham and the Dudleys it underlies a tenuous hope through which the poet self-consciously unites the theme of civic virtue with the Orphic powers of verse. The elegiac passages, of course, do anachronistic violence to the archaeological decorum of ruins poetry, but at the same time they suggest that the Orphic poet through whom the Muses "vnto men eternitie do giue" (367) may also become the Orpheus who builds cities. His memorializing function, through which he returns the dead to the world of light, is also a civic act, a creation of exemplary images whose suasive powers can reorder society. By distinguishing between the falsity of the "courting masker" (202) and the "great good deeds" that true statesmen perform "in countrey and in towne" (263), the poet reenacts the very civic virtue he recalls. In the hands of such a poet, fame ceases to be an idle name, a relic of the past, and becomes instead the stimulus to renewed virtue. For Spenser, political virtue takes a variety of forms, most of them courtly or imperial rather than civic in character; but for the Orphic virtue of the poet, the city, remembered in its glory, is a consummate symbol: "The restored city is a palace of art." This is indeed why, after the emblematic visions or "tragicke Pageants" (490) which depict the fall of urban splendor in the Pharos of Alexander, the gardens of Semiramis, and the bridge of Trajan, Spenser turns to consoling visions that include a symbol of the stellified Sidney, "a signe" that "in heauen . . . doth appeare" (615): "The harpe, on which *Dan Orpheus* was seene / Wylde beasts and forrests after him to lead" (607–8).

For Spenser, the way out of the wilderness begins in the poetry of ruins—*la letteratura delle rovine*—in which the basic configuration of river and city prefigures what the later Orphic reconstruction of the city will mean. One image in *The Ruines of Time* points strikingly in this direction: when the nymph who once wore the garland of Britain's pride laments beside the river, she recalls how the Rome to which she once belonged "in the necke of all the world did ride" (74). Her recollection anticipates several later recurrences of this triumphal posture in *The Faerie Queene*, including Britomart's civilizing mastery of the crocodile at Isis Church, Mercilla's mastery of the lion beneath her throne, and the triumph of their countertype, Lucifera, over the dragon at her feet. But the most important of these postures involves the city Britomart calls Troynovant,

> that with the waues
> Of wealthy *Thamis* washed is along,
> Vpon whose stubborne neck, whereat he raues
> With roring rage, and sore him selfe does throng,
> That all men feare to tempt his billowes strong,
> She fastned hath her foot, which standes so hy,
> That it a wonder of the world is song. . . .
>
> (3.9.45)

This avatar reverses the earlier configurations of city and river and presents the city as a symbol of the human triumph over time. Britomart offers
the vision as an implicit criticism of Paridell's view of history, which, in
focusing on the "idle name" of "*Priams* Citie sackt" (3.9.33, 38), overlooks
the consolation of Troynovant, the power of the city to regenerate itself.
Obsessed with the ruin of their city, Paridell's ancestors "Gathred the
Troian reliques sau'd from flame" (3.9.36) and from them built the idle
civilization of Paros, which, like Buthrotum and the other false cities of
Vergil's *Aeneid*, is merely a regressive simulacrum of a lost past. As
Britomart points out, the true successor of Troy is not reconstructed
around relics but "built of old *Troyes* ashes cold" (3.9.38); like a giant
tree, it grows organically "out of her dust" and from the seed of her
"scattered of spring" (3.9.44).

In *The Ruines of Time*, Spenser seems to direct a similar critique at
the poetry of ruins. Unlike the Rome he translated out of Du Bellay,
Spenser's Verulamium is a city "Of which there now remaines no memorie, /
Nor anie little moniment to see" (4–5). Verulamium's "High towers, faire
temples, goodly theaters" exist not as ruins but as poetic fabrications; like
the elegiac recollection of Walsingham and the Dudleys, they substitute for
the idolatry of visible desolation an inner sense of history as potentially
renewable. The many sieges of Verulamium and its utter destruction by
the Saxons (104–14) accord almost perfectly with Merlin's prophecy to
Britomart, in which he says that though the Saxons "all thy Cities . . .
shall sacke and race" (3.3.34), yet history shall preserve "The royall seed,
the antique *Troian* blood" (3.3.42). Britomart's description of Troynovant
is a perfect symbol of this preservation; standing with its foot fastened on
the neck of the Thames, the city emblematically adopts a posture once
held by Verulamium's mistress, Rome. The genius of Verulamium might
well be jealous, for she recalls that in her days of glory

> In *Britannie* was none to match with mee,
> That manie often did abie full sore:
> Ne *Troynouant*, though elder sister shee. . . .
> (100–102)

Indeed, as William Harrison explains in his *Description of England* (1577),
Verulamium was "preferred before" London "bicause it was newer, and
made a Municipium of the Romans, whereas the other was old and
ruinous" (*Minor Poems*, II, 286). Seen in the proper historical perspective,
being "old and ruinous" would not be a condition to be lamented; but,
like a conventional ruins-poet, the genius of Verulamium concludes, "Ne
ought to me remaines, but to lament / My long decay" (156–57). She

places particular emphasis on the supposed change in the course of the Thames, which has long since left her side:

> Seemes, that that gentle Riuer for great griefe
> Of my mishaps, which oft I to him plained; . . .
> From my vnhappie neighborhood farre fled,
> And his sweete waters away with him led.
>
> (141–47)

But as Spenser knows, this is a cataclysm that only "seemes" as a fiction in his poem, for by his time Leland, Harrison, and Camden had thoroughly discredited the myth that the Thames once flowed by Verulamium. Spenser needs the myth in order to retain the river-city figure already established in his ruins poetry. He chooses a particularly questionable myth so that he may begin to move beyond it. The true course of history, like the true course of the river, is less spectacularly erratic than in some myths of change. The Thames flows where it always flowed, past the city older than Verulamium and still standing.

Britomart's description of Troynovant symbolizes this endurance, and later in *The Faerie Queene*, at the pageant of the Thames and Medway, the city emerges as the crowning expression of a humanized, historic time. Troynovant arises on the flowing, princely Thames

> like to a Coronet
> He wore, that seemed strange to common vew,
> In which were many towres and castels set,
> That it encompast round as with a golden fret.
>
> Like as the mother of the Gods, they say,
> In her great iron charet wonts to ride,
> When to *Ioues* pallace she doth take her way:
> Old *Cybele*, arayd with pompous pride,
> Wearing a Diademe embattild wide
> With hundred turrets, like a Turribant.
> With such an one was Thamis beautifide;
> That was to weet the famous Troynouant,
> In which her kingdomes throne is chiefly resiant.
>
> (4.11.27–28)

"Like as the mother of Gods . . . Old *Cybele*": like, indeed, to the city once thought to lie in irreparable ruin:

> Such as the *Berecynthian* Goddesse bright
> In her swift charret with high turrets crownde,
> Proud that so manie Gods she brought to light;
> Such was this Citie in her good daies fownd:

> This Citie, more than that great *Phrygian* mother
> Renowm'd for fruite of famous progenie,
> Whose greatnes by the greatnes of none other,
> But by her selfe her equall match could see:
> *Rome* onely might to *Rome* compared bee. . . .
> (*Ruines of Rome*, 6.71–79)

The emergence of Troynovant in the guise of Cybele is thus a true *renovatio*, a triumph over history. It fulfills the promise of the *Ruines of Rome*, recovering the Orphic power by the circuitous Vergilian process of *translatio*: the westward progress of the Phrygian mother, arrested for a time in ruins, is carried on in epic movement toward Troynovant. As the major focus of this epic movement, the city symbolically embodies historic destiny; it extends the life of civilization and forms the basis of human culture. This is reflected in Spenser's use of Cybele, mother of civilization, for her diadem exalts the city as the crowning expression of earthly life:

> her stately sitting [in her chariot] betokeneth the firme ground whereon
> is builded Cityes and townes: by her Crown so signified. . . .
> On her head . . . she weareth a stately crowne, made in the forme of
> many towers and castles, in that the circuit and compasse of the earth is
> round, like the shape of a crowne, and is replenished and filled with
> Citties, Castles, and Villages. . . .

Cybele has, of course, other, less congenial associations. Her exotic "Turribant" recalls her priests, the corybants, whose "franticke rites" Spenser compares to those of Bacchus (*FQ*,1.6.15), and Cambina's arrival in the guise of Cybele unleashes a Dionysian violence, a "rude confusion," that breaks the "bonds of peace" (4.3.41). To ride the river as Cybele's crown is to stand in a precarious relation to gigantic powers. But like the powers of Love and Hate held in reconciling tension by Concord (4.10.32–34), such dynamism lies at the heart of civilized order. *The Faerie Queene* thus realizes (albeit in a problematic way, because the New Jerusalem sets its signature on all the urban visions of the poem) a potential thematically implicit even in Spenser's poetry of ruins, where the glory of the city appears as a worldly vanity, but also as the "fairest of all earthly thing" (*Ruines of Rome*, 1.14).

This latter view Spenser significantly maintains in his two marriage odes. In contrast to the reflective mode of the ruins poetry, the celebratory mode of these poems closes—with varying success—the temporal disjunction that had earlier separated the moment of Spenser's poetic utterance from the actual civilized life of the city. As a result, the city, elsewhere a disembodied ghost, becomes a solid and living social context in which both poem and poet can participate: indeed, it functions in these poems not simply as a stage or frame but as an informing principle in their dramatic movement. In the *Epithalamion*, this recovery may even echo, by structural parallel, the first Orphic gesture toward the city in the *Theatre*. Thomas M. Greene notes that the serio-temporal succession from the dawn of anticipation to the evening of consummation is also structured by a concentric system that surrounds the central event in the personal drama—the marriage ceremony—with several other contexts, social, natural, cosmic, and divine. Most nearly adjacent to the ceremony, and forming as it were the immediate threshold and environment for this climactic event, is a social context colorfully staged as an urban drama, with boys who "run vp and downe the street, / Crying aloud with strong confused noyce" (137–38), with "people standing all about" (143), with "many gazers, as on [the bride] do stare" (160), and with the "merchants daughters" who never saw "So fayre a creature in your towne before" (167–68). These celebrants, together with the "yong men of the towne" who "Ring . . . the bels" and "bonefiers make all day" (261, 275), contribute to an over- whelming impression of crowded, bustling life and bourgeois prosperity. The gaily bedecked temple, the "sacred ceremonies" with their "roring Organs" and "Choristers" singing the "ioyous Antheme" (216–21), the young men released from their "wonted labors for this day" (262)—all witness that "This day is holy" (263), not just for the poet but for the community. And though the poem's descrescendo moves toward the silence of private joys, the poet's thrice-repeated command, "bring home the bride againe, / Bring home . . . / Bring home" (242–44), ties a sense of place to a sense of community. This link insures that "sacred peace" that makes the marriage night "From feare of perrill and foule horror free" (354, 322); it inspires the poet's final prayer for "a large posterity" to inherit "the earth, which they may long possesse, / With lasting happinesse" (427–19).

Thus, at the climactic moment of this social drama, Spenser simultaneously celebrates the foundation of human society in marriage and its culmination in the city. He shows that marriage not only is "the fountain of humanitie," but also leads to a larger civic destiny as "the Seminary of the Commonwealth . . . the foundation of Countries, Cities, Universities." Because it is, among other things, the "foundation of . . . Cities," marriage shares an Orphic role with poetry in the life of civiliza- tion. Spenser's conscious exploration of this parallel, and not merely the important biographical coincidence of his roles as husband and poet, motivates his participation in the poem. Thus, when Spenser as husband undertakes at the beginning of the poem to sing as "Orpheus did for his owne bride" (16), he also takes upon himself the poetic role sought but not assumed in the *Ruines of Rome*: he sings a city into being. Melancholy reflection on the city gives way to a participatory celebration which overcomes history by closing the temporal disjunction between what was and is. Certainly the "bourgeois milieu" (Greene, p. 223) of the poem contributes to its unconventional decorum; but it also expresses the momentary confidence Spenser reposes in a vision of the city closer to contemporary reality than to Roman glory.

Indeed, it is partly the bourgeois transformation of urban culture that enables Spenser to transcend the melancholy reflection on antique ruins. Unlike Rome or London, the simple town of the *Epithalamion* has no imperial destiny; but if its provincial and burgherly atmosphere seems remote from the refinements of civilization, it should be remembered that Spenser explicitly connects the two in *A View of the Present State of Ireland*. Once Ireland is "subdewed and reformed," he observes, the measures for "the good establishment of that Realme" will include the reedification of its neglected towns, for

> theare is nothinge dothe soner Cause Civilitye in anye Countrye then manye market Townes by reason that people repairinge often thither for theire nedes will dailye see and learne Civill manners of the better sorte . . . theare is nothinge dothe more enriche anye Country or Realme then manye Townes for to them will all people drawe and bringe the fruites of theire trades. . . .

As Spenser notes in *The Faerie Queene*, Trojan Brute founded Troynovant not only "To be the compasse of his kingdomes seat" (3.9.46), but also to be "sought / Of marchants farre, for profits therein praysd" (2.10.5). The poem's chivalric decorum, of course, thrusts such concerns from the center to the periphery of vision, but in many of the values it celebrates, *The Faerie Queene* is truly a citizen's allegory. The New Jerusalem, not imperial Rome, is the threshold to the poem, and the way to it is pointed by the figures of Charity and the Seven Corporal Works of Mercy. The books that follow explore in various ways excess and deficiency, profit and loss, chastity, charity, marriage, family, concord, inheritance, and property.

To turn from Spenser's courtly heroes to his minor figures is to discover the breadth of the poem's social orientation. It includes or alludes to clerks and a bailiff-errant; a surgeon, a schoolmistress, and beadsmen; a master-cook and a kitchen-clerk; watchmen and keepers and messengers; monks and priests; bargemen, a boatman, and pilots and sailors and beaten mariners; fishermen and merchants and a butcher; many instances of the "cunning Craftesman" (2.9.41)—blacksmiths and goldsmiths, a painter, a mason, and a carver; porters, a footman, and tax collectors; widows and orphans and beggars and courtesans and thieves. "Sky-threatening towres" (5.10.23) and courtly palaces dominate Spenser's architectural vistas, but his landscape also includes inns and churches, schools and a hospital, bridges and harbors, a storehouse and sheds, walls and pillars and steeples and gates and streets. And for this landscape there is a material substratum of brick and mortar and timber and glass and nails and conduit pipe; brass, iron, steel, lead, and copper-wire; cheese and bread and milk and wine and tobacco; coaches and wagons and wheels; clocks and compasses and cobbled shoes; linen, arras, and silk. Most often such "merchandize" (2.12.19) appears in completed form as material prepared for consumption by the poem's heroes and emptied of the history of its own production by the use of a participial construction: Artegall thus wields a sword "garnisht all with gold" (5.1.10), and Britomart sleeps beneath an "embrodered quilt" (3.1.61). But at times Spenser pauses to remember the history of labor and the work of the "cunning Craftesman": gold is "Framed in goldsmithes forge" (4.6.20), and arras is "made in painefull loome" (3.11.51).

In *The Faerie Queene* as in the *Epithalamion*, Spenser frequently stages urban festivals to celebrate the love and labor that together make society. Like the Bible, which compares the restored Jerusalem to Eden, Spenser's Legend of Holiness celebrates the restoration of Eden with an urban procession in which "all the way the ioyous people sings, / And with their garments strowes the paued street" (1.12.13). As the poem moves closer to contemporary history, Arthur himself walks on the incarnate stage of a historic city's streets:

> Then all the people, which beheld that day,
>   Gan shout aloud, that vnto heauen it rong;
>   And all the damzels of that towne in ray,
>   Came dauncing forth, and ioyous carrols song:
>   So him they led through all their streetes along,
>   Crowned with girlonds of immortall baies,
>   And all the vulgar did about them throng,
>   To see the man, whose euerlasting praise
> They all were bound to all posterities to rasie.
>   (5.11.34)

Joined by "all the vulgar," this celebration emerges out of Arthur's "toylesome paine" and "great trauell" (5.10.21). Like that "worke great *Troynouant*," which brings to fruition Brute's "labours long" (3.9.50–51), this urban festival underlines the extent to which the worlds of hero, poet, and citizen are coessential fabrications, coequal expressions of all that lies within the powers of man.

That is why in the *Prothalamion* as in the *Epithalamion*, the poet participates in the civic order, in the progress of the poem toward the city. The progress, significantly, is by water, and begins

> When I whom sullein care,
> Through discontent of my long fruitlesse stay
> In Princes Court, and expectation vayne
> Of idle hopes, which still doe fly away,
> Like empty shaddowes, did aflict my brayne,
> Walkt forth to ease my payne
> Along the shoare of siluer streaming *Themmes*. . . .
> (5–11)

In the temporal flow of "streaming *Themmes*" the poet seeks release from the time-serving cares of his "fruitlesse stay." At the same time, however, the river ironically mirrors the mutable world he seeks to abandon, and both the river's bank, "paynted all with variable flowers, / And all the meades adornd with daintie gemmes" (13–14) betray the poet's gesture toward Ovidian idyl as an escape into artifice. The arrival of the two swans in the third stanza, however, initiates a process of recovery, through which the poet, celebrating their impending marriage and the society to which it leads, returns himself to the life of culture. The return, following the flow of the river, gradually purges the poem of its Ovidian elements and culminates in a vision of the city real enough, secure enough, to be named:

> At length they all to mery *London* came,
> To mery London, my most kyndly Nurse,
> That to me gaue this Lifes first natiue sourse:
> Though from another place I take my name,
> An house of auncient fame.
> There when they came, whereas those bricky towres,
> The which on *Themmes* brode aged backe doe ryde,
> Where now the studious Lawyers haue their bowers
> There whylome wont the Templer Knights to byde,
> Till they decayd through pride:
> Next whereunto there standes a stately place,
> Where oft I gayned giftes and goodly grace
> Of that great Lord, which therein wont to dwell. . . .
> (127–39)

In certain respects, this vision of the city is less inviting than its homely, provincial counterpart in the *Epithalamion*. Less exclusive in its focus than that poem, the *Prothalamion* incorporates, through the poet's plaint and the flowing river, many of the negative implications associated with the cities of the ruins poetry. The Knights Templars, who "decayd through pride," seem to justify the poet's opening flight from "Princes Court," and though the poet names the city, he is careful to trace his own name to other sources. Nonetheless, both the naming of "mery *London*" and its personification as "my most kyndly Nurse" contribute to the consoling and relatively unguarded moment when the poet unveils his name and accepts the city as his cultural heritage. This moment, like the visions of Troynovant in *The Faerie Queene*, significantly reverses the configuration of river and city, so that the city's "bricky towres . . . on *Themmes* brode aged backe doe ryde." In this symbolic triumph over mutability, London is invested with the power of cultural endurance; as Harry Berger, Jr., has said, it "figures man's historical environment" and, as the objectification of the human spirit, "outlasts its makers" (p. 519). This is confirmed by the otherwise strange mention of the "studious Lawyers" who succeed the Knights Templars and thus replace "chivalric force" with "legal persuasion" (Berger, p. 519).

It is confirmed also by the imaginative succession of Essex to Leicester in the role of patron. On the one hand, Spenser laments the passing of Leicester, "Whose want too well now feeles my freendles case"; but on the other hand, he concedes that "here fits not well / Olde woes but ioyes to tell" (140–42). The reason lies not so much in the decorum of the occasion, which should separate the concerns of poets and brides, as in the meaning of the occasion, which ultimately unites them. Just as the marriages find their ultimate significance in the city toward which they lead, so the poet finds in the cultural and historical endurance figured by the city a consoling counterbalance to mutability. Like the poet, Leicester House has seen its changes:

> Yet therein now doth lodge a noble Peer,
> Great *Englands* glory and the Worlds wide wonder,
> Whose dreadfull name, late through all *Spaine* did thunder,
> And *Hercules* two pillors standing neere,
> Did make to quake and feare:
> Faire branch of Honor, flower of Cheualrie,
> That fillest *England* with thy triumphs fame,
> Ioy haue thou of thy noble victorie,
> And endlesse happinesse of thine owne name
> That promiseth the same:
> That through thy prowesse and victorious armes,
> Thy country may be freed from forraine harmes:
> And great *Elisaes* glorious name may ring

> Through al the world, fil'd with thy wide Alarmes,
> Which some braue muse may sing
> To ages following. . . .
>
> (145–60)

Essex's succession at Leicester House is both a personal and cultural consolation. Spenser's praise of the noble peer who "therein *now* doth lodge" (145) succeeds the earlier "now" of his friendless case (140) and thus transforms his idle hopes, "still" afflicting his utterance at the beginning of the poem (8), into "Olde woes" (142). His idyllic flight from court, moreover, gives way to a reassurance whose imperial sweep is truly a *translatio* carried forward from the *Ruines of Rome*. Moreover, as Spenser turns to his projected patron's achievements and to the glory of his Queen spread through "al the world," he purges his own poem of its earlier Ovidian fancies, moves toward the contemporary world, and thereby consciously parallels the structure of the final book of the *Metamorphoses* in which Ovid turns from myth to history, passing first from the death of cities past to "The citty *Rome*" which "of the uniuersall world in time to come shall hold / The soueraignty," and then moving forward to the stellification of Julius Caesar, who will "euermore looke downe / Upon our royall Capitall and Court within Rome towne," and to his succession by the poet's contemporary patron, Augustus, who established "peace in all the world" (15.422–860). The encomium is not, therefore, merely a perfunctory and hyperbolic gesture of reverence; it is, like the encomia of Walsingham and the Dudleys in *The Ruines of Time*, an essential element in the Orphic logic of the poem. Through its praise of brides and statesmen, the poem participates in the very process of culture-building that it celebrates and locates in the city.

Spenser's awareness of this link is borne out in the final stanza, in which

> From those high Towers, this noble Lord issuing,
> Like Radiant *Hesper* when his golden hayre
> In th'*Ocean* billowes he hath Bathed fayre,
> Descended to the Riuers open vewing. . . .
>
> (163–66)

This descent of the stellified patron from tower to river reintegrates the praise of Essex with the configuration of river and city organizing the poem. It places the life of culture in a perspective of mutability even wider than the personal disappointment with which the poem began, and it seemingly argues for the ultimate triumph of time. The eternal oceanic rhythm associated with the river is further reinforced by the final description of the marriages as taking place "at th'appointed tyde" (177). While implying subjection to time and the river, however, this image also suggests the potential for a timely mastery of mutability and thus supports the cultural triumph earlier figured in the city, whose towers "on *Themmes* brode aged backe doe ryde." This cultural mastery finds its poetic counterpart in the refrain of the poem, "Sweete *Themmes* runne softly, till I end my Song." The refrain, like the city itself, is a consoling if partial triumph over mutability, and together both consolations express the symbiotic relation between poetry and the city. The Orphic poet who civilized with his song, it was said, possessed as well the power to halt the flow of rivers. Cesare Ripa interprets this latter power as a variation of the former, for when Orpheus "stops the flow of rivers," he demonstrates the power of poets to curb "dishonest and lustful men who, when they are not kept back by the force of language from their infamous lives, run without any restraint as far as the sea, which is the regret and bitterness which usually come suddenly upon the carnal pleasures." In the *Prothalamion*, the city only manages to ride the river's back, and the poet only momentarily retards and tames its flow; but these achievements balance the tide of mutability and human failure with consoling hopes for cultural endurance.

These hopes, like the ghostly melancholy of the ruins poetry, center on the city. They confirm the extent to which the city shapes Spenser's reflection on the life of poetry in the life of culture. The cities of *The Faerie Queene*—Troy, Thebes, Rome, Antwerp, Troynovant, Cleopolis, Babylon, Nineveh, Salem, and the New Jerusalem—thus bring to fruition both a Vergilian career and an Orphic preoccupation with the city that began when Spenser, like the Camden whom he praises, first tried "To see the light of simple veritie, / Buried in ruines" (*The Ruines of Time*, 171–72). Fittingly, this basic continuity inspired one of the unknown encomiasts of *The Faerie Queene* to pass over the Vergilian claims of the Proem and to praise its author as "this Bryttane *Orpheus*." In so doing, he wisely adopted Spenser's own configuration of city and river and thus portrayed the writing of *The Faerie Queene* as a triumphant act of Orphic reconstruction, a recreation of a city that will stand against the flow of time:

> Fayre *Thamis* streame, that from *Ludds* stately towne,
> Runst paying tribute to the Ocean seas,
> Let all thy Nymphes and Syrens of renowne
> Be silent, whyle this Bryttane *Orpheus* playes.

KENNETH GROSS

Mythologies and
Metrics in Spenser

The poet of *The Faerie Queene* seems to
have had a preternatural dislike not only of chaotic change but of stasis
and sharp closure as well. His stanza organizes the continuum of language
in such a way as to resist both random succession and abrupt cessation and
blurs any absolute boundaries between its unfolding, interlocked, and
echoing sections. As Angus Fletcher observes, the complex rhyme scheme
of the stanza has the effect of marrying the archetypal structures of quest
romance, the temple and the labyrinth. From a historical point of view,
Spenser seems to evade two of the most typical uses of stanzaic form in
English Renaissance poetry. On the one hand, his stanza is never merely a
neat, closed frame for a pictorial or emblematic content, a self-sufficient
order or closed knot of ambiguities like that of a paradox or an epigram.
On the other, as Paul Alpers amply shows, the stanza never accommodates itself to that "internalization" of dramatic speech, with its rapid
movement of voice and attitude, which so characterizes English poetry
from Wyatt to Donne. Spenser in fact subordinates any such decisive
movement to the steady piling up of independent images and verbal
formulas, each of which is free to counterpoint and even to refigure those
that come before and after it. In this reading, Spenser's master trope
becomes aporia, or *dubitatio*, that is, the presentation within a discourse of
so many alternative perspectives that any radical choice among them
becomes difficult or delayed. This sovereign multiplicity of image and

From *PMLA* 1, vol. 98 (January 1983). Copyright © 1983 by Modern Language Association
of America.

reference, which continually puts off all absolute gestures of ending, is what lends the strange sense of freedom to Spenser's intricately structured, even overdetermined poetry. Alpers examines Spenser's writing primarily by analyzing its grammar and diction, but the conclusions he draws can be applied directly to the poet's multiplied and interwoven rhymes. At this local level Alpers' arguments suggest a coherent, even a dialectical intention behind the seeming hypertrophy of dramatic speech in what G. Wilson Knight calls "the Spenserian fluidity."

Beyond his use of rhymes, however, Spenser's most surprising prosodic innovation is the final hexameter, of which George Saintsbury gives the following account:

> The long alexandrine at the close seems to launch each stanza on towards it successor, *ripae ulterioris amore,* or rather, with the desire of fresh striking out in the unbroken though waveswept sea of poetry. Each is a great stroke by a mighty swimmer; it furthers the progress for the next as well as in itself. And it is greatly in this that the *untiring* character of The Faerie Queene consists.

Saintsbury's quaint and rather Whitmanesque imagery may embarrass us, and certainly the sense of muscularity the critic imparts to the stanza seems out of key. But his central insight is powerful: the prosodic movement of the poem does indeed image the progress of desire, the search for fulfillment and continuity of being that is so strong in Spenser's poem. At least one of Saintsbury's tropes deserves serious consideration—namely, the suggestion of an almost eschatological longing in the quotation from the *Aeneid*, taken from the lines in book 6 that tell of souls trapped on the nether bank of the Styx stretching their hands over it "out of love for the further shore." If Saintsbury's account were put in less affective terms, however, one might begin to qualify it by saying that Spenser's final hexameter subtly extends the prosodic and syntactic movement before the verse comes to rest on the final rhyme. Nor do readers cross the slight but inevitable abyss of white space that divides stanza from stanza until they have gained a sense of secure, full, and yet dilated energy. The hexameter thus diffuses (and defuses) the crisis moment of closure by delicately balancing ending and continuity. It provides a still point in a turning world, but in the double sense of "still" on which Spenser repeatedly puns in the Mutability Cantos. As an adjective or an intransitive verb, "still" refers to a state of motionlessness and rest—"still music," "still thoughts." But as an adverb it suggests not the cessation of a process but the perpetuation and repetition, as in the Elizabethan phrase "still again," where "still" has the strong sense of "yet."

The hexameter rhymes with and yet goes beyond the preceding line, distinguishing itself not only metrically but rhetorically from the body of the stanza. For the alexandrine commonly amplifies, qualifies, or under-cuts the previous lines, continually opening up broader moral, metaphori-cal, and psychological perspectives. Perhaps the most frequently cited instance of this effect is the parenthetical "God helpe the man so wrapt in *Errours* endless traine" (1.1.18), in which the reader stumbles suddenly from the concrete monster to the ordinarily hidden metaphors of common speech. Other examples are:

> And in her cheekes the vermeill red did shew
> Like roses in a bed of lillies shed,
> The which ambrosiall odours from them threw,
> And gazers sense with double pleasure fed,
> Hable to heale the sicke, and to review the ded.
> (2.3.22)

> With that a ioyous fellowship issewd
> Of Minstrals, making goodly meriment,
> With wanton Bardes, and Rymers impudent,
> All which together sung full chearefully
> A lay of loves delight, with sweet concent:
> After whom marcht a iolly company,
> In manner of a maske, enranged orderly.
> (3.12.5)

> He pypt apace, whilest they him daunst about.
> Pype iolly shepheard, pype thou now apace
> Unto thy love, that made thee low to lout:
> Thy love is present there with thee in place,
> Thy love is there advaunst to be another Grace.
> (6.10.16)

> Upon a Crab he rode, that him did beare
> With crooked crawling steps on uncouth pase,
> And backward yode, as Bargemen wont to fare
> Bending their force contrary to their face,
> Like that ungracious crew which faines demurest grace.
> (7.7.35)

This sample does small justice to the wide range of modulations that the final alexandrine can produce: only the first two quotations, for instance, illustrate its tendency to fall into two subtly differentiated hemistiches. The phenomenon that concerns me, however, is at once so elementary and protean that I hesitate to assemble any further examples, especially since I reserve for my discussion of the marriage odes most of my more detailed

formal discriminations regarding Spenser's art of closure. Suffice it to say
here that the hexameter not only ends but fulfills the entire movement of
the stanza; in its momentary rhetorical shift, together with the delayed
final rhyme, it embodies a motion resembling the redeemed form of
"mutabilitie" described by Dame Nature in the last book of the poem:

> . . . by their change their being doe dilate:
> And turning to themselves at length againe,
> Doe worke their owne perfection so by fate.
> (7.7.58)

  Thus Spenser's most characteristic metrical invention at least potentially represents his vision of change, continuity, and fate . . . I want
to discuss two other instances of what I have called the "mythologization"
of prosodic form in the poetry of Spenser: the refrains of the great
marriage odes, "Prothalamion" and "Epithalamion." The dialectic of ending and ongoing in these poems is, to a certain degree, present in any
poem with refrains, since this formal device both marks the closure of
individual strophes and provides a regular focus for memory and anticipation in the temporal unfolding of the poem as a whole. But Spenser
transforms these purely formal features of the refrain by associating them
with the odes' two most crucial images of poetic communion, the river
Thames and echo.
  With slight variations in tense and reference, the refrain of "Prothalamion" is "Against the wedding day which is not long; / Sweete
Themmes ronne softly till I end my song." While the second line is not a
hexameter, as in "Epithalamion" (unless one pronounces the final e's in
"Themmes" and "ronne"), it has somewhat the same effect, being one of
the slowest and most fluent verses in all English poetry. The couplet as a
whole builds on the contrast between the climactic awareness of time
leading up to the marriage ceremony and the gentler time frame implied
by the flowing Thames, as well as the more uncertain temporality of the
poet's own song. The poet sets out to reconcile the sense of climax and
the sense of flow, to unite them in a marriage larger than the historical
event that occasions the poem. For as the poem progresses, the marriage
itself becomes the axis of a number of unusual anxieties—related to
Spenser's personal loss of patronage (st. 1), the excessive purity of the
swans (st. 3), references to Jove's rape of Leda (st. 3) and to the fallen
condition of the Knights Templar (st. 8)—and the happy expectation of
the nuptial rites is marred by a strange fear. A portion of the poet's
consciousness seems to be writing the poem not "against" (in preparation
for) but "against" (in resistance to) the wedding day, as if with an obscure

foreboding that the ineluctable moment of marriage will be not so much a joining as a rupture, a sudden break with the past and a destruction of all future hopes. In "Spenser's 'Prothalamion,' " Harry Berger, Jr., analyzes these darker layerings of the poem in great detail and concludes that Spenser overcomes his anxieties only when he can see the marriage as the promise of an ongoing, imaginative transformation of actuality rather than as a singular event. One of Spenser's strategies is to elide the crisis, for in the closing stanza the marriage anticipated throughout the preceding lines is suddenly spoken of in the past tense, as already consummated and thus domesticated within the calmer time consciousness of retrospection. In the refrain itself, the main symbolic agent of this transformation is the river Thames, an image of natural power and continuity that relieves the mounting fears registered in the proleptic vision of the "against" line, a therapeutic repetition that counters the neurotic or compulsive one. The Thames (= times) also serves as a measure of the poet's own literary continuity, and Geoffrey Hartman fittingly invokes the refrain of "Prothalamion" as a precedent for the antiapocalyptic implications of Wordsworth's water and river imagery. He points out that Spenser's refrain "indicates by its steady return how much time is at man's disposal, how everything will flow along in order and degree, and how the world is too well established on the flood for any 'end' to be feared." One must add, however, that the poem's concluding repetition of the unaltered line "Against the wedding day which is not long" obscurely points beyond the already accomplished historical wedding toward an occulted, apocalyptic union.

"Epithalamion," too, as A. Kent Hieatt has shown, presents the marriage of ceremonial and natural temporality; it recovers what Spenser wonderfully calls "that sweet paradise of day and night." The mythological and numerological materials of the poem undoubtedly set the marriage celebration within a cosmic frame, but the refrain itself, not unlike that of "Prothalamion," also limits the movement toward the transcendence of ordinary, successive time. For the final hexameter of each refrain diffuses the pressure of the moment, securing for the poet not only a ritualized time but an expansive, numinous, yet grounded space (again, "that sweet *paradise* of day and night"). The mediator of space and time in this poem is "Eccho," not so much the classical nymph as a more generalized power of repetition, a god in and of the refrain; the trope informs the metrical and verbal scheme so fully that even the common splitting up of the long line into hemistiches is subtly figured as a relation between echoes and answers. The woods in which this echo abides is asked to perpetuate by turns the music of goddesses, angels, and bridesmaids, but primarily it serves to contain that echo which is a metaphor for the poet's own expansive powers of voice. This *topos*, of course, goes back to Vergil's *First Eclogue*, in which the shepherd Tityrus "teaches the woods to re-echo 'fair Amaryllis'."(3). But in Spenser, this singular moment has been expanded into a massive poetic fabric in which the poet, taking a stance at once self-effacing and self-exalting, sets himself the task of singing his own epithalamion. No other formalities are required; indeed, Spenser's envoi claims that it was the proleptic urgency of his song, rather than material necessity, that was responsible for "cutting off" any more ample or literal pageantry. The poem thus restitutes the poet's own self-created loss, draws from his poverty a more liberated symbolic pageant—a "song made in lieu of many ornaments"—in which he himself (qua bridegroom) is effaced behind his own enlarged poetic voice and will: "So I unto myself alone will sing, / The woods shall to me answer and my Eccho ring."

The desire for echo here is fundamentally a desire for response, the poet's desire to marry his epithalamion to the powers and presences of the surrounding world. Repetition becomes a way of overcoming isolation ("my selfe alone") and establishing not only poetic identity but poetic relatedness ("the woods shall to me answer"). It is as if Echo were being asked to liberate Narcissus, both to purify and to strengthen the selfhood in preparation for marriage (even at the cost of splitting the poetic from the natural or sexual self).

Although referring directly to Ovid's mythologizing of visual and verbal reflection helps expose the dialectics of Spenser's invocation, it also does some violence to the work; for Spenser's figure of echo is a very tentative piece of mythmaking, one that perhaps depends specifically on his not naming the tragic heroine of Ovid's fable (in which Echo becomes an emblem of erotic loss, rather than of the sort of erotic affirmation associated with Vergil's echoing name). Thus generalized, this Spenserian echo remains virtual, and hence a less constricted and more virtuous trope through which to frame an idea of erotic continuity. Such strategies of naming and unnaming are, of course, dialectical in their workings. In "Prothalamion," for instance, it is the *insistence* on naming the Thames that allows the river, addressed as friend and even as beloved, to be raised from its merely historical status to a quasi-mythological power without being fully (and awkwardly) anthropomorphosed. Like the river, Spenser's "Eccho" becomes a highly subjective numen, a figure both powerful and placid. Her dismissal from the poem after stanza 17, when the refrain turns to "Ne let the woods them answer, nor theyr eccho ring," coincides with the onset of night and a retreat from public celebration; but Spenser's command of her fictive presence, or present absence, is secure enough that this change in no way dislocates the poem's magisterial progress. One cannot imagine the traditional god of the epithalamion, whose name echoes in the old refrain of "O Hymen, Hymenaee," suffering the poet to banish him thus.

The refrain of "Epithalamion" appropriates for the poet a dilated, earthly space; that of "Prothalamion" asks for a secure, continuous, and natural form of time. The space is sacred, and the time partakes of its own sort of moving eternity; but the echo and the river remain relatively fragile presences, lacking any truly divine authority and "endlesse" only within the "short time" of the world. In fact, Spenser's mythic forms here resist any attempts we might make to valorize them by appealing to an apocalyptic ending or a timeless eternity, which would empty them of all their poignancy. Echo and the river are more than naive, natural daimons; they are presences restored to the landscape by the poet's personal, if belated, act of mythmaking. They remain mythologized, however, largely because they appropriate certain otherwise transcendental or supernatural characteristics within a lower realm of human time and becoming. But this transposition of mythological elements suggests a temporality that is congruent with the redeemed form of "mutabilitie," which I mention above to illustrate the movement of the Spenserian hexameter:

> But by their change their being doe dilate:
> And turning to themselves at length againe,
> Doe worke their owne perfection so by fate.

Not only do these lines describe the Aristotelian concept that all organisms are subject to a teleological drive to fulfill their innate form, but the wording precisely recalls Plotinus' doctrine that the descending hypostases and states of existence that make up the cosmos are created by the "dilation" (diastasis) of being from the transcendent Logos, the fixed, immutable source of all forms and the point to which all substance ultimately returns in love. In Spenser, however, this ontologically transcendent movement has paradoxically become the basis for the less absolute and more temporalized cycle of mutability that rules nature, humanity, and poetry. The process by which God's creatures dilate their being and return to, or turn into, themselves is bounded within the same dimension as are the laterally resounding echo and the onward flowing river. While this orderly movement partially redeems the flux of time and language, it still allows the poet no direct access to the higher sources of timeless reality and rest that he invokes at the end of his epic. The last lines of *The Faerie Queene* serve both to distance and to reduce the apocalyptic Sabbath to a point of still unrealized desire placed wholly beyond the realm of dilation and becoming. The mythopoesis of mutability, even if it recompenses us for the unreachableness of the final end, gains autonomy only at the expense of authenticity, since it sacrifices the certainty of divine revelation.

The simultaneous necessity and inaccessibility of an endless Sabbath call into question the ability of any poetry to ground its moral argument on "the pillars of eternity." A corollary to this idea is Spenser's apparent conviction (widely testified to throughout *The Faerie Queene*) that any discourse claiming to lay hold of Apocalypse in less ambivalent fashion is bound to collapse or calcify into naive chiliasm, false prophecy, or imaginative tyranny. And yet this very skepticism, directed as much at nonliterary religious writing as at secular poetry, seems one of the motives for what I call Spenser's "domestication" of supernatural modes of vision within gentler and more continuous dimensions. To put it another way, the Mutability Cantos are a stay not just against the return of chaotic change but against the disturbing prospect of unmitigable closure, a "Last End," or else some catastrophic imitation of it. As the final movement of Spenser's secular scripture, the trial of the Titaness Mutability serves as a last judgment "in lieu of" an apocalypse, since it attempts to locate some sufficient form of restitution and justification within the cycles of time rather than beyond them. In fact, as a discrete fragment ending an unfinished epic, book 7 might be said to expand the mode of closure developed in the Spenserian stanza to cosmic proportions. Dilating itself on the verge of that fearful gap which opens up between the final Sabbath and the realm of becoming, the closing vision of canto 7 strangely resembles the slightly extended hexameter that both rounds off a stanzaic period and mitigates the inevitable disjunction between one stanza and another, that simultaneously delays and reaches out toward the words that follow.

JOHN GUILLORY

The Image of Source in "The Faerie Queene"

The passage quoted here, from Book IV [of *The Faerie Queene*], follows the long catalogue of rivers comprising the pageant that celebrates the marriage of the Thames and the Medway:

> O what an endlesse worke haue I in hand,
>   To count the seas abundant progeny,
>   Whose fruitfull seede farre passeth those in land,
>   And also those which wonne in th'asure sky?
>   For much more eath to tell the starres on hy,
>   Albe they endlesse seeme in estimation,
>   Then to recount the Seas posterity;
>   So fertile be the flouds in generation,
> So huge their numbers, and so numberlesse their nation.
>
> Therefore the antique wisards well inuented,
>   That Venus of the fomy sea was bred;
>   For that the seas by her are most augmented.
>   (*FQ* IV.xii.1–2)

The marriage of the Thames and the Medway is a Spenserian "invention," a myth of origination, and perhaps also one of the generative pre-texts of *The Faerie Queene*. The apparent hopelessness of the task set out in these lines is belied by the fact that Spenser has already named ("contained") a number of rivers large enough to counterfeit the infinity that he seems to argue lies beyond the power of the artist to represent. The act of naming is

---

From *Poetic Authority: Spenser, Milton, and Literary History*. Copyright © 1983 by Columbia University Press.

"endlesse" but very engaging because it perpetuates the beginning of poetry in a recognition of mere naming as the aboriginal poetic achievement. The function of this naming excursus is not difficult to determine: The will to write is regenerated in a regression to archaic poetic acts, or returns to origins.

Returning to the source in order to feed, as it were, raises an interesting question about what we may call the "economy" of origins. As a poet, Spenser might be said to ally himself with "antique wisards," whom he sees as inventors of the myth of Venus. Their myth possesses a certain logic perceived after the fact as analogous to the logic behind Spenser's own story of the Thames and the Medway. The ocean in the Venus story becomes identified with the infinity of the rivers or the stars, giving us an idealized, because inexhaustible, image of source. What is taken from this source cannot really subtract from it. At the same time, however, the linking of the Venus story to the catalogue of rivers forces Spenser to equate the fictionality of both tales; they are both "invented," and the origins they are meant to discover are in fact devised for the occasion. The choice of Venus' birth as a complement to the marriage of rivers brilliantly defends against the inherent danger of the fictional origin by implying that *generation itself* is born of that source (Spenser's *Venus genetrix*). Generation is a self-sustaining power that, once free of its origin, can return in order to augment, not subtract: "For that the seas by her are most augmented." As I shall argue presently, Spenser usually represents origins in *The Faerie Queene* as watery sources, but the interest of this tactic lies in its relation to the economy by which energy, moral or poetic, is dispersed through the massive structure of the poem.

Hannah Arendt, in a fine essay entitled "What is Authority?" constructs a genealogy of the concept, whose roots she locates in Roman conceptions of a political order. The word *auctoritas*, from which we derive our terms for author and authority, is further traced to the verb *augere*, "to augment." I introduce this etymology following upon Spenser's association of origin and augmentation not only to make a polemical point but to stress that this connection is not fortuitous. With the first words of *The Faerie Queene*, Spenser places himself within the Virgilian tradition, or at least attempts to impose upon his poetic career a Virgilian structure. Whatever Virgil's *Aeneid* may actually say about the origins of the Roman nation, his epic is usually perceived as a sanctification of Roman origins, hence an affirmation of an authority (Augustus) in the present. The impulse emanates from the most entrenched beliefs of the Roman citizen:

> At the heart of Roman politics, from the beginning of the republic until virtually the end of the imperial era, stands the conviction of the

sacredness of foundation, in the sense that once something has been
founded it remains binding for all future generations . . . The foundation
of a new body politic—to the Greeks an almost commonplace experience—
became to the Romans the central, decisive, *unrepeatable beginning* of
their whole history, a unique event. And the most deeply Roman
divinities were Janus, the god of beginning, with whom, as it were, we
still begin our year, and Minerva, the goddess of remembrance.

The derivation of authority from augmentation leads to the conclusion that "what authority or those in authority constantly augment is
the foundation." Additions or extensions must be submitted to the authorizing model of an "unrepeatable beginning," for the obvious reason
that any new beginning is permanently excluded from the process of
Roman politics. In this context it is not difficult to understand why the
inception of an imperial order should generate a comprehensive anxiety
and defense of authority, one result of which is the *Aeneid*. Spenser puzzles
his critics by grafting himself upon the Virgilian lineage, but his problem
is so very like Virgil's: he too is committed to a conception of an
unrepeatable beginning, a sacred source. The difference lies in the
greater uncertainty he experiences about the nature of this source. Beginnings multiply themselves wildly in the romance form, which conversely
admits a casual disregard for "loose ends." The multiplicity of these
beginnings invites dissociation from origins that Spenser points to as his
own, especially if those origins are represented as sacred.

The ostensible commitment of *The Faerie Queene* to its biblical,
"sacred" pre-text emerges from this context as extremely problematic. The
wandering of the narrative farther and farther away from the redaction of
the Book of Revelation (which is the "origin" of Book I) can also be
construed as an approach (albeit reluctant) to the truer and more dangerous origin of romance. The closure of Book I, unlike the closure of
Revelation, which completes the biblical canon, is broken by the continued wandering of Redcrosse Knight, and every closure thereafter is broken
more violently than the one before. Spenser desires to ground his text in
the origin of the sacred pre-text, but the romance origin must be seen as a
powerfully sustained challenge to that aspiration—indeed, as the inevitable displacement of sacred origin. The multiplicity of beginnings in *The
Faerie Queene* is one effect of the failure of the sacred origin to move
toward a repetition in the later text of its own completion. Every reader of
Book VI knows how radically broken Spenser's ending becomes.

What Hannah Arendt calls an "unrepeatable beginning," Edward
Said calls an *origin*, and I follow Said here in desynonymizing the two
terms. The confusion of the words has served a useful purpose, however, if

we are legitimately to conclude that a poetic text desires to support their synonymy. Some such distinction will emerge out of the vicissitudes of Spenser's habitual recourse to origins, whether or not we shade in the historical background. Said distinguishes between a beginning and an origin as, most basically, the difference between an active and a passive relationship in a sequence of terms: "X is the origin of Y" while "the beginning of A leads to B." Why should an author wish to ground his work in the passivity of an origin? This question would be meaningless outside of the context of authority, as Said himself recognizes in a further attempt to distinguish these concepts: "The state of mind that is concerned with origins is, I have said, theological. By contrast, and this is the [historical] shift, beginnings are eminently secular, or gentile, continuing activities." I am, of course, more than willing to affirm the relation of the sacred/secular dichotomy to the problem of origins/beginnings, as well as the intrinsic association of sacred, "inspired" origins with the desire to inflate the authority of a text. The historicist argument is something else altogether, and it is much more difficult to verify.

The shift from sacred to secular can be seen to coincide with the supercession of beginnings, but when does this happen? One would like to say: when the secular text no longer exhibits anxiety about its relation to the sacred. At this point the parallel distinctions resist translation into historical terms, and at least one of the conclusions to be drawn from this study is that this resistance in poetic texts is a permanent feature of literary history. Under the covering fiction of inspiration, and its later permutations, the idea of the sacred origin lingers in the secular text. The problem for the poet writing in the ruins of exploded mythologies is not markedly different from that experienced by Spenser, a fact that may now be demonstrated.

The strongest temptation to which the heroes of *The Faerie Queene* are subject is denominated in the medieval system of vices as *accidie*, sloth. The temptation is simply to rest, in its most radical form, to give up. The pervasiveness of this arch-evil impresses the reader as an odd restructuring of the traditional hierarchy of vices. In Canto vii of Book I, Redcrosse drinks from a well whose effects are immediately enervating; he is subsequently seized by Orgoglio, against whom he is now defenceless. We are told in Stanza 4 that the nymph who was "wont to dwell" in this fountain was "out of Dian's favour":

> The cause was this: one day when Phoebe fayre
> With all her band was following the chace,
> This Nymph, quite tyr'd with heat of scorching ayre
> Sat downe to rest in middest of the race:

The goddesse wroth gan fowly her disgrace,
And bad the waters, which from her did flow,
Be such as she her selfe was then in place.
Thenceforth her waters waxed dull and slow,
And all that drunke thereof, did faint and feeble grow.

(I.vii.5)

As an allegorical image, the Nymph is intended to objectify a state of moral lassitude in the Knight, corresponding to the fact that Redcrosse has removed his armor, and further emphasized by the editorializing allusion to the pool of Salmacis in Ovid's *Metamorphoses*. The allegory of *The Faerie Queene*, as James Nohrnberg has argued, proceeds by exhaustive analogy, and here the reader is invited to examine what seems to be one example of a complete analogy between two sets of terms. What defeats an examination conducted along these lines, however, is the fact that the two stories, of the Nymph and of the Knight, are not merely adjacent; they intersect causally. In the narrative the fountain is a "source" of Redcrosse's fall to Orgoglio, but morally this makes no sense at all; that is, if we are inclined to see Redcrosse's fall as a moral failure. A conception of purely allegorical causation entails no such problem: the Nymph's failure to participate in the hunt "causes" the fountain's transformation. The first cause in the series, the ultimate "source," is Diana, who would presumably correspond to a divine or providential principle in the allegorical order to which Redcrosse belongs. Spenser's use of "disgrace," cut off from grace, describes the vulnerable condition of the Knight's luxuriation in a pastoral pleasance, and reminds us of the theological analogue; but Spenser does not need to name the analogue for Diana and this is important. The only represented "source" on one side of the analogy is Redcrosse's moral act, the putting off of his armor, which repeats, perhaps, his earlier failure in the House of Pride. The supposed providential source is the allegory itself: the enervating well. Later in the book, when Redcrosse falls into the "Well of Life" during the fight with the Dragon, the intervention of Providence through the source image itself is made more explicit. Here I wish to emphasize the uneven effect of the analogy, intelligible as the intersection of allegorical causation with a problem of representation. The representation of the source is given in the narrative the power of causation as well.

Readers who are schooled in the conventions of allegory usually have no difficulty accepting what Angus Fletcher sees as its "magical causation." The episode of the enfeebling well is an example of the subclass "imitative magic," which "tries to bring real events which the magician wants to control into parallel with symbolic events. The analogy of the Nymph and Redcrosse (with Spenser as the magician-allegorist) is clear, but also perhaps misleading, as all analogies between magic and art disintegrate with further elaboration. The premise of magic is that the world contains no uncaused event. Magic makes available to the allegorist other systems of causation, but no system, by definition, can represent the indeterminacy of a moral act. If the poet does not wish to identify the act itself, which has the traits of a beginning, with a virtual unprecedented origin, then the moment of choice tends to drift out of the range of representation. Redcrosse's sudden decision to rest is given a moral value only to provoke an explanatory fiction of origin ("the cause was this . . .") that attempts to incorporate the indeterminacy of the act into the system of allegorical causation. The reader is not sure, however, that the story of the Nymph, in *repeating* Redcrosse's action, helps to *explain* it. What I mean to suggest by recomplicating an apparently basic example of an allegorical action is that images of origin in *The Faerie Queene* are imbued with a secondariness that cannot be said to characterize the idea of the true origin. The well or stream as image of origin participates in the causative structure of the poem by immediately becoming secondary, just as in the story of the Nymph the spring is easily associated with the *effect* of Redcrosse's moral lapse but continually resists what seems to be its identification with the cause. The *origin*, like the undetermined act, remains unrepresentable except as something that has already happened, but there is no reason to believe that the poet is unaware that the image of the origin moves by a kind of linguistic inertia into the category of the secondary. That secondariness is exploited in what I have referred to as the economy of origins, the subject I would like to examine in the context of another passage.

In Canto ii of Book II, Guyon and the Palmer encounter three victims of Acrasia's enchantments. Amavia is dying beside the body of her lover, Mordant, who is already dead, and she holds in her lap their baby, who plunges his hands into the blood streaming from its mother's wounds. Amavia tells her story and dies, and Guyon takes the baby to a nearby fountain to wash its hands of blood. But the blood will not wash away, a fact that elicits this explanation from the Palmer:

> But know, that secret vertues are infusd
> In euery fountaine, and in euery lake,
> Which who hath skill them rightly to haue chusd,
> To proofe of passing wonders hath full often vsd.

> Of those some were so from their source indewd
> By great Dame Nature, from whose fruitfull pap
> Their welheads spring, and are with moisture deawd;

Which feedes each liuing plant with liquid sap,
And filles with flowres faire Floraies painted lap;
But other some by gift of later grace,
Or by good prayers, or by other hap,
Had vertue pourd into their waters bace,
And thenceforth were renowned, and sought from place to place.
(II.ii.5–6)

The situation repeats with greater complexity the episode of the enfeebling well. More interestingly the fountain genealogy delineates in a very displaced idiom the relationship between Guyon, whose name is taken from the river Gihon, and the Palmer, whose purpose is the continued purification of that source. Guyon's problem, as we learn later during his period of separation from the Palmer, is an unacknowledged dependency, related, though not with immediate clarity, to the need for temperate behavior. The Palmer hints that fountain sources are available to the temperate only, those who "hath skill them rightly to have chusd." When we recall that Gihon means "to burst forth," at least part of the Palmer's digression about watery sources comes into focus. Guyon, of course, does not "burst forth" until he is released like a "tempest" (II.xii.83) upon the Bower of Bliss. Until then, his greatest temptation is to revert to a more dangerous fluidity, like Redcrosse at the well, "poured out in looseness on the grassy ground."

Fountains in *The Faerie Queene* are usually reservoirs of energy, sources of power. But true to the secondariness of the image the power ("vertue") comes from elsewhere, from a transcendent source, Dame Nature, whose indescribable otherness, maintained through the end of the *Mutabilitie Cantos*, is one of the marvels of the poem. Her introduction here as the source of sources, from whom "welheads spring," anticipates the theme of generation that more and more overwhelms the poem as it progresses. In this context, however, the proleptic celebration of generative nature highlights the exceptional status of his fountain, which is not an image of fecundity, but of the frozen chastity that follows an attempted rape. The Palmer tells us, after expounding the general subject of water sources, that a Nymph of Diana was pursued by the lusty Dan Faunus (again, we will meet him in the *Mutabilitie Cantos*). She prays to Diana to let her die a maid, and in response to her prayer she is metamorphosed into a stone, "from whose two heads / As from two weeping eyes, fresh streams do flow."

And yet her vertues in her waters byde
For it is chaste and pure, as purest snow
Ne lets her waues with any filth be dyde,
But euer like her selfe vnstained hath beene tryde.
(II.ii.9)

The fountain is easily located within the thematics of Book II, since temperance is opposed not only to the kind of lust displayed by Faunus but also to the immovable chastity of the Nymph, a fact which determines the negative virtue of this watery source. Temperance is a form of pure generation, a medium between chaste sterility and sterile self-indulgence. In accordance with the rigorous logic of the Canto, the Bloody Babe is given to Medina, a rather dry personification of the Golden Mean.

At this point the Nymph's fountain seems to be reduced to a negative image of a true source, and the reader may wonder exactly what relation Spenser is trying to establish between the idea of generation and the streams and wells pervading the poem. Where are the streams that flow directly from the "source," Dame Nature? Book II has perhaps already evolved beyond the point where allegorical representations of this order (the "Well of Life") are possible. Generation, as we have already argued, contributes to an economy of origins by establishing a continuity of the source and its effluent, which exchanges its pretension to primary status for a privileged relation to a transcendent and unrepresented source. In the proem to Book VI, this economy is spelled out as a system of interchange:

> So from the Ocean all rivers spring
> And tribute backe repay as to their king.
> (VI.Pr.7)

This ocean is associated with an authority in the present, Elizabeth, and the poet accepts the risk implied by the location of his authorizing origin in a very accessible present. I raise this point perhaps prematurely in order to expose a presupposition underlying much of the concern with origins in *The Faerie Queene*: Is the transcendence of the origin indicated by its pastness? Here we must return to the Palmer's explanation of virtuous fountains in order to recover the temporal aspect of Spenser's argument. The Palmer makes a significant distinction between wells deriving their virtue immediately from Dame Nature, and a second, mediated variety of source:

> But other some by gift of later grace,
> Or by good prayers, or by other hap,
> Had vertue pourd into their waters bace,
> And thenceforth were renowned, and sought from place to place.

Guyon and the Palmer live in a world (our world) of *later grace*, clearly distinguishable in this stanza from the virtues flowing out of more primitive sources. "Later grace" is almost redundant, since the word "grace" draws into the context of the argument the recollection of the radical discontinuity that made grace necessary. The hypothesis emerging here is that this world, in its very presentness, contains sources of power that are newly made, whose authority derives from a vertical descent of a higher power. It is this origin that becomes the object of quest ("and sought from place to place"), also the quest of *The Faerie Queene*. Arthur seeks Gloriana, and Spenser "seeks" an apotheosized Elizabeth. These origins may promise nothing more than strength to continue, but because they do not derive from an irrecoverable past, they seem to escape the critique of origins founded upon a resolute doubt at the core of representation. Spenser's acceptance of the secondariness of his water sources is to be equated with his willingness to subsist beneath, as it were, the priority of a transcendent power. The quest for an origin outside of, but cotemporal with, the production of the poem encounters a problem of great significance for literary history: the tendency of the sacred source to degenerate into the secular beginning. The sacred other feeding energy into the poem, whose traces I have described in the image of the source, defines the ideal of "generation." Other tracks might also have been followed, but here I can only suggest that all such paths would lead to the Garden of Venus and Adonis, the ideological crest of the poem, and the most elaborated of Spenser's mythopoetic scenes of generation. It is not my intention to analyze the erotic cores of these central books (such analysis would indefinitely extend my argument) but rather to follow like Alpheus my critique of origin, as it finally emerges fully apparent in the displaced "core" of Book VI. I believe this critique will uncover an alternative, and intractably "secular" origin: the fact of desire.

II

Discourse, according to Michel Foucault, is composed of statements, whose formations are various, almost innumerable. One such variant form of statement, the list, will provide us with a means of understanding some currents of significance that run in *The Faerie Queene* well below the level of the sentence. Here is the list: *gens, genus, genius, generation, general, gentile, gentle, gentleman, generous, genealogy, gender, genesis, genital*. Such a list has a *prima facie* relevance in the vastly stratified language of Spenser's epic. The non-English of the poem, like Joyce's non-English, requires of its readers habitual attention to the agglutinative properties of an etymon as important in the Romance languages as *genus*. The cognates in this list develop over a great stretch of time, and for that reason may also be said to comprise a historical argument. For example, the list seems to assert an intrinsic connection between a process of abstraction (the naming of kinds) and the activity of reproduction. The smallest kind may be the clan, or extended family, united by a purely reproductive pattern. Hence the development of "generalizing" as abstraction of apprehended likeness. (Something like this process has been examined in Wittgenstein's analogy of "family resemblances.") A second notion arising from this list is the idea of *gentility*, the *gentleman*, with the corollary *generosity*, a subject that exercises Spenser in Book VI of *The Faerie Queene* and leads him inevitably into the dismantling and reconstruction of genealogical fictions (*vide* the romance of Pastorella). Genealogies are crucial to gentlemen, and in the Renaissance to the tensions heating up the issue of primogeniture. Ideas of origin intersect with this semantic field producing more abstract conceptions of genealogy and genesis, to some of which I have already alluded. At the moment we may allow the word list to recede into the middleground in order to bracket two words that are drawn together by Spenser in the passage I would like next to examine: *genius* and *generation*.

At the entrance to the Bower of Bliss stands a figure called Genius, an effeminate young man who is one of many Acrasian representatives of unproductive lust. He is contrasted with another figure, also a Genius, whose identity is difficult to determine precisely. Spenser identifies this positive figure with the god Agdistes, who is a

> celestial powre, to whom the care
> Of life, and generation of all
> That liues, pertains in charge particulare,
> Who wondrous things concerning our welfare,
>   And strange phantomes doth let vs oft forsee,
>   And oft of secret ill bids vs beware:
>   That is our Selfe, whom though we do not see,
> Yet each doth in him selfe it well perceiue to bee.
>
> (II.xii.47)

C. S. Lewis, who puzzled over this stanza in *The Allegory of Love*, was confident that up to the line ending "welfare," Spenser is speaking about the "universal god of generation," a familiar figure in medieval literature. But there is another distinct kind of Genius, which is the "tutelary spirit" or "external soul" of individual men. Spenser seems to be saying that Agdistes is also this Genius, and Lewis finds the composite creature "unimaginable." The problem is not resolved by the usual recourse to Renaissance syncretism because there remains a logical objection to the confusing of a "universal" demigod and daemons who are defined by the particularity of "individual souls." There must be considerable pressure behind the fusion of the two figures, and a clue to the source of that pressure is provided by the intrusion into this text of yet another allegorical precursor. The "strange phantomes" which Agdistes "doth let vs oft forsee" recall the description of Phantastes in the Castle of Alma; "he could things to come forsee." "Genius" and the correlative "fantasy" are waiting in the wings of Renaissance poetic theory, although Spenser is very careful to subordinate imagination to reason and memory in his anatomy of the mind. The allusion to Phantastes in this passage is attributable, I believe, largely to his elective affinity for the evil *Doppelgänger* of the Good Genius. Villains of imagination in *The Faerie Queene*, of whom the archetype is Archimago (arch-magus and arch-image), often recreate themselves as the *Doppelgänger* of an innocent victim, or produce such figures from their stock of evil spirits. Under the aegis of Agdistes, genius and generation are drawn together as a means of counteracting the power of the double, whose identity is simply desire itself. The problem is once again the Renaissance dilemma of distinguishing sacred and profane love. The Good Genius comes between the converging impules of desire and imagination, preempting the false reproduction (of shadows, shows) that would result from, as it were, their copulation. The problem of desire enters the poetics of allegory as the possibility of this false image. The language of allegory, however, with its "shadows" and "outward shows," can exactly duplicate an "idle fantasy," and this dangerous similitude needs to be examined now. I offer as context a second word list: *fain, feign, fancy,* and *fantasy.*

The involvement of imagination in desire is confirmed for Spenser by one of those linguistic accidents of which he takes full advantage. *Fain* and *feign*, despite the absence of distinction in Renaissance orthography, are derived from two quite different sources. *Fain* is from Old High German and means "wont, longing, desire." *Feign* is taken from the Latin *fingere,* "to shape or to form," and hence to pretend or to produce a fiction. Spenser puns in a similar fashion on the words *concept* and *conception.* Fancy can of course be used to mean either a desire or love object, or a contraction of fantasy. *Phantoms, phantasms, fantasies,* and *fancies* are then the correlative objects of desire and imagination. Usually Spenser will use one word in the context of the other, in order to suggest a mutual intensification of "affect." For example, Britomart's conversation with Redcrosse about Arthegall in Canto iv of Book III:

> But *Britomart* kept on her former course,
>   Ne euer dofte her armes, but all the way
> Grew pensiue through that amorous discourse,
>   By which the *Redcrosse* knight did earst display

> Her louers shape, and cheualrous aray;
> A thousand thoughts she fashioned in her mind,
> And in her feigning fancie did pourtray
> Him such, as fittest she for loue could find,
> Wise, warlike, personable, curteous, and kind.
>
> (III.iv.5)

Britomart "fashions" in her mind a duplicate (but better) image of Arthegall based on Redcrosse's description, thereby placing at still another remove the object of desire. In this context, we remember that her feelings were first aroused by an image in Merlin's glass. The reader is inclined to the conclusion that whatever system of mutual intensification exists between desire and imagination, the earliest movement of feeling is preceded by a still earlier act of imagination. For many reasons, Spenser remains fearfully ambivalent about this fact. Modern readers have been lectured in the complex self-delusions attending "object choice," to the extent, possibly, that our lack of surprise at the conventional wisdom of Spenser's analysis of desire obstructs a more important insight: a critique of origins (in a more hidden sense, of allegorical origins) is embedded in this language. Coinciding with the allegorist's expressed intention in the letter to Raleigh, Britomart "*fashions a gentleman*" in her mind—"wise, warlike, personable, curteous, kind"—but out of what? Arthegall's failure to correspond to the ideal image makes his portrait vulnerable to ironic reduction, but Britomart cannot know this. Irony is the occupational hazard of allegory, or as its contemporary champions maintain, allegory's true value and distinction. For Spenser the question is whether imagination represents an object or begets it. The betrayal into irony (or the failure of allegorical representation) is in fact a less feared alternative than the prospect of the imagination as beginning, displacing some other and more valued origin.

The power of imagination is therefore reduced by linking it to failed representations, the lesser of two evils. Hence the easy derogation of

> idle thoughts and fantasies
> Devices, dreams, opinions unsound,
> Shewes, visions, soothsayes, and prophecies
> All that fained is, as leasings, tales and lies.
>
> (II.ix.51)

This is Phantastes, to whom any power of origination is being denied. The digression through the Castle of Alma in Book II provides Spenser with a needed defense against Phantastes the Poet—*his* double. Spenser is thoroughly conventional in tracing his poetry to the more authoritative quarters of Reason, who is in charge of "all artes, all science, all philosophy." Reason is also a censor, a "magistrate," ruling and overruling the false productions of the magus, his unauthorized double. The legal analogue fits into the general scheme of repressed imagination, as Phantastes himself is a typical example of the Renaissance neurotic, the melancholy man. At this point in the poem (but not later) Spenser finds a purer origin in the personification of memory, Eumnestes ("good memory"), who might also be called "true re-presentation." In the proem to Book II, allegory is associated with *anamnesis*, and Canto x elaborately unfolds a version of "antique history" in the chronicles of England and Faery land. These texts are read like scripture; they are prophetic revelations, and they are included in *The Faerie Queene* as a kind of model of what a sacred origin would be. It is as though the narrative cord of the Bible had been unwound into constituent mythical and historical strands. Guyon and Arthur read the stories of the past relevant to themselves, unconscious of the status of the text in which they do this reading. That text must one day be added to the books in Eumnestes' chamber, the same text for *both* books. Spenser cannot, of course, add to the words of the Bible; and yet this is what any sacred text must do, by however remote a process of translation, allegorization, interpretation.

Spenser need not deny the power of imagination to intensify desire, or even its subversive effect upon allegory, but he must resist desire as a source that draws him to the dangerous priority of the "unprecedented" act of imagination. The antecedent of Arthur's dream, which, as the origin of the quest, is the pre-text of the poem itself, risks the truth claims of the allegory in an episode of desire. Arthur wonders "whether dreams delude, or true it were," that is, whether he really was visited by the Faery Queen and not sleeping with an image of his own mind. Some observations on two other episodes of desire—the Bower of Bliss and the Dance of the Graces on Mt. Acidale—will open the question of what gratification might mean in relation to allegorical intentions. Curiously, this end is perceived as an origin: *there was a time in which desire was gratified*. The quest for origins becomes a quest for the gratification of desire. Spenser is eventually disillusioned about the possibilities of anamnesis but his poem continually sets up scenes of possible gratification, or scenes in which such a possibility is explored. From the first of my two examples, Acrasia's Bower, we should not expect any gratification that can be considered authentic within the categories of the poem. But that is not to say that Spenser (as well as Guyon) is not tempted. The following stanza is worth consideration:

> Her snowy brest was bare to readie spoyle
>   Of hungry eies, which n'ote therewith be fild,
>   And yet through langour of her late sweet toyle,
>   Few drops, more cleare then Nectar, forth distild,
>   That like pure Orient perles adowne it trild,
>   And her faire eyes sweet smyling in delight,
>   Moystened their fierie beames, with which she thrild
>   Fraile harts, yet quenched not; like starry light
> Which sparckling on the silent waues, does seeme more bright.
>   (II.xii.78)

Many scenes in *The Faerie Queene*, quoted "out of context," are not very far from pornographic, as critics have almost acknowledged in comments on Spenser's sensuality. The problem here, as with pornography, is precisely the nature of the visual image as a stimulus to desire. C. S. Lewis seized upon what seems to be the exclusively visual nature of the erotic stimulus to conclude that there are in fact no sexual relations at all in the Bower of Bliss, an interesting misreading since we are not told that the lover sleeping in Acrasia's lap has always been so immobile. In the stanza quoted above Acrasia is shedding tears "through langour of her late sweet toyle." This would have to be post-coital *tristesse*, an image of gratified desire. The image *of* gratification places the scene of sexual consummation in a past that the voyeur (Guyon, the reader) has no wish to recover. The fire that quenches not is the desire *of* desire, like the reflection of the starry light that seems *more* bright than the stars themselves. The simile also links the duplication of desire to the idea of representation, or the seductiveness of the mere image. The erotic "fantasy" is desire folding back upon itself, completely emancipated from its object. And this process of duplication or folding back bears a structural similarity, which the poem must deny, to the approved concept of generation, represented in various places as the hermaphrodite, or the snake biting its tail, or the ocean-river interchange. The middle books of *The Faerie Queene* worry this distinction, an undertaking that is analogous to the process of distinguishing the true from the false Florimel.

Allegorical characters are conventionally "seduced" by images, and Spenser only literalizes this metaphor by writing it into a narrative of seduction. Guyon is not finally seduced but the Knight called Verdant is, and it is important to observe what this means in the larger thematic scheme of Book II:

> His warlike armes, the idle instruments
>   Of sleeping praise, were hong vpon a tree,

And his brave shield, full of old moniments,
Was fowly ra'st, that none the signes might see. . .
(II.xii.80)

Vergant is plainly cut off from his especial origins, the implicit argument of the erased "moniments." These are "memorials" of a general nature, or specifically marks on a shield. The legendary "Briton moniments" establish Canto x as the context for determining the relation between memory and desire. The self-activating complex of desire-fantasy comes between the present moment and a past origin, establishing, by virtue of this discontinuity, an aimless and undesirable beginning. This beginning is completely static, like the still postures in the Bower of Bliss; the Knight sleeps, his instruments are idle. Loss of origin is analogous to the blankness of the shield, from which the memory signs are obliterated. This condition of obliteration, the letter erased, is almost the worst evil Spenser can conceive.

The *worst* evil is embodied by the Blatant Beast, who does not so much erase letters as write over them or displace them. He is intended to figure calumny, which supersedes sloth as the most dangerous of vices in Spenser's allegory. I have already suggested that all the monsters in *The Faerie Queene* are prototypes of the Blatant Beast and I want to emphasize here his possible relation to the fantasy by way of introduction to a problem in the interpretation of the Dance of the Graces on Mt. Acidale, the most fully rendered episode of the "lineaments of gratified desire." The Blatant Beast has no overtly erotic signification, but his presence in a book highly charged with sexual themes requires comment. Here is an early adumbration of the Beast in *The Teares of the Muses*:

> For the sweet numbers and melodious measures
> With which I wont the winged words to tie
> And make a tuneful diapase of pleasures
> Now being let to run at libertie
> By those which have no skill to rule them right
> Have now quite lost their natural delight.
>
> Heaps of huge words uphoorded hideously
> With horrid sound though having little sense
> They thinke to be chief praise of Poetry
> And thereby wanting due intelligence
> Have mard the face of goodly Poesie
> And made a monster of their fantasie. . .
> (547–58)

These stanzas are sung by Polyhymnia, who, as a principle of integration or harmony, is a foreshadowing of the kind of infolded complexity visible in the Dance of the Graces. The poem ends with all of the muses breaking their "learned instruments," a recurrent motif in Spenser's poetry, culminating in the breaking of Colin Clout's bagpipes after Calidore's unwelcome intrusion. The "monster" can be language or even poetry, "let to run at libertie," as though mere words proliferate meaninglessly of themselves unless subject to a perpetual effort of restraint. A certain parallel is established very early in Spenser's career between restraint as a poetic necessity and restraint as a principle of sexual morality. These two themes are usually equated allegorically only where they both fail: in the disastrous collapsing together of desire and fantasy. In Book VI, the two themes belong to different sets of allegorical fictions, which Spenser is very careful to keep apart. The necessity of their distinction arises because he is led in Book VI to consider the possibility of representing the "lineaments of gratified desire" as itself the pure origin he seeks. In other words, he is no longer determined to distinguish the abstract conception of generation from the motivating principle of a desire that could be experientially associated with the will to write. This is a more direct poetic strategy, as the strict recourse to the romance form evidences; romance is the genre of return, of finding the lost origin. It is also a secular form, and I am inclined to believe that at this point Spenser is willing to accept an origin that is secular—the experience of desire— provided that origin can be purified by an uninvoked agency of mediation (let us call it "grace") whose source is unimpeachable. This much of my argument has been implied by Harry Berger, Jr., and other critics, who read Book VI as a book of origins and sources. My second hypothesis, however, departs from the reading of the Mt. Acidale episode now current.

Let me defer for the moment a statement of this hypothesis in order to set down some sentences by two of Spenser's critics, passages intended to epitomize the thematic significance of the Dance of the Graces:

> In the intersection between visible actuality and invisible transcendence, where agape merges with eros, poetry has its life. Spenser's visionary stanzas allow us to see the dance of imagination, the concrete universal emerging from the figure the poem makes.

> Only by turning inward, by self-creation, by tirelessly seeking and wooing and invoking the muses, or eros, or what lies behind them all—only thus do we regain our long-lost heritage. By some process akin to anamnesis we withdraw, we retire, we return to the nursery, we close the circle of beginnings and endings, we come finally to that first Idea, that pure grace which has always moved us. . .

It is important to take into account the presence of Rosalind as a simple country lass and poor handmaid of Gloriana, if one is to do justice to the realistic basis of Spenser's vision. The triumph of imagination is partly measured by the extent to which it has converted frustration, brute fact, the world of first sight and first nature, into a symbolic intuition of the real. . .

Admirable as Isabel MacCaffrey's and Harry Berger's ecstatic readings of Spenser's famous climax may be, it should be remembered that Spenser could not have meant by "imagination" anything like what these readings imply. Nevertheless both statements go to the heart of the matter, which is the question of origin. Spenser does seem to locate in this episode an erotic origin of the poetic text, and this origin does also allow for the subsumption of the image of desire into a transcendent source. If there is any "triumph," however, it is in the poem's movement *against* imagination, and this is where formulations like those quoted above are misleading. Berger argues (and his analysis is substantially reaffirmed by MacCaffrey) that Spenser achieves his triumph by bracketing, as it were, the activity of imagination, without losing sight of the possible and imminent impingement of the "real" world. This acknowledgment of the real context permits a free flight of imagining and even the touching of the imaginary image to the real (figured as the country lass, Rosalind). The idealized representation is a victory won at the cost of an ultimate defeat, since the immediate vision is dissolved by Calidore, the Blatant Beast returns, and then the poem itself disintegrates at the ungentle touch of this reality.

And yet the persuasiveness of this particular interpretation is dependent upon a mutual exclusivity of imagination and reality that is completely foreign to Spenser's poetic. Imagination is *not* equivalent to the activity of making poems and poetic self-consciousness cannot be assumed in this poet to mean reflection on the opposition or supposed reconciliation of the imagined and the real (the functional opposition is between the fantastic and the *true*). A triumph of imagination can be conceived by Spenser only as a reduction, a loss of authority, the poem as a mere "heap of words." I cannot find any passage in the poem where imagination is given a positive meaning, nor does the historical background sketched in chapter 1 provide us with a contemporary consensus for interpreting imagination as anything but the usurper of textual authority, the intruder into the sequence of representation. The fantasy has much more to do with the "real" in Berger's phrase (or MacCaffrey's "visible actuality") since that world is riddled with delusion. Calidore brings with him a tendency to be seduced by the mere image, and surprisingly he does not unlearn this mistake in his encounter with the

Graces. He begins in the state of infolded desire ("he himselfe his eyes envued") and even Colin's sage discourse is said to feed his "greedy fancy," possibly because he still has one eye on the "place, whose pleasures rare / With such regard his senses ravished." We recall his attention was similarly divided in an earlier episode between Meliboe's sermon and Pastorella's beauty. The "dance of imagination" that MacCaffrey sees, or Berger's "triumph of imagination," begs the question of exactly what is being "represented" in this passage, and what relation this representation bears to the allegorical image.

The object of representation is precisely what precedes the fiction and strictly speaking does not *need* representation. Spenser gambles on the absolute priority of desire in order to exclude the autonomous self-generation of the image and place the activity of the poet under the authority of a transcendent agency. In short, he stages a scene of pure inspiration, excluding entirely from this scene its consequence: the poem. We do not hear what Colin Clout sings, only that he is singing. His experience is visionary, not imagining but pure *seeing*, and not subject to the temporal displacements of representation. The singing and the seeing of his beloved are simultaneous: "Thy loue is present there with thee in place" (VI.x.16). Colin Clout is addressed as the other by the poet at this point (like Coleridge's daemonic Kubla poet, who also sings and sees at once, he is most "other" precisely at the moment of vision). And we, the poet, the reader, the voyeur Calidore, must remain outside of that coincidence of time and place within the charmed circle of the dancing graces. Colin experiences pure presence in its temporal and spatial manifestations but to the reader that presence is already *there* and not here. The gratification of desire is represented deliberately at this remove because it is sheer priority. We may feel that we are the excluded other because we are "outside," but it is Colin who is truly other, and Rosalind, and Gloriana. The dance of the Graces on Mt. Acidale is a moment of "inside-out," an expression that might be offered for the topography of inspiration, if such a thing could be.

Is this the origin of Spenser's allegorical image? The reader must certainly suspect that he has never read any poem written by Colin Clout in a state of rapture, "in the midst," of an epiphany. The poem we read begins with *the experience of an imagined loss*, not the loss of any gratification really experienced, but the loss of the "lineaments of gratified desire." The origin is preserved as a pure "idea of origin" and as such is removed from the temporal sequence of poetic composition. Spenser stages the scene of his inspiration, knowing he was never inspired. The poem therefore begins with any Calidore-like transgression, which is to say, anywhere, because *The Faerie Queene* is the record of perpetual *erring*. The poet has a vision of a vision—he sees himself inspired—but the experience he needs to recover is the loss itself, the moment at which the sanctity of the poetic origin could still be upheld not because the content of a vision is remembered but because a feeling of loss is remembered, the feeling of the vanished god, or the violated sacred place.

To admit the need for loss, for the experience of longing rather than the experience of vision, is to propose a fact about the nature of poetry that the sacred poet would not be inclined to accept. The transgression of Calidore leaves open the possibility that the graces may never return, which does not mean that Spenser loses faith in his inspiration but that he may never again be able to reexperience its loss:

> For being gone, none can them bring in place,
> But whom they of themselves list so to grace
> Right sorry I (said then sir Calidore)
> That my ill fortune did them hence displace.
>
> (VI.x.20)

The final displacement of the sacred place delivers the poem over to the world, the secular, the ultimate effect of this event is the breakdown of the narrative (the freedom of the Blatant Beast) and the dismay of the poet. The modern reader may find the pathos of this loss truly moving, but that pathos might be too easily tempered by such theories as that of Northrop Frye, whose notion of displacement I mention here in order to dissociate it from the kind of event taking place in Spenser's poem. It is true that the great ambition of allegory, as its etymology indicates, is to bring sacred mysteries into the marketplace, to make the "displacement" of the sacred a triumph. For the critic who locates the value of secular literature in its displacements of the sacred, an allegorical conception of poetic meaning will inevitably be pulled toward the center of critical theory, as has certainly happened in Frye's *Anatomy*. The decay and final collapse of this ideal in *The Faerie Queene* should not be glossed over, nor need it be offered as evidence that the poem fails. The last movement of *The Faerie Queene* completes its critique of origins by giving up the truth claims of allegory as a veil behind which lies a putative sacred origin. The text that emerges from this critique is the secular text, and the question that immediately presents itself concerns the authority of these human words. What authority can such a text have if it is created in the continual absence of a speaking God?

PETER SACKS

"Astrophel"

The most obvious change as one
moves from Spenser's earlier elegiac works to "Astrophel" is that the poet
seems to have crossed into an apparently less unreal world. The pastoral
garb is more loosely worn, and the poem is not as enclosed as the
Calender, with its cycle of months and its entire cast of shepherds. Nor is
it located within the realm of quasi-visionary encounters such as in "The
Ruines of Time" or "Daphnaida." The mourning voice is that of the poet
himself, and he seems to speak from within our world:

> Shepheards that wont on pipes of oaten reed,
> Oft times to plaine your loves concealed smart:
> And with your piteous layes have learnd to breed
> Compassion in a countrey lasses hart
> Hearken ye gentle shepheards to my song,
> And place my dolefull plaint your plaints emong.
>
> To you alone I sing this mournfull verse,
> The mournfulst verse that ever man heard tell:
> To you whose softened hearts it may empierse,
> With dolours dart for death of Astrophel.
> (lines 1–10)

This is clearly an assured bid for inclusion in the company of poets.
Unlike the isolated Colin Clout addressing Pan, Spenser is now speaking
directly to his fellow poets, commanding their audience. Some of these
poets are the other elegists whose poems are published here with Spenser's.
In fact, Spenser has maneuvered these poets, all of whose elegies preceded

his in time, into a position of posteriority and dependency. It is he now who leads the mourning, introducing their poems after his.

Also within this introduction we recognize the familiar motif of piercing and breeding. The poem's power to impregnate suggests the surviving poet's ongoing, if displaced, sexual energy, his assertion of a thrusting force that one already feels must carry him beyond the weaker introversions of melancholy. This force is complicated by its aggressiveness. The figurative resemblance between the poet's piercing power and the power that killed Astrophel suggests that a part of the elegy's motive, however troped, lies in an impulse to wound almost as death wounds. It is as though some of the violence of death's power enters man's anger against that power. But this anger is as much a rage against man's own susceptibility to death, hence a rage against the self. And it is not surprising to hear that rage take on the characteristics of death itself. . . . The purpose of raising the subject [of the psychological background of the tendency to self-injury] in discussing "Astrophel" is not merely to delve beneath that otherwise apparently fortuitous similarity between the piercing power of the elegist and that of death (compare the related anger and destructive power of the elegist in the opening of "Lycidas"). It is also to make some sense of the surprisingly vicious fury of Astrophel's foreign campaign:

> Eftsoones all heedlesse of his dearest hale,
> Full greedily into the heard he thrust:
> To slaughter them, and worke their finall bale,
> Least that his toyle should of their troups be brust.
> Wide wounds emongst them many one he made,
> Now with his sharp borespear, now with his blade.
>
> His care was all how he them all might kill,
> That none might scape (so partiall unto none).
>
> (103–10)

The distaste that many readers feel for this passage stems, I think, from a failure to read beyond its surface, and even beyond the allegorization of Sidney's battle against the Spanish. It is true that after the evocation, earlier in the poem, of the perfect "gentle" shepherd, this may seem an incongruously harsh picture, but there are several ways to understand its significance. Most important of these is to consider what the poem tells us of Astrophel's disdain for the world. His unhappiness is in fact presented as his only "fayling," and we are shown how it relates to his unassuageable devotion to the ethereal Stella. So exclusively is Stella presented as a star that this figure entirely occludes any human referent. It is this very occluding or excluding quality that marks the attitude of her adorer. As star she is immortal, attracting Astrophel away from the mortal world. It is in relation to this dislocative *contemptus mundi* that Astrophel's violence takes on some of its meaning, for it is thus seen as a channeling of what we may suppose to be the wrath enfolded within his contempt. Astrophel's heedlessness toward the world is directed no less against his own nature ("All heedlesse of his dearest hale"). Just as suggested, he takes on a role not unlike that of Death itself, whence the description of his thorough and impartial slaughter.

Added to the impulse behind this depiction of Astrophel's rage against mortality is of course Spenser's own fury against death, both as mortality and as event. The violent lines therefore bear the weight of his own anger and sorrow. There is, however, a further element at work here: Spenser's hostility or at least ambivalence toward Astrophel's lethal pursuit. At an obvious level, Spenser finds it difficult to approve the very choice that led to Sidney's death. His criticism is pointed in the language of "Did prick him forth with proud desire of praise" and in the query "What needeth peril to be sought abroad?" More interesting yet is the way Spenser displays how Astrophel becomes reduced to the very savagery that kills him. Spenser captures the way violence recoils on the self, and by a momentary ambiguity he blurs the identities of the hunter and the beast:

> So as he rag'd emongst that beastly rout,
> A cruell beast of most accursed brood
> Upon him turnd (despeyre makes cowards stout)
>
> (115–17)

The case of Spenser's critique assumes added interest when one recalls that Astrophel's choice is equated by Spenser with a rejection of language. For Astrophel was not content with a merely verbal wooing or praising of Stella, and chose instead the unmediated and here almost suicidal pursuit of violent action. Spenser's ambivalence poises on one of those reversals so typical of this poem: "Ne her with ydle words alone he wowed, / And verses vaine (yet verses are not vaine)" (67–68). Do we hear the note of an inner debate within whose dialectic the voice of Sidney had come to play its associated part? Does Spenser's parenthesis answer that side of the poet that shares Sidney's skepticism? The issue goes to the core of "Astrophel," for as suggested earlier, the poem achieves its work of mourning precisely by resolving this question of the adequacy of language and its figures of consolation.

To sketch it most simply, this resolution comes about by the thorough way in which the second part of the poem, "The Lay of Clorinda," questions and moves beyond the consolation figured in the earlier part. The withdrawal from or rather rejection of the figure of the Astrophel flower, and the substitution for it of a further, more advanced consolatory figure (the soul as celestial infant) performs a process similar in form to the work of mourning itself—the undoing of a prior position or attachment and the substitution for it of a fresh attachment. The problematic intervening phase involving as it does a temporary return of affect and interest upon the self, is also present in the poem. The remainder of this [essay] will elaborate upon this schema.

The first part of the poem moves from the introductory self-presentation of the elegist to a picture of the young Astrophel. The conventional enumeration of the qualities of the deceased goes back to the earliest attempts to perpetuate the powers or virtues of the dead in the bodies, and later in the minds, of the living. But as we read Spenser's evocation of the young Astrophel, we are reminded of another motive for this kind of repetition: the retrospective creation of a defense against shock. This is especially evident in the way Spenser seeds the early part of the poem with warning signals, miniature reversals that prepare us for the catastrophic reversal to come. The characteristic form of these reversals is the turning of a word or line against itself: "Both wise and hardie (too hardie alas)" (72); "Besides in hunting, such felicities, / Or rather infelicitie he found" (79–80). This creates a cushion of expectation, but it also instills a vertiginous instability, as though within language, as in life, there were this sudden tendency for reversal or cancellation, the sudden opening of a chasm. Hardiness threatens to collapse upon its own excess, felicity hovers over infelicity, the word lies on its shadow or negation.

The account of Astrophel complicates itself, as his life did, with the turn to Stella. And as we have seen in our view of that love's associations and implications, this leads in turn to the narrative of his death. A sense of causality and plot, even of fatality, thus emerges, and as one rereads, details of this plotting declare themselves. An example of the careful timing of such details is the implicit comparison of Astrophel to Orpheus, "And many a nymph . . . both crystall wells and shadie groves forsooke, / To heare the charmes of his enchanting skill" (43–46), which comes just before the reorienting of the poem toward the otherworldly Stella. By associating Astrophel with Orpheus, the poet casts a little more premonitory shade upon his shepherd, moving him a step further toward his doom, and toward his fictional assimilation to that other vegetation god, Adonis.

We have already observed the account of battle following this, and we come thence to the wounded Astrophel, pouring forth "huge streams of blood" upon the "cold deare earth." The image of the vegetation god

giving his warm blood to the cold earth is obvious, but Spenser delays any
suggestion of the fertilizing consequences of this martyrdom. Such consequences will come only with the metamorphosis of victim to flower later
in the first part of the poem, and even that consolatory figure will prove
short-lived. As we shall see, the delay is deliberate, for it allows Spenser
to show to what extent the pastoral world, together with its resources for
cure or comfort, has been disrupted.

For the moment, Spenser turns to the conventional questions
addressed to those who might have prevented the death. We have already
discussed such conventional elegiac questioning, and it is unnecessary to
repeat all its determinants and effects here. One aspect does, however,
stand out in Spenser's use of the convention—the fact that his addresses
are not the traditional gods or nymphs of preceding elegies but rather
Astrophel's "shepheard peares" and companions. While this departure may
indicate Spenser's unease with the inherited fictions, it also reinforces our
suspicion that much elegiac questioning is designed to avert an angry or
guilty self-questioning. The distance between Spenser and Astrophel's
peers is, after all, relatively slight. And recalling Spenser's unease regarding his long-delayed elegy, the words *unpitied* and *unplayned* lend a specific
edge to this aspect of his questioning.

But Spenser is also drawing attention to the way in which Sidney's
pursuits as a soldier cut him off from those of his peers who were devoted
to poetry. This focus points toward the question, and the complaint,
regarding the difficult relation between poetry, particularly pastoral poetry,
and historical events—an issue that the poem now turns to address.

In the passage describing the foreign shepherds' discovery of the
wounded Astrophel, Spenser surely suggests that even if Sidney's friends
had been there, they might not have saved him. The shepherds have been
following the hunt. This alerts us to the polarity of shepherds and hunters,
a polarity as old as the Adonis myth itself and one that Spenser uses to
focus the unhappy relation between pastoral and history, between a realm
of fiction and one of action and death. The crucial point is that the
pastoral world can neither cure itself nor defend itself against the violence
of history.

As Astrophel bleeds to death—"They stopt his wound (too late to
stop it was)" (145)—the pastoral world has certainly been "launched" by
the "cruell beast" of history. The implications for pastoral elegy are
especially dire, and they go to the heart of Spenser's clear-eyed and
original relation to his tradition. For how can a conventional pastoral
elegy find comfort for a death inflicted by a world whose realities have so
clearly ravaged the realm of pastoral itself? Spenser's answer will require

his revision of the tradition, including the myth of Adonis. But that revision comes much later in the poem.

Like Adonis, Astrophel is mourned by his Venus figure, Stella. But something very odd happens in this second representation of Stella. What we see is no less than the utter disintegration of the figure of the star into that of a grieving woman. She who was "the fairest star in skie" is suddenly tearing her "yellow locks," rending the roses in her "red cheeks," and despoiling the treasury of her "fair brest." The figure of a woman now occludes that of the star, thus continuing to undermine any dubious or facile substitution of figures like that of the star for human individuals. While thus undoing the tropes of conventional elegy, Spenser pursues a decidedly Ovidian account of inadequate mourning. Like the models by which it is influenced, Spenser's account combines psychological acuity with metamorphic figurations. As Stella weeps over her beloved, she "deformes" her face "like him to bee." Instead of withdrawing from the dead, Stella makes the common psychological response of identification, a response which, as Ovid and Spenser knew, may involve a lethal deformation of the self. Stella dies "untimely" and flies off like a turtledove to join her mate. Even though that "untimely" may be read as an expression of the poet's sorrow, it tends to confirm our suspicion that Stella is not designed to serve as an example of successful mourning.

It is against this negative example that the mourning of Clorinda will be dramatically counterpoised. In this progressive, oppositional structure, Spenser is again ensuring that the development of his poem enacts the work of mourning. Stella represents the part of the self that adopts an untenable position beyond which the mourning self must move. She is like Alcyon or the city of Verulam in this respect, but in "Astrophel" Spenser is able to move beyond them to a positive inventor of consolations. And it is precisely this surpassing movement that is so crucial to effective mourning.

The surpassal consists in more than merely replacing Stella by Clorinda. More significantly, it has to do with how Clorinda rejects and surpasses the attempted consolation that initially followed the deaths of Astrophel and Stella. The gods, we are told, pitied the dead lovers and transformed them into a single flower, henceforth given the name of Astrophel. The figuration here is not a little contrived, working as it does to include both lovers in a single emblem which changes from red to blue, which carries the star insignia of Stella, and which darts forth beams of light from the dew that represents her tears! Added to this are the variety of names by which the plant is called—Penthia (from the Greek word meaning "tearful sorrow"), Starlight, and Astrophel. Clearly, there is an extreme self-consciousness about the positing of this figure. Nor is one's belief in its substantiality reinforced by the bewildering series of dis-figurations that have preceded it. Stella the star, we recall, became the grieving woman who became a turtledove that then gave way to a flower that in turn resembles the original star.

This instability of the figure is intensified by the poem's departure from what might have been its guiding myth or framework of figuration, the myth of Adonis as transmitted by Bion, Ovid, and Ronsard. Such departures will become even more obvious as the poem continues, but already we notice that Stella is at a far remove from the Venus figure who would normally be grieving over the dying Adonis. We have seen Stella subjected to fluctuations of form and identity, and she finally dies, unlike her immortal model.

At the same time, the movement beyond the figure of Venus, associated as she is with the mother as lover, performs the mourner's essential detachment from such a figure—his recapitulation, in the act of mourning, of the disjoining from his original attachments. "Lycidas" and "Adonais" will offer clear repetitions of this, and we shall study the movement more closely in those poems. For the moment, we may notice how thoroughly Spenser has thus far revised his myth, reducing Venus to this metamorphic Stella, who survives only as a highly contrived and decorative flower. The mourner's movement beyond the Venus figure would thus seem to go hand in hand with the skeptical attack on inade-quate fictions. And it is at this critical point that Spenser closes the first part of the poem, introducing the subsequent mourners who come to bewail the double death. By an almost eclogic succession, he turns from Stella to Clorinda's more adequate voice of mourning.

The switch toward a new mourner, opening up a distance from the unfortunate Stella and from the figures discussed above, begins with a section corresponding to the intermediate phase of mourning mentioned earlier, in which there is a detachment of affections and interest from the lost love-object and a temporary return of these upon the self. From this stage the mourner works outward once more, trying to find or invent a new object of attachment. It is, therefore, fascinating to note how thor-oughly Spenser's poem works *through* this very process. Clorinda's lay begins with an intense withdrawal from the external world and a return inward to the self:

> Or where shall I enfold my inward paine,
> That my enriven heart may find reliefe?
> Shall I unto the heavenly powres it show?
> Or unto earthly men that dwell below?

To heavens? ah they alas the authors were,
And workers of my unremedied wo: . . .
To men? ah they alas like wretched bee,
And subject to the heavens ordinance: . . .
Then to myselfe will I my sorrow mourne,
Sith none alive like sorrowfull remaines:
And to my selfe my plaints shall back retourne,
To pay their usury with doubled paines
(3–22)

In these lines we notice, too, that Clorinda has undone the fiction of divine benevolence posited earlier by the pitying gods' transformation of the lovers into a flower. As she continues her lament, she undoes the consolatory flower figure itself: she grieves for Astrophel as a flower that has been cruelly and "untimely cropt." Twice she says that death has totally "defaced" the flower, thereby defacing by association the supposedly immortalizing figure as well. This undoing is, however, far more rigorous, as Clorinda actually turns to analyze and then reject the earlier figure:

What is become of him whose flowre here left
Is but the shadow of his likenesse gone.
 Scarce like the shadow of that which he was,
 Nought like, but that he like a shade did pas.
(57–60)

The flower is therefore discarded as quite incapable of figuring Astrophel. It is "the shadow of his likenesse gone," in other words, an image merely of his vanished appearance. Even the resemblance is inadequate ("Scarce like . . . Nought like"), except that its very shadowiness gives it a claim of comparison. For Astrophel resembled a shadow only in his ephemerality. So it is not the content of the figure (the flower) but rather its status *as figure* or shadow that gives it title to an admittedly far from consoling resemblance. Not only has the figure thus been exposed for what it is but the very tenor of its function has been scorned and discarded.

This is an extraordinary example of Spenser's revisionary power over his received myth. What we previously called a departure, Venus's death, is here followed by a radical rejection of the mythical transformation of the god into a flower. An unmistakable feature of this rejection is the similarity of its condemnatory language to the language of Plato's attack on the poets: "but the shadow of his likenesse." But more important is the Platonic bias against the merely physical body of likeness of which that flower figure was a shadow. With this double degradation of both the figure and the merely physical existence of Astrophel, the poem moves to its final invention, the consolatory figure of the heavenly infant. It is to this new-found or rather newly created object that the mourner can now transfer her feelings and thereby complete the work of mourning.

As one might expect from what we have already seen of this Neo-Platonic revision of the Adonis myth, the new consolation is also determined by Spenser's philosopher. For by way of a near-Socratic *but*, Clorinda moves immediately from the inferior world of shadows and likenesses of embodied life to the pure world of the liberated soul:

> But that immortall spirit, which was deckt
> With all the dowries of celestiall grace:
> By soveraine choyce from th'hevenly quires select,
> And lineally deriv'd from Angels race,
>   O what is now of it become, aread.
>   Ay me, can so divine a thing be dead?
>
> Ah no: it is not dead, ne can it die,
> But lives for aie, in blisfull Paradise:
> Where like a new-borne babe it soft doth lie.
>   (61–69)

As one moves from the discarded Adonis myth to these lines, one is traversing the history of religious philosophy. . . . We saw how the primitive vegetation deities such as Adonis were spiritualized by the Orphic sects, who substituted ideas of the resurrection of the soul for the mere notion of a returning principle of fertility and who made use of the infant deity figure to represent the newborn soul in the next world pleading its claim of divine lineage: "I am the son of earth and starry heaven, and by birth I come from God: ye know this well yourselves." These Orphic beliefs in turn influenced Plato, who associated the figure of the infant with his notion of the soul in full possession of all it will lose in earthly life. Spenser's Neo-Platonic use of this consoling figure of the soul as infant— hitherto unseen in elegies for persons other than children—originates its own tradition, influencing such elegists as Wordsworth, Shelley, and Yeats.

Although it is not quite as explicit here as in later elegies, we should note the particular current of sexuality that plays such a powerful and inescapable role in elegy, as in the work of mourning. In the previous chapter, I suggested that the mourner must, in deference to death, sacrifice not only the lost object but also his own primary sexual desire. The sacrifice, not unlike a symbolic self-castration, is necessary not only as a defense against death but also as the means of erecting the *figure* for what survives—a figure that, however spiritualized, retains its connection with the phallic power of the vegetation god. The consolation in elegy will, therefore, include the mourner's assertion of an ongoing but displaced and troped sexuality. Like a maturing child, he must discover a substitute love-object; he must invent or inherit a figure for his own potency and for his own association with images of return or resurrection.

To sketch this in "Astrophel" (for we shall see it more dramatically in "Lycidas"), Astrophel suffers a mortal, castrative wound, and the flowers that image him are themselves either plucked or "untimely cropt." This cropping of Astrophel is in turn matched by the mourners' own castrative gestures as they break their garlands and break the bitter alder from the boughs. In addition, we have already noted how the poem reduces and effectively discards the Venus figure of the eternal, loving mother. The movement beyond Venus-Stella toward the sister, Clorinda, strongly suggests a deliberate purging or chastening of the maternal or erotic connection. It is in relation to this movement, together with the many castrative gestures, that the final consolation asserts its recovery of a figurative sexual power.

The image of the infant not only represents an originally phallic power, as it did in the reborn Dionysian infant figure, the fig-wood phallus in the basket, and in the derivative figure of the Christ child in the manger. It also surely reflects the metaphorical sexual power of the poet who has engendered it. The elegist has thus moved from the cropt flower and broken garlands of loss to the resurgent "making" of this newborn infant. We are returned to the poem's introductory mention of the elegist's power to pierce and breed, while the image of the child itself returns us to the opening line of the elegy proper ("A gentle shepheard born in Arcady"). Spenser has thus feigned a spiraling return, from the infant born in Arcady to the child that the poet has figured forth in Paradise.

Despite this achievement, Spenser is inexorably still within the realm of figures. But as the consolatory figure is spelled out, we see how carefully Spenser treads. The soul is "like" an infant, and what the infant sees is, unlike the parallel situation in the more naive "November" elegy, expressly invisible to us ("which no eye can see"). The child itself sees these "immortall beauties" only in dream. Hence Spenser does not sacrifice his poem's hard-won sophistication as regards the unavoidable presence of figuration. He allows Clorinda to mourn effectively, without trapping her in the blindness of false claims. Her status as a critic of figures is unimpaired. Spenser has thus performed the work of mourning and moved from discarded to reinvented figures; but he has done so in a manner that, by bringing that very critique and reinvention into the poem, could satisfy his skepticism regarding the nature of fictions and might well have satisfied even Sidney himself.

The poem continues with a brief surge in celebration of celestial love before wisely subsiding with a recognition of limits and a shift of focus back to the mourner, who, no longer isolated, speaks from within a community: "But live thou there still happie, happie spirit, / And give us leave thee here thus to lament" (C91–92). A healthy division of the "there" from "here" assures us that in contrast to the case of Stella, no dangerous identifications are being made. And finally, with clear self-knowledge regarding the true motives of man's mourning ("mourning in others, our owne miseries"), the poem comes to its close.

JOHN HOLLANDER

"The Footing of His Feet": Spenser's Early Error

It is by now a commonplace that even ordinary errors, misstatements or misrememberings of the most un-eventful sort, can be usefully construed as metaphors which correct something wrong in the representations we make to ourselves in our inner lives, even as they get something outside us palpably wrong. The mistakes made by a great imagination can enact very powerful tropes. Even though the point of error may be minute, it may be speaking for a matter of great consequence. Such is the case with a fruitful mistake made by Spenser as a very young poet. I shall discuss it shortly, but it will be instructive to approach it through a similar mistake made by Spenser's greatest follower, Milton.

Milton's mistake occurs in a line from *Il Penseroso*, in the passage celebrating the Imagination's nighttime at the heart of the poem. This section, running roughly from lines 75 through 122, has obsessed English and American poetry from Collins to Yeats and Stevens; from

> I hear the far off *Curfew* sound
> Over some wide-water'd shore,
> Swinging low with sullen roar

—whose echoes are heard in the "sullen horn" of the may-fly in Collins' "Ode to Evening" and in the repeated "wide water, without sound" of Stevens' "Sunday Morning"—through the place

From *On Poetry and Poetics*, edited by Richard Waswo. Copyright © 1985 by John Hollander. Gunter Narr Verlag, Tübingen, 1984.

> Where glowing Embers through the room
> Teach light to counterfeit a gloom

and to generate the interior illumination of the figurative, the passage then continues into the realms of tragedy and romance.

But at this point, the power of Melancholy is invoked as being unable to call up the power and the persons of poets in the way in which the figure of "Gorgeous Tragedy" had been able to represent tragic poets by presenting their plays

> But, O sad Virgin, that thy power
> Might raise *Musaeus* from his bower,
> Or bid the soul of *Orpheus* sing
> Such notes as, warbled to the string,
> Drew Iron tears down *Pluto's* cheek,
> And made Hell grant what Love did seek.

It is interesting to observe that the parallel evocation of Orpheus, in the closing lines of *L'Allegro*, calls up music and lyric poetry to make one

> hear
> Such strains as would have won the ear
> Of *Pluto*, to have quite set free
> His half-regained *Eurydice*.

We are reminded that the formulation in *Il Penseroso* suppresses the fact that Hell granted to poetic power only half of what Love did seek, and it is all the more touching that, as Milton's meditative consciousness moves on, the matter of suppression, of telling half a tale—or perhaps half a truth—of poetic incompleteness, in short, emerges as a central question. The lines continue:

> And made Hell grant what Love did seek.
> Or call up him who left half told
> The story of *Cambuscan* bold,
> Of *Camball*, and of *Algarsife*,
> And who had *Canace* to wife,
> That own'd the virtuous Ring and Glass,
> And of the wondrous Horse of Brass,
> On which the *Tartar* King did ride . . .

The poet invoked here is of course Chaucer, but as author of the half-told *Squire's Tale*—a very strange choice indeed to juxtapose with the exemplary works of the tragic dramatists, those central matters of Thebes (for Sophocles), the line of Pelops (for Aeschylus) and of Troy (for Euripides). We may well ask why this is so, and a glance at the following lines will lead to an answer, as well as to the problematic line of my title:

> And if aught else great Bards beside
> In sage and solemn tunes have sung,
> Of Tourneys and of Trophies hung,
> Of Forests, and enchantments drear,
> Where more is meant than meets the ear.
> Thus night oft see me in thy pale career . . .

The "great Bards" are only one, Spenser, the suppression of whose name is a very different matter from reducing Chaucer's to "him that left half told . . ." It has been frequently remarked that the epithet "sage and solemn" was one which Milton himself recalled, probably a decade or more later, in a passage in *Areopagitica* to which we must return, when he invoked "our sage and serious poet Spenser." Indeed, possible allusions to Ariosto and Tasso fade before the strength of Spenser's presence here. "And who had *Canace* to wife" is itself answered by the text it echoes, from Book IV, canto iii of *The Faerie Queene*: "For Triamond had Canacee to wife" (st. 52), and the importance of the allusion to *The Squire's Tale* is now apparent. It is that half-told story which Spenser completes in Book IV of *The Faerie Queene*, and which he uses as an occasion for acknowledgment of his major precursor, Chaucer, "Well of English vndefyled." Milton chooses the half-told tale of Chaucer because of its influential power on Spenser, as well as for its incompleteness; at the same time, Spenser is himself unnamed and undesignated here. Given that, as Dryden observed in a famous moment in the preface to the *Fables*, Chaucer's relation to Spenser was that of Spenser to Milton (his "original"), it would seem that this whole passage would constitute an important constellation of acknowledgments.

That Spenser goes unacknowledged, then, save perhaps through the screen of Chaucer's presence, is strange. Spenser confessed that he could not dare to strive for poetic eminence "but through infusion sweete / Of thine owne spirit, which doth in me surviue" as he says to Chaucer, adding that

> I follow here the footing of thy feete,
> That with thy meaning so I may the rather meete.
>   (IV.iii.34)

But at the analogous point of acknowledgment, Milton loses his own footing, in all the senses of the word which Spenser had employed. When he moves away from a half-avowed Spenserian scene "Where more is meant that meets the ear," he does so with a curious metrical limps, a lapse of an almost unique sort in all of Milton's verse. The hypermetrical line, "Thus night oft see me in thy pale career" is egregious not only for its extra syllables—it is a strict iambic pentameter thrusting out from the well-trained herd of octosyllabics in both *L'Allegro* and *Il Penseroso*—but also because it continues on with the rhymes of the previous couplet, an infelicity elsewhere scrupulously avoided. I find it interesting that no editor since the eighteenth century has remarked on the line, and then only to observe that its role was to introduce a new section. But no new section in either of the companion poems is introduced in this fashion, and we are clearly dealing with a matter of meeting meaning in a deeper way.

For Milton's is no ordinary error, no mere lapse in prosodic control nor violation of his own carefully drawn ground-rules. Rather it is itself an interpretive reminiscence of Spenser, and a strong defense against the very defensive suppression of acknowledgment which has just occurred. Like the one other, far better known slip of Milton's, which also occurs with respect to Spenser, some slight souring of the "infusion sweete" is going on, though ultimately with an even more quickening effect. In the most famous passage, perhaps, in *Areopagitica* which I mentioned earlier, Milton's celebrated lapse of memory causes him to include Guyon's Palmer on the excursion into the Cave of Mammon (as Spenser does not) as well as into the Bower of Bliss. The whole passage, which starts out with celebrated dispraise of the "fugitive and cloistered virtue, unexercis'd and unbreath'd," deals with necessities of moral and spiritual risk, of imaginative enterprise; "that which purifies us is triall, and triall is by what is contrary." I continue with the famous sentences:

> That virtue therefore which is but a youngling in the contemplation of evil, and knows not the utmost that vice promises to her followers, and rejects it, is but a blank virtue, not a pure; her whiteness is but an excremental whiteness; which was the reason why our sage and serious Poet Spenser, whom I dare to be known to think a better teacher than Scotus or Aquinas, describing true temperance under the person of Guyon, brings him in with his palmer through the cave of Mammon, and the bower of earthly bliss, that he might see and know, and yet abstain.

It is not surprising that, at such a crucial imaginative moment, Milton, whose earthly father was a musician and a money-lender, and whose spiritual or poetical father was Spenser, might reach out for a succedaneum and prop by remembering one—the assistance of the reasonable palmer—that had not been there. The cave of Mammon, in particular, is charged for Milton with implicit significance: it probably plays a greater formative role in the generation of the Hell of *Paradise Lost* than has been acknowledged, and is in any case a highly-charged *topos* for an ambitious poet.

The significance of Milton's mistake has been variously discussed by historical scholars like Ernest Sirluck, and poetic interpreters—Harold Bloom and, more recently, John Guillory. I shall not dwell on it any further, but return to the long line in *Il Penseroso*. In its Spenserian environment, it presents as many features of a fiction as of an error (like the cave of Mammon slip and, indeed, like any dream). Looked at more closely, it can be seen to seal a kind of closure as much as to commence what Warton in the eighteenth century called the "second part or division of the poem . . . ushered in with a long verse."

> Of Forests, and enchantments drear,
> Where more is meant than meets the ear.
> Thus night oft see me in thy pale career . . .

The "thus" can look backward, syntactically, as well as forward, and the repeated rhyme of the previous couplet, carried through in the following long line, suggests a compelling and familiar way of closing down a stanza. Suppose that we pad out the lines as follows:

> Of forests and of dire enchantments drear,
> Where more is meant than merely meets the ear—
> Thus night thou oft dost see me in thy pale career.

The Spenserian closure, which had operated so strongly on Milton in "On the Morning of Christ's Nativity" as Kenneth Gross has so admirably shown, returns here in synecdoche: a triad of lines of 8, 8 and 10 syllables, linked in rhyme to what proceeds, is here made to represent what had been 10, 10 and 12. The line in which the speaker rejoins the text of *Il Penseroso* after leaving it at night in his high, lonely tower "Where I may oft outwatch the *Bear*" (line 87) is not merely hypermetrical, but Spenserianly so. Stylistically speaking, the absence of Spenser's name even in pronominal allusion (as with Chaucer's) is a question of suppression; poetically it is another matter, and the Spenserian close enters the poem in a return of the repressed.

Milton's line, then, is in itself a metaphoric version of Spenser's alexandrine, and is, in its role in *Il Penseroso*, playing an important part in the drama of authorial priority in that poem, and in Milton's early career generally. Humphrey Moseley, the publisher of Milton's 1645 *Poems* in which it appears, boasts of having been able to bring "into the Light as true a Birth, as the Muses have brought forth since our famous Spencer wrote; whose poems in these English ones are as rarely imitated, as sweetly excell'd." And while neither of these is strictly or significantly true, it is clearly the Spenserian presence which shadows so much of the light of these poems. It may seem strange to suggest that Spenser—or his return-ing shade—can enter them by the waving of so slender a wand as a single alexandrine. For a historian of form, identifying Spenser with the English hexameter line might seem irresponsible or capricious. Yet for English poetry from the mid-1580's on, this identification, was clearly at work: poets grasped and wielded the minutiae which later learning might overlook.

In early Tudor poetry, the hexameter line introduced the rhyming couplet form called by George Gascoigne the "poulter's measure," the twelve-syllable six stressed line rhyming with the following fourteener. (We may remind ourselves of the rhythmic effect of this by distinguishing between the full couplet of fourteen-syllable lines: "Fourteeners, cut from ballad stanzas, don't seem right for song: / Their measure rumbles on like this for just a bit too long" and "A poulter's measure (like a "baker's dozen") cut / One foot off a fourteener couplet, ended in a rut.") But the independence of the six-foot line would not emerge until well after the Earl of Surrey had given the English pentameter a canonical form. The first English poem in alexandrines I know of is Surrey's translation of Psalm 55; the first original one is George Turberville's "Of Ladie Venus" (a version, perhaps via Poliziano, of Moschus' "Idyllion of wandring Love"—as E. K. calls it in a note on the "March" eclogue of *The Shepheardes Calendar*), published in 1567. Ten years after that, we find Sidney and Spenser first employing the line at about the same time: Sidney in several places in the original *Arcadia*, and Spenser, for the first avowed time, as the closing line of the opening "January" eclogue of *SC*. This last instance is most significant: Spenser associates the alexandrine with closure of a pentameter rhymed stanza, albeit only once, at the very end of the whole poem, which is itself by way of being the entire *Shepheardes Calender* in prefatory microcosm. The anticipation of the ultimate shaping of the alexandrine and its role in the stanza-form of *The Faerie Queene* is clear.

Sidney used alexandrines not infrequently in the sonnets of *Astrophel and Stella* (sonnets 1, 6, 8, 76, 77, 102, as well as the first and third songs), but more and more, particularly after the publication of *The Faerie Queene* and of *Epithalamion*, the English alexandrine seems to ring with Spenser's name. The intricately rhymed alexandrines of the lament for Sir Philip Sidney, *The Mourning Muse of Thestylis*, by Spenser's friend Lodowick Bryskett (written in 1587 or after); the choice by the devotedly Spenserian poet Michael Drayton of alexandrines for his devotedly Spenserian topographico-mythographic *Poly-Olbion*; the use, by even so anti-Spenserian poets as Donne and Jonson, of alexandrines to terminate strophes of epithalamia and odes—in all of these instances there is some echo, however muffled or suppressed, of the older poet. Milton's self-consciously Spenserian alexandrines have recently been discussed in detail. Abraham Cowley used the alexandrine frequently among the heroic couplets of his youthful *Davideis*, not with an eye to their power of closure, but, interestingly enough, to trope augmentation. In a note to one of these lines in Book I, Cowley apologizes for the intrusion of the long line, protesting that "it is not by negligence that this verse is so loose, long, and as it were, vast; it is to paint in the number the nature of the thing which it describes." Cowley cites at this point a number of such lines, including one from the fourth book, "Like some fair pine o'erlooking all th'ignobler wood," which caused Dr. Johnson, in his "Life of Cowley," to observe that he could not discover "why the *pine* is *taller* in an Alexandrine than in ten syllables." But Johnson went on to praise, as an example of "representative versification," the conclusion of these couplets:

> He who defers this work from day to day,
> Does on a river's bank expecting stay
> Till the whole stream which stopp'd him should be gone
> Which runs, and, as it runs, for ever will run on.

Here, the last line so clearly applies to itself, to verse in general, and to running water as an ancient figure of eloquence, that Johnson's conviction that verse "can imitate only sound and motion" gives way. Cowley used the alexandrine, later on, conspicuously to terminate strophes of his "Pindarick" odes, and from a remark by the poetaster Dogrel in his play *The Guardian* (1650), in reference to one of his own lines of verse ("The last is a little too long: but I imitate *Spenser*"), the association remains strong for him.

When John Dryden comes to discuss the alexandrine's use as the third line of the occasional, pace-modulating triplet in Augustan verse, he makes clear this same association: "Spenser has also given me boldness to make use sometimes of his *Alexandrin* line, which we call, tho' improperly, the Pindaric, because Mr. Cowley has often employ'd it in his *Odes*," he observes in his dedicatory essay prefixed to his translation of the *Aeneid*. He goes on to add that it gives "a certain majesty to the verse, when 't is us'd with judgment, and stops the sense from overflowing into another line." Dryden's triplets that conclude with hexameters, then, are like the closes of Spenserian stanzas: the effect of an alexandrine for him is clearly cadential. It is perhaps more than merely amusing to note what may be the earliest instance of an alexandrine at the end of one of Dryden's triplets; in 1670, in the fourth act of his heroic drama *The Conquest of Granada*, his hero Alamanzor counsels the Queen of Granada not to look before she leaps:

> True, 'tis a narrow path that leads to bliss,
> But right before there is no precipice:
> Fear makes men look aside, and then their footing miss.

Dryden knew well the passage in *The Faerie Queene* Book IV cited earlier, and seems here to be following the "footing" of Spenser's "feete" in a way that strangely surfaces, some twenty-seven years before he wrote the introduction to his translation of Virgil. In his nondramatic verse, Dryden seems not to have used the longer line to complete a triplet much before 1682 (lines 90 and 166 of "The Medal"). In the following year, he concludes the final couplet of the great elegy on John Oldham that begins "Farewell, too little, and too lately known" with a line imitated from Virgil (having used one for a triplet earlier in the poem): "Thy brows with ivy, and with laurels bound, / But fate and gloomy night encompass thee around." Here, the echo of Virgil's specific account of the shade of Marcellus in Book VI of the *Aeneid* ("sed nox atra caput tristi circumvolat umbra." This line is translated by Dryden later on as "and night, with sable shades, involves his head,") points back to the mention of Marcellus by Dryden earlier, and itself *circumvolat*, wraps up, the whole poem in the Spenserian closure.

During the next twenty-five years, the cadential power of the alexandrine at the end of the occasional triplet in Augustan heroic couplets had become weakened by convention. Pope, in the famous passage from *An Essay on Criticism*, heaps his scorn on such concluding devices: "A needless Alexandrine ends the Song, / That like a wounded Snake, drags its slow length along," brilliantly slowing up his own line with the "slow length." It is interesting to observe that, less than twenty lines later (370–73), when Pope is using the same sorts of self-descriptive lines to represent beneficial, rather than harmful phonetic devices, he introduces a "quick" rather than a "slow" alexandrine. Like all the lines in this passage, it directs its energies toward a particular bit of narrative:

> When Ajax strives, some Rock's vast weight to throw,
> The Line too labours, and the Words move slow;
> Not so, when swift Camilla scours the Plain,
> Flies oe'r th'unbending Corn, and skims along the Main.

Swift Camilla's fast six feet are uncontaminated by any belatedly Spenserian closure here, and one can't help wondering whether the serpentine presence in the bad, slow "closing" alexandrine has not wandered into the example from Spenser, via Milton: the stanza in *F.Q.I.vii.31*, describing Arthur's helmet, ends with the dragon on it, "And scaly tayle was stretcht adowne his backe full low." The "old Dragon under ground," in stanza 18 of Milton's Nativity Hymn, at stanza's end "Swinges the scaly Horror of his folded tail" in echo of Spenser. Pope's needless alexandrine is related to these lines; his effectively swift one has been purified by Virgil, and by Dryden.

In any event, the alexandrine continued to resonate, however faintly, with Spenserian allusiveness, throughout the seventeenth century. We may well want to ask if Spenser himself even gives evidence of being aware of his own possession, as it were, and, if so, where and when. Without knowing anything of the formal structure of Spenser's "lost works" like the *Dying Pellicano* or the *Dreames*, we may turn to the verse epilogue to *The Shepheardes Calender*, in six alexandrine couplets, beginning "Loe! I have made a Calender for every yeare, / That steele in strength, and time in durance, shall outweare." (The poem is divided in two by the opening of the fourth couplet, "Goe, lytle Calender! thou hast a free passeporte," which echoes the already formulaic "Goe, little booke: thy self present . . ." of the opening invocation "To His Booke." It is interesting to observe that the six tetrameter triplets of the opening invocation contain the same number of syllables as the six hexameter couplets of the closing one.) The form to which that epilogue is attuned is by no means a trivial matter; but in any case, I should like to consider one unique earlier instance of an alexandrine line in Spenser's earliest published writing. Both for the remarkable question of the occasion of its occurrence, and for the uncanny relation it bears to the egregious pentameter line of Milton's, it deserves the attention it never seems to have received.

In 1569, Spenser at the age of seventeen had graduated from school and was on his way to university, and it is at this early moment in his far from pale career that he translated some poems of Marot and Du Bellay for an English edition of Jan van der Noot's *Theatre for Voluptuous Worldlings*—a kind of emblem book with woodcuts accompanying the poems and an extended, polemically protestant, commentary. Spenser's version of the Marot lines (themselves a translation of Petrarch's "Standomi un giorno solo a la finestra") is in rhymed iambic pentameter. But in the fourth of the so-called "epigrams" into which it is divided, a "spring of water" is described,

> Whereto approched not in any wise
> The homely shepherde, nor the ruder clowne,
> But many Muses, and the Nymphes withall,

> That sweetely in accorde did tune their voice
> Unto the gentle sounding of the waters fall . . .

Here once more (for us), but first (for Spenser) is an egregious alexandrine, the only one in all of the 294 lines which Spenser contributed to
the *Theatre*. It represents a strange sort of mistake, for the French to
decasyllabic:

> N'osoient pasteurs ne bouviers approcher,
> Mais mainte Muse et Nymphe seulement,
> Qui de leurs voix accordoient doulcement
> Au son de l'eau . . .

Spenser radically expands Marot's half-line in what is his first, apparently
unwitting, alexandrine. This would be of little interest were it not for its
origination, for the rest of the poet's *oeuvre*, of a thematic *topos* as well as
a formal one. A singer "tuning" his or her voice to the fall of water—
where "tune" means both to sing or sound (*OED* sense 3) as well as to
attune or adapt to (*OED* 1a or b, *accorder*)—is a recurring presence. Ten
years later, in the "Aprill" eclogue of *The Shepheardes Calender*, the
shepherd called Hobbinol says of his friend Colin Clout,

> then will I sing his laye
> Of fayre Eliza, queene of shepherdes all,
> Which once he made, as by a spring he laye,
> And tuned it unto the waters fall.

This was an important trope for the young poet. In an ambitious and
radically experimental book, Colin, the figure "under whose person the
Author selfe is shadowed," both intones his song to the moving water,
and accords his singing with it. Tityrus, in Virgil's first eclogue, "at ease
in the shade teaches [with his piping and signing] the Woods to re-echo
the name of lovely Amaryllis" ("lentus in umbra / formosam resonare
doces Amaryllida silvas"). In the *Calender*, "Tityrus" stands for Virgil, and
the Virgilian trope of imprinting human significance on the mute nature
of the pastoral world—the institution of the pathetic fallacy, as it were—is
powerfully revised in Spenser's transumption of it. Colin addresses—and
thereby extends authorial power over—the moving water of poetic tradition, even as he accommodates to it. (One of these senses of "tune" makes
this an emblem of Eliot's "Tradition and the Individual Talent," the
other, of Bloom's *The Anxiety of Influence*: Spenser's figure subsumes the
dialectic between these views.) Hobbinol tells us that the "laye" so
attuned was not about Colin's love Rosalind, but of "fayre Eliza" herself,
which suggests a major consecration to a Muse outside the "greene cabi-

net" of the *Calender*. In addition, the quatrain's *rime riche*, unusual in that book, of "laye" (poem) and "laye" (reclined) underscores the trope of according, and the association of pastoral *otium* and pastoral poetry.

The figure returns in the "June" eclogue of *SC* (11.7–8): "The bramble bush where byrdes of every kynde / To the water fall their tunes attemper right." It reappears in *Virgils Gnat* (Spenser's translation of the pseudo-Virgilian *Culex*) where, at the opening, the falling water is clearly revealed as poetic tradition: "We now have playde (Augustus) wantonly, / Tuning our song unto a tender Muse." And at a high and important moment in Book VI of *The Faerie Queene*, Sir Calidore encounters a stream at the foot of Mt. Acidale, where he is about to be vouchsafed one of the poem's major and central visions:

> Ne mote wylde beastes, ne mote the ruder clowne
> Thereto approach, ne filth mote therein drowne:
> But nymphes and faeries by the bancks did sit,
> In the woods shade, which did the waters crowne,
> Keeping all noysome things away from it,
> And to the waters fall tuning their accents fit.
>
> (VI.x.7)

Here there is a direct reminiscence of the Marot translation, of the privileged scene of a vision of eloquence not to be transgressed upon by "the ruder clowne," the bad poets. Spenser had, probably in the early 1580's, reworked his contributions to the *Theatre* volume, and these revised poems were published much later in his volume entitled *Complaints*. In this later version, the lines about the nymphs read "That sweetly in accord did tune their voyce / To the soft sounding of the waters fall," the alexandrine being corrected. In addition, his later *Visions of Bellay* recast into sonnet form the blank verse he had originally used for them in the van der Noot book. In the early, unrhymed Englishing of one of the *Songe* sonnets, the same figure turns up:

> Hard by a rivers side, a waling nymphe
> Folding her armes with thousand sighs to heaven
> Did tune her plaint to falling rivers sound.

In the later text, this becomes

> Hard by a rivers side a virgin faire
> Folding her armes to heaven with thousand throbs
> And outraging her cheekes and golden haire
> To falling rivers sound thus tun'd her sobs.

Du Bellay's French seems to provide a possible paradigm for the alexan-drine expansion of the Marot turning-to-the-water line: his "Nymphe esploree . . . / Accordeit ceste plainte au murmure des flotz," and Spenser may have had the cadence of the French *alexandrin* in his ear as he worked with the uncannily similar text from Petrarch via Marot, where one "waling nymphe" gave way to many.

Be that as may be, their song was in his line; and just as the terminal alexandrine would always seem a Spenserian echo, the trope of tuning poetry to the flow of poetic waters became, for many of Spenser's followers, a kind of colophon or signature to be acknowledged. Thus, three years after the publication of the first edition of *The Shepheardes Calender*, Thomas Blenerhassot (in *A Revelation of the True Minerva*, 1582): "Take lute in hand, tune to the waters fall." Lodowick Bryskett's elegy for Sir Philip Sidney in alexandrines, mentioned earlier, makes the water that of his local, Irish poetic river; the nymphs he invokes at his poem's opening seem figures for the poetic of his friend Spenser: "Help me to tune my dolefull notes to gurgling sound / Of *Liffies* tumbling streams . . ." George Peele's *A Farewell* (1589): "So couth he sing his layes among them all / And tune his pype unto the waters fall." William Vallans (*A Tale of Two Swans*, 1590): "Where Venus . . . / Sate lovely by the running river side, / Tuning her Lute unto the waters fall." *The Returne from Parnassus* (Part II, 1606) invokes Spenser directly: "While to the waters fall he tun'd her fame" (Act I, ii), and, later on (Act IV, iv): "Weele tune our sorrows to the waters fall." Spenserians like Drayton, William Browne and George Wither repeat the figure several times.

What we have seen in the resonance of Spenser's early, mistakenly long alexandrine exhibits a somewhat ghostly quality: the anticipation, at an early point an artist's work, of what might come to seem synecdochic of it by others. There are other such instances of overprivileged—and perhaps over-determined—minutiae in Spenser which, by self-echoing, he seemed to avow. One of these is the rhetorical formula, used in a quasi-mythographic context. "Who knows not X?" Spenser uses it to institute a central fiction—to introduce it and to make an ironically guarded claim for its prior establishment by the two-edged means of a rhetorical question. Its first use in the "August" eclogue of *The Shepheardes Calender* involves "a doeleful verse / Of Rosalend (whe knowes not Rosalend?) / That Colin made." (Colin-Spenser has a "love and mistresse" with the "feigned name" of Rosalind.) This initial instance of the little scheme is protected by the fictional extension of the question "Who knows not?" That question is uttered by Cuddie, one of the shepherds in the eclogue, about another, Colin, and his mistress: in Cuddie's world, her name is echoed by every stream. When Spenser comes later on to echo his own formula, the two other occasions, while evoking versions of a Colin-Rosalind situation, are nonetheless far more audacious.

In the first of the *Cantos of Mutabilitie* (VII.vi.36), Spenser as narrator first names the sacred spot, the hilltop whereon a legal proceeding with cosmic consequences is to take place. The hilltop "shadowed," as Spenser would have said, by the hill in the poem was a place near and dear to him—Gullymore, near his own home at Kilcolman—but renamed in the poem from the valley beneath it, and thereby refigured. The spot "That was, to weet, upon the highest hights / Of Arlo-hill (who knows not Arlo-hill?)" stands to the poet as Rosalind to his own persona, Colin; it bears a feigned name which also, "being wel ordered, will bewray the very name" of a personal place. The rhetoric of questioning here is much more complex than in the first instance. Firstly, the height has been re-named from a stream of water at its base: readers could be said to know and not know it at once, depending upon whether what Spenser elsewhere calls the "feigned colours" or the "true case" is meant. Secondly, the narrator here, unlike the naif Cuddie in the *Calender*, knows well that the scoffing answer ("Nobody"), the plain answer ("I don't"), are both subsumed by the wise answer ("We all do, now that you mention it").

The second re-echoing of the formula occurs in Book VI of *The Faerie Queene*, a few stanzas after the reoccurrence of the tuning-song-to-the-waters'-fall figure we just considered. The scene is the top of Mt. Acidale itself, where Sir Calidore has come upon his fragile vision of the hundred naked girls dancing in a ring around the Graces, who concentrically surround an unnamed lady in the process of being "advaunst to be another Grace":

> She was, to weete, that jolly shepheards lasse,
> Which piped there unto the merry rout;
> That jolly shepheard which there piped was
> Poore Colin Clout (who knows not Colin Clout?)
> (VI.x.16)

And who remembers not Rosalind, who need not be named? At this astonishing moment of encounter between a pure fiction (Sir Calidore) and his own persona, the narrator names that persona by means of the formula applied to his "love and mistress" by a surrogate shepherd-poet earlier in Spenser's career.

It is no wonder, then, that this poignantly returning figure should have picked up—as the tuning-to-the-water had not been—by Milton, at a moment of flagrantly Spenserian mythopoeia. In discoursing of the genealogy of his version of Comus in *A Masque Presented at Ludlow Castle*, the Attendant Spirit tells of how Bacchus

> On *Circe's* island fell: (Who knows not *Circe*,
> The daughter of the Sun? Whose charmed Cup
> Whoever tasted, lost his upright shape
> And downward fell into a groveling Swine.)

The long parenthesis, incorporating the mythographic footnote into the text itself, anticipates what would be a major strategy in *Paradise Lost*. The allusive use of the Spenserian device is rhetorically complex as well: by interpretively echoing Spenser's rhetorical question, Milton can displace his own mythographic uneasiness. Instead of asking "Who knows not Comus?" about his masque's character (the one he had so radically transformed from the belly-god of Ben Jonson and the delicate youth of Philostratus), he can re-direct the question to one about Circe. He is thus able to ask it with the singular candor of Spenser's Cuddie.

The Spenserian *topos* of tuning-to-the-water is, like the "who knows not?" scheme, more than merely one of what Thomas Warton called "Spenser's imitations of himself": it was recognized as such, as we have seen, by subsequent poets of the kind whose ear is tuned to the frequency at which poetic echo is transmitted. What seems so strange about the original alexandrine in the 1596 *Theatre* is that the young poet's schoolboy pentameters should stumble over just that place. When Colin Clout, ten years later in the *Calender*, can tune in on his central precursors through the tutelage of a "Tityrus" who is both Virgil and Chaucer, Spenser is troping the pastoral convention of the accord between natural voice and shepherd's piping. The "water's fall" had not yet become the major stream of full, assured poetic eloquence, the Thames, which would provide for the poet at the end of his life so resonant an undersong. But this poignant moment of being metrically out of tune would in fact generate just such a figuration of poetic accord. Both the long line and the trope of tuning poetry to moving water would always stay with him.

Even if the alexandrine seems to remain Spenser's property in subsequent verse, I do not mean to suggest that all egregious long lines, or versions of them like the one of Milton's that has led us to this pass, are willful and manifest Spenserian allusions. But for a certain kind of English poetic ear, the very line is like a spell. Even after the flood of eighteenth-century Spenserian verse had turned the stanza-form into a trivial container, Wordsworth, Blake, Byron, Shelley and Keats could reanimate it in powerfully different ways. Keats, in particular, returned to the Augustan practice of pacing heroic couplets with the occasional alexandrine (in

Lamia Part II). But one particular instance of an egregious alexandrine is, in light of the previous discussion, a most touching one.

Keats's line—or rather lines, for it is a pair of them, a Drayton-like *Poly-Olbion* alexandrine couplet, in fact—reaches out from the metre of his 1816 verse *lettre* to Charles Cowden Clarke, who, Keats says,

> first taught me all the sweets of song.
> The grand, the sweet, the terse, the free, the fine;
> What swelled with pathos, and what right divine;
> Spenserian vowels that elope with ease,
> And float along like birds o'er summer seas;
> *Miltonian storms, and more, Miltonian tenderness;*
> *Michael in arms, and more, meek Eve's fair slenderness.*
> (11.53–59)

The alexandrine couplet is interestingly displaced here from the lines which invoke, with a sort of Popean "representative versification," Spenserian vocalic prominence, onto those lines characterizing Milton's style. Secondly, they are far from Miltonic in themselves: the architectonic quality of the couplet resounds with Sidney and Spenser. The pattern in which the stylistic modes (concrete "storms," abstract "tenderness") are exemplified in the following line by the near-rhyming instances (concrete "arms," slightly more general "slenderness") can be rendered thus:

Miltonian storms	(and more)	Miltonian tenderness
Michael in arms	(and more)	meek Eve's fair slenderness

The more precise (masculine?) rhythmic echo of the first four syllables of line two is modulated by the slower, rhythmically more ambiguous (feminine?) half-line about Eve. And yet they are both aspects of the Miltonic voice, even as they are revealed in a Spenserian schematic pattern, arrayed in the alexandrine line that for poets would always be Spenser's own. As we have seen, Milton himself, at a moment of authorial anxiety, of suppression of the proper acknowledgment of his poetic father, himself falls into the "footing" of his precursor's "feete" and causes his verse to cast a shortened but unmistakable shadow of the Spenserian line. The line from *Il Penseroso* is a momentary revisionary version—I should call it a metalepsis—of a line of Spenser's whose own origination lies in a mysterious moment of over-determined error.

In following the thread of Milton's line, we may seem to have wandered into, rather than out of, a labyrinth; I hope it has not been too confusing to discover that one was holding on to a line of Spenser's for most of the journey. One of the dangers has been the risk of concern with the sort of historical detail that caricatures philological research—the risk of becoming what Pope called one "who reads not, but who scans and spells," a "word-catcher that lives on syllables." Formal matters of prosody and versification concern verse, not poetry, which is to say that poetics is involved with trope, rather than with theme or scheme. But the mysterious way in which poetry animates the otherwise lifeless image of verse-form has always been something that poets have perceived in each other's work, and have been reticent about addressing openly. Occasionally, as at moments of metrical pathology like the two we have pursued so relentlessly, these perceptions may surface, and we may conclude that the loss of footing has been a slip not of ordinary nor of unusual skill or craft, but a stumbling over a block set up by the Imagination itself.

DONALD CHENEY

Envy in the Middest of the 1596 "Faerie Queene"

It is not easy to make generalizations about the overall structure of Spenser's *Faerie Queene*. Whether we ascribe this fact to the problems of allegory or symbolism, of epic or romance, or to Spenser's amiable mixing of various modes and genres, probably every reader of the poem has had the experience of seeming to find a pattern there which lasts long enough to quicken his pulse and kindle his ambition, but which then vanishes by the time he has gotten to the next canto or book, or to his index cards, or his typewriter, or his colleagues. Even Milton, that fittest member of Spenser's audience, may be expressing a similar experience of his great predecessor when he speaks of a belated peasant who "sees, / Or dreams he sees" the midnight revels of faerie elves, "numberless" to his ignorant eyes, intent on their dance, charming his ear with their music "while overhead the moon / Sits arbitress"; a sight which finally eludes his comprehension:

> . . . far within
> And in their own dimensions like themselves
> The great seraphic lords and cherubim
> In close recess and secret conclave sat
> A thousand demi-gods on golden seats,
> Frequent and full.

We can sense the grace and purposeful energy of Spenser's antique images; but he has not made it easy for us to take their measure, or his. Frequently we feel excluded from the inner conclave of his deliberations. Perhaps he does not want us to get his number, to map his territory, to possess his text.

Yet there have been some advances in our understanding of the poem's structure; and I should like to begin today by examining one of these. In an article on "Placement 'in the middest' in *The Faerie Queene*," Baybeck, Delany, and Hieatt have called our attention to Spenser's use of center-points in the first three books. One of their discoveries is startling in its numerological explicitness. Book III, as first published in the three-book installment of the poem in 1590, contains twelve cantos of varying lengths, for a total of 679 stanzas. The central stanza, number 340, appears in the description of the Gardens of Adonis, in canto vi, stanza 43, and describes the center of Venus's garden in terms which identify it with the center of the female body, the *mons veneris*:

> Right in the middest of that Paradise,
>> There stood a stately Mount, on whose round top
>> A gloomy groue of mirtle trees did rise,
>> Whose shadie boughes sharpe steele did neuer lop,
>> Nor wicked beasts their tender buds did crop,
>> But like a girlond compassed the hight,
>> And from their fruitful sides sweet gum did drop,
>> That all the ground with precious deaw bedight,
> Threw forth most dainty odours, and most sweet delight.

This stanza calls attention to its "centrality" in too many ways for me to believe that Spenser did not calculate its precise position in terms of stanza count. Here in Book III Spenser gives us a *locus amoenus* which is clearly the best, the purest, the most natural, the most Edenic (as he seems to be punning with his use of the shortened form of Adonis as Adon), the most authentic of the various bowers and gardens of delight which have appeared previously in the poem. He has stressed the secret apartness of this garden, the sequential acts of the understanding and imagination by which one can reach the center of the garden. He emphasizes the "garland" of myrtle trees (sacred to Venus) which encompass— form a circle around—the Mount. And he opens the stanza with the phrase, "Right in the middest . . . ." Surely we are meant to respond to this stanza as meaningfully central to Spenser's book.

Baybeck, Delany, and Hieatt go on to find analogous center-points in Books I and II. Counting stanzas in the earlier books as they had done with Book III, they find the phrase "in the middest" occurring near—but unfortunately not quite at—the central stanza in both cases. In Book I, for example, the center appears at stanzas 12 and 13 of canto vii, just as Orgoglio has knocked down Red Cross, "And all his sences stound, that still he lay full low" (I. vii. 12. 9). Some seven stanzas earlier, the bower in which Red Cross pours himself out in looseness to Duessa has been identified with the nymph who has displeased Diana by sitting down to rest "in middest of her race." Like her, Red Cross subsequently interrupts his quest to drink of her enervating fount and finds himself (stanza 11) "Disarmd, disgrast, and inwardly dismayde" when Orgoglio attacks. In Book II, the central stanza is canto vii, stanza 54, describing the apples in the Garden of Proserpina. Here, it is the preceding stanza which mentions the silver seat "in the midst" of the garden, where Proserpina "often usd from open heat / Her selfe to shrowd, and pleasures to entreat." In both books, there is certainly a plausible case for the thematic or narrative centrality of the episode as a whole; and the two episodes are clearly comparable. Red Cross is tempted to stop in the middle of his race, and falls to that temptation; Guyon does not. Still, from the point of view of the numerically precise centering found in Book III, it must be confessed that Books I and II do not respond unambiguously to the stanza-counting which has paid off so handsomely in Book III. It would seem, in fact, that the midpoints or turning-points of Books I and II are to be perceived in terms of canto-count, not stanza-count. A crucial event occurs in the seventh canto, at the beginning of the second half of the book. Perhaps an analogous structure would be those plays of Shakespeare in which a turning point occurs "around the middle of the play," in the third act if the audience is aware of act divisions. Mercutio and Tybalt are killed at such a point, wedding Romeo to Fury and setting the play on a clearly tragic course.

But it is entirely possible in any case that Spenser felt under no obligation to adhere strictly to a numerological pattern. Probably as we expand our understanding of the ways in which numerological awareness pervaded the literature of the Renaissance we shall find it less difficult to believe that symmetries of this sort could be adopted casually and inter-mittently. If a sense of the harmonies of the macrocosm is shared by an entire culture, then it may be matter for allusion rather than persistent and consistent imitation in a work of art. By demanding that our col-leagues should be consistent in their numerical readings of literature, we have probably taken necessary steps against critical caprice; but we should not assume that Renaissance poets or critics were constrained to any similar consistency.

Having said this, however, I would go on to suggest that Spenser's use of center-points in Books I–III may well be seen in terms of signifi-cantly increasing precision and emphasis. So far as the proposed clue is concerned—the phrase "in the middest"—we see that this phrase actually occurs twice in canto vii of Book I (it also appears some thirty other times in the poem, usually without any apparent role as a clue to stanza-centering). Red Cross falls prey to the curse directed against the nymph who stopped in middest of her race (canto vii, stanza 5); he is then rescued by Prince Arthur whose armor is described (canto vii, stanza 30) as having one precious stone shaped like a Lady's head "in the midst thereof." For the reader of Book I the centrality of Red Cross's fall is to be weighed against the centrality of his rescue; and as we read on in the poem we find that Arthur's role in rescuing the hero of the book is more clearly crucial in Book I than in subsequent books. So it is appropriate that there should be two centers or focal points in Book I. In Book II, where the hero does not fall in the narrative sense of the term, then the center of the temptation may be more clearly identified, perhaps, and the phrase "in the midst" moves closer to the center of the book in proportion as Guyon's response to temptation is less in question. But in Book III, the midpoint is not a center of temptation but a central focus of the poem's meditation on the role of Venus in this world. Only in Book III, by this logic, does Spenser place us "*right* in the middest." Even without reference to any question of mid-points, readers have generally sensed that Spenser's description of the Gardens of Adonis was somehow distinct from its surroundings, an anthology piece on grounds of its philosophical content or its bravura treatment of literary antecedents or its relation to personal experience ("Well *I* wote by tryall," says the poet, "that this same / All other pleasant places doth excell"). So it is appropriate in different ways that Spenser should have placed his description in the poem with especial care.

I have taken time to discuss this article in some detail, and even to carry its argument further than its authors had done (and further, I suspect, than some of you might choose to follow me), because I believe that it points to an element in the 1590, three-book version of the *Faerie Queene* which distinguishes it from the expanded, six-book poem which Spenser published in 1596. As Baybeck, Delany, and Hieatt point out, Spenser seems to have abandoned any over-riding interest in organizing his later books around precisely numerical center-points; an exception may be Book V, where Alastair Fowler (by a different method of calculating stanza-count) locates the midpoint at the stanza (V. vii. 4) where Isis and Osiris are identified with the Moon and Sun "For that they both like race in equall iustice runne." Even this, however, is not placement "in the middest" as seen in Books I–III, but concern with parallel races to be run—a culmination, with the union of Britomart and Artegall, of a quite different, though equally Spenserian motif. What is more, Spenser disturbs some of the earlier symmetry by changes in the 1596 edition of the earlier books: Book I gains a stanza and Book III ends with two fewer so that its precise midpoint is now less precise. It would seem then that the secret of Book III's symmetry, which was to pass unobserved for nearly four centuries, had been forgotten or come to be despised by its author after only six years; or that the haste of publishing in 1596 led to a number of solecisms in both the earlier and the later installments. I should like today to propose an approach to the 1596 poem which sees its more notorious "errors" as something other than the unintended or unobserved consequences of Spenser's need to combine his poetic career with his obligations in Ireland. Instead, I would suggest that the *Faerie Queene* of 1596 is concerned—"obsessed" would not be too strong a word—with the ubiquitous and ultimately insuperable threat posed to poet, poem, and commonwealth by Envy.

As a bridge between the numerical concerns which I have been discussing thus far and the largely thematic ones which will concern me from now on, I should like to call your attention (as mine was kindly called by Gillian Adams in a graduate seminar last Fall) to a classical lyric which conveniently expresses some of these concerns.

> Let us live, my Lesbia, and let us love, and let's not give a farthing for all the gossip of complaining old men. Suns may set and rise again; but once our brief day has set we shall have a single eternal night to sleep through. Give me a thousand kisses, then a hundred, then another thousand, then a second hundred, then still another thousand, then a hundred. Then, when we have completed many thousands, we shall confuse them, so that we shall not know, and so that no malevolent person may envy us when he knows, how many kisses there have been.

Time has not been uniformly kind to this lyric by Catullus, and it has frequently received the malice which it tries to avoid. Some readers have expressed the judgment which Catullus elsewhere attributes to Aurelius and Furius, and surmised that the poet is suspiciously willing to confine himself to kissing instead of moving on to more central concerns. More directly offensive to numerologists, however, is the judgment attributed to Martial: What must Lesbia have made of these demands? Only a cold lover could count at a time like this. *Pauca cupit qui numerare potest:* well may we be meeting today in deepest winter. Both of these criticisms, however, are responsive to the anxiety which pervades the poem. The lover is looking over his shoulder, first at the threat of time's winged chariot and then at the more immediate threat of envious onlookers whom he had at first dismissed out of hand. As the source of his concern changes, his defense subtly changes too. While time/death was the enemy, the response was not merely to make the most of one's brief day but to amass a patterned and perceived number of "kisses": to set a record of monumental scale. But when the poet's critical onlookers are the ultimate threat, then pattern and number are themselves risky: the alternative is to break the measure, confuse the number, and seek to veil not only the spectators but the lovers themselves in a saving ignorance. Even the lovers must be protected from the paralyzing self-consciousness which might attend knowledge of the full measure of their love. It seems that Catullus would agree with Martial: *pauca cupit qui numerare potest.*

Catullus's poem expresses more directly and emphatically a contrast which could be illustrated more subtly and obliquely from several of Donne's lyrics: the lovers create a perfect, ample, circular and therefore endless microcosmic pattern of their love as a response to both time and envy—enemies which are sometimes seen in one and the same figure such as the "unruly Sunne." There, however, the poet's faith in the efficacy of his well-wrought creation remains at most slightly questionable. Catullus, by contrast, frankly abandons his original strategem and chooses to reject his role as exemplary lover in the hope of evading envy.

I would suggest that the dominant tone of the 1590 *Faerie Queene* is close to that which I have just ascribed to Donne. At the end of Book III in its 1590 version, Amoret has been restored to Scudamour by Britomart; and the reader is invited to look on (as Britomart is looking on, "half envying" them) and identify the embracing lovers with an imagined or recollected model of "that faire *Hermaphrodite*"—an archetypal image of two bodies and two sexes become as one. As Merritt Hughes noted in 1960, Spenser's presentation of the two lovers is analogous to that of Donne's "Extasie": in both cases the poet calls attention to the onlooker's viewpoint and thereby creates a dramatic context for the lovers' intimacy. But although there is an opportunity for dramatic irony, this is not exploited very emphatically.

> And if some lover, such as we,
>   Have heard this dialogue of one,
> Let him still mark us, he shall see
>   Small change when we'are to bodies gone.

This has not been taken as a very big "if"; readers have tended to disregard the small change; and the *Songs and Sonnets* seem to do a tidy business as instruments of seduction. Similarly, the half-envious attitude of Britomart in 1590 has not bothered readers who knew of Merlin's prophecy and could reasonably expect wedding bells for her in 1596.

But what readers were given in 1596 did not entirely fulfil these expectations. Spenser removed the stanzas describing the union of Amoret and Scudamour, presumably in order to provide a narrative link to the opening of Book IV; but he unaccountably failed to reinsert them later in the poem, or at any point to describe the union of those two lovers. "Whatever happened to Amoret?" is the title of Judith Anderson's 1971 essay on Book IV; and it is a question to which there can be no definite answer. Most readers assume that Spenser was somehow distracted from tying this narrative thread, somewhere presumably before canto x when Scudamour remarks that at last he rests assured of his love, "That to disloyalty she will not be allured." But this is not the only puzzling aspect of Book IV. When Britomart sets off with Amoret at the beginning of canto i, she takes on herself some of the qualities of that Busyrane from whom she has just rescued her. Practicing a "fine abusion" on her, Britomart is content to magnify Amoret's fears by pretending that she is as she seems, a male knight eager to claim his reward from the maiden whom he has just rescued. In this climate of rather mischievous double-entendre, the two women reach a nameless castle which resembles Malecasta's Castle Joyous in the first canto of Book III. Here too there is the compulsory jousting to gain admission; the doffing of Britomart's helmet and revelation of her feminine beauty; the ambiguous love-complaints which are taken with unintended applications. But Britomart and Amoret are the only named participants in this episode, and Britomart now enacts in part the role originally attributed to Malecasta and indignantly rejected by the chaste, more naive maiden of Book III. Without meaning for an instant to slander her willingness to share her bed with another woman, this time around, I would suggest that the episode—if only by virtue of its implied comparison with the earlier one—raises more questions as to its possible implications than it bothers to resolve. And the same, I think, can be said increasingly of the episodes which follow.

But Britomart is no longer the patron of the Fourth Book, which is devoted to the Legend of Cambel and Telamond. Alone of all the six books, its title page names a pair of patrons rather than a single individual; and although this is the book of Friendship so the patronage of a pair of friends might seem unremarkable, the book is also unique in giving its titular patronage to individuals who appear briefly and peripherally to the main action of the book. Cambel and Telamond (or Triamond as he is named in the text of the poem) are apparently meant to serve as paradigmatic figures, representative of *discordia concors*, friendship coming as a resolution to strife, friendship reconciled with love. But since their story is explicitly presented as Spenser's tribute to Chaucer, as a completion and elaboration of the unfinished *Squire's Tale*, we may wonder why Spenser has chosen to break deliberately with the established pattern of his fiction at least partly in the name of his relationship to Chaucer. Let us consider briefly the roles played by squires in the two poems.

From the General Prologue to the *Canterbury Tales* we learn that the Squire is the Knight's son, "A lovyere and a lusty bachelor," fresh as the month of May and as eager to win his lady's grace as his father has been to win his Lord's war. Twenty lines are devoted to a description of his youthful jollity; only a final couplet characterizes his subordinate relation to his father:

> Curteis he was, lowely, and servysable,
> And carf biforn his fader at the table.

Chaucer's squire, then, may be the glass of fashion and the mould of youthful form; but he can not carve for himself: he is in an honored but secondary position in his father's house. Like Chaucer, Spenser opens his poem with the picture of a knight; but the figure who is pricking on the plain in Book I is no seasoned veteran whose gray sobriety suits his age. The earnestness of Red Cross is made clear at the end of the first canto, when he rejects indignantly—though perhaps "with wonted feare of doing ought amis"—Archimago's vision of an erotic Una at his bedside. So the enchanter next fashions a figure of the antithesis of this solemn young knight:

> Like a young Squire, in loues and lust-hed
> His wanton dayes that euer loosely led,
> Without regard of armes and dreaded fight.

The sight of this squire in the arms of Una fills him with abhorrence and sends him into the wilderness without his lady. The psychology of the episode seems clear enough. By denying his own libidinous fancy, the knight projects it upon his lady and upon a "squire" who is everything Red Cross denies in himself. By this route, the imagination separates Red Cross from Una. The contrary route by which such division may take place is shown in canto ii, when Fradubio tells his story. He too was once such a squire:

> In prime of youthly yeares, when corage hot
> The fire of loue and ioy of chevalree
> First kindled in my brest, it was my lot
> To loue this gentle Lady . . .

Fradubio—"Brother Doubt"—is the expanded image of the wanton boy whom Red Cross has rejected and ejected from himself. Both halves of the divided self, Red Cross and Fradubio, are similarly and equally the victims of Duessa: for her twoness is a figure of their twinning.

Not all of Spenser's squires are so narrowly conceived as projections of a knight's libido. Timias, Prince Arthur's squire, is loyal and serviceable to his master and also (though not usually at the same time) devoutly committed to the Platonic courtship of his lady, Belphoebe. And as we shall see, the tale of this squire will figure prominently in the action of Book IV. In his overt behavior, Timias is certainly a far cry from that demonic, lustful figure described above; and by the same token he is far closer to the attractive, gentlemanly figure portrayed by Chaucer. The Franklin would be proud to have Timias as his son, no doubt. But Spenser makes clear that he is intensely vulnerable to dirty fighting and low blows. In Book I, Duessa needs only to sprinkle her poison lightly on his "weaker partes" and he is instantly "dismayd" and subject to Orgoglio: in one stanza she accomplishes what had taken her half a book with Red Cross. And in Book VI, he is still being treated for festering wounds, this time from the Blatant Beast. No character in the *Faerie Queene* has a lengthier medical history than Timias. It would seem that his hot youth makes him susceptible to lust and to the suspicion of lust; and in this he is not unlike other of Spenser's squires. Furthermore, his love for the determinedly, even ferociously chaste Belphoebe can only add to his discomfort. Other lovers in the *Faerie Queene* may follow long and circuitous routes to their beloved; but for Timias there is no place to go. We have no reason to believe that Belphoebe will ever abandon her virginity; indeed, her virginity is what defines her. Or as Spenser puts it, Belphoebe is a shadowing forth of Elizabeth's virginity. So Timias is condemned to the total continence of a Guyon without showing any of Guyon's natural talents in that direction.

The problem of Timias comes to a crisis in the seventh canto of Book IV. He encounters Amoret in the arms of a villainous figure of Lust, and attempts to rescue her. But the villain uses Amoret as his shield, so that Timias cannot avoid wounding her as he strikes at her enemy. Finally (if we can trust our reading of Spenser's ambiguous pronouns) Timias does deal Lust a significant blow:

> Yet he his hand so carefully did beare,
> That at the last he did himselfe attaine,
> And therein left the pike head of his speare.
> A streame of coleblacke bloud thence gusht amaine,
> That all her silken garments did with bloud bestaine.

At this point the villain throws Amoret to the ground; and when Belphoebe arrives on the scene shortly thereafter, he flees to his cave where Belphoebe kills him with an arrow. Inside the cave she finds the still intact Aemylia alongside a vile Hag who has been performing the friendly service of satisfying the villain's lust in Aemylia's place. Moved by sympathy for Aemylia and loathing for the Hag, Belphoebe returns to Timias:

> There she him found by that new louely mate,
> Who lay the whiles in swoune, full sadly set,
> From her faire eyes wiping the deawy wet,
> Which softly stild, and kissing them atweene,
> And handling soft the hurts, which she did get.
> For of that Carle she sorely bruz'd had beene,
> Als of his owne rash hand one wound was to be seene.

In a sequence of events which resembles Red Cross's vision of Una in the arms of that Squire in Book I, Belphoebe is filled with wrath, considers killing the pair ("With that selfe arrow, which the Carle had kild"), but contents herself finally with rebuking the Squire ("Is this the faith, she said, and said no more"), and flees the scene.

The reader may pause to wonder what exactly has happened in this episode. The answer will depend on the particular narrative thread which one chooses to pursue. If we focus on Belphoebe, as her presence in the immediately preceding stanzas encourages us to do, then we may say that the situation does resemble that of Red Cross earlier. Her reaction to the figures in the villain's den shows that she makes an absolute distinction between chaste and unchaste women, as her education under Diana might have led us to expect. Furthermore, although she does not know this, the apparently wanton girl in her lover's arms is in fact her twin sister; so the twinning process discussed earlier is even more explicitly and literally at work here. By this logic, one might assume that Belphoebe is simply in error, mistakenly projecting her own divided feelings as Red Cross had done; that Timias is merely attending to Amoret's wounds and there is no more actual eroticism in the scene than had been the case (for example) with Britomart and Amoret in their shared bed in canto i—a scene which had also given rise to misdeeming and slander. Since the aftermath of this present episode shows Timias pining away alone in the wilderness, the bare outline of the narrative seems to support this interpretation.

But there are complicating factors. For one thing, the Argument to canto vii says outright that "The Squire her loues." For another, we have observed the battle between Timias and the villain, as Belphoebe has not, and the imagery has encouraged us to consider this an encounter with Lust on the part of both Amoret and Timias—with lust as an internal force. And finally, we have the long critical tradition by which this episode is seen as alluding to Raleigh's marriage to Elizabeth Throckmorton and his consequent fall from grace in Elizabeth's court. All of these factors point to an alternative reading: that Belphoebe's invincible chastity has caused *Timias* to seek a twin sister of Belphoebe who has been trained in womanhood rather than virginity. In the case of the putative identification with Raleigh, the maiden in question is named Elizabeth and so shares a Christian name with Raleigh's royal mistress if not a common parentage.

Timias combines two meanings in his name, the English "Time" and the Greek *timē*, honor; and it is time which restores him to honor at court, as it did (much later) Raleigh. But time has seriously encroached on the fabric of Spenser's fiction. In the more orderly narrative of Book I, Red Cross is reunited with Una only after he has experienced the consequences of his error; he wanders to a full understanding of himself, and is made whole at the House of Holiness. Belphoebe's error, if it is that, is never corrected; she merely abates her rage. And whatever may be the cause of Amoret's disappearance from the poem, it is not that Belphoebe has assimilated her values into herself; Timias is reunited with the same chaste figure he had known previously, and on the same terms as before. And when Spenser describes the reunion he rather surprisingly suggests that Timias' service of Belphoebe is an abandonment of his master:

> In which he long time afterwards did lead
> An happie life with grace and good accord,
> Fearlesse of fortunes chaunge or enuies dread,
> And eke all mindlesse of his owne deare Lord
> The noble Prince . . .
>
> (IV. viii. 18)

Only a part of the earlier pattern has been restored; the gentle Squire is seen now for the first time as neglecting his duties as a man of action. Perhaps in 1596 Spenser has come to look on Elizabeth's court as a place of sterile dalliance not far removed from Phaedria's or even Acrasia's bower. Timias seems here to resemble that negative view of Adonis, Verdant in the Bowre of Bliss, his armor rusty from long disuse.

The story of Timias is of a Squire whose situation is finally one of stalemate: a lovely boy (as he is called) who has no prospect of growing up; in terms of Spenser's mythological patterns, Timias is to Belphoebe as Hippolytus was to Diana, the counterpart of the Adonis-Venus relationship. But in his continuation of Chaucer's Squire's Tale, Spenser invents a story in which resolution and marriage are made possible for two pairs of lovers. At the end of Chaucer's fragment, the Squire was promising to

> . . . speke of Cambalo,
> That faught in lystes with the bretheren two
> For Canacee er that he myghte hire wynne . . .

Since Cambalo is the brother of Canacee, this seems to imply an incestuous marriage; perhaps as has been suggested this was part of some oriental
source for the tale. In any case, when Spenser chooses this single motif
out of the tale for his elaboration, he invents a resolution which avoids
incest. To begin with, he invents a story of three brothers (not two),
Priamond, Diamond, and Triamond, whose mother has won for them the
promise from the Fates that the life of each shall pass, on his death, to his
surviving brothers. Secondly, Cambell enjoys the apparently insuperable
advantage of a magic ring which will cure all his wounds—a ring with
similarly curative powers also appears in Chaucer's fragment. Finally,
when Cambell has killed the first two brothers and seems about to kill the
triple-lived Triamond, there appears on the scene a new character, Cambina,
sister of the three brothers, bearing a cup of nepenthe to calm Cambell's
wrath. The upshot is that two pairs of brother and sister intermarry and
the threat of incest (or permanent spinsterhood for Canacee) is averted.
One marries one's friend's sister, not one's own.

The tale seems scarcely more edifying than this summary would
suggest. Spenser has succeeded in capturing some of the naive discontinuity that appears in Chaucer's tale. As one recent Chaucerian (P. M.
Kean) has remarked about the Squire's announced intention, it "suggests a
composite romance of the scope of a *Faerie Queene*, and it is hard to
believe that Chaucer ever seriously considered including anything on this
scale in the *Canterbury Tales*. It seems more likely that the exuberance of
the project is intended to match the exuberance of the Squire's youth and
inexperience." This may not have been Spenser's judgment of the tale
(although it is tempting to imagine that he saw the Squire as proposing
and failing to write the *Faerie Queene*, as Pamela Steiner has suggested
in an essay which she is at present revising for publication), but there is
one possible clue to the way he saw himself in relation both to Chaucer
and to the Squire's Tale. Addressing his predecessor, he laments that
time has defaced the *Canterbury Tales* and robbed posterity of much
treasure:

> Then pardon, O most sacred happie spirit,
>   That I thy labours lost may thus reuiue,
>   And steale from thee the meede of thy due merit,
>   That none durst euer whilest thou wast aliue,
>   And being dead in vaine yet many striue;
>   Ne dare I like, but through infusion sweete

Of thine owne spirit, which doth in me surviue,
I follow here the footing of thy feete,
That with thy meaning so I may the rather meete.
(IV. ii. 34)

The "infusion" of Chaucer's spirit into the surviving Spenser seems strikingly close to the passage of life from brother to brother in his story of the three -mond brothers—and the story of those brothers seems more one of continuity from generation to generation, in any case. So perhaps Spenser is in some sense the third of the "brethren" to confront Cambell. And there is another curious possible link to the world of the Faerie Queene. Canace's name was known to both Chaucer and Spenser from Ovid's Heroides xi and other sources, as the name of a daughter of Aeolus who fell in love with her brother. According to one version of the tale, both brother and sister were killed by their father, and their child thrown to dogs; but according to another version, they married and their daughter Amphisa was later beloved by Apollo. Spenser has an Amphisa who was the mother of Chrysogone, who was in turn impregnated by the sun and bore Belphoebe and Amoret. So it seems possible that Spenser's relation to Chaucer is based on a shared sense of the possibilities and limitations of fantasy. Chaucer's Squire as story-teller is a figure of the youthful poet, bursting with energies and enthusiasm, filled with stories of magical power which imperfectly disguise his own desire for actual power. He is a potent dreamer because he is not a free agent. He is a squire, a scudarius or shield-bearer, carrying the name of another than himself. And his tale breaks off when its protagonist is incautiously revealed as proposing a marriage of a sort permitted only to the gods. Spenser's revision of the Squire's Tale extricates him from this difficulty, by inventing a plot in which brothers and sisters intermarry instead of marrying, and in which a supernatural drug is produced, nepenthe, which will calm Cambell's wrath and make peace, friendship, and intermarriage possible.

But the pattern which I have been describing is obscure and elusive at best; and the same must be said of other hints of meaningful patterns of harmony in the Fourth Book. The gap between Britain and Fairyland is opening up, and Spenser's identification with the Squire's world of ineffectual fancy underscores this fact. The story of Cambell and Triamond may possibly carry meanings far below the surface of the sort which I have just described, obscure and heavily censored intimations of generational rivalry and forbidden unions. Possibly the poem's allusions to other incestuous figures reinforce such hints: among the similes, the recurrent allusions to Myrrha, or to the mysteriously fertile world of Egypt; among the characters of the poem itself, the incestuous twins Argante and

Ollyphant in Book III, whose names are derived from faerie myth and Chaucerian sources respectively—Argante being an alternative name for the demonic faerie queen, Morgan le Fay, and Ollyphant a monster mentioned in *Sir Thopas*. But on the surface the Cambell-Triamond story traces a tetradic pattern of love and friendship which seems far removed from everyday human relationships. By contrast, the experience of Timias is much closer to reality, and much less clearly susceptible of resolution.

There is one large-scale picture of marriage and union in Book IV, and I mention it at this point because it represents a similar "infusion" of vitality from generation to generation. At the end of Book IV, Spenser describes the marriage of the Thames and the Medway. Critics have remarked that earlier poems had celebrated the marriage of the Thames, but with the Isis as bride rather than the Medway. In fact, Spenser sees this marriage as one in which the bridegroom is now the *son* of that Thames who had married the Isis long ago, far upstream. And so at the wedding his parents flow before him in the procession. For the pattern which Spenser has tried to trace with Cambell and Triamond, rivers are a far more apt medium than humans. In their natural confluence they exist easily with change. In fact, the central river here, the Thames, *is* a figure of Time as Spenser plays on its name. And when the elder Thame sees his son marrying the Medway, he may also reflect that his wife and his new daughter-in-law are bearers of comparable names—Isis from the Greek *isos*, equal, and Medway with its related sense of marking a midpoint. And yet historical time has passed as well when this new marriage takes place. As Alastair Fowler argues persuasively, the Medway was identified during the 1590's with Elizabethan naval operations; so the wedding is expressive of an armed peace for contemporary England. For an earlier generation, the center of things may have been at Oxford, but now modern Englishmen must gather their forces downstream and be prepared for possible invasion from without. Spenser has chosen a final episode for Book IV which clearly suggests the conflicts between the ideal and the actual which dominate his vision in 1596.

I have been speaking chiefly with reference to Book IV; but the principal episodes of Books V and VI similarly demonstrate Spenser's increasing sense of a gap between literature and life. In the proem to Book IV he protests against the "rugged forehead" which has criticized him for writing of love, and he urges Elizabeth to banish her "imperious feare" and "hearke to loue, and read this lesson often." But it is clear that Elizabeth will not do so. In Book IV, as Belphoebe, she banishes Timias. In Book V, as Mercilla, she presides over Duessa's execution. To destroy a principle of psychic action like Duessa is virtually to commit suicide. The Fifth

Book is filled with intimations of the dismantling of Spenser's world. We are not surprised to see a poet's tongue nailed to Mercilla's doorpost, and the poet's name changed from Bonfont to Malfont. Justice is shown as operating harshly in a harsh world, most notably in Ireland, and with imperfect success; as the book ends, Envy, Detraction, and the Blatant Beast (and, one might add, many readers) vilify Artegall as he passes by, cool and unconcerned.

Book IV offers a somewhat more benign view of England than had prevailed in Book V; but its prime antagonist, the Blatant Beast, roams the countryside as well as the court. And here Spenser has constructed a myth of his own life which parallels the story of Timias: where Raleigh had offended Elizabeth by marrying another, "lower" Elizabeth, now Spenser publicly does the same thing. In fact, he goes Raleigh one better: in *Amoretti* 74, he informs us that he is thrice blessed by Elizabeths: his mother, his queen, and his new love all bear that name. And in *Amoretti* 80, as in Book VI, canto x, he explicitly calls attention to his temporary abandonment of the Faerie Queene in order to celebrate her "handmayd":

> After so long a race as I haue run
> Through Faery land, which those six books compile
> Giue leaue to rest me being halfe fordonne,
> And gather to my selfe new breath awhile.

When Colin's celebration of his lady is interrupted by Calidore, it is clearly no act of conscious malice which causes the poet's grief. Frequently in Book VI, it seems that well-intentioned blundering is as dangerous as malice or conscious envy. The results are as invidious in either case. Calidore stumbles on a knight and his lady at an intimate moment; but Calidore is no figure of Lust. Instead, he is (at this point, anyway) a model of polite mankind trying to avoid abrasive acts in an overcrowded world. And when he sees Colin and the Graces, he is at worst guilty of curiosity. But in any case, the damage is done, the vision is destroyed and Colin breaks his pipes. By the end of Book VI, it appears that Spenser is suggesting that poetry is radically private in nature. Not even a "homely verse, of many meanest" can escape backbiting commentary. Perhaps the final lines of Book VI are the equivalent of Colin's pipe-breaking:

> Therfore do you my rimes keep better measure,
> And seeke to please, that now is counted wisemens threasure.

We should recognize that the end of Book VI creates a final symmetry to Spenser's poetic career. In the prefatory poem "To His Booke" at the opening of the *Shepheardes Calender*, Spenser expressed a fear lest "Enuie

barke at thee, / As sure it will." It is only at the end of Book VI that this
barking is fully actualized in the figure of the Blatant Beast. And in the
Envoy to the *Shepheardes Calender* he expressed confidence that his poem
would serve as

> . . . a Calender for euery yeare,
> That steele in strength, and time in durance shall outweare:
> And if I marked well the starres reuolution,
>   It shall continewe till the worlds dissolution.

By 1596, as I have tried to show, Spenser has come round once again to
his sense of the omnipresence of Envy, both in its overtly malevolent
forms and also as a mis-deeming or mis-taking attendant on any act of
comprehensive vision. So he has abandoned the optimism of this Envoy,
both in its belief that accurate measure can assure poetic survival, and in
its concluding appeal to informed judgment: "The better please, the worse
despise, I aske no more." In 1596, Spenser turns away from the epic
programme which he had enunciated in his 1590 Letter to Raleigh, and
begins to devise more devious methods of expressing his sense of a
threatened universe. He ceases to create a model of the universe, with its
central points centrally located and marked, and begins to create a model
of the poet seeking a private refuge in that universe.

One final example may help to show the difference between the
First and the Sixth Books. In 1596, Spenser added a single new stanza to
the First Book. It ties up no loose ends, adds no new topical meaning that
I can see; but it does call attention to the existence of a vitally interested
and appreciative audience for Red Cross's fight with the dragon. It appears
now in canto xi as the third stanza:

> And pointing forth, lo yonder is (said she)
>   The brasen towre in which my parents deare
>   For dread of that huge feend emprisond be,
>   Whom I from far see on the walles appeare,
>   Whose sight my feeble soule doth greatly cheere:
>   And on the top of all I do espye
>   The watchman wayting tydings glad to heare,
>   That O my parents might I happily
> Vnto you bring, to ease you of your misery.

In 1596 Spenser is acutely aware of being watched and judged, especially
by figures of authority. Red Cross in Book I, and Artegall in Book V,
perform their climactic deeds of monster-killing in public, before an
audience. By contrast, when Calidore meets Artegall at the beginning of
Book VI, he stresses the loneliness of his quest "In which although good

Fortune me befall, / Yet shall it not by none be testifyde." In point of literal narrative fact, this is not the case, for Calidore does lead the Beast back to court to show him off; but it seems ultimately true as an expression of the personal, inwardly turned nature of Spenser's poem in 1596, when he finds that it is he, himself, who is now in the middest of the race, and strongly tempted to rest.

Chronology

1552   Edmund Spenser probably born either in this year or in 1553 (date deduced from a reference in the *Amoretti*, sonnet 60), in London, to Elizabeth and John (?) Spenser, about whom nothing is known

1561–69   Attends the newly-founded Merchant Taylors School, in London, probably entering as one of the poor men's sons, who pays no admission. Is a student of the school's Headmaster, the famous educational theorist Richard Mulcaster. In 1569, while still at the school, Spenser publishes twenty-two translations from Joachim du Bellay and a French translation of Petrarch in Jan Ver der Noodt's anti-Catholic *Theatre for Worldings*.

1569–76   Attends Pembroke College, Cambridge, as a Sizar, or scholarship student. Receives his B.A. in 1573, and his M.A. in 1576.

1578   Becomes secretary to the former Master of Pembroke College, John Young, now bishop of Rochester.

1579   Publishes *The Shepheardes Calender* anonymously. Marries Machabyas Childe on October 27. Joins the household of Robert Dudley, Earl of Leicester, where he meets Leicester's nephew Sir Philip Sidney.

1580   Appointed secretary to the Lord Deputy of Ireland, Arthur, Lord Grey de Wilton. Arrives in Dublin on August 12.

1581–88   Holds the Clerkship in Chancery for Faculties; as Clerk, Spenser oversees ecclesiastical licenses and dispensations.

1582–84   Lord Grey leaves Ireland, but Spenser stays, leasing New Abbey, a house south of Dublin, near the great Bog of Allen. Sometime before 1582, a son, Sylvanus, is born. In summer of 1584, Spenser becomes deputy to Lodowick Bryskett, Clerk of the Council of Munster, and a friend of Sidney's.

1588–89   Acquires estate in Munster, Kilcolman. Possibly a daughter, Katherine, born around this time. Friendship with Sir Walter

Raleigh, whose estate neighbors his. Returns to the Court of Queen Elizabeth with Raleigh in 1589, and in December of that year, enters Books I–III of *The Faerie Queene* on the Stationer's Register.

1590   Publication of Books I–III of *The Faerie Queene*, including the *Letter to Raleigh*, in which Spenser outlines the plan of the whole *Faerie Queene*. Publishes *Muiopotmos*. Death of wife Machabyas Spenser (?).

1591   Publishes *Complaints* and *Daphnaida*. Granted a life income of £50 by Queen Elizabeth.

1594   Spenser returns to Ireland, marries Elizabeth Boyle on June 11, in Cork.

1595   Publishes *Amoretti* and *Epithalamion* (which celebrates his courtship of and marriage to Elizabeth Boyle) and *Colin Clouts Come Home Again*. Returns to London in the winter.

1596   Publishes Books I–VI of *The Faerie Queene* (adding Books IV–VI, and changing the ending of Book III to accommodate them), as well as *Prothalamion* and *Fowre Hymnes*. Sometime during this time, a son, Peregrine, is born. Spenser returns to Ireland in late autumn.

1598   Enters *A Vewe of the present state of Irelande* in the Stationer's Register (published 1633). Rebellion breaks out in Ireland led by Tyrone and O'Neill, which has some success. Spenser's estate is sacked, and he moves family to Cork, going himself to London with letters from the Lord President of Munster for the Privy Council.

1599   Spenser dies on January 13 in London. He is buried in Westminster Abbey.

1609   New edition of *The Faerie Queene*, which includes the *Mutabilitie Cantos*.

Contributors

HAROLD BLOOM, Sterling Professor of the Humanities at Yale University, is the author of *The Anxiety of Influence, Poetry and Repression* and many other volumes of literary criticism. His forthcoming study, *Freud: Transference and Authority*, attempts a full-scale reading of all of Freud's major writings. A MacArthur Prize Fellow, he is the general editor of *The Chelsea House Library of Literary Criticism*.

NORTHROP FRYE is University Professor Emeritus at the University of Toronto. His major books include *Anatomy of Criticism* and *Fables of Identity*.

A. C. HAMILTON is Professor of English at Queen's University, Kingston, Ontario, and the author of *The Structure of Allegory in "The Faerie Queene."*

THOMAS GREENE is Professor of Comparative Literature and Renaissance Studies at Yale University. His books include *The Descent from Heaven, Rabelais: A Study in Comic Courage* and *A Light in Troy*.

THOMAS P. ROCHE, JR. is Professor of English at Princeton University, and the author of *The Kindly Flame*.

DONALD CHENEY is Professor of English at the University of Massachusetts, Amherst, and the author of *Spenser's Image of Nature*.

A. BARTLETT GIAMATTI is President of Yale University. His books include *The University and the Public Interest, Exile and Change in Renaissance Literature* and a study of Spenser.

HARRY BERGER, JR. is Professor of English at Cowell College, University of California, Santa Cruz. He is the author of *The Allegorical Temper*.

ISABEL G. MacCAFFREY was Professor of History and Literature at Harvard University. Among her writings are critical studies of Spenser and Milton and essays on Wallace Stevens.

ANGUS FLETCHER is Professor of English at the Graduate School of the City University of New York. His books include *Allegory: The Theory of a Symbolic Mode* and studies of Spenser and of Milton's *Comus*.

PATRICA A. PARKER is Associate Professor of Comparative Literature at the University of Toronto, and the author of *Inescapable Romance*.

LAWRENCE MANLEY is Associate Professor of English at Yale University, and the author of *Convention: 1500–1750*.

KENNETH GROSS is Assistant Professor of English at the University of Rochester, and the author of a forthcoming book on Spenser, *Spenser's Poetics*.

JOHN GUILLORY, Associate Professor of English at Yale University, has written *Poetic Authority* and a forthcoming study of canon-formation.

PETER SACKS is Associate Professor in the Writing Seminars at Johns Hopkins University, and the author of *The English Elegy*.

JOHN HOLLANDER is Professor of English and Poet-in-Residence at Yale University. His many books include *Spectral Emanations: New and Selected Poems*, *The Figure of Echo* and *Rhyme's Reason*.

Bibliography

Allen, D. C. "On Spenser's *Muiopotmos*." *Studies in Philology* 53 (1956): 141–58.

Alpers, Paul J. *The Poetry of "The Faerie Queene."* Princeton: Princeton University Press, 1967.

————. "The Eclogue Tradition and the Nature of Pastoral." *College English* 34 (1972): 352–71.

————. "Narration in *The Faerie Queene*." *English Literary History* 44 (1977): 19–39.

Anderson, Judith H. *The Growth of a Personal Voice: "Piers Plowman" and "The Faerie Queene."* New Haven: Yale University Press, 1976.

————." 'Nor Man It Is': The Knight of Justice in *The Faerie Queene* V." *PMLA* 85 (1970): 65–77.

Aptekar, Jane. *Icons of Justice: Iconography and Thematic Imagery in "The Faerie Queene"* V. New York: Columbia University Press, 1969.

Arthos, John. *On the Poetry of Spenser and the Form of Romances.* Freeport, N.Y.: Books for Librairies Press, 1956.

Atchity, K. J., ed. *Eterne in Mutabilitie: The Unity of "The Faerie Queene": Essays Published in Memory of Davis Philoon Harding, 1914–1970.* Hamden, Conn.: Archon Books, 1972.

Bean, John C. "Making the Daimonic Personal: Britomart and Love's Assault in *The Faerie Queene*." *Modern Language Quarterly* 40 (1979): 237–55.

Berger, Harry, Jr. *The Allegorical Temper: Vision and Reality in Book II of Spenser's "Faerie Queene."* New Haven: Yale University Press, 1957.

————. "Spenser's *Prothalamion*: An Interpretation." *Essays in Criticism* 15 (1965): 363–80.

————, ed. *Spenser: A Collection of Critical Essays.* Englewood Cliffs, N.J.: Prentice-Hall, Inc., 1968.

————. "Two Spenserian Retrospects: The Antique Temple of Venus and the Primitive Marriage of Two Rivers." *Texas Studies in Literature and Language* 10 (1969): 5–25.

Bieman, Elizabeth. "Britomart in Book V of *The Faerie Queene*." *University of Toronto Quarterly* 37 (1968): 156–74.

Blisset, William. "Florimell and Marinell." *Studies in English Literature, 1500–1900* 5 (1965): 87–104.

Braden, Gordon. " 'Riverrun': An Epic Catalogue in *The Faerie Queene*." *English Literary Renaissance* 5 (1975): 25–48.

Brill, Lesley. " 'Battles that Need Not be Fought': *The Faerie Queene* IIII." *English Literary Renaissance* 5 (1975): 198–211.

Bush, Douglas. *Mythology and the Renaissance Tradition in English Poetry*. New York: Pageant Book Co., 1963.

Cain, Thomas H. *Praise in "The Faerie Queene."* Lincoln: University of Nebraska Press, 1978.

Carscallen, James. "The Goodly Frame of Temperance: The Metaphor of Cosmos in *The Faerie Queene*, Book II." *University of Toronto Quarterly* 37 (1968): 136–55.

Cheney, Donald. *Spenser's Image of Nature: Wild Man and Shepherd in "The Faerie Queene."* New Haven: Yale University Press, 1966.

———. "Spenser's Hermaphrodite and the 1590 *Faerie Queene*." *PMLA* 80 (1972): 192–200.

Cooper, Helen. *Pastoral: Medieval into Renaissance*. Totowa, N.J.: D. S. Brewer, 1977.

Craig, Joanne, "The Image of Mortality: Myth and History in *The Faery Queene*." *English Literary History* 39 (1972): 520–44.

Crampton, Georgia Ronan. *The Condition of Creatures: Suffering and Action in Chaucer and Spenser*. New Haven: Yale University Press, 1974.

Cullen, Patrick. *Spenser, Marvell and Renaissance Pastoral*. Cambridge, Mass.: Harvard University Press, 1970.

Cummings, R. M., ed. *Spenser: The Critical Heritage*. London: Routledge & Kegan Paul, 1971.

Davis, Walter R. "Arthur, Partial Exegesis, and the Reader." *Texas Studies in Literature and Language* 18 (1977): 553–76.

Dees, Jerome S. "The Narrator of *The Faerie Queene*: Patterns of Response." *Texas Studies in Literature and Language* 12 (1971): 537–68.

Dundas, Judith. "*The Faerie Queene*: The Incomplete Poem and the Whole Meaning." *Modern Philology* 71 (1971): 157–65.

Dunlop, Alexander. "The Unity of Spenser's *Amoretti*." In *Silent Poetry: Essays in Numerological Analysis*. Edited by Alastair Fowler. London: Routledge & Kegan Paul, 1970.

Dunseath, T. K. *Spenser's Allegory of Justice in Book Five of "The Faerie Queene."* Princeton: Princeton University Press, 1968.

Durling, Robert. *The Figure of the Poet in the Renaissance Epic*. Cambridge, Mass.: Harvard University Press, 1965.

Edwards, Calvin. "The Narcissus Myth in Spenser's Poetry." *Studies in Philology* 74 (1977): 63–88.

Ellrodt, Robert. *Neoplatonism in the Poetry of Spenser*. Geneva: Folcroft Library Editions, 1960.

Fletcher, Angus. *The Prophetic Moment: An Essay on Spenser*. Chicago: The University of Chicago Press, 1971.

Fowler, Alastair. *Spenser and the Numbers of Time*. New York: Barnes & Noble, 1964.

———. *Triumphal Forms: Structural Patterns in Elizabethan Poetry*. Cambridge: At the University Press, 1970.

Freeman, Rosemary. "*The Faerie Queene*": A Companion for Readers. London: Chatto & Windus, 1970.

Frushell, Richard C. and Bernard J. Vandersmith, eds. *Contemporary Thought on Edmund Spenser.* Carbondale: Southern Illinois University Press, 1975.

Frye, Northrop. *Anatomy of Criticism: Four Essays.* Princeton: Princeton University Press, 1957.

Giamatti, A. Bartlett. *The Earthly Paradise and the Renaissance Epic.* Princeton: Princeton University Press, 1966.

————. *Play of Double Senses: Spenser's "Faerie Queene."* Englewood Cliffs, N.J.: Prentice-Hall, Inc., 1975.

Gohlke, Madelon S. "Embattled Allegory: Book II of *The Faerie Queene.*" *English Literary Renaissance* 8 (1978): 123–40.

Goldberg, Jonathan. *Endless Worke.* Baltimore and London: The Johns Hopkins University Press, 1981.

Greene, Thomas M. *The Descent from Heaven: A Study in Epic Continuity.* New Haven: Yale University Press, 1963.

Guillory, John. *Poetic Authority.* New York: Columbia University Press, 1983.

Hamilton, A. C. *The Structure of Allegory in "The Faerie Queene."* Oxford: At the Clarendon Press, 1961.

————, ed. *Essential Articles for the Study of Edmund Spenser.* Hamden, Conn.: Archon Books, 1972.

Hankins, John E. *Source and Meaning of Spenser's Allegory: A Study of "The Faerie Queene."* Oxford: At the Clarendon Press, 1971.

Helgerson, Richard. "The New Poet Presents Himself: Spenser and the Idea of a Literary Career." *PMLA* 93 (1978): 893–911.

Heninger, S. K., Jr. "The Implications of Form for the *Shepheardes Calender.*" *Studies in the Renaissance* 9 (1962): 309–21.

Hieatt, A. Kent. *Short Time's Endless Monument: The Symbolism of the Numbers in Edmund Spenser's "Epithalamion."* New York: Columbia University Press, 1960.

————. *Chaucer, Spenser, Milton: Mythopoeic Continuities and Transformations.* Montreal: McGill-Queens University Press, 1975.

Hill, Iris T. "Britomart and 'Be Bold, Be Not Too Bold'." *English Literary History* 38 (1971): 173–87.

Hill, R. F. "Colin Clout's Courtesy." *Modern Language Review* 57 (1962): 492–503.

Hoffman, Nancy Jo. *Spenser's Pastorals.* Baltimore: The Johns Hopkins University Press, 1971.

Holahan, Michael. "*Iamque Opus Exegi*: Ovid's Changes and Spenser's Brief Epic of Mutability." *English Literary Renaissance* 6 (1976): 244–70.

Hyman, L. W. "Structure and Meaning in Spenser's *Epithalamion.*" *Tennesee Studies in Literature* 3 (1958): 37–42.

Kaske, Carol V. "Spenser's *Amoretti* and *Epithalamion* of 1595: Structure, Genre, and Numerology." *English Literary Renaissance* 8 (1978): 271–95.

Kennedy, Judith, and Reither, James A. *A Theatre for Spenserians.* Toronto: University of Toronto Press, 1973.

Kermode, Frank. *Shakespeare, Spenser, Donne.* London: Routledge & Kegan Paul, 1971.

Knight, W. Nicholas. "The Narrative Unity of Book V of *The Faerie Queene*: 'That Part of Justice Which is Equity'." *Review of English Studies* 21 (1970): 267–94.

Lewis, C. S. *The Allegory of Love*. Oxford: At the Clarendon Press, 1936.

———. *English Literature in the Sixteenth Century Excluding Drama*. Oxford: At the Clarendon Press, 1954.

———. *Spenser's Images of Life*. Edited by Alastair Fowler. Cambridge: At the University Press, 1967.

MacCaffrey, Isabel G. *Spenser's Allegory: The Anatomy of Imagination*. Princeton: Princeton University Press, 1976.

Mack, Maynard, and George deForest Lord, eds. *Poetic Traditions of the English Renaissance*. New Haven: Yale University Press, 1982.

Mallette, Richard. "The Poet and the Hero in Book VI of *The Faerie Queene*." *Modern Language Review* 72 (1977): 257–67.

Miller, David. "Abandoning the Quest." *English Literary History* 46 (1979): 173–92.

Miller, Lewis H., Jr. "The Ironic Mode in Books I and II of *The Faerie Queene*." *Papers on Language and Literature* 7 (1971): 133–49.

Mills, Jerry Leah. "Spenser and the Numbers of History: A Note on the British and Elfin Chronicles in *The Faerie Queene*." *Philological Quarterly* 60 (1976): 281–87.

Miskimin, Alice S. "Britomart's Crocodile and the Legends of Chastity." *Journal of English and Germanic Philology* 77 (1978): 17–36.

Montrose, Louis A. " 'The Perfecte Patterne': The Poetics of Courtship in *The Shepheardes Calender*." *Texas Studies in Literature and Language* 21 (1979): 34–67.

Moore, John W., Jr. "Colin Breaks his Pipe: A Reading of the 'January' Eclogue." *English Literary Renaissance* 5 (1975): 3–24.

Mueller, W. R., and Allen, D. C., eds. *That Soveraine Light: Essays in Honor of Edmund Spenser*. Baltimore: The Johns Hopkins University Press, 1952.

Murrin, Michael. *The Veil of Allegory*. Chicago: The University of Chicago Press, 1969.

———. *The Allegorical Epic: Essays in its Rise and Decline*. Chicago: The University of Chicago Press, 1980.

Nelson, William. *The Poetry of Spenser: A Study*. New York: Columbia University Press, 1963.

———, ed. *Form and Convention in the Poetry of Edmund Spenser: Selected Papers from the English Institute*. New York: Columbia University Press, 1961.

Nestrick, William V. "Spenser and the Renaissance Mythology of Love." *Literary Monographs* 6 (1975): 37–50.

Neuse, Richard. "Triumph Over Hasty Accidents: A Note on the Symbolic Mode of the *Epithalamion*." *Modern Language Review* 41 (1966): 163–74.

———. "Milton and Spenser: The Virgilian Triad Revisited." *English Literary History* 45 (1978): 606–39.

Nohrnberg, James. *The Analogy of "The Faerie Queene."* Princeton: Princeton University Press, 1976.

O'Connell, Michael. *Mirror and Veil: The Historical Dimension of Spenser's "Faerie Queene."* Chapel Hill: University of North Carolina Press, 1977.

Owen, Lewis J. "Mutable in Eternity: Spenser's Despair and the Multiple Forms of Mutabilitie." *Journal of Medieval and Renaissance Studies* 2 (1972): 49–68.

Paglia, Camille A. "The Apolonian Androgyne and *The Faerie Queene.*" *English Literary Renaissance* 9 (1979): 42–63.

Parker, Mother Mary Pauline. *The Allegory of "The Faerie Queene."* Oxford: At the Clarendon Press, 1960.

Parker, Patricia A. *Inescapable Romance: Studies in the Poetics of a Mode.* Princeton: Princeton University Press, 1979.

Phillips, James E. "Spenser's Syncretistic Religious Imagery." *English Literary History* 36 (1969): 110–30.

———. "Renaissance Concepts of Justice and the Structure of Book V of *The Faerie Queene.*" *Huntington Library Quarterly* 34 (1970): 103–120.

Richardson, David. "Duality in Spenser's Archaisms." *Studies in the Literary Imagination* 11 (1978): 81–98.

Roche, Thomas P., Jr. *The Kindly Flame: A Study of the Third and Fourth Books of Spenser's "Faerie Queene."* Princeton: Princeton University Press, 1964.

———, ed. *Essays: Spenser, Herbert, Milton.* Princeton: Princeton University Press, 1970.

Rollinson, Phillip. "A Generic View of Spenser's *Fowre Hymnes.*" *Studies in Philology* 68 (1971): 292–304.

Rose, Mark. *Heroic Love: Studies in Sidney and Spenser.* Cambridge, Mass.: Harvard University Press, 1968.

Rusche, Harry. "The Lesson of Calidore's Truancy." *Studies in Philology* 76 (1979): 149–61.

Sims, Dwight. "The Syncretic Myth of Venus in Spenser's Legend of Chastity." *Studies in Philology* 61 (1974): 427–50.

Skulsky, Harold. "Spenser's Despair Episode and the Theology of Doubt." *Modern Philology* 78 (1981): 227–42.

Smith, Hallet. *Elizabethan Poetry: A Study in Conventions, Meaning, and Expression.* Cambridge, Mass.: Harvard University Press, 1952.

Tonkin, Humphrey. *Spenser's Courteous Pastoral: Book VI of "The Faerie Queene."* Oxford: At the Clarendon Press, 1972.

Tufte, Virginia. " 'High Wedlock Then Be Honored': Rhetoric and the *Epithalamion.*" *Pacific Coast Philology* 1 (1966): 32–41.

Tuve, Rosemond. *Elizabethan and Metaphysical Imagery.* Chicago: The University of Chicago Press, 1947.

———. *Allegorical Imagery: Some Medieval Books and Their Posterity.* Princeton: Princeton University Press, 1966.

Watkins, W. B. C. *Shakespeare and Spenser.* Princeton: Princeton University Press, 1950.

Weiner, Andrew D. " 'Fierce Warres and Faithful Loves': Pattern as Structure in *The Faerie Queene,* I." *Huntington Library Quarterly* 37 (1974): 33–57.

Wells, Robin. "*Semper Eadem*: Spenser's 'Legend of Constancie'." *Modern Language Review* 73 (1978): 250–55.

West, Michael. "Spenser and the Renaissance Ideal of Christian Heroism." *PMLA* 88 (1973): 1013–32.

Wickert, Max A. "Structure and Ceremony in Spenser's *Epithalamion*." *English Literary History* 35 (1968): 135–67.

Williams, Arnold. *Flower on a Lowly Stalk: The Sixth Book of "The Faerie Queene."* East Lansing: Michigan State University Press, 1967.

Williams, Kathleen. *Spenser's "Faerie Queene": The World of Glass.* Berkeley: University of California Press, 1966.

———. "Spenser and the Metaphor of Sight." In *Renaissance Studies in Honor of Carroll Camden.* Edited by J. A. Ward. Houston: Rice University Press, 1974.

Woodhouse, A. S. P. *The Poet and his Faith: Religion and Poetry from Spenser to Eliot and Auden.* Chicago: The University of Chicago Press, 1965.

Woodward, Daniel H. "Some Themes in Spenser's *Prothalamion*." *English Literary History* 29 (1962): 34–46.

Yeats, W. B. "Edmund Spenser: The Cutting of an Agate." In *Essays and Introductions.* New York: MacMillan & Co., 1961.

Acknowledgments

"The Structure of Imagery in *The Faerie Queene*" by Northrop Frye from *Fables of Identity: Studies in Poetic Mythology* by Northrop Frye, copyright © 1963 by Harcourt, Brace & World, Inc. Reprinted by permission.

"The Structure of Allegory in Books I and II of *The Faerie Queene*" by A. C. Hamilton from *The Structure of Allegory in "The Faerie Queene"* by A. C. Hamilton, copyright © 1961 by Oxford University Press. Reprinted by permission.

"Mutability and the Theme of Process" by Thomas Greene from *The Descent from Heaven: A Study in Epic Continuity* by Thomas Greene, copyright © 1963 by Thomas Greene. Reprinted by permission.

"The Marriage of the Thames and Medway" by Thomas P. Roche, Jr. from *The Kindly Flame: A Study of the Third and Fourth Books of Spenser's "Faerie Queene"* by Thomas P. Roche, Jr., copyright © 1964 by Princeton University Press. Reprinted by permission.

"Gardens of Adonis" by Donald Cheney from *Spenser's Image of Nature: Wild Man and Shepherd in "The Faerie Queene"* by Donald Cheney, copyright © 1966 by Yale University Press. Reprinted by permission.

"The Bower of Bliss" by A. Bartlett Giamatti from *The Earthly Paradise and the Renaissance Epic* by A. Bartlett Giamatti, copyright © 1966 by Princeton University Press. Reprinted by permission.

"The *Mutabilitie Cantos*: Archaism and Evolution in Retrospect" by Harry Berger, Jr. from *Spenser: A Collection of Critical Essays* edited by Harry Berger, Jr., copyright © 1968 by Prentice-Hall, Inc. Reprinted by permission.

"Allegory and Pastoral in *The Shepheardes Calender*" by Isabel G. MacCaffrey from *English Literary History* 1, vol. 36 (March 1969), copyright © 1969 by The Johns Hopkins University Press. Reprinted by permission.

"Imagery and Prophecy in *The Faerie Queene*" by Angus Fletcher from *The Prophetic Moment: An Essay on Spenser* by Angus Fletcher, copyright © 1971 by The University of Chicago Press. Reprinted by permission.

"The Romance of Romance" by Patricia A. Parker from *Inescapable Romance: Studies in the Poetics of a Mode* by Patricia A. Parker, copyright © 1979 by Princeton University Press. Reprinted by permission.

"Spenser and the City: The Minor Poems" by Lawrence Manley from *Modern Language Quarterly* 3, vol. 43 (September 1982), copyright © 1983 by University of Washington. Reprinted by permission.

"Mythologies and Metrics in Spenser" by Kenneth Gross from *PMLA* 1, vol. 98 (January 1983), copyright © 1983 by Modern Language Association of America. Reprinted by permission.

"The Image of Source in *The Faerie Queene*" by John Guillory from *Poetic Authority: Spenser, Milton, and Literary History* by John Guillory, copyright © 1983 by Columbia University Press. Reprinted by permission.

"Astrophel" by Peter Sacks from *The English Elegy: Studies in the Genre from Spenser to Yeats* by Peter Sacks, copyright © 1985 by The Johns Hopkins University Press. Reprinted by permission.

" 'The Footing of his Feet': Spenser's Early Error" by John Hollander from *On Poetry and Poetics* edited by Richard Waswo, copyright © 1985 by John Hollander. Reprinted by permission.

"Envy in the Middest of the 1596 *Faerie Queene*" by Donald Cheney, copyright © 1986 by Donald Cheney. Published for the first time in this volume.

Index